THE MYSTERIOUS SOFÍA

THE MEXICAN EXPERIENCE
William H. Beezley, series editor

THE MYSTERIOUS SOFÍA

～

One Woman's Mission to
Save Catholicism in
Twentieth-Century Mexico

STEPHEN J. C. ANDES

University of Nebraska Press | Lincoln

© 2019 by the Board of Regents of the University of Nebraska. All rights reserved ∞

Library of Congress Cataloging-in-Publication Data
Names: Andes, Stephen J. C. (Stephen Joseph Carl), author.
Title: The mysterious Sofia: a Catholic woman's story through a century of change / Stephen J. C. Andes.
Description: Lincoln: University of Nebraska Press, [2019] | Series: The Mexican experience | Includes bibliographical references and index.
Identifiers: LCCN 2019003680
ISBN 9781496214669 (cloth: alk. paper)
ISBN 9781496217608 (pbk)
ISBN 9781496218186 (epub)
ISBN 9781496218193 (mobi)
ISBN 9781496218209 (pdf)
Subjects: LCSH: Valle, Sophia del, 1891–1982. | Catholic women—Mexico—Biography. | Catholic Action—Mexico—History—20th century. | Catholic labor unions—Mexico—20th century. | Catholic Church—Mexico—History—20th century.
Classification: LCC BX1428.3 .A53 2019 | DDC 282.092 [B]—dc23
LC record available at https://lccn.loc.gov/2019003680

Set in Arno Pro by Mikala R. Kolander.

For my father, Fred Stephen Andes III

Contents

List of Illustrations	ix
Acknowledgments	xi
Nota Bene, Dear Reader	xv
Prologue: *De te fabula narratur*	xvii

PART 1. THE MYSTERIOUS SOFÍA

1. Days of the Dead	3
2. The Sophie Letters	8
3. Miss del Valle	9
4. The Mastermind	11
Interlude: Tere Huidobro	15

PART 2. A FAMILY ROMANCE

5. Little Flowers	19
6. Sofía's Belle Époque	33
7. Vocation	43
8. Respectable Telephone Operator	52
9. Preparing the Future	68
Interlude: Family Albums	81

PART 3. MEXICAN ODYSSEY

10. The Catacombs	91
11. The Voyage	99
12. The Test	112
13. Gasparri's Parrots	131
14. A Long, Hot Roman Summer	139
15. The Return	152
16. The Peace	164
Interlude: *Las viejitas*	170

PART 4. A WOMAN ALONE

17. Out of the Shadows — 185
18. The New Woman — 191
19. Resistance — 200
20. *Les femmes internationales* — 204
21. Terrible Beasts — 218
22. Winter in the City of Light — 220
23. Doubt — 231
24. Lourdes — 239
25. The Road to Warsaw — 242
26. Borders — 248
27. Bridges — 252
    Interlude: Walls — 260

PART 5. CATHOLIC VAGABOND

28. Miss del Valle Goes to Washington — 265
29. The Plan — 272
30. The Deception of Miss Duffy — 281
31. Consider the Lobster — 288
32. Golden Hour of the Little Flower — 294
33. On the Road — 305
34. *La patria* Calls — 328
    Postlude: Day's End — 341
    Matins: A Few Days After — 353
    Postscript — 358

Notes — 359
Bibliography — 393
Index — 407

Illustrations

1. Sofía Goeury Smith and Francisco del Valle Ballina, ca. 1887 — 23
2. Sofía del Valle at play as a child, undated — 27
3. Family del Valle, ca. 1900 — 29
4. Sofía del Valle with her maternal grandmother, Sofía Smith de Goeury, date unknown — 30
5. Family del Valle, behind the ideal, early 1900s — 32
6. Sofía del Valle in a European school, ca. 1908 — 35
7. Matilde, Sofía, and an unidentified friend, ca. 1910–12 — 37
8. Alfredo Méndez Medina, founder and first director of the Mexican Social Secretariat, ca. 1920 — 48
9. The Mexican Social Secretariat at 9 Motolinía Street, ca. 1923 — 56
10. Ericsson telephone operators at the main exchange in Mexico City — 60
11. "Respectable" Ericsson telephone operators in the Rest and Recreation Room, ca. 1926 — 61
12. Sofía del Valle and "Catholic couture," ca. 1926 — 70
13. Elena Lascuráin de Silva and Clara Arce, leaders of the Damas Católicas — 71
14. Sofía del Valle, ca. 1926 — 73
15. Miguel Darío Miranda in the Social Secretariat, ca. 1926 — 75
16. The trial of Madre Conchita and José de León Toral, 1928 — 148
17. Sofía del Valle, ca. 1930 — 192
18. Students of Cultura Femenina on field day, ca. 1930–32 — 194
19. Students at Cultura Femenina, ca. 1930 — 196

20. "Respectable" students in class at Cultura Femenina, ca. 1930 — 197
21. Sofía del Valle reading with a student of Cultura Femenina, ca. 1934 — 266
22. Sofía del Valle sitting on steps, ca. 1934 — 267
23. "The clerical reaction" cartoon, ca. 1934 — 270
24. "Freedom in Mexico" drawing, November 1934 — 303
25. Family del Valle with Miguel Miranda, ca. 1937 — 318
26. *Juventud* cover, "A member of the JCFM knows how to smile" — 332
27. *Juventud* cover, "Feminine intelligence and study" — 334
28. Sofía del Valle, 1950 — 337
29. Sofía del Valle with members of the African delegation of the WUCWO, 1961 — 339

Acknowledgments

"For me," Sofía del Valle once wrote, "one of the most valuable and least practiced virtues is gratitude."

I am thankful.

People first.

The extended del Valle family—the Ruiz de Huidobros and Rule Carrazas—immediately welcomed me, shared with me, and provided the true heart and soul of this book.

Jason Glaspey has a habit of saving me; Holly Glaspey, too. Ben and Becca Begley always let me read to them what I'd written. Yves Solis and his amazing family hosted me in Mexico City way too many times.

When the project was just ink and notebook paper, James Wilkey read the ill-formed, unfinished pages. He read draft after draft. I have on my computer a MS Word document titled "James Wilkey Encouragement."

Andrew Johnson, Tom Barber, and Michael Pasquier read very early chapters. They spared me from making a fool of myself.

The Junior Faculty Writing Group at LSU said both *yes* and *no*. (I'm probably more grateful for the *no*.) Thank you: Catherine Jacquet, Sherri Franks Johnson, Zevi Gutfreund, Kodi Roberts, Brendan Karch, Asiya Alam, and Devyn Spence Benson.

Aaron Sheehan-Dean read the entire manuscript. I can't tell you how many times I refreshed my email inbox waiting for his perfectly on-point, incredibly informed, comments. (Sorry for the adverbs, Aaron.) Suzanne Marchand told me to write the book I wanted to write, but to be ready for the consequences. Andrew Burstein and Nancy Isenberg always gave good advice. Victor Stater supported the project with funds from the History Department. My graduate seminar, "Biography of Latin America," learned it all with me. They had to read the manuscript as an assignment for class. They made the book better. Thank you: Rosa Lázaro Lugo, Pedro Ramos Vélez, Edrea Mendoza, Juan Rodríguez Cepero, María Anna Zazzarino, Chase Tomlin, Negar Basiri, Anwita Ray, Natalie D'Auvergne-LaMotte, and Liz Johnston.

Charles Shindo always had his office door open for me. And all my colleagues at LSU have made the job pretty great.

So many *Mexicanistas* shaped my thinking, corrected my writing, and reminded me of what I'd forgotten. Julia Young read the whole manuscript. Her advice was just in time. Matthew Butler, whose research is all over this book, challenged me to be a better historian. Jaime Pensado, Timothy Matovina, Maggie Elmore, and many others at Notre Dame, kindly listened and told me it made sense. The book relies on the work of many historians. I'm certain I didn't credit them nearly enough: Susie S. Porter, Robert Curley, Matthew Butler, Julia Young, Yves Solis, Valentina Torres Septién, Ben Fallaw, Edward Wright-Rios, David Kertzer, Kristina Boylan, Patience Schell, Paolo Valvo, Massimo de Giuseppe, Joanne Hershfield, Maurice Demers, Ann S. Blum, Jocelyn Olcott, Nichole Sanders, Stephanie Mitchell, Stephanie Smith, Silvia Arrom, Margaret Chowning, and Kathleen Sprows Cummings.

Research assistance in Mexico City was provided by Cristina García. Shane MacDonald scanned files from the National Catholic Welfare Conference (NCWC) archives at the Catholic University of America. Marco Antonio Pérez Iturbe at the Archivo Histórico del Arzobispado de México (AHAM) is the most helpful, and nicest, archivist you'll ever meet.

Now, institutions.

LSU provided a year-long ATLAS Fellowship for writers and artists. I wrote the bulk of the manuscript during that year. The Manship Summer Research Fellowship and the Council on Research Summer Research Stipend helped get me to archives in Mexico City and Rome. The Cushwa Center for the Study of American Catholicism at Notre Dame enthusiastically supported the project with a travel grant to their archives. LSU's History Department kindly paid several publication subventions. Thank you.

The University of Nebraska Press is the only one that said yes. Bridget Barry and Emily Wendell are amazing to work with. The two anonymous reviewers told me what to lose and what I couldn't do without. Martha Ash is an artist at copyediting. Of course, any mistakes that remain are my own.

My father and mother, Steve and Susan Andes, always taught me to say thank you. Be kind, they said, accept others, and think of others. Opal, Silas, and Mercer have a better father because of them.

And to you, Sarilyn, everything is because of you and for you.

Nota Bene, Dear Reader

> In most books, the I, or first person,
> is omitted; in this it will be retained.
>
> Henry David Thoreau, *Walden*

How Do You Tell the Story of a Life?

This is a work of history. It's nonfiction. All the quotes in the book—even dialogue—come from historical documents: letters, memoir, interviews. I started out trying to write a book useful for scholars. But what about a good story? One that people want to read; a story that informs and—God forbid—moves your nerve endings.

Can a good story be useful to scholars?

I can foresee what some of your critiques may be. There are these odd interludes throughout the book where I interject myself, the author, into the narrative. Scholarly biographies don't usually do that. The authorial "I" is a no-no. What, then, is this author-interjection all about?

The interludes, in part, exist as a narrative technique. They walk you, the reader, through Sofía del Valle's life and through my, the author's, process in interpreting her life. I met Sofía's surviving family when I was three-quarters of the way done with the manuscript. It made Sofía's existence as a person seem real, maybe for the first time. She was no longer just words on a dusty document. So I wrote about those encounters with Sofía's family, and it seemed appropriate to include them in the story.

There's an ethical rationale for the interludes, too. As we walk through Sofía's life we also experience my day with one of Sofía's grandnieces, Tere Huidobro. I hope the interludes provide an alternative to the straight-armed, palm-in-your-face objective distancing of much historical narrative. I hope they reveal my awareness that I, as a white, male American, am particularly ill-suited to tell the story of a Mexican, Catholic woman.

I thought quite a lot about whether to call our protagonist by her first name. There are good reasons to refer to female historical subjects by their *surnames*. Women have been minimized, infantilized, and marginalized in stories told by historians: first names for women, surnames for men—dismissal and erasure for the first, respect and reverence for the second. That was not my desire for Sofía del Valle. But it soon became clear that "Sofía," as the protagonist's name and identifier, fit the intimate tone of the book. It felt right. It felt, in fact, that after spending so much time with Sofía del Valle, learning her story, Sofía and I had moved past the formality of surnames. Each of you will judge whether I made the right choice.[1]

I'm fully aware that bringing you with me on my pilgrimage is dangerous. As you sit beside me, as you look over my shoulder, as you hear my inner thoughts, the spell of historical objectivity will be broken. You'll see my lapses, I'm afraid—my bias, my ignorance. But that's okay.

Where the book lacks objectivity it offers transparency. Maybe the interludes give some insight into the fragility of memory, perhaps a better measure as to the true weight of representation.

There's no definitive Sofía del Valle. But we, you and I, can say something about Sofía. This book is my something.

Do historians imagine anything anymore?

All good stories are true.

Prologue

DE TE FABULA NARRATUR

It's May 2005.

I feel like a man drowning in the dark subterranean sea that is Rome's subway system. The Metropolitana di Roma.

The underground sea foams with tourists, slick-suited Italians, nuns in full habit, priests in cassocks. This human wave buoys me to the surface and finally to fresh air.

I look up. A sign reads Via Ottaviano. The street will take me straight on to St. Peter's Square and to the colossal basilica that looms in the distance. Lingering doubts poke at me. You're a historian of Mexico. Why are you studying in Rome?

Caught in a meandering flotsam of humanity, I push onward to Vatican City. The smallest national territory in the world, Vatican City is a 109-acre Catholic island anchored in the heart of Rome. Before I reach the Bernini Colonnade that rings St. Peter's Square I see a gate, the Porta Angelica. A detail of Swiss Guard—six feet tall and decked out in pantaloons designed by Michelangelo—protects the entrance to Vatican City. They salute priests and bishops who splash out of the human surf on the street and into the gated world beyond. Thinking I'm just another curious tourist, a Swiss Guard points me toward St. Peter's Square.

"The basilica is that way," the blue-eyed blockade tells me in perfect English.

I shake my head and show my passport, imploring in labored Italian. "*Archeeve-oh Segree-toh Vatican-oh.*"

The guard smiles wryly and diverts me to a kind of border checkpoint. At last I stagger into Vatican City—one step closer to the Vatican Secret Archive.

I was a young graduate student then, working on a master's degree in history. It was my first experience in an archive. I was sweating.

Dan Brown's novels be damned, entrance to the Vatican Secret Archive is open to all researchers. "Secret" is perhaps one of those unintentionally provocative words that give an aura of mystery to the archive. It simply means private or reserved, not clandestine or inaccessible. There are ancient documents stretching back a millennium, but also documents of modern vintage.

I came to Rome for one reason. I wanted to be among the first scholars to look at recently declassified files held in the Vatican about Mexico's national revolution and the religious conflict that followed in its wake (ca. 1910–40).

In the archive I entered a marble-floored index room. There, scholars and students find the precise file name and number they need to call up the documents from storage. Some of the indexes give an exact idea as to what the folders contain. Some do not.

Often only *miscellaneous* is listed. For these unidentified files, an act of faith is required. Requesting them might reveal a momentous find, some newly unearthed document, or, perhaps nothing: an irrelevant list or a dull note.

"When doing research in the archives, always look under miscellaneous."

My academic advisor gave me this nugget of wisdom before I embarked on that first research trip. I have always remembered it, even now more than a decade later. It turned out to be good advice.

I made several return trips to the Vatican archive over the next ten years. I figured looking under *miscellaneous* probably meant also looking at similarly neglected headings like *appendix*. And so it was that I encountered a dossier of letters written by a Mexican woman named Sofía del Valle (born, 1891; died, 1982). Her file was in the appendix. Traces of Sofía del Valle's story had shown up before, but only as one of the many active Catholic women during the period.

Or so I thought . . .

My view changed as I read Sofía's Vatican file. She was the daughter of European immigrants to Mexico. As a devout Catholic, a single woman, neither nun nor mother, she resisted religious persecution in an era of revolutionary upheaval. She became a labor activist in a time of class conflict. She founded an educational movement, toured the United States as public lecturer, and raised money for Catholic ministries—all in an age dominated by economic depression, gender prejudice, and racial discrimination. During the Cold War, she campaigned for development in an era of revolution and anti-Americanism. Sofía del Valle's Vatican letters reveal a history that reaches far beyond Mexico.

Following Sofía's archival footprint I discovered thousands of pages of her correspondence and oral memoir. I soon found material not only in Rome, but also in Mexico and the United States. The sources describe Sofía del Valle's remarkable, though relatively unknown, life of activism.

But who was she?

The only way I know how to begin is with Sofía's life in sketch. Sofía del Valle lived through most of the twentieth century, from her birth in 1891 to her death in 1982. She was the daughter of immigrants: a Spanish father and a Mexican-born mother of French and English heritage. Sofía was birthed into a world where large Catholic families were common. The del Valle family had eight children. Sofía was second in birth order. Of six daughters two would become nuns, two would marry and have children of their own, and two—including Sofía—would never marry. She wasn't a nun. She never married and she never had children. Even so, she devoted her life to work for the Catholic Church.

War and revolution, global in their reach, didn't leave the del Valle family unaffected. The family left Mexico City for Europe in 1907, before the country plummeted into revolution. Sofía's father, a rising merchant in the Mexican capital, had the means and wherewithal to leave Mexico in a time of crisis. Most weren't so lucky. Class would always be a pronounced feature of Sofía's family, as was race—Sofía had light skin and a decidedly European heritage. The tangle of class and race provided privilege and opportunity for Sofía. First among these was education. Sofía spent her formative years in European schools, primarily Catholic, but even a Jewish school, in Lausanne, Switzerland. Sofía mastered Spanish, French, and English. She earned a teaching certificate. When

World War I broke out in 1914, the family migrated back to Spain, then later to New Orleans, Louisiana. Finally they returned to Mexico City in 1922. Sofía was thirty years old at the time. As a single woman, she worked. She used her language skills as a personal assistant to the Swedish managers of the Mexican branch of Ericsson Telephones.

Sofía's class status was subject to her Catholicism, and Catholicism was itself undergoing a social revival in the early twentieth century. Traditional Catholic charity—the rich simply giving to the poor—was no longer enough, according to the new thinking. Many Catholics had woken to the idea that the church needed to do something to fix the problems of the Industrial Revolution.[2] Poverty couldn't just be righted through alms. As Sofía surveyed Mexico in the aftermath of revolution—some two million dead in a decade of civil war—she threw herself into the Catholic social movement percolating in the capital. She organized women in the factories of the city. A night school followed, where she taught literacy and basic jobs skills to workingwomen. In 1926 Sofía established the first Catholic women's liberal arts college in Mexico. Then, war came yet again.

For the next three years (1926–29) Sofía lived through a bloody conflict called the Cristero War. It pitted the Mexican government—former revolutionaries turned politicians—against a Catholic Church unwilling to accept the political and cultural changes wrought by revolution. Thousands of Catholics rebelled. They fought, killed, and died in the name of Christ, all to force the government to change its laws, which prohibited religious liberty. For Sofía, a self-proclaimed pacifist, it meant perseverance, practicing her faith in private homes, and struggling to keep her new liberal arts college going.

Today, many Americans and Europeans have forgotten the Cristero War. But in the 1920s and 1930s the religious conflict in Mexico made international headlines.[3] The Cristero War was Mexican Catholicism's entrée to global notoriety. And in this too, Sofía del Valle would play a role.

After the Cristero War, peace visited Mexico. But the resparking of religious conflict in the 1930s inaugurated the next period of Sofía's life—peripatetic travel. For the next three decades she found herself in Rome, Paris, and Washington DC. But her journeys weren't only in great capitals. She traveled through Mexico's pueblos and cities; she visited Havana, Des Moines, and Warsaw and scores of cities and towns in between. Her job was fundraising and raising awareness of the plight of Mexican Catholics. Sofía del Valle—not a bishop, a priest, or nun, but a single woman—became the leading spokesperson for the Mexican Catholic Church in the United States and Europe.

When Sofía del Valle wasn't traveling, she led a Catholic association for young women in Mexico. It had only 8 members in 1926; by 1942 it had 102,491, and by 1960 it had 110,000. Sofía seemed to show up everywhere. In Vatican circles several popes over her lifetime knew her by name. For a time, she served as Latin America's sole member on the leadership council of the International Union of Catholic Women's Leagues, an organization that, by 1939, represented 25 million women. In the United States millions heard information she provided about Mexico on a well-known radio show, hosted by Father Charles Coughlin, America's first right-wing radio personality. She appeared on the front page of the *New York Times* as a supposed secret agent of the Mexican clergy in the United States. Her female friends and acquaintances were on the A-list of famous Catholics, including Dorothy Day and Maria von Trapp (of *Sound of Music* fame). There's even some evidence that she met Mother Teresa. Catholic women like Sofía were developing a global vision at the same time as literary, feminist, socialist, and civil rights movements. The collective portrait reveals a new model of piety and activism for Catholic women: publicly confident and culturally up-to-date, intellectually driven, professionally trained and accomplished. And more important still, these Catholic women developed careers as individuals. They weren't merely complements to famous men.

By the 1950s and 1960s Sofía's work went in new directions, in education and economic development primarily, with the United Nations Educational, Social, and Cultural Organization (UNESCO) and the Alliance for Progress. Sofía's work, she believed, was always *Catholic*, even if, increasingly, her work took her outside of Catholic organizations. In retirement, after 1972, she devoted her time to social service organizations, many of them interfaith groups, and some with feminist leadership. Sofía died in Cuernavaca, Mexico, in 1982.

Between these boldly sketched lines there are the finer details that often don't make it into the historian's portrait. There's a story of family and heartache; of memory and misremembering. There's a story of love and celibacy and what it felt like to choose. There are missions and tests, voyages and returns.

Sofía's life in sketch is not enough. Her story demands a retelling.

Unearthing Sofía del Valle's documents in the Vatican sparked my imagination. I knew that the Catholic Church experienced momentous transformations during the twentieth century. Many of those changes bracketed Sofía's own story, shaping the contours of her life. In the same year of Sofía's birth (1891), Pope Leo XIII published *Rerum Novarum*, the Catholic Church's first clear articulation of a mission to help solve working-class poverty through organized activism. The document represented a "call-to-arms" against both state socialism and laissez faire capitalism. It motivated the laity to develop a Catholic "third way," a middle path between the two systems. The century saw Catholic activists become increasingly involved in missions to peasants, urban workers, and the poor. Women like Sofía took on a pronounced role as leaders in social and missionary work—not just in Mexico, but around the globe. The Catholic Church responded—perhaps *reacted* might be a better word—to revolution, communism, and fascism. Incipient ecumenical relations with Protestants, Muslims, and Jews developed, albeit slowly, resulting in increased introspection, especially in postwar Europe. A landmark council, known as Vatican II (1962–65), retooled the very definition of what characterized the church. It had been conceived as an unassailable hierarchy of men; the council redefined it as the Pilgrim People of God, composed of all the faithful.

De te fabula narratur . . . about you the story is told.

Through Sofía's life we can see a world. And women like Sofía stood at its center. Women like Sofía carried the Catholic faith through the Cristero era, the Great Depression, World War II, the Cold War, and the building of a new world order. Her biography is a prism for the transformations in twentieth-century Catholicism.

Sofía's story uncovers how Catholic women became creative agents in shaping twentieth-century Catholicism. Worldwide, ordinary Catholics—especially women—led the church in new ways in the twentieth century. An increased focus on social justice, lay organizing, and female activism didn't suddenly appear in the 1960s. Catholics like Sofía del Valle seeded these transformations in the late nineteenth and early twentieth centuries.[4]

Sofía's life shows the remarkable rise of Latin America onto a global stage. The twentieth century saw a shift in population, and eventually power, from the Global North to the Global South.[5] Almost half of the world's Catholics now live in Latin America. The election of Pope Francis in 2013, the first pope from the region, reveals the surprising inversion of power. North America and Europe were at one time the center of global Catholicism. That is no longer the case. There are now more Catholics in Latin America than the total population of Western Europe combined. Catholicism in Latin America has become a sustaining force for the global church. Latin American activism, devotion, and charisma define the church of the present and will shape the church of the future.

Bridges and borders both make appearances in our story. Religion was a bridge connecting people and ideas across borders. Shared religious devotion, gender norms, and organizational networks linked activists across national frontiers. What Sofía's story evokes is the search for home amid rapid social and cultural change. She was a devout Catholic seeking a place in a revolutionary society, a single woman searching for a role in a male-driven religious institution, a Mexican looking for solidarity with American and European Catholics. She lived at a time when—even in the 1920s and 1930s—technology and communication were challenging the borders nations constructed. Travel, migration, culture, business, and even religious activism were just some of the transnational (or border-challenging) features of that century. Understanding how a Catholic woman such as Sofía del Valle encountered those features before the 1970s provides a greater perspective on our own increasingly interconnected world. International links were changing Catholicism long before our own digital age.

And yet, for all the important cross-border interconnection, nationalism still mattered. A key supporting cast member in our story is the Mexico Sofía knew and experienced. *Her* Mexico was in a process of reconstruction in the aftermath of the twentieth century's first great social revolution. At the very core of Sofía's motivation for action lay a love for that Mexico, to see Catholicism vindicated as a true wellspring of *Mexicanidad*, Mexican identity. Told through her eyes, the story of Mexico-in-the-world was always a Catholic story, one of hope, trial, and redemption, despite the winding roads that Providence seemed to have marked out for her nation.

And Sofía's journey says something about America's own religious evolution. Mexicans, and those of Mexican descent, have always been a part of America's religious landscape. Today, Latino Catholics in the United States have come to make up a growing majority of the most active and dynamic faith communities in the country. The vibrancy of these communities—just like the vibrancy of Sofía's life—was made richer through cross-cultural exchanges. If America is an immigrant nation, and all the better for it, then Christianity, too, in America is all the better when building bridges than when guarding borders.

Sofía's story is told not through the eyes of bishops or popes, nor prominent Catholic men from Europe or the United States, but through a little-known woman from Mexico. History can be made in the appendix as well. Sofía's story begins in Mexico City. The year is 1934.

THE MYSTERIOUS SOFÍA

PART 1

The Mysterious Sofía

1

Days of the Dead

Días de Muertos, 1934
Mexico City

News of a conspiracy to overthrow the Mexican government made headlines on the morning of October 27, 1934. The alleged conspirators were Catholic priests and a woman referred to in the press only as the "Mysterious Sofía."

The story broke as multitudes of Mexican Catholics prepared to celebrate the Days of the Dead, a traditional time of remembrance and devotion to departed loved ones. The days correspond to the ritual Catholic feasts called All Saints and All Souls in the Roman calendar, the first and second of November.

El Nacional, a newspaper funded and sponsored by the Mexican government, published the charges of conspiracy to coincide with the upcoming holiday. It was no coincidence.

The editors of *El Nacional* knew what they were doing. Publishing the allegations during the Days of the Dead would give the story maximum impact. Banks and businesses would be closed. Hundreds of earnest fathers and mothers would seek to baptize their children at the National Cathedral. Some fifty thousand pilgrims would stream to the shrine of the Virgin of Guadalupe on Tepeyac hill overlooking the city. News of a clerical conspiracy was intended to provide a stark reminder to the Mexican public that their pious pastors were not what they seemed. It was to remind citizens of the capital who in fact administered their lives. Not the clergy, but a revolutionary state that could arrest rogue priests, even bishops—a revolutionary state intent on beating religious sympathies out of the populace and instilling new civic loyalties and rituals, without reference to Mexico's Catholic past.[1]

El Nacional claimed the masterminds of the rebellion were Mexico's two most important bishops: Pascual Díaz and Leopoldo Ruiz y Flores. Their supposed goal was the overthrow of the Mexican government. Their crime, it was said, was seeking American military intervention to do so. According to the newspaper, the bishops and their accomplice—the Mysterious Sofía—had committed national betrayal.

Rumors and recriminations such as these were nothing new. Two years earlier, Leopoldo Ruiz y Flores—one of the alleged conspirators—had been forcibly exiled to the United States by the Mexican government for similar accusations. He'd been taken into custody, made to surrender his passport, and escorted by plane and then by train to Texas.[2] Ruiz, now in exile, operated as the pope's representative to Mexico while living in San Antonio.

El Nacional, and with it the Mexican government, was not just insinuating the involvement of the clergy, but outright stating it. They linked the clergy's activities at present to the tragic events of 1926 to 1929, a rebellion by the so-called *cristeros*—Catholic insurgents who led an armed uprising against the Mexican state.[3]

More than a dozen states in the country's center-west region saw rebel activity during the Cristero War of the late twenties. At its peak, some fifty thousand Catholics fought in small bands and militia detachments. Their war cry was "Long Live Christ the King!" Almost one hundred thousand combatants and civilians died in the civil war. Peace came in June 1929, but soon new bands of Catholics were once again armed. Insurgency again stalked the Mexican countryside in 1934. Catholicism would not go away.

The Catholic faith had been there since 1521, when Cortés and his marauding conquistadors laid waste to the Aztecs. They introduced guns, germs, and steel, certainly, but also the cross. Perhaps Christianity would have remained a religion of pure conquest, making disciples at the point of sword and spike. Then it happened.

A dark-skinned virgin appeared to a Nahua convert, Juan Cuauhtlatoatzin, better known by his Christian name, Juan Diego. The apparition and her message—"build a temple of worship"—happened on the very spot, Tepeyac hill, where the Aztec earth goddess Tonantzin had been venerated by natives before the conquest.[4]

The Virgin of Guadalupe, as this avatar of Mary the Mother of Jesus would be known, became a foundation myth before Mexico was Mexico. It was proof, so the story went, that God had come to this place not through European intermediaries, but directly—a dark-skinned virgin revealing Christian truth to an Indian.[5] The Catholic faith adapted to its Mexican environment, allowing it to flourish, but changing it nonetheless. The history of the spread of Christianity had always been so.

The faith practiced by most Mexicans was local. It was rooted to a shrine, a bleeding crucifix, a talking Christ, a miraculous saint. Throughout the colonial era (1521–1810) local religion administered villagers' lives and routines. Clerical reform was slow. The so-called "Rosary Belt" of Mexico's center-west didn't strengthen ties to sacramental, orthodox, and institutionally mandated rituals of the faith until the late nineteenth century.[6]

Church and state had often been at odds in Mexico. Anticlerical reform came in the mid-1800s, and again with the revolutionary generation of the 1910s. Conflict between the church and state didn't always touch the lives of average Mexicans. Yet the newest revival of anticlericalism, during the 1920s, touched off something new and more acute. The revolutionary government sought to eliminate the sacramental routines that connected Catholics to community and nation. That was the meaning of the Cristero Rebellion. The religious issue was not about "smells and bells" or seemingly inconsequential ritual issues of little import. It was a crisis of identity.

What would this new Mexico become in the aftermath of social revolution?

That was the question foremost on the minds of politically minded Mexicans. Many radicals, anticlericals, and revolutionaries envisioned a secular Mexico, without reference to God in public life: a lay state, where the streets and political forums were emptied of God-talk. At the very least, they hoped for a pliant church, committed to a religion purified of its past intrusions into Mexican politics.[7] For many Catholics, especially those mobilized amid revolutionary upheaval, the secular revolutionary vision was a denial of Mexico's history—of the very founding stories that gave meaning and movement to their lives.

And so during the Days of the Dead in 1934, religion again made headlines. "Now as previously," raged the editorial in *El Nacional*, "[Archbishop Díaz's] words are of peace but his acts and deeds are of war." The Catholic leadership was carrying out a "clerical adventure," but the government, and by extension the very revolution itself, would emerge victorious against this internal threat. "The directors of the Catholic clergy in Mexico must understand they are playing their last card."[8]

Proof of sedition and conspiracy came in the form of anecdotal thinking. Near the small town of Tanhuato, in the state of Michoacán south of Mexico City, Catholics had skirmished with a federal army detachment: eight civilians, eight rank-and-file soldiers, and one army lieutenant lay dead.[9] This was proof, to the newspaper, that the cristeros had not stopped their fighting even now in 1934. And the clergy was certainly behind it, the editorial fumed, especially as Michoacán was the same state where Ruiz was archbishop before his promotion as Vatican representative.

If correlation was not enough, *El Nacional* produced a series of letters, obtained by surreptitious means, intercepted by a web of Mexican agents who operated on both sides of the border.[10] A letter by Ruiz surfaced, where he wrote about the defense of religion in Mexico. The newspaper surmised that this could only mean *armed* defense. But a certain "Sofía" wrote the letter that attracted the most attention.

The unidentified woman's surname wasn't provided in the intercepted correspondence. She'd contacted prominent American Catholic leaders, according to one letter, on some sort of mission to the United States: "In today's edition we publish the facsimile of a letter that one of the 'agents,' named Sofía, mysteriously wrote to a recipient dubbed simply 'Doctor.' The letter came from Washington and is dated the 10th of the present month."[11]

Here then, in Sofía's own words stated the newspaper, Sofía met with the Reverend John J. Burke and William F. Montavon, both Americans, individuals the newspaper described as carrying out activities against the Mexican government during the recent Cristero Rebellion. Burke was secretary of the National Catholic Welfare Conference (NCWC) in the United States, and Montavon was in charge of the organization's propaganda. The NCWC was the leadership umbrella of the U.S. Catholic Church (a forerunner to the current United States Conference of Catholic Bishops). The NCWC, in charge of coordinating much Catholic public opinion, had important contacts in the American government. It was reported that Rev. Burke had met with American president Franklin Roosevelt just days after his conference with the Mysterious Sofía. The content of the conference was unknown, but *El Nacional* saw this as a clear invitation for American intervention, perhaps even military intervention, in the internal affairs of Mexico. "Today, as yesterday, the Mexican Revolution is confident that history will repeat itself and that the 'cristeros,' even though spilling innocent blood, will not be able to obtain their object, the control of temporal power."[12]

Who was this Sofía? the editorial asked. Through clerical agents such as Sofía, the newspaper argued, the clergy was carrying on its antigovernment campaign, perhaps organizing an "armed revolt" or even a "political assassination." At the very least the work of Sofía and the "intrigues of the directors of the clergy" were seeking to "betray the fatherland."[13]

El Nacional linked cristero insurgents, Mexican bishops, and American intervention in one sprawling clandestine conspiracy. The conspiracy's linchpin was the Mysterious Sofía.

2

The Sophie Letters

All Saints, 1934
Library of Congress, Washington DC

Miss Elizabeth Kite was worried about her friend, Sofía del Valle. While on a break from her secretarial duties at the Library of Congress, a front-page headline in the *New York Times* had caught her attention: "Ruiz Denies Catholic Plot; Mexican President Strikes at Church."[1]

Kite scanned the article. Archbishop Ruiz had written a statement—a denial of the clergy's involvement in the conspiracy. The Associated Press had picked up the statement and now the story was being splashed everywhere in the international media. The Catholic leadership of Mexico, Ruiz insisted, neither advocated armed resistance nor sought American intervention.

Accompanying Ruiz's denial was a mention of certain "Sophie" letters. The letters, Kite read, had been published in Mexico City. "Sophie" was allegedly a Catholic agent in Washington working to get the U.S. government to intervene in Mexico.

Kite dashed off a letter to the American National Council of Catholic Women (NCCW). She hoped Agnes Regan and Margaret Lynch, the NCCW's directors who administered all affairs for Catholic women in the United States, already had a handle on the situation.

Kite added a last line, a prayer for Sofía del Valle: "May Heaven protect her and the Catholics of Mexico!"[2]

3

Miss del Valle

November 5, 1934
Offices of the National Council of Catholic Women, Washington DC

Agnes Regan and Margaret Lynch were well aware of the scandal created by "Sophie," as the *New York Times* had incorrectly referred to Sofía del Valle. The "Sophie" letters had rendered Regan and Lynch's already difficult job as directors of women's ministries and a social service school that much more time consuming.

Miss del Valle was becoming a headache.

Sofía's mission had been dumped on their desk back in May. The American bishops, as well as Father Ernest G. Tagle of Catholic University of America, had insisted that they coordinate Miss del Valle's speaking tour, make contacts for her, handle arrangements and logistics, and so on.

Margaret Lynch pushed back. Wouldn't it "be better to have Miss del Valle do all of this herself?" Lynch wrote in one memorandum. "With a map of the United States, anyone could handle engagements," she drolled to her male superiors.

Miss del Valle was "entirely too busy" came the reply from Father Tagle. The groundwork and the preparation would have to be done for her, he insisted. Seeing Lynch's reluctance, Father Tagle added that he assumed Lynch would want to keep the matter "centralized" at the offices of the National Council of Catholic Women.

The priest's not-so-subtle power play worked, as it often did when a member of the male clergy requested a Catholic laywoman to follow directives. Lynch agreed, albeit grudgingly, to coordinate a plan of action and respond to Father Tagle within the week.[1]

The Mysterious Sofía public relations fiasco loomed as a new obstacle for Regan and Lynch. The increased workload it would take to coordinate Miss del Valle's lecture tour would take time away from the Catholic School of Social Service, the real heart and vision of Agnes Regan and Margaret Lynch. The school trained women in the techniques and know-how necessary to minister to the working poor, especially mothers.

After the *Times* article ran, Father Joseph Muckle, a Basilian priest in Canada, invited Sofía for an extended trip to Toronto. Lynch and Regan agreed that the nuisance of Miss del Valle had been solved.

4

The Mastermind

November 13, 1934
Convent of the Incarnate Word, San Antonio, Texas

Archbishop Leopoldo Ruiz y Flores—at age sixty-nine mostly bald, spectacled, bookish, even diminutive—seemed the least likely mastermind of a clerical plot.

He bristled at the thought of being labeled a rebel. Even apart from appearances, his theology and, more important, his practice, had never been hawkish. If anything, militant Catholics—cristeros—had blamed him for selling out, giving up on armed defense, spinning a yarn to the Vatican back in 1929 that the rebellion was doomed to fail.

Ruiz had been a realist, one of those in the clergy, along with Pascual Díaz, to help broker a peace agreement with the Mexican government. And now it was Ruiz and Pascual Díaz whom the government accused of conspiracy. To Ruiz it was, at best, a wry irony; at worst, a tragic consequence of negotiating with the Mexican government.

Ruiz, as well as Díaz, saw the cristeros as fundamentally unable to keep a key requirement of "Just War" doctrine: a possibility of success. Vatican officials believed that no revolution in Mexico could succeed without American support. Once Rome completely withdrew support for armed defense, Ruiz had backed the Vatican's line. He issued a public letter to the clergy and faithful, urging Catholics in Mexico to seek resistance to antireligious laws, but not to take up arms.[1]

But now Ruiz was the scapegoat for the Mexican government's latest charges—that he had requested American military intervention.[2]

He felt he had to respond, to make clear that the clerical conspiracy was simply a ruse, timed wisely to coincide with the government's latest ungodly proposal: socialist and sexual education in Mexico's schools. The clerical conspiracy, so-called, had merely been a distraction.[3]

He'd written as much in his statement to the Associated Press: "*El Nacional* . . . seems to be preparing the ground for charging the Catholic clergy with any excess that may break out from people provoked by this persecution."[4] The clerical conspiracy was a convenient way to blame the clergy for potential violence caused by the implementation of socialist and sexual education in Mexican schools—the educational reform intended to curtail the influence of the Roman Catholic Church. Curriculum would be absolutely secular; the ideological thrust of it was scientific and, often, antagonistic toward religious traditions. A basic sex education component was included, which horrified Catholic parents.[5]

Handling Sofía's mission to the United States would be trickier.[6] Ruiz knew that Sofía's work, to collect money for Catholic ministries in Mexico, was a fundraising mission plain and simple. It wasn't an attempt to provoke American intervention in Mexico's internal affairs.

And yet, Ruiz's denials of military intervention could not hide the evidence of American meddling in Mexican politics. In the 1840s, for instance, Mexico lost half its territory to the Manifest Destiny "visionaries" of the North. As for the Catholic Church, Mexican bishops in the 1860s helped mastermind a French invasion. The U.S. ambassador, Henry Lane Wilson, connived to see President Francisco Madero removed from power in 1913. Just a year later, U.S. Marines took the port of Veracruz for seven months.[7] In 1916 General John "Black Jack" Pershing and the so-called Punitive Expedition led the original American manhunt to track down Pancho Villa.

Pershing's raid was a disaster. Villa led Pershing and his doughboys on a wild goose chase through Mexico's north before the Great War called Pershing to help fight in the trenches of France. The Americans gained some military experience; Mexicans, especially the revolutionary government, rekindled their memories of U.S. interference. For the government's newspaper, *El Nacional*, the threat of a Catholic-led American intervention was a further way to paint the church as a traitor, playing into the longstanding nightmare of the boogeyman to the north.

For Leopoldo Ruiz, the problem was how to protect his own political cachet. Painted as a rebel by the government and perceived by the Vatican as inept, his options as an intermediary were narrowing. The *New York Times* parading Sofía's name imperiled her fundraising abilities. Ruiz considered Sofía's efforts valiant. Sofía's work was, Ruiz thought, a fundamental priority for post-cristero Mexico. Ruiz's vision was a Catholic Church in reconstruction, building for the future, growing its base through religious education and spiritual formation.

Still, Ruiz had to make sure that that his authority was not undermined by the charge that a laywoman was carrying out a clandestine mission in the United States. He crafted his statement accordingly: "No lady nor layman nor cleric has any authority to speak for the Mexican bishops, or to ask the Bishops of the United States to seek any intervention on their part, either armed or moral, in the affairs of Mexico. I myself am the only one who has authority to speak on matters Mexican, and I think I need not say I have made no such request, nor anything like it."[8]

The statement was technically correct, but it also left room for Sofía's mission in the United States. She was not speaking officially for the church, but as a Catholic activist of her own accord; the lectures she was giving were her own, not scripted by Ruiz. It was a fine line to be sure. Women like Sofía were increasingly active in Catholic lay organizations. And in Mexico's case, the activity of women was an asset. Mexican Catholic men were more easily flagged for political activism. Because of their gender, churchwomen like Sofía had the potential to operate without suspicion, not appearing to "do" politics as such.[9] Women in Mexico still did not have the right to vote, and their organizing for the church was often perceived as pious superstition by revolutionary politicians. Yet the greater significance of her mission should not be missed. In an era of revolutionary upheaval and political unrest, a Catholic woman was at the vanguard of church renewal. This carried with it an inherent tension. Theological principles mandated the maintenance of hierarchy and gender division. But theology had to be balanced against the practical advantages women could win in their increasingly public role as leaders in the church.

The question remained about the future of Sofía's mission. Ruiz had luckily been in Washington when the news broke in *El Nacional*. On his visit to the Washington offices of the NCWC, Ruiz officiated Mass the morning after his arrival.

From where Ruiz stood, vestment-clad and consecrating wafers and wine, he could see the Mysterious Sofía. The woman before him was forty-three, almost five feet, six inches tall, and, Ruiz knew, made thin from a chronic liver condition. A prayer shawl covered coal-black hair, which she left braided and clipped close in the back, a nod to the short hairstyles of the day. She had an oval face, a slightly receding chin, a determined, downturned nose.

After Mass, Ruiz told Sofía that *El Nacional* had publicized a letter from her to Rev. Miguel Miranda, the "Doctor" cited in the newspaper's editorial—that it had revealed some of her activities in the United States. He showed her the article: "Conspiracy of the Mexican Clergy to Obtain the Intervention of the United States in Mexico: Mysterious Sofía Agent."[10]

She became anxious for her family. Could there be reprisals against her parents? She left her surname off the letter. It seemed safe to suppose that her real identity was not publicly known in Mexico.[11]

Certainly the authorities knew?

Ruiz couldn't be sure but, just to be safe, counseled Sofía that it would be wise for her to go to Canada for the time being, and hopefully, the affair would be resolved.

In November 1934, during Mexico's Days of the Dead, it was neither clear whether Sofía's mission would succeed nor whether the religious troubles of Mexico would ever end.

Interlude

TERE HUIDOBRO

Recently

Paseo de la Reforma, Mexico City, 8:44 a.m.

This is where I've come to end my search for Sofía del Valle.

A Starbucks.

And it's all wrong.

The Starbucks is counter only, none of those ubiquitous café chairs. It won't do for this meeting. I'm supposed to have an interview with Tere Huidobro, Sofía del Valle's grandniece, to talk about Tía Popi, the name Tere always uses to refer to Sofía.

I'm struck that this moment is actually pretty funny.

As I'm starting to look on my phone for suitable locations with actual chairs I hear a voice. "¿Estephan?"

I realize I'm completely engrossed in my smartphone. I look either severely sight impaired or, at the very least, weirdly unprofessional.

Wheeling in the direction of the voice, I shove the phone in my pocket. I respond in Spanish (as all our conversations will be in Spanish) and contort surprise into an awkward smile.

Tere Huidobro comes into view. *This is Sofía del Valle's grandniece.* She's a woman nearing fifty. Dark hair and light complexion. Honestly, Tere looks nothing like Sofía, but her face seems to share some indefinable family resemblance. Maybe the eyes? I think. Yes, perhaps the eyes, slightly hooded; those long smile lines on her cheeks . . .

I greet Tere with outstretched hand. A man, presumably her husband, is with her.

"Héctor," he introduces himself formally, without so much as another word. I wonder whether Tere's husband is skeptical of this whole interview thing.

I don't pursue the thought because I see an enormous, brightly colored sewn handbag under Tere's arm. Photo albums. She's messaged me about these photos; she inherited them from her father, José Luis Ruiz de Huidobro del Valle, Sofía's nephew. José Luis died in 2010. He was Sofía's godson, born in 1930. His mother, Ana María, was Sofía's sister.[1]

The only reason I know any of this, that I'm even in touch with Sofía's extended family at all, is due to the miracle of modern internet connectivity. By which I mean Facebook. Six months previous, I Googled "Sofía del Valle" and went through almost every result that came back. One of the hits led me to a web-based genealogy site. It provided a partial list of del Valle descendants. From there I contacted the account holder. Turns out he's a professor at Johns Hopkins University. His wife, named Ana María like her grandmother, also teachers at Hopkins. She's Ana María del Valle's granddaughter and grandniece to Sofía. Ana María kindly spoke to me and directed me to Tere Huidobro in Mexico City. Ana and Tere are cousins, but Tere possesses most of the material remains of Sofía's memory, most of which fits inside that brightly colored sewn handbag under her arm. *I really want to see what's inside that bag.*

Tere doesn't have internet or a computer at her home, but she's sent photos by her phone. Photos of photos are what I've seen, and only a few, for that matter.

And so we're here, the three of us, on the sidewalk of Mexico City's grand thoroughfare, Paseo de la Reforma. Reforma Boulevard.

"*¿Qué hacemos?*" What should we do now? Tere asks the question to no one in particular. She realizes the Starbucks I've chosen is not apt for an interview. We start walking.

From a roundabout in the middle of Reforma Boulevard, the Angel of Independence, a 311-foot victory column, stares down at us as if waiting for my reply. Its wings unfurled all in gold, bare breasted, the angel reaches out with laurel crown in hand.

Perhaps this is where my pilgrimage to find Sofía del Valle ends. But the day has only just started. *Origins*, I think. Begin at the beginning.

PART 2

A Family Romance

5

Little Flowers

"Well look," Sofía told an interviewer in 1972, "I was born on October 18, 1891, so I am eighty-one years old. I was born in Mexico City. My father Spanish, based in Mexico, my mother born in Mexico, of an English mother and French father of Belgian origin... that is the hodgepodge of which I was made."[1]

The mysterious Sofía's family heritage, the "hodgepodge" from which she descended, was decidedly European and staunchly Catholic in origin. Both put her at odds with the revolutionary vision of Mexican identity.

Sofía's family first arrived in Mexico during the turmoil of the French Intervention (1862–67). They were immigrants who came to the country in the wake of an imperial dream. Sofía was the daughter of an Anglo-French, though Mexican-born, mother named Sofía Goeury Smith. Her maternal grandfather was Henri Goeury, a Parisian furniture maker. In the 1860s Henri was wooed by Mexican monarchists into leaving his successful shop in Paris in order to assist in the decoration of the Palacio Nacional and Chapultepec Castle. Only the best French styles would do for the newly arrived Emperor Maximilian. Family lore had it that Sofía's grandfather was never formally paid for his work; that as the political winds began to turn against the emperor, and financial resources became scant, Henri received just one cup, albeit a cup used by Maximilian as he breakfasted each morning. Henri died soon after, and Sofía's grandmother decided to remain in Mexico to raise her two daughters.[2]

Sofía's mother's family had arrived in Mexico at an important moment in the country's national story. Debate over whom or what made Mexico *Mexico* fueled the social and political fights of the nineteenth century. On paper the demographics were clear. When Mexico achieved its independence from Spain in 1821, approximately 60 percent of its population was considered "Indian." The trend extended well into the nineteenth century. Early national leaders and intellectuals set policies to incorporate and amalgamate Mexico's indigenous population. It was less a policy of "whitening" than a drive to *mexicanizar*—to Mexicanize—unacculturated and unincorporated groups. The so-called Wild Indians, the *Indios Bárbaros* of the great northern frontier, were one important target of conquest and later assimilation. Teaching Spanish language and promoting productive industry and agriculture were part of the assimilation strategy. The dream of the yeoman farmer tilling small plots of land was the vision of many of Mexico's early political class just as it was with their Jeffersonian neighbors to the north. In Argentina and Brazil, leaders courted European immigrants to model industriousness. But Mexico's particular social and political milieu presented obstacles to attracting foreigners.[3]

The nineteenth-century project of Mexicanization sputtered as large swaths of Mexico's north remained ungovernable. The Apache and Comanche forged their own empires with no regard for Mexico's desire to build a nation.[4] A century filled with civil war and foreign interventions did nothing to create a hospitable environment for European immigrants seeking new lives across the seas. Mexico lost half its territory in the Mexican-American war of 1846–48. Conservatives and liberals duked it out in a bloody civil conflict over a series of reform laws and a new Constitution in 1857. Conservatives felt themselves the protectors of the colonial heritage; this included the legacy and institutional interests of the Catholic Church. And conservatives didn't go down without a fight. For a time conservatives were victorious over the liberals led by Benito Juárez. Conservatives, in league with the Catholic hierarchy, invited Napoleon III of France to name a foreign emperor to rule Mexico. This was the French Intervention that prompted some of Sofía del Valle's family to immigrate. The European noble secured was Maximilian, of Austrian Hapsburg stock. Maximilian set up his imperial court in Mexico City and ruled for less than five years in a kind of colonial pastiche.

This was the twilight of the monarchs on both sides of the Atlantic. Maximilian disappointed his conservative and Catholic suitors, having himself taken a shine to many of the liberal policies that the Mexican monarchists so loathed. Benito Juárez and his radical liberals continued their march to the capital, and a promising young general named Porfirio Díaz rode in front of a proud cavalry, taking back power from the foreign interlopers. And Sofía's grandfather was thus left with an emperor's breakfast cup for services rendered.

Porfirio Díaz leveraged his own rising popularity from the nationalist victory, eventually taking the presidency in 1876. Maximilian was shot, and his wife Carlotta spent the rest of her years back in Europe. If anything, xenophobia solidified in the nineteenth century. Militant antiforeign sentiment hardly left room for the European immigrant to constitute any meaningful element of Mexican identity. And while French fashion and culture made their mark on Mexican consumerism during the long dictatorship of Porfirio Díaz (1876–1911), Victorian culture—and English pounds—arguably held a stronger pull for many in the fallout from the French imperial disaster.[5]

If the French Intervention colored Sofía's mother's family, her father had an equally important link to prerevolutionary Mexico. Sofía's father, Francisco del Valle Ballina, was one of the relatively few Spanish immigrants who came from Spain to Mexico during the Porfiriato. Several factors favored European immigration to the United States rather than Mexico. American immigration policies lured Europeans with looser restrictions, higher wages, and the promise of work, as there was far less labor competition from indigenous groups in the United States than in Mexico.[6] Before 1876 only some 25,000–35,000 foreigners had immigrated to Mexico; that number would climb to 116,527 by 1910 and reach 270,000 by the end of the Great Depression. Scant figures when compared to the United States from 1820 to 1932 (32.5 million), Argentina (6.5 million), and Brazil (4.3 million).[7] Given Mexico's policies, it's interesting that Sofía del Valle's Spanish father made it to Mexico at all. But Mexico held one attraction for Francisco that the United States couldn't provide: an uncle who already owned a successful grocery store in Toluca, a town outside the Mexican capital. When his uncle offered him a job, Francisco made the decision to immigrate to Mexico, in the hopes of improving his economic and social status.[8]

Francisco was capable and hard working. In little over a year, he was able to relocate to Mexico City with the money and contacts he had gained through his uncle. He was eventually named manager of a factory of wines and liquor, called La Casa Colorada. Through his importation of European methods of distillation, Francisco expanded the factory's business and his own personal wealth. At thirty-two Francisco married Sofía Goeury and children quickly followed.

Their second daughter was given the name María Sofía Victoria del Valle. In public she would go by Sofía del Valle. Friends and family simply called her by the nickname "Chofi."

Sofía's family heritage placed her on a particular side of Mexican history: conservative, linked to the old regime, organizational Catholics of an antirevolutionary stripe. She belonged to an elite social class in Mexico, extremely wealthy compared to the majority. But according to her, Sofía's father endeavored to wield his financial success without aristocratic pretentions or ostentation.[9] Francisco del Valle dressed in English suits with tailored jackets and high-collared shirts. As he aged he grew a white walrus mustache and walked with an elegant cane. Securing a comfortable home for his large family—six daughters and two sons—and educating them remained his chief concerns.

Disciplined, industrious, and successful in business, Francisco del Valle was also deeply religious. He and his wife endeavored to pass on their spiritual commitments to their children. Like many Catholics of the day—Mexican Catholics included—Sofía del Valle and her family were especially devoted to the newly canonized Thérèse of Lisieux. Catholics called Thérèse "the Little Flower." Although she lived a cloistered life, Santa Teresita, as she was known in Spanish, inspired worldwide affection and became a model of female piety suited to contemporary Catholic sensibilities.

Born Thérèse Martin in 1873 to pious parents, she grew up in northern France, where she would spend most of her short life. Thérèse was

1. Sofía Goeury Smith and Francisco del Valle Ballina, ca. 1887. Personal collection of Adriana Garza Ramos.

the youngest of five living children. Her mother, Zelie Martin, died of breast cancer when Thérèse was only four-and-a-half years old. At thirteen Thérèse expressed her desire to enter the Carmelite order at Lisieux, following the example of several older siblings. But the rules of the religious order stated that novices had to be sixteen. At fifteen she took the most important trip of her life, a pilgrimage to Rome, where she accompanied her father and one of her sisters. During an audience with Pope Leo XIII (1878–1903), arranged by her father, Thérèse, in disobedience to an express order by the papal staff to remain quiet during the meeting, fell before the pope, clung to his knees, and did not let go until Leo permitted her to enter the Carmelites early. She got her way, and on returning to France, she joined the religious community at the Lisieux Carmel. She took the name Thérèse of the Child Jesus and the Holy Face (Thérèse de l'Enfant-Jésus et de la Sainte-Face). For the remaining nine years of her life she lived within the cloister, until her premature death of tuberculosis at twenty-four years old in 1897.[10]

Thérèse's brand of spirituality consisted of prayer, self-abnegation, and daily sacrifice. She rejected the idea of becoming a great saint, instead endeavoring to gain union with God through the ordinary duties and routines of life. And although Thérèse repudiated the notion of pursuing sainthood, saintliness remained her central focus. She likened the status of her soul to that of a daisy or violet in the world of flowers, not comparable to magnificent lilies or roses. If she were not a great soul, just as daisies and violets were not great flowers, she would still seek to give joy to "God's glances when He looks down at His feet."[11] From this reference came her name "the Little Flower," by which millions of Catholics would come to know her. The Little Flower promoted a "little way," a path that recognized "complicated methods are not for simple souls," and she would write in her autobiography, begun just two years before her death, that "I am one of those."[12] Her mysticism, then, was not that of ecstatic experience or soaring visions. She emphasized holiness as union with God. It was achieved through performing the ordinary tasks of life, but doing them in love. Her diary attests to this, highlighting some of the menial tasks in which God could be found, including reading, folding clothes, daydreaming, and observing nature.[13] The "little way" was about daily self-sacrifices, the lack of spiritual consolation, hiding pain—mental and physical—behind a smile, reveling in one's smallness, hiddenness, and obscurity. As historian Barbara Pope describes, "because God watched every act, no matter how small, each act became a kind of drama."[14] Thérèse's spiritual quest "offered a balance against the rational organization which so powerfully shaped late nineteenth- and early twentieth-century piety, allowing a growing number of individuals to transcend the ordered drive of modernity and attain a profoundly personal union with the divine."[15] Thérèse's emphasis on her interior life, self-transformation, personal experience, suffering, and innocence provided a powerful devotional repertoire mounted against the skepticism, materialism, and rationalism ascendant in contemporary culture. Thérèse's little way "described how Catholics could act 'in the world' without being harmed by it."[16]

The Little Flower's precipitous growth from obscure nun at her death in 1897 to canonization and acclaim by Catholics worldwide by 1925 can be explained through a combination of savvy marketing and genuine appeal. The Lisieux Carmelites distributed two thousand copies of a portion of her autobiography along with some of Thérèse's correspondence after her untimely death. The autobiography would later comprise three parts and be published as *The Story of a Soul*. By 1909 the Carmelite community at Lisieux received fifty letters a day describing miracles and favors attributed to Thérèse's intercession. This was in keeping with the assertion of Thérèse's companions, who claimed that on her deathbed, Thérèse stated that she would spend her time in heaven doing good on earth. By 1914 these letters reached approximately five hundred a day. In 1925, the year of her canonization, *The Story of a Soul* had been translated into thirty-five different languages.

Thérèse's popularity was further aided by millions of devotional prayer cards. Her sisters had dutifully collected her eyelashes and tears as relics even before her untimely death. As her fame spread, newly erected statues of the saint holding a bouquet of roses popped up in parish churches and chapels across Europe and the Americas. The large propaganda effort was assisted by the Carmelites' dogged determination to see the process completed. Although Thérèse fit the ideal of female piety, she also fit the statistic: "since the eighteenth century as Rome bureaucratized the process, 80% of saints were members of the clergy or religious orders and 65% of those came from France, Spain, and Italy."[17]

Thérèse helped bring the world of the contemplative cloister into the realm of popular piety.[18] Her autobiography had something for everyone. It was part family romance, depicting a model Catholic family; part clerical portrait; part ethical and theological rumination—even a compelling narrative of female autonomy in a male-dominated religious world. She was the perfect heroine. Catholics saw her as an innocent, suffering, and miracle-working girl. She reflected the early twentieth-century Catholic disposition of withdrawal inward. But Catholics found hope in Thérèse's vibrant, intimate relationship with Jesus—hope that intimacy with God could bring about salvation not only for the individual soul, but for the family, the nation, and the world.[19]

We can catch a glimpse of Thérèse reflected in the life of Sofía del Valle. Thérèse, the Little Flower, became the patroness of the Mexican Young Women's Catholic Association (Juventud Católica Femenina Mexicana or JCFM), which Sofía helped establish. Sofía's hardships, small sufferings, even the monotony of her journeys—all recorded in her long correspondence with various priests and bishops—give us a sense of a spiritual simulacrum reenacted in Sofía's daily search for union with God and a mission to sanctify the worlds surrounding her. Sofía's letters evoke a deep intimacy with God, whom she constantly referred to as "Diosito" (dear little God). Like Thérèse, Sofía was often self-effacing. Sofía described herself as no one special, but still someone through whom God could do great things.

Yet there were important differences. Unlike Thérèse, Sofía decided to live out her devotion and activism in the world. Mexican women were never neatly confined to the traditional spheres of acceptable female piety: the convent, on the one end, and conjugal domesticity, on the other.[20] Revolution in Mexico and total war in Europe, whatever political reorganizations these processes set in motion, had likewise opened up new possibilities for women.[21] While for Catholic women these possibilities remained bounded by a male-dominated hierarchy, these same church leaders promoted female activism. Male clergy encouraged a robust Catholic femininity as a counterbalance to the perceived threat of liberal feminism.[22] Moreover, in Latin America, the mobilization of the laity, and especially women, was in large part a development stemming from the realities of priestly scarcity. There weren't enough priests, and so laymen and laywomen had to fill the

2. Sofía del Valle (*left*) imagining dramatic worlds to inhabit. Date unknown. Personal collection of María Teresa Ruiz de Huidobro Márquez.

gaps. Behind the call-to-arms, so to speak, was the church's fear of losing members to Protestant evangelization and to socialists. Catholic women especially were seen as educators. They could defend the young from non-Catholic influences by providing moral and religious training.[23] Catholic activist women, like Sofía, did not promote radical egalitarian gender relations. But their activity and leadership commonly undermined the stereotype of the pliant religious woman. Sofía del Valle, like many of her counterparts in Europe and the Americas, helped shape a public role for Catholic women: little flowers growing wild outside cloistered walls.

Sofía del Valle's memories of childhood read like a family romance. They could be taken from the pages of Thérèse of Lisieux's autobiography, *The Story of a Soul.*

Catholics loved the family romance genre. It provided an ideal model of paternal provision, maternal sacrifice, a family built on domestic stability, founded in daily devotional practices such as the rosary, quotidian Communion, and corporate prayer. The family romance operated as a critique of the social disintegration lamented by Catholics in Europe and the Americas. Forces eroding the family included crowded urban centers, industrial wage labor, women working outside the home, and a rising secular state.[24]

Sofía wrote fondly of the del Valle home in an unfinished memoir. The del Valle residence was one of the first to be built in the Colonia Roma neighborhood of Mexico City, an area of the capital soon to be associated with the urban, Catholic lay elite. A new church, run by the Jesuit order called La Sagrada Familia (The Holy Family), would be built in Colonia Roma in 1910.[25] It offered brick-and-mortar proof of the idealized Catholic family's power in that era.

One of the earliest surviving family portraits of the del Valles reflects the Catholic ideal. The del Valles are respectable: thoroughly well-to-do with pretty dresses and neat suits in Victorian style. Francisco del Valle's growing business allowed the family to afford a nanny as well as the means to educate the children at home with a personal tutor.

In addition to the intimate atmosphere and the happy family meals, Sofía recalled the influence of her maternal grandmother, who lived with the family. Sofía's grandmother spoke Spanish only partially, a product of the French enclave in which she remained after the death of her husband. Sofía remembered her fortitude, as well as her sense of humor. "*¡Hija sé fuerte!*" (Be strong, girl!) she often heard her grandmother say.[26] Yet Sofía's grandmother mixed her exhortations with levity; she always had some joke or funny story to tell the children. It was her grandmother who taught Sofía to pray and to recognize that spiritual realities surrounded life on earth. Prayer was about fostering gratitude according to Sofía's grandmother: "To pray not only asking, as if God were a chest full of stuff available to suit my tastes, but joy-

3. Family del Valle, ca. 1900: Sofía Goeury de del Valle (Sofía's mother, *standing*); Francisco del Valle Ballina (Sofía's father, *seated*). Children (*left to right*): Francisco "Paco," age 5; Hortensia, age 3; Sofía, age 9; Clara, age 7; Matilde, age 12. Three more children, not pictured, would be added: Ana María, Enrique, and Consuelo. Personal collection of María Teresa Ruiz de Huidobro Márquez.

ously giving thanks for the beauty that surrounded me in the rain, for flowers, for the birds, for the children who sang and played around me and invited me to their games, the joy of a home in peace."[27] Sofía's memories of her family reflect an ideal. The del Valles were inward without being insular. They sought to be ordered and happy. Families like hers, Sofía believed, were families that could lay a foundation for peace in chaotic modern cities and strife-ridden nations.

How do we get at the del Valle family behind the ideal?

Sofía's letters, as well as her unfinished memoir, provide intimations of life behind the veneer. There are clues that Sofía often battled with her mother and that these frequent clashes developed in Sofía an acutely resilient will. A strict disciplinarian, the elder Sofía loved order. Francisco mainly provided the tenderness. He doted on his children; he was affable and approachable. Tenderness also came from Sofía's

Little Flowers   29

4. Sofía del Valle with her maternal grandmother, Sofía Smith de Goeury. Date unknown. Personal collection of María Teresa Ruiz de Huidobro Márquez.

grandmother, who taught her grandchildren to pray as well as to play. Nurture came from the family's *nanita*, an endearing name Sofía used for their nanny. Sofía recalled in a 1972 interview with historian Alicia Olivera that the nanny "lived with us her whole life and died in my house at the age of seventy."[28] The nanny—Sofía never gave her name—was a woman of the working class, dark skinned, originally from the state of Guanajuato. It was common for poor, mestiza women to work as domestic servants. She traveled with the del Valles to Europe, still wearing her "sandals and sombrero" and her jacket made of leather. The del Valle children teased their nanny about her Mexican clothes in comparison to the European fashions. "She was one of the ugliest people I have ever known in my life," Sofía remembered, perhaps reflecting the racist stereotypes of her era when beauty was associated with lighter skin tones. "But," Sofía continued, "also one of the best and the smartest."[29] Sofía may have learned discipline from her mother, inherited her mother's tenacity, and taken up her mother's love of learning, but the early nurture Sofía received came from her *nanita*.

The two Sofías, mother and daughter, seemed to butt heads. Much later, when Sofía was a woman of forty, she hinted at the family dynamic established between her, her father, and her mother. Sofía was then in Belgium, studying the latest methods of Catholic organizing. While in Bruges, Sofía stayed with a Catholic family whose daughter Sofía had come to know. Sofía saw her own story played out at dinner one evening. She observed the young woman's interactions with her father and mother. "I ate with the family," Sofía described in a letter to a friend, "and I encountered a Father del Valle who supports his daughter and I found a Mother del Valle who at times *repels her*." Sofía made sure to underline the phrase. "It is always the same!!" Sofía commented.[30]

Sofía's description, at forty, is brief but telling: easy support and acceptance from her father, demanding expectations and resistance from her mother. Whatever childhood and adolescent battle of wills lay behind Sofía's comment, and perhaps they extended even into adulthood, Sofía came to possess fortitude, derived, in part, from battling with her mother. Sofía's personality was not one of withdrawal from

5. *Left to right*: Sofia Goeury de del Valle, Hortensia, Sofía, Matilde, Consuelo, Francisco del Valle, Enrique (*seated*), Ana María, Francisco, Clara. Date unknown. Personal collection of Adriana Garza Ramos.

conflict, but confrontation. She learned early to hold her opinions, even under resistance. She learned she would have to fight to keep them.

Another photograph, this one of the now completed del Valle family—all eight children appear—hints strongly at the family dynamic. They are ordered, but playful. Sofía is at the center, smiling happily, with her head nearly resting on her sister Hortensia's shoulder. Francisco, the father, is amid the children; the youngest, Consuelo, is on his lap. Francisco is enthralled by Clara's piano playing, as perhaps he is by all the doings of his eight children. The elder Sofía, the mother, looks up from her open newspaper, darting a look both stern and annoyed to her oblivious children.

As with saints so with Sofía . . . it's difficult to disentangle the ideal and the real.

6

Sofía's Belle Époque

> What of chastity? It confers a particular strength.
>
> Marianne Moore

One of the del Valle family's early neighbors in Colonia Roma was Pedro Lascuráin, a conservative Catholic. After the start of the Mexican Revolution in 1910, Lascuráin served as foreign secretary under President Francisco I. Madero (1911–13). Pedro Lascuráin then played an infamous role in General Victoriano Huerta's coup d'état in 1913.[1] The del Valles weren't in Mexico to experience their neighbor's notorious role in the revolution. Francisco del Valle moved his family to Europe in 1907, when Sofía was sixteen. Yet, the course and process of the revolution left an indelible mark on Sofía; her later work as a Catholic social activist was conceived in response to a society in reconstruction, where Catholics endeavored to forward their own plan for Mexico's future. The Catholic alternative to revolution would emphasize the integrity of the family, from resisting socialist education to promoting protection for a family wage.[2]

As the Mexican Revolution developed, Sofía del Valle spent her remaining formative years in Europe, alternating between Villaviciosa, Asturias (Spain), her father's hometown, and Lausanne, Switzerland. In Lausanne Sofía encountered a cosmopolitan world; in school she met students from various parts of Europe. She learned to command French and English and developed friendships with girls from diverse religious traditions, especially Jewish émigrés to the city.[3] Sofía recounted, "We had contact with young people from different European countries and different religions. This helped us to expand our view of life, to understand better what the world is and more than once, to get some good little lesson helpful for the future." These lessons came not only through her studies at the Catholic Institute of Lausanne, which she attended every morning, but also through her studies at a Jewish school called "Bonne Brise." There she recalled a friendship with a young Jewish girl who challenged her character: "I find that your judgments in general are very quick; you don't wait to have all the necessary information before airing them. I recommend this phrase that has helped me in life: *D'abord comprendre et ensuite juger*" (First understand and then judge).[4]

Sofía recalled that her friend's words affected her deeply. Speaking her mind was never a problem for the young Sofía. But, even as a young woman, she realized her judgments had to be based in real facts. Sofía later remembered her friend was not just recommending the adage, "think before you speak." She was telling Sofía to *understand*. For Sofía, that meant education, reading, consultation, introspection, and investigation. Sofía came to believe her opinions were only as good as her preparation.

But how close to that ideal did she come in her younger years? Certainly as an old woman she looked back on the incident as significant, a "good little lesson helpful for the future." Perhaps over time she came to develop a reserve in airing her opinions in the pursuit of a just appraisal of people and circumstances. And yet the experience of failure to keep an ideal is a painful teacher. Sofía, to at least one young Jewish girl, was not only quick to make judgments, but also unafraid to voice unfounded opinions. We don't know what the interaction entailed. Was Sofía brash? Was it simply teenage arrogance? Backbiting? Gossip? Or was it religiously motivated, fueled by awkward misunderstandings and prejudices between a Jewish girl and a Catholic one? At any rate, this didn't seem to be the first time Sofía's judgments and opinions had caused conflict with those around her. Sofía often had strong words with her sisters. She could be short with them—even in later years members of the del Valle family would remember Sofía's clashes with her younger siblings. Sofía, in her late teens and early twenties, was a young woman with a sharp mind and, at times, a sharp tongue. She believed her opinions should be heard, even when the demands of deference recommended silence.

6. Sofía (*far left, second row*); Matilde (*first row, kneeling*), holding hands, wearing white blouse with collar, ca. 1908. Personal collection of María Teresa Ruiz de Huidobro Márquez.

Sofía's years in Europe tell us also about Sofía as a developing woman: her emerging understanding of femininity and sexuality. The ideal of feminine beauty was in flux when Sofía arrived in Lausanne in 1907. The Victorian era had been all about tiny waists, large busts, and still larger behinds—an illusion kept up, quite literally, through corsets, bustles, and crinoline underskirts. By the first decade of the 1900s more slender silhouettes appeared, still with accentuated bust and hips, but more statuesque. Dresses became slightly more functional and bell shaped. In America the new look was called the Gibson Girl. The Gibson Girl ideal encompassed both a new fashion sense and a new sense of freedom. She was athletic, flirty, independent—a woman with a larger say in her sexual choices. Women's hairstyles were swept up in bouffant, pompadour style or worn as loose curls piled atop the head. Shirtwaist blouses hung over cinched waistlines. Suit jackets for women fitted over skirts that exposed shoes and even showed some ankle. Hats expanded.[5]

Sofía's Belle Époque

The real, shocking change was in undergarments as designers began dispensing with corsets. Female bust support needed a new garment. It was called the bandeaux, the bust extender, the bust supporter, the bust shaper, and most commonly, the bust bodice or the *Soutien-gorge*. Finally, by the onset of World War I, "brassiere" became the conventional name.[6]

Hats, hairdos, and "bras" defined the changes in fashion Sofía encountered through her own emergence into early womanhood. The hats and hairdos are easily identified in photographs of Sofía from the era; the undergarments, less so. In one picture, Sofía appears with her schoolmates shortly after her arrival in Lausanne. It was probably taken around 1908. She would've been seventeen. Sofía and the other young women have big hair, puffed and curled and back brushed to achieve the bouffant, pompadour style. Some of the younger girls still have braided hair; they wear sailor suits indicative of styles for children. But not Sofía. She wears a shirtwaist blouse, billowing over a belted waist. Whether she wore a bust bodice or simple corset is unclear. But her silhouette is certainly not the exaggerated S-curve of the late Victorian era.

Another photograph shows Sofía and her sister, Matilde, a few years later, probably between 1910 and 1912. She would've been around twenty. Their silhouettes are straighter, their suit jackets tailored, but without the severely cinched waist of a few years earlier. Their hats and hairdos are still big. They were clearly within the fashion stream of their day, but in a comfortable mainstream. They weren't pushing the boundaries of acceptable wear for respectable young women, nor were they lagging behind.

Hats, hairdos, guesses about undergarments—what do these tell us about Sofía as a young woman? They signal class and social status. She was firmly in the upper crust of society. Her family had the means to educate Sofía at good schools. Sofía had the resources to pay attention to fashion trends and to wear fashionable clothes, even selectively. Yet Sofía was also a *Catholic* young woman. She wasn't at the avant-garde of fashion fads; her manner of dress wasn't scandalizing to her parents. Still, she paid attention to beauty, to presenting herself as distinctly feminine within the conventions of feminine beauty at the time. She

7. Matilde (*left*), Sofía, and an unidentified friend. "Memories of the old days in Lausanne," ca. 1910–12. Personal collection of María Teresa Ruiz de Huidobro Márquez.

wasn't a liberated bon vivant of the Belle Époque. But neither was she a homely schoolmarm-in-training; she wasn't prudish and unconcerned with worldly beauty. The stereotypes don't fit Sofía—liberated or repressed. She was probably a better representation of a young woman of her class and religion than either of the two extremes.

Choices about fashion and beauty call to mind other choices Sofía made as a young woman: choices about sexuality.

Wouldn't a pretty and fashionable young woman desire marriage?

The question assumes the stereotypes of Sofía's own day: that an eligible young lady would surely want to marry. Catholicism in that era urged either marriage or the convent. But Sofía seemed unafraid to postpone a decision on the issue. She remembered vividly how her father, when the family lived in Lausanne, received an offer of marriage for Sofía from a distant family relative. Because Sofía was just sixteen, her father didn't believe she was ready for an engagement and politely refused the proposal. Later he humorously recounted the proposal to his daughter. Sofía herself was relieved; romantic attachment was not on her mind at the time.[7]

It seems reasonable enough that Sofía, at sixteen, didn't want an engagement to a distant relative. The situation, however, does speak volumes about Francisco del Valle. He appeared cognizant of what his daughter might want or not want in the matter, instead of being overbearing. What he sought for his children was a good education. Francisco was in the habit of saying, Sofía recalled, "I am not going to leave my children money, because money can be robbed from anyone, or someone could marry one of my daughters for it, whatever it might be . . . no . . . I will leave my children education."[8] Education for daughters was not a foregone conclusion in 1910. Sofía's father valued the development of his daughters' minds, not as a function of attracting a mate, but as an asset they might hold for whatever the future would bring.

What, if anything, do we learn of Sofía's choices about sexuality?

Apart from this early proposal, Sofía never spoke about any romantic attachments, potential or otherwise. Her later interviews are silent on the issue, other than to say she didn't feel a call to marriage. Sofía's letters make no allusion to a boyfriend or to young infatuation. On the other side of the spectrum, Sofía never expressed a desire to be a nun, to join a religious order like her sisters Hortensia and Consuelo. In fact, she made sure to distinguish herself from the consecrated life, often taking offense at the suggestion that she was a nun, as she later traveled alone, as a single woman past the age when most women had already married. When faced with the conventional choices of a Catholic young woman—marriage or the convent—she would end up choosing neither. What she chose was celibacy, to live a celibate life of service.

Although modern readers may suspect otherwise, Sofía's celibacy didn't cover for something else, whether it be homosexual attraction, an asexual orientation, or a negative view of married, heterosexual intercourse.[9] Her choice for celibacy was a sign of her power to decide. Past generations of young women might've become nuns to experience a life free from the responsibilities of marriage and children. Sofía didn't have to make that choice. Society was shifting. Women went to university. They became doctors, lawyers, teachers, and office workers. Women, especially single ones from well-established families, could become professionals. The church, for its part, gradually and over time accepted the role of young single women as activists.[10]

The life of a single woman had its benefits. Nuns were free from family responsibility, but were the object of tighter scrutiny, more surveillance, than laywomen. They rarely, for instance, were allowed to travel alone. Although the church desired young women to see themselves as mothers-in-the-making, male clergy could be pragmatic too. Single laywomen, argued an increasing number of churchmen, were needed to speak in public defense of the church, even to devote all their activities to the effort.[11] The church needed women, and this opened a space for them to take up leadership roles. But there was a caveat: Sofía's independence, as a lay celibate woman, was bounded by the recognition of her parents' authority—which she always foregrounded—as well as by the close relationships she formed with Mexican clergy. She nodded to the spiritual direction of prominent bishops and priests. She always finished her letters to spiritual leaders by signing off as *"una hija en el Señor"* (a daughter in the Lord).[12] Sofía's choice for celibacy, although not without its Catholic limitations, empowered her unlike her married and consecrated sisters.

The del Valle's spent seven years in Lausanne. Matilde and Sofía, the two eldest, were close in age and developed a tight bond. They worked teaching catechism to children in Lausanne from 1910 to 1914. With the outbreak of war in 1914, the family fled Switzerland through France and on to Spain via train. The war-wounded crowded the train cars, many scarred from battle, leaving a deep impression on the del Valle children. Sofía remembered that Providence helped the family pass safely through France and finally to Asturias. They remained only briefly in Villaviciosa and soon relocated to Gijón, Spain, for the remainder of the war. In Gijón, Sofía and her sister Matilde began to work in social Catholic projects, assisting the wives of fishermen in religious education and providing fiestas for young people, giving them healthy pastimes, as she later described. She worked closely with a Jesuit in Gijón, Ángel Elorriaga, who provided her with freedom to develop her ministries with a degree of autonomy.[13]

The Mexico of Sofía del Valle's youth had become a faint memory. Her immediate concerns lay before her, the ministries to which she and her sisters gave the better part of their time. If war in Europe caused the family to abandon Switzerland, revolution in Mexico would soon direct the course of her life.

From 1910 to 1917 revolution convulsed Mexican society. The 1910s produced a trio of agrarian and popular civil wars, the displacement and migration of hundreds of thousands, and the deaths of approximately two million Mexicans. President Porfirio Díaz's long, authoritarian rule came to an end in 1911. Local experiences of Porfirian rule throughout the nation produced grievances along a spectrum of society, touching different social classes and regions. Southern peasant communities and northern cowboys and ranchers opposed the regime on issues related to land and autonomy. Urban middle-class liberals, artisans, and workers sought new opportunities for employment, political inclusion, and labor rights. Wealthy land-owning elites wanted an end to the political incumbency and the lack of democracy inherent in the Porfiriato.[14]

One of these elites from the northern state of Coahuila, Francisco I. Madero, galvanized the opposition. Madero's early plans for reform gave way to calls for revolution by late 1910. But the fighting—and winning—was done by intrepid cowboys in the state of Chihuahua, Pascual Orozco and Francisco "Pancho" Villa among them. The south, too, was in rebellion. Emiliano Zapata, village chief of tiny Anenecuilco, started his own revolution, taking back lands robbed by neighboring Hacienda El Hospital, in what had been a centuries-long fight to maintain village lands against the planters' progress.[15]

The denouement of the Porfiriato came in May 1911. Ciudad Juárez, on the northern border, surrendered to revolutionary forces. Díaz resigned, sailed to exile in France, and died there in 1915—his tomb remains in the Parisian cemetery at Montparnasse.

Cracked, crumbling, but not yet destroyed, Díaz's old regime hung on tenaciously. Madero called for presidential elections, set for October 1911. The election, freer and fairer than had been seen before in Mexico, catapulted Madero to the presidency. His fifteen months in office would be an experiment in democracy that the Porfirian elite would fight tooth and nail. Madero's failures, his fatal flaws so to speak, were twofold. The Porfirian congress and politicos remained even while the Porfirian army hung on. A second civil war was touched off in 1913 when one of those Porfirian generals, Victoriano Huerta, orchestrated a coup that left Madero and his vice president, José Pino Suárez, dead. Military underlings shot the president and vice president on the way to prison.

Followers of Madero, called Maderistas after their leader, rose up against Huerta. Another revolutionary from Coahuila, Venustiano Carranza, emerged as the leader of a new revolutionary force—the Constitutionalists—so named for their call to write a new constitution to replace the one from 1857. Villa and Zapata loosely aligned with Carranza, at least until Huerta too was driven from power in 1914. The "winners"—Carranza's Constitutionalists, Zapatistas, Villistas—turned on one another. A third civil war in 1915 ended in a Constitutionalist victory. Zapata was assassinated in 1919 and Villa in 1923. Carranza's revolutionary faction consolidated power and emerged with their new constitution in 1917. Carranza became the new president (1917–20). The 1917 Constitution provided protection for labor rights, laid plans for a massive land reform, and guaranteed public education. The document was also anticlerical. It outlawed religious instruction in public schools, took away the clergy's free speech rights, prohibited the church from owning property, and banned religious worship outside of church buildings. The revolution meant to assert its authority over the rhythms and rituals of Mexican life.

Although a measure of national stability gradually returned, conflict, especially of a religious nature, marked the subsequent two decades.

In 1918 Sofía's father returned to Mexico. Francisco del Valle didn't feel it safe for the family to return at that time and instead moved them to New Orleans. The family remained in Louisiana until 1922. While in New Orleans, the eldest son, named Francisco after his father, died in an accident.[16] Sofía's sister Clara married in New Orleans and started life with her new husband, Alfonso. Another sister, Hortensia, entered the Assumptionist order in Philadelphia. Matilde, the oldest, stayed in Spain to take care of Francisco's aged mother. Thus, when the family finally returned to Mexico in 1922, only four siblings made the journey—Sofía, Ana María, Enrique, and Consuelo. Although the family unit had contracted, Sofía recalled that the return to Mexico brought a sense of stability; Don Francisco bought a house outside Mexico City in Tlacopac, then an unincorporated part of the city, which today has been absorbed into the urban sprawl. The house was dubbed "Quinta Sofía" after Sofía's mother, her namesake. A small garden, planted with fruit trees, cactus, and flowers helped provide a note of tranquility, an oasis separate from the bustle of the city and the postrevolutionary political, social, and cultural reconstruction in the capital.[17] It became a point of departure and return for Sofía, who quickly integrated herself in the Catholic renewal movement in Mexico.

Even as she embarked on greater apostolic endeavors, the family remained the core of her enlarging networks: "I can never sufficiently thank Our Lord for the parents he gave me who allowed me to enjoy an atmosphere of peace, tranquility, love, joy, and service, as my family and my home were always the great school of my life."[18] Within the boundaries of family, gender, and social class, Sofía endeavored to serve and to participate in the Catholic movement. For her, these boundaries did not represent restrictions on her freedom. They were firm bases from which to act in the social and cultural worlds outside her safe garden home.

7

Vocation

Sofía explained in an interview in 1972 that many women in her family had taken religious vows and became nuns. The Assumptionist order, Sofía said, had been the calling of two of her sisters and two of her nieces. Hortensia—one of the sisters—had entered the order and served for many years in Philadelphia, Europe, and Brazil. Hortensia, known as Mother François, became assistant general—second-in-charge—of the entire Assumptionist order. One of Clara's daughters lived in Rwanda as a medical missionary; one of Ana María's daughters served as a principal for several Assumptionist schools.

"I am going to ask you a question out of curiosity," probed Alicia Olivera, the historian who conducted the 1972 interview with Sofía. "Why didn't you ever become a nun?"

A bulky recording device sat on the table between them. On one side of the floral couch sat the young investigator, Alicia Olivera; on the other, the old woman, Sofía del Valle, age eighty-one.

"Because I never had a calling," Sofía answered, "a vocation." Sofía laughed slightly at this. It was almost rehearsed, an answer prepared and given to a question that had come many times over the years.

"I'm also asked something similar," Sofía continued after a brief pause. "Why did you never marry? Because I didn't have that calling, that vocation, either."

"No, but it's interesting," the interviewer continued, almost uncomfortable that she'd brought up the subject, "that some of your sisters dedicated themselves to religious service."

"That is to say, to serve others," Sofía corrected, "but I believed I could serve them very well. I'll tell you why I never became [a nun]."[1]

Sofía del Valle returned to Mexico some fourteen years after her departure. When she left with her family for Europe in 1907 she had been a teenager of around sixteen. She lived in Spain and Switzerland, developed new relationships, and built a life surrounded by her family. She cultivated her intellectual interests; she obtained a degree in French for which she was certified to teach. Sofía ventured into a world of service to others. A profound need to participate in helping the culture she found herself in was awakened through the example of her parents as well as the active priests and laypeople that she came to know. She worked as a catechist in Switzerland and as a social worker in the fishing community in Gijón, Spain. In New Orleans she entered the professional world. She used her language skills to secure a job at Hibernia Bank, in the international transactions division. The Mexican Revolution reached into her family's personal wealth, causing Sofía's father to lose his property and assets. This is why the family had to leave Europe and relocate to New Orleans. She returned to Mexico a woman of thirty, full of "so many memories, of all the things that had been done in so many places," she later recalled.[2] Her friends, acquaintances, and relatives in Mexico City—the networks of her youth—had not remained intact after so many years abroad.

The Mexico of Sofía's youth had changed too. Mexico City was bursting at its borders. Population had swelled rapidly since the 1870s. From 1870 to 1910 the city's inhabitants tripled to 729,153. By 1921 the population had reached 903,063. The commercialization of agriculture, railroad building, and the growth of a land monopoly by relatively few hacendados forced scores of peasants to the capital. Rapid industrialization, fueled by American and European investment, brought wealth and prosperity to merchants, property owners, and import-export companies. Many newly arrived migrants and small-scale artisans did not fare so well.[3]

Population growth and the new prosperity split the city into an affluent west side and a poor, miserable east side. Mexico City's central plaza, the Zócalo, became a dividing line. As new workshops and small industries such as textiles grew in the 1880s, the middle and upper classes retreated west of the central plaza. The Federal District received some 80 percent of all national expenditures, and those were mainly spent west of the Zócalo. Plateros Street, stretching south and west of the Zócalo to Alameda Park, became a commercial symbol of Porfirian progress. Cafés, boutiques, fancy shops, restaurants, and business offices lined the street. Alameda Park, seven hundred feet wide and fifteen hundred feet long, contained bronze fountains, music stands, aviaries, and trees of all kinds: poplar, eucalyptus, palm, cypress, and pepper. One fourth of all Mexico's retail purchases were made between the Zócalo and Alameda Park.[4]

While the wealthy lived west of the Zócalo, neighborhoods to the east developed in varying degrees of misery. Artisan professions had been replaced by small warehouses, then by larger ones, and finally by factories. Property ownership increasingly came into the hands of fewer and fewer individuals. Urban migration sent property rates soaring, pricing many working families out of the housing market. New tenement houses, *vecindades* as they were known, replaced home ownership for many. By 1900 the overcrowded city averaged seven inhabitants to a room. Some 16 percent of the population had no room at all; they paid pennies per night to stay in vast public lodgings for the homeless. They labored in textiles, soap making, the perfume business, cigarette production, seamstress work, laundry, and the like. For fortunate women with some education, clerical work and telephone operating were more common by the 1920s.[5] But formal employment couldn't keep up with demand, especially as revolution increased the city's population. A vast informal economy boomed. Street vendors, tortilla makers, and domestic servants tried to make ends meet. Before the revolution already 3 percent of the population were legally registered as prostitutes. That number only increased as chaos in the countryside brought more women to the capital in search of a livelihood—women who lacked the skills, education, and opportunity to find work elsewhere.[6]

Further east of the Zócalo, and increasingly to the far north and south as well, tenement houses gave way to slums. Dilapidated hovels stood on thoroughfares named Dog Lane, Rat's Alley, and Pulque Place. On every few streets one could find a saloon selling pulque. The acrid-smelling substance came from fermenting *aguamiel*, the sap collected from the underground bulbs of the cactus-like maguey plant. The milky white substance was the drink of the people. Relatively low in alcohol content, but cheap, it contributed to public drunkenness, swelling the population of public jails in the city when consumed in mass quantities.[7]

A consumer culture rebounded after 1920.[8] It added to the visual disparity and income inequality of the city. Ready-made fashions were marketed in Mexico City as in New York, Buenos Aires, and Rio de Janeiro. Colgate Ribbon Dental Cream could be purchased at any pharmacy. Feminine napkins, sold by Johnson & Johnson, could be bought at local drugstores. Claveles cigarettes ran advertisements with women who were thin, light-skinned, and projected flapper freedom and self-indulgence.[9] Newly arrived peasants to the capital—wearing white trousers, straw sombreros, and huaraches—contrasted sharply with the new, modern styles on the streets and in the boutiques. The east side's dirty skirts, loose cotton blouses, and worn leather sandals gave way to the west side's ready-made skirts, chiffon blouses, and silk brocade one-strap high heels.[10]

It was a time of transition for Sofía del Valle. When the city of her birth seemed different, and life's direction unclear, Sofía noticed a strong, but familiar desire.

"I began to want to do something," she told Alicia Olivera in 1972.[11]

If her vocation had been to serve others, that call came in an internal longing. It wasn't a divine voice from on high that invited her to service. It was subtler than that.

"One day," Sofía remembered, "someone told me that Father Méndez Medina, Alfredo Méndez Medina, the director of the Mexican Social Secretariat, was going to speak at [the Church of] la Profesa. Go hear him."[12]

An interior desire and an invitation to the event led Sofía to the calling that would direct the course of her life.

Alfredo Méndez Medina was a figure of some renown in the Mexican Catholic movement when Sofía encountered him at La Profesa Church. And like Sofía, he too had spent quite some time in Europe.

Méndez Medina's sojourn across the Atlantic was undertaken as part of his training to become a Jesuit.[13]

Europe was alive with the latest teaching on the social mission of the church. Méndez Medina read voraciously the newest journals devoted to society's social problems: urbanization, wage labor, conditions of factory work, the plight of the working poor. Socialism provided an answer. Class conflict, strike, labor demands—all these were being held out to workers as a strategy to improve their lot. What options might there be for a Catholic solution? Méndez Medina asked. One that was in line with the church's idea of class harmony, a corporate society, working together to restore the dignity of work? Méndez Medina read that economic liberalism, the total deregulation of markets, had likewise been a driver of so much contemporary misery. Socialism *and* free market economics both seemed vastly deficient, Méndez Medina came to believe in Europe.

Ordained a priest in 1910, Méndez Medina had only his final period of formation remaining: the tertianship. It was envisioned as a final moment of decision for a man to make before taking his fourth vow. This was a distinctly Jesuit vow: obedience to the pope in regards to missions. It meant that the Jesuit would go anywhere and do anything that the church called him to do.

Méndez Medina's tertianship confirmed his vocation for social work. In May 1912 he wrote a manifesto on the work that should guide the Catholic movement in Mexico. The church, he wrote, should reach out not simply by "Christianizing the worker, or attracting him to religion through material support." Instead, Méndez Medina envisioned a *"radical transformation"* that would produce a "Christian sense" of work. This meant organizing workers into professional unions that respected authority and endeavored to harmonize the goals of labor and capital. The church would be the galvanizing force uniting conflicting interests in society. Professional organizations were the key to a Christian reordering of work. Méndez Medina saw that these unions had to become "more democratic, broader, free and unimpregnated by outside domination over the worker." His social vision had crystalized: unions professionally organized, Catholic in spirit. Arbitra-

8. Alfredo Méndez Medina, ca. 1920. SINAFO, INAH, Fototeca Nacional, Archivo Casasola, "Retrato de un Sacerdote," num Inv: 45684.

tion and negotiation would guide the unions, not violent strikes or class conflict.

Méndez Medina returned to Mexico from Europe in 1913, trained in social Catholic techniques and a broad vision to organize workers. The Jesuit joined the Catholic movement already in motion. Four social congresses had convened in the first decade of the twentieth century, seconded by a multitude of smaller conferences called "social weeks," held in various locations around the republic. These events, while mainly intellectual endeavors, helped lay the foundation for numerous lay associations by 1910. Méndez Medina's participation in one of these gatherings in 1913 catapulted him to fame within the Catholic activist community. He assisted in founding workers' associations, helped draft social legislation, and convened social study groups. But, as Mexico's democratic aperture under Francisco Madero rapidly closed with the coup d'état led by Victoriano Huerta, Méndez Medina was reassigned to the seminary in San Salvador.[14]

By 1920, with a measure of stability returning to Mexico, the bishops named Méndez Medina director of a new institute called the Mexican Social Secretariat (Secretariado Social Mexicano). Intelligent, charismatic, and driven, Méndez Medina had dark receding hair, an intellectual's broad forehead, and eyes like a sad poet. He was the unanimous choice of the Mexican bishops to lead the new Social Secretariat. The institute was based on the Belgian social secretariat founded by Father Georges Rutten. Its mission, like its European model, would be to provide resources and technical direction to social Catholic projects. But how to implement it?

Méndez Medina felt strongly that before an office was opened there needed to be further preparation. For the next two years Méndez Medina visited some thirteen Mexican states and fifty cities. The fight against socialism, he believed, should be waged through constructive, positive means. He would show Catholics, and whoever might hear him speak, that the church had a plan to solve their problems. He would unify and systematize Catholic efforts, restructuring the vast network of pious and charitable organizations into modern, professional unions. He traveled the country giving public conferences and established fledgling unions. He dialogued and debated with any and all who would listen.[15]

Organizing women workers was a concern for the Jesuit. He focused on the Association of Catholic Ladies (Asociación de las Damas Católicas), trying to show them they had a responsibility to reach out to working class women. He even argued that they drop the word *Dámas*—Ladies—from their name. It implied a middle- and upper-class association, as though wealthy women alone were the focus of church efforts. Their members were extraordinarily rich compared with most of Mexico City's workingwomen. Méndez Medina argued that these women had a Christian duty to use their resources for the cause of the working poor.

And so it was to these women, the Damas Católicas, that Méndez Medina spoke at La Profesa in Mexico City. Sofía del Valle heard Méndez Medina preach the same message he'd given throughout Mexico's north, center-west, and south. After speaking, Méndez Medina came down from the pulpit, said Mass, and went to the sacristy. Sofía made her way there and introduced herself.

"*Padre*, I am Sofía del Valle and I'm interested in what you said." Méndez Medina turned to look at the woman who'd boldly come to speak with him. "I just arrived in Mexico," Sofía continued, "and I would like to do something and I heard that you are orienting *las señoras*. I worked over there with Father Elorriaga in the Professional Unions."

"Ángel Elorriaga?" This piqued Méndez Medina's interest.

"Yes."

"In fact he's an old partner of mine, *hija*," Méndez Medina smiled.

"*Ay, padre* that's wonderful, I worked with him in this way."

"Ah, very well, we should work together," the priest said. He continued putting his vestments away. "We haven't had anyone to organize the women." Méndez Medina looked back at Sofía. "We already have professional unions for men, but we don't have any for women because we haven't had the person do it; but you might just be that person."

"*Ay, padre* it would be my pleasure."[16]

Sofía del Valle found her vocation. Her calling was to serve others—workingwomen, the poor, and educating women would come to play an important role in this calling. She found she could do this "something" without becoming a nun or a wife and a mother.

8

Respectable Telephone Operator

Sofía del Valle quickly got to work after her encounter with Alfredo Méndez Medina. But that work straddled social worlds in Mexico City. When the del Valle family returned to Mexico in 1922, they returned in different economic circumstances. Francisco del Valle had lost the family's home in Colonia Roma, and the family spent a year renting a house closer to the heart of downtown. In 1924 the del Valle's new home in the far outskirts of the capital was finally ready. The new Quinta Sofía was surrounded by a pastoral landscape, and Francisco set about planting trees and a vegetable garden for the family's personal use. The neighbors of Quinta Sofía were the holiday residences of foreign capitalists. Despite the growing presence of the wealthy, the pueblo of Tlacopac maintained a community of rural farmers; a small chapel dedicated to the Most Holy Conception provided services only on Sundays. The del Valle family had to venture further into San Ángel for daily Communion.[1]

Quinta Sofía was located some eight miles from the recently inaugurated offices of the Mexican Social Secretariat at 9 Motolinía Street in the city's downtown. Electric trolley was the main transport in the 1920s. A commuter train also ran from the far suburbs to the city proper. By the late twenties a fleet of independently owned buses clogged the urban landscape. Taxicabs and private vehicles increased the congestion as well.[2] Each day Sofía traveled north and east, crossing from the prosperous side of the city into the poorer, working-class boroughs. Crossing geographic boundaries meant crossing class ones.

The economic losses suffered by Francisco del Valle required Sofía to find paid work to help support the family. This she had already done in New Orleans. In Mexico she again leveraged her education, language skills, and the connections of her father in finding employment. During the morning she was a personal assistant, first at La Corona, a petroleum company, and later for the manager of the Ericsson telephone company, who was the del Valle's neighbor in Tlacopac. Sofía's knowledge of Spanish, French, and English allowed her to translate for the company leadership. Her experience and time in Lausanne made her an excellent choice as the personal assistant to the foreign manager of Ericsson.[3] With afternoons free, she devoted her time to Méndez Medina's Social Secretariat as head of feminine works.

But where to begin? "Absent from Mexico for so many years," Sofía later remembered, "I had no idea of the condition of the working woman in Mexico."[4] She knew something of the lives of women in Switzerland and something also of fishwives in Spain. Mexico was an unknown quantity for Sofía. She turned to her father and Méndez Medina. The three drew up a list of factories and workshops where women found employment in the city as a place to start. They listed El Buen Tono, a cigar maker. And as seamstresses and needleworkers were abundant at the time, they made sure to add High Life and La Britania, makers of high-quality shirts for men, as well as the seamstress workshop, El Nuevo Mundo. The perfumer Casa Bourgeois also figured on the list, as did several urban schools, which employed a growing number of female teachers.[5] With the list drawn up, Francisco del Valle approached the leadership of each factory or workshop. He was an established business presence in the city with a good reputation. Sofía's mission, Francisco told the managers, was to provide religious education and professional skills to female workers, not to form unions with the power of collective bargaining. Her work, Francisco assured, would serve only to better relations between management and labor; Sofía was not inflaming class antagonism.

Whether it was through the force of Francisco's persuasion, or because Catholic-based labor organizing promised not to disturb company productivity, the managers gave Sofía access. She went to each factory, workshop, and school in turn. Her anxiety grew as she would step on each new factory floor, enter a busy workshop, or walk the halls of a school. On one early visit Sofía felt strange as "the order was given to stop the machines and a table was provided for my use to stand on and from there to address the workingwomen." Knowing what to say was difficult at first, Sofía recalled. Sofía was a stranger there, removed from the problems of women who had to live hand-to-mouth, supporting children or extended families through a meager wage. "Alien" was the word Sofía used to describe her feeling as she looked out at the women gathered around her table.[6] Who was she to help them?

Each visit grew easier. She learned to make her voice carry. She spoke of benefits for the women. She was starting a Professional Employees Union for Women (Unión Profesional de Empleadas), she told the factory women. To the seamstresses and needleworkers she spoke of a new association for them, the Needleworkers Union (Obreras de la Aguja); and to the teachers, she offered the Teachers Professional Union (Unión Profesional de Maestras). She invited those who wanted to learn to read, write, or do basic arithmetic to a night school hosted by the Social Secretariat and assisted by the Damas Católicas. The classes were held after hours so the women could continue working and still learn new skills. By joining the associations, for a small fee, their money could be pooled, which paid for day care. A food pantry was opened as well: rice, beans, and corn could be purchased at reduced prices. A savings and loan program was also made available to the women. Women joined the new associations and Sofía's confidence grew. The night school was in high demand. The day-care provisions were among the first of their kind offered to women in Mexico City. As the Professional Employees Union for Women began to operate, Sofía was learning the problems of Mexican women. She visited them at work; she taught them classes in the night school. Sofía became convinced that education was what these women wanted and needed. She was determined to provide that opportunity.[7]

The work of Sofía del Valle was structured within a gendered social world. Her activities at the secretariat were officially directed by Father Méndez Medina and, after 1925, by his successor, Father Miguel Darío Miranda. Sofía's father facilitated her entrée into professional organizing. At La Britania, for instance, distant relatives held partial ownership in the textile company. Because she was a single woman, her father would take her home at the end of the day, or if this wasn't possible, a male member of the Social Secretariat would accompany her to the electric train that traveled from the city center to her home in Tlacopac. Her family would be advised when she left, and the family's gardener would wait for her at the stop with a lantern, as electric lighting had not yet been installed in the community. Sofía remembered that one time she encountered the gardener asleep on a bench beside the stop, apparently affected by too much pulque. "*Ya llegué*" (I've arrived), Sofía said tersely, waking up the embarrassed gardener.[8]

By early 1923 the Mexican Social Secretariat was in full swing. It became a library resource as well as a cache of technical assistance. Méndez Medina wrote and published a variety of manuals providing the "how to" of labor unionization with a Catholic thrust. The secretariat published its own journal, *La Paz Social* (Social peace), which reached a modest circulation of two thousand. The office was busy. It was part resource center, part staging headquarters for Catholic unionization efforts, and part hub for social Catholic associations that shared the space, such as the Damas Católicas and the Young Men's Catholic Association (Asociación Católica de la Juventud Mexicana).[9]

Mexican social Catholic thinking was premised on the reform of capitalism, not its destruction. To get capital in the hands of the people, limiting the disastrous debt that could come from loan sharks, was a key plank in the Social Secretariat's vision. Toward this end, a savings and loan fund was founded to provide working families access to credit at little or no interest. A financial committee composed of laymen directed the funds for the Social Secretariat's savings and loan bank called the Cajas de Ahorros León XIII. This committee included Sofía's father, Francisco del Valle Ballina.[10]

Méndez Medina divided the remaining work of the secretariat among a group of active laypeople. There were lawyers like José Villela, who wrote for *La Paz Social* and was in charge of outreach to men. René Capistrán Garza, a zealous leader of the Young Men's Association, facilitated links between his coterie of passionate youth and the secretariat's social strategy. Luis Bustos, at the time head of the Knights of Columbus in Mexico City, marshaled that group's links

9. The Mexican Social Secretariat at 9 Motolinía Street, ca. 1923. Alfredo Méndez Medina, seated center. Sofía del Valle stands behind Méndez Medina in bell-shaped hat. Francisco del Valle seated with white walrus mustache and cane. Photograph, Archivo Histórico del Arzobispado de México, base Miguel Darío Miranda, caja 9.

to business, channeling charitable donations to social efforts. And there was Sofía del Valle, busy giving night classes to workingwomen and networking through her father's business contacts.[11] But what did the social Catholic alternative look like in practice? What gains did it achieve?

Although Méndez Medina's secretariat was established in Mexico City, the real strength of the Catholic union movement was farther west, in the state of Jalisco.[12] It was there in 1922 that the National Confederation of Catholic Workers had come into being. A congress of thirteen hundred Catholic labor associations from twelve states and the national capital met to coordinate local and regional movements into one confederated body. The major debate centered on the Catholic identity of unions. From a practical standpoint, getting legal recognition meant organizing along professional lines—carpenters, bricklayers, textile workers—not along religious lines. The Mexican government began prohibiting such confessional groups soon after they formed. Legal recognition had to be achieved by making them appear less overtly Catholic. Méndez Medina, who helped organize the congress, felt that demanding workers be Catholic to join unions would potentially mean excluding potential members. A compromise on the issues was reached. The Catholic religion would be respected among union members, avowed socialists would not be admitted, and union leaders would be individuals of high moral repute. Religion was indeed crucial to the Catholic union movement, but pragmatic strategies would help them maneuver in an increasingly hostile labor environment prevailing in Mexico at the time.[13]

The National Workers Confederation scored its biggest victories in Jalisco. Salary increases, benefits, and job security were won through negotiation and, as a last resort, strikes. The gains there showed the real viability, the competing power, of Catholic labor. But two competing movements proved stronger: the government-sponsored labor confederation—CROM—and the more radical CGT.

In Mexico City, the Catholic union movement was not nearly as strong as in Jalisco nor as radical. Francisco and Sofía del Valle focused on education and uplift, rather than salary increases or benefits. And they had fierce competition. The government's Regional Confederation of Mexican Workers (Confederación Regional Obrera Mexicana or CROM) grew in strength in the 1920s, as presidents Alvaro Obregón (1920–24) and Plutarco Elías Calles (1924–28) favored CROM's willingness to bend to government priorities. The General Labor Confederation (Confederación General del Trabajo or CGT)—a home for radicals, communists, anarchists—had no such compunction to government collaboration. These three movements (CROM, CGT, and Catholics) battled for the working classes of Mexico City.[14] Sofía del Valle would soon be in the middle of the fight.

Sofía del Valle arrived to work every day at 8:00 a.m. The offices of the Empresa de Teléfonos Ericsson, S.A. were located just on the west side of the Zócalo in downtown Mexico City. Ericsson international was located in Stockholm. Founded in 1876 by Lars Magnus Ericsson, the multinational telecommunications business grew quickly worldwide.[15]

Ericsson had been in Mexico for over two decades by the time Sofía del Valle began her job.[16] The company managed to weather the worst of the revolution with a larger subscriber base. In 1910 Ericsson had 3,781 subscribers in the Federal District. That number more than tripled by 1919, to 12,680. Upward growth continued, reaching 17,581 subscribers at the end of 1923. Ericsson had twice the subscribers of its rival, Telefonía y Telegrafía Mexicana.[17]

Sofía del Valle's job was far different from most Ericsson workers. As a personal assistant, she translated for the Swedish management, liaised with the plant supervisors, and handled job applications for potential telephone operators. Sofía's skills and family connections afforded her opportunities that other workers didn't have.

Both men and women worked for Ericsson in Mexico. Men were mostly in their twenties and thirties and worked as engineers, technicians, repairmen, construction workers, and line installers. Most male employees worked for a daily wage that ranged between 1.00, 2.50, and 5.75 pesos. It would've been half that amount in American dollars at the time. Women worked as telephone operators. In the 1920s very few women began a career as a telephone operator and then worked their way up to a position held by a more educated woman such as Sofía del Valle. Ericsson paid female telephone operators hourly—between 0.14, 0.22, and 0.78 centavos—based on their job experience. The female employees were younger than the men, most between eighteen and twenty-five years old, the oldest around thirty-five.[18] It's unclear what Sofía made in salary. But as a personal assistant it probably dwarfed the wage of the average female employee of Ericsson.

Like Ericsson in Mexico, telephone companies worldwide hired women almost exclusively for the position of telephone operator. In the early days of the telephone men had been hired, but that experiment quickly failed. Historian David Mercer writes: "Managers quickly came to view young women as more articulate, polite, and more likely to follow instructions, than male operators."[19] Service, indeed, became the key reason why women quickly filled the ranks of telephone operators.

Early manual telephone systems required human assistance to make a phone call. The subscriber picked up the handset on their telephone and were connected to an operator. The customer spoke briefly to the operator, who received the numerical code of the person to be reached, and then manually plugged in a line to a switchboard in front of them. Only then could the call be connected. Early systems even required an A-Operator to take care of the outgoing call and a B-Operator to handle the incoming call. As the number of lines in any one network increased, the number of possible switches likewise increased. The job required fast, accurate movements. A level of basic literacy and numeracy was essential, usually a high-school level of education, although this varied from market to market. Telephone operators became an extension of the ideal household maid or servant. The bulk of early customers were well-off, upper-middle-class businessmen. They were used to receiving fast, efficient service at home and in the office. And that same fast, efficient service extended to the telephone network.[20] Subscribers came to demand a level of respectability among telephone operators, which companies like Ericsson endeavored to uphold.

Telephone operators were to reflect middle-class values of discipline, modest dress, and sexual propriety. Women worked in an area separate from men. Telephone operators sat in long rows in front of long banks of telephone switches, each handling a number of switches. A female supervisor walked up and down the rows of operators. A quality assurance operator listened in on the service each employee provided. The gendered workspace also meant women did different work than men did. "Women's work" was largely defined in relation to physical labor.[21] The factory, the workshop, and the telephone exchange endeavored to protect the ideal female respectability of women workers.

Protection of respectability even extended into the private lives of telephone operators. Bell Telephone in the United States, for instance, occasionally sent "medical matrons" to investigate the homes of its telephone operators. Ericsson in Mexico set similar policies. They required telephone operators to remain unmarried and to be without children. Unsurprisingly, a 1920 survey of Ericsson's employees found that none of the telephone operators reported having dependent children. Even in revolutionary Mexico, work outside of the home and

10. Ericsson telephone operators at the main exchange. *L. M. Ericsson Review* 3, nos. 3–4 (March–April 1926): 28, www.ericsson.com/history.

motherhood were often viewed as mutually exclusive. Ideal families consisted of a working, virtuous father who earned enough money to cover the expenses of a dependent wife and children. Mothers were the at-home teachers, the housekeepers, the domestic guardian. Upholding respectability in the home and at the office was key to the customer service mandate. If a woman got married, she was supposed to leave employment. If she was found to be pregnant and unmarried, she was fired.[22] At Ericsson this is precisely what happened during Sofía del Valle's period of employment.

The reality of 1920s Mexico shattered the middle-class ideal of family respectability. In 1921 14.6 percent of women in the capital were between the ages of twenty and twenty-nine: 82 percent of these women had at least one child and were either divorced, widowed, or separated from their husbands as a result of the revolution.[23] The 1917 Mexican Constitution went a long way in trying to close the gap between ideal and

11. "Respectable" Ericsson telephone operators in the Rest and Recreation Room, ca. 1926. *L. M. Ericsson Review* 3, nos. 3–4 (March–April 1926): 28, www.ericsson.com/history.

reality. It had provided for the protection of workingwomen and children, demanding labor practices that gave maternity leave, breaks for nursing mothers, and light work duty for women in the last trimester of pregnancy.[24] Ericsson's management didn't automatically grant these concessions. Throughout the 1920s the policy of only hiring unmarried women with no children continued. Union organization among telephone operators in the capital increased as a response.

Already in 1921, preceding Sofía del Valle's return to Mexico, telephone operators were throwing their lot in with striking workers in Mexico City. In February of that year 350 workers from Ericsson affiliated with the CGT, the radical labor confederation. A much smaller number—51—did not join. Instead, some affiliated with a Catholic labor association organized with the help of two male Catholic associations, the Knights of Columbus for men and the Catholic Association of Mexican Youth (Asociación Católica de la Juventud Mexicana or

ACJM) for youths. And so two unions emerged within Ericsson, one linked to the CGT and the other to the Catholic movement.[25]

By May 1921 Ericsson telephone operators associated with the CGT went on strike. The walkout brought 50 percent of telephone service in the capital to a halt. Other "service industry" workers joined: bakers, waiters, and tram drivers. Ericsson's management was forced to negotiate a new labor contract. The majority of the telephone operators voted in favor of the new agreement. Members of the Catholic union—many of whom were engineers, some telephone operators, and other supervisors—did not. They preferred to maintain the status quo. Ericsson dragged its feet in enforcing the new labor contract. The managers argued that the labor provisions in the Constitution, as well as the new labor contract, did not apply to telephone operators. The Constitution, argued Ericsson management, had afforded labor protection to "obreras" (workingwomen), not its telephone operators, which Ericsson classified as "señoritas" (young ladies). The telephone operators, according to management, were respectable young ladies, not workingwomen. In 1923 Ericsson workers joined another CGT-led strike in the capital.[26]

Sofía began her job for Ericsson in 1924. She worked for a management that supported policies of female morality, decorum, and respectability. Señorita del Valle was herself unmarried, without children, educated, and respectable. In many ways she was the female ideal of the workingwoman Ericsson desired to promote. Yet the culture of work at Ericsson—separating "señoritas" from "obreras"—became a way to deny telephone operators improved working conditions, maternity rights, and salary increases. The irony was that telephone operators actually had quite strenuous jobs. Often operators had little time off; it wasn't unusual for women to work around the clock, even bringing cots into the exchange room to work the switchboards in the wee hours of the morning.[27]

The radical CGT-affiliated union brought the case of two women in particular before the Mexico City Labor Arbitration Board. The two women—both unmarried and found to be pregnant—had been promptly fired from their positions as Ericsson telephone operators.

Bertil Flyckt, an Ericsson manager, testified before the Labor Arbitration Board. He provided the company line on the issue:

> As a general rule, the Company only admits to this type of work single women who, therefore, are not liable to become pregnant; and all the employees of the indicated work are warned that contracting legal marriage or entering any other illicit union will be a justifiable cause for termination, since the policy of the Company is that they do not have small children, since it is demonstrated that during pregnancy and child-rearing, the efficiency of women at work, for reasons of the significant change in their mental and moral faculties, decreases [so much] that service is seriously compromised.[28]

Elsewhere, Ericsson's management claimed that unmarried and pregnant telephone operators created a moral scandal within the workplace. Flyckt's rationale says a lot about how the project of safeguarding female respectability was one that worked to Ericsson's advantage. It was couched in sexist language. It showcased a prevailing view that pregnancy diminished women's ability to work. It revealed that behind the veneer of family protection lay the priority of profits over persons.

The case of the two women, who failed to regain their jobs, dragged on until late in the 1920s. Finally in 1929, the Mexico City Labor Arbitration Board granted Ericsson telephone operators the maternity rights they had fought for.[29] But this was an ephemeral victory. Ericsson was even then building a fully automatic exchange station, which had no need for telephone operators.

Sofía del Valle didn't remember Ericsson management as profit hungry and misogynist. Except for a few brief mentions of Ericsson, her job as a paid employee is rather murky. She never related Ericsson's policies on maternity in later interviews, in her correspondence, or in the large paper trail that made it into the archives. She focused her memories on her work as a Catholic activist, not as a paid employee. And even then, when recalling her Catholic work, Sofía spoke about the practical needs she was trying to meet. She never had much to say about grand theory.

"What most interested us at this moment," she recalled, "wasn't so much the question of improving work conditions, but bettering the women themselves."[30]

The vision to improve the workingwomen first prompted her to start the night school. "We gave classes in reading and writing, and to those that didn't know how, in arithmetic; in sum the essential things to these women and classes, we should say of personal identity, of knowing that they were people, that they had to develop, they had obligations to themselves and to their families, to their society, to their church and to everything, in sum a development of the human person."[31] Sofía's passion was education, to improve the lives of workingwomen by teaching them skills like reading, writing, and basic mathematics. The women who worked at Ericsson already had these skills, but tobacco workers and needleworkers often did not. She didn't see her role as organizing the picket line, the labor shutdown, or the strike. Sofía's role, as she saw it, was one-on-one, face-to-face interaction with women, helping them to help themselves by educating them.

The night school Sofía started included multiple socioeconomic classes. The needleworkers and the women who worked in the tobacco industry were poorer, less educated, and had fewer prospects than did telephone operators, teachers, and clerical workers. But they rubbed elbows in the school. Sofía and her partner in the night school, Elena Lascuráin de Silva, connected less educated women to teachers and white-collar workers in mentoring relationships. The workingwomen in Sofía's night school initiated many of the activities. They planned day trips to San Ángel, near Sofía's home. They went on a group pilgrimage to the shrine of the Virgin of Guadalupe, where they prayed for favor in job prospects.[32]

Sofía's passion for education says something about the Catholic alternative to socialism and unbridled capitalism. It was evolutionary. Méndez Medina certainly pushed a more radical campaign to improve labor conditions. And there were gains in this area, especially in Jalisco, but the improvement of labor conditions was only a piece of the Catholic vision. That vision embraced a cross-class component and religious devotion. The Catholic union movement involved mutual aid societies, credit cooperatives, night schools, and catechism.[33] There was a concern for material conditions. But labor conditions weren't improved through class warfare, but through harmony. Training, education, a robust spiritual dimension—these aimed at building up the whole man, the whole woman, through sacrament, through devotion. How was this vision applied to Ericsson workers?

Sofía was involved with them to some degree. She invited them to the night school and spiritual meetings. Her name comes up in relation to the ongoing dispute between the CGT-affiliated union and the Catholic union. Ericsson's management preferred the Catholic union because many belonged to it. The company's leadership tried to ban the CGT union from representing telephone operators, and the CGT union appealed to the Labor Arbitration Board. In that appeal, the CGT-union leadership wrote that Señorita del Valle "hinted to the señoritas that applied for the job of telephone operator to affiliate first to [the Catholic union], a practice that Señora Terrazas and other employees from the central office continue to follow, such as Señorita Elguero that leads this union and is also a supervisor."[34] The claim was that Sofía and her successors had implied to job applicants that joining the Catholic union would improve their job prospects at Ericsson. That was the worst charge leveled against Sofía in particular—one that reveals a conflict of interest, using her position at Ericsson to expand the Catholic union's membership. But the appeal listed other general grievances against the company: work contracts were being negotiated on an individual basis between management and telephone operators, the operators did not have job security, and they had to submit to a medical exam before being hired. The implication was that Ericsson didn't want the responsibility of employees with health problems or who were pregnant or had dependent children.

It is no stretch of the imagination to see Sofía upholding company policy. Ericsson's policies squared with much Catholic teaching on the family. Marriage was a sacramental union. Breaking that union, or tarnishing it through sex or childbirth outside of marriage, was sin. And these activities, Catholics believed, were detrimental to society in general. The family was the foundational starting point of Catholic renewal. Sofía del Valle was no feminist. She wasn't radical or revolutionary on the issue of sexual mores. But she was evolutionary on relations between the sexes. "There is no superiority, there are differences," she would tell Alicia Olivera in 1972. "I have this conviction that in a home where the mother is good and the father bad, in the majority of cases the home is saved by that mother; in a home where the father is good and the mother bad the home can't be saved despite the father."[35]

Sofía was holding various motivations in tension at Ericsson. In her night school we see Sofía's desire for women to improve themselves through education. We see her bringing women together across class distinctions, united by Catholic devotion. We see Sofía working against gender superiority. But at Ericsson, Sofía labored for the individual woman, not for women as a gender category. We see her upholding a woman's right to work, yet also protective of a Catholic ideal of femininity. She was cautious to preserve a woman's respectability in the workplace. We see Sofía learning to present herself as a fashionable, modest woman, aware of her femininity, confident working with male bosses, and resolute that women should improve their lives, their families, and their society through education.

But the window of opportunity for Catholic labor activism was closing in Mexico City by 1924. Plutarco Elías Calles became president. The government-backed labor confederation—the CROM—grew in strength. It began forcibly excluding both the more radical CGT and Catholic unions from many of the factories where Sofía had been free to organize previously. Cigarette and garment industry workers who refused to affiliate with CROM were fired. After receiving several donated Singer sewing machines, Sofía set about providing these women with piecework to supplement their salary losses.[36] As the doors to Mexico City's factories began to close for Sofía, the Social Secretariat also experienced a crisis. Alfredo Méndez Medina was fired as director of the institute. There were allegations that he had become too autonomous from church leadership in his role. But there were also accusations of sexual misconduct, for which he was officially exonerated.[37] Rumors followed Méndez Medina. He was transferred out of Mexico City. The Catholic alternative to revolution seemed to be faltering.

By May 1925 the Social Secretariat was left without its director. While important, Méndez Medina was only one part of the Catholic movement; the activities of the numerous laypeople and associations continued in his absence. And by June 1925, a new director showed up at the offices of 9 Motolinía Street, Father Miguel Darío Miranda. For Sofía, a lifelong friend and spiritual confidante had arrived.

The friendship between Sofía and Miranda was forged amid a coming maelstrom: the bloody Cristero War of 1926–29. Sofía del Valle's future mission beyond the borders of Mexico was launched in the aftermath of this religious crisis. Amid the civil war, as Catholics rebelled against the Mexican government, martyrs would be made and so too would murderers. It was a conflict that left an indelible mark on Sofía, her vision for Mexico, and on her role in bringing that vision to reality.

9

Preparing the Future

In May 1925 Sofía del Valle met a man who, more than anyone else, brought her close to romantic love. That man was Miguel Darío Miranda, the new director of the Mexican Social Secretariat. In May 1925 President Calles had been in office for six months. Religious tensions increased precipitously in that space of time.

Miguel Miranda was cut from a different cloth than the secretariat's former director, Alfredo Méndez Medina. Whereas Méndez Medina emphasized action, organizing, and the expansion of Catholic labor unions, Miranda valued study, consolidation, and the establishment of a strong Catholic training. Where Méndez Medina was brash and daring, Miranda was studied and cautious. The activity of the secretariat slowed almost immediately. The new director's first month at the secretariat was spent observing the institution's ministries, speaking with its lay leaders, and developing an educational strategy.[1] Miranda envisioned the secretariat as a catalyst for Catholic education—forming the Catholic conscience—of priests and lay activists. He saw Sofía as an integral part of that mission.

Their relationship began conventionally enough. Miranda, as the secretariat's manager, recognized in Sofía a key asset to the organization. After his month of observation, Miranda called Sofía for an interview.

"What you are doing is very laudable," he said, "but it has one great defect: your function in my opinion is to multiply Sofías."[2]

After the meeting, Sofía del Valle's efforts redoubled in the area of women's education. Together, after a year of planning, Miranda and Sofía founded the Instituto Superior de Cultura Femenina—Advanced Institute of Feminine Culture—in June 1926, even as church-state tensions began to boil. With Miranda at the helm of the Mexican

Social Secretariat, a new mission for Sofía del Valle emerged, one that focused her vision on creating a national education project for Catholic women.

Again, Sofía's father assisted his daughter's mission. The residence on Motolinía Street already hosted the Social Secretariat and several other Catholic associations. Sofía's father, Francisco del Valle, negotiated with Miranda and the owner of the headquarters at Motolinía Street the construction of a second floor with classrooms, a bathroom, and a patio for breaks between courses. There, on the renovated second floor, Cultura Femenina opened for instruction.

The school's mission was to provide young women an advanced liberal arts education with a Catholic foundation.[3] Subjects included theology, journalism, photography, philosophy, history (both national and universal), French and English language training, as well as practical skills like typing. Courses in religion were offered, but they went beyond the basics of catechism, covering ethics, psychology, and logic.[4] The small project of the night school for workingwomen now began blossoming into a robust intellectual curriculum. Courses in domestic training and morality were confined to only the first two years. The vision was not to train housewives, but to produce dynamic, well-read, and equipped women. The skills they learned would serve them, Sofía believed, whether they remained at home with children or entered the growing marketplace for female labor.

Sofía also helped establish a sister organization, the Mexican Young Women's Catholic Association (Juventud Católica Femenina Mexicana or JCFM) also headquartered at Motolinía Street. The group focused on putting Catholic education into practice through social works.[5] There had always been a critique of Catholic women's associations: they were simply pious groups for *niñas de bien*, rich good girls. Sofía believed that Cultura Femenina and the JCFM could prove that reputation incorrect. Both organizations would be the major works she devoted her energies to for the next thirty years. It was her efforts for these institutions that would lead her to the United States, Canada, and on to Europe.

12. Teachers at the Advanced Institute for Feminine Culture—Cultura Femenina, ca. 1926: (*left to right*) Father Luis Gómez, Sofía del Valle, Rafael Dávila Vilchis, Father Jesús García Gutiérrez, Father Dionisio Saavedra. Photograph, Archivo Histórico del Arzobispado de México, base Miguel Darío Miranda, caja 8a.

Sofía del Valle was no *chica moderna*—the Mexican version of a 1920s flapper—but she also set herself apart from the drab, veiled, traditional Catholic garb of her day. Sofía self-consciously appropriated aspects of consumer fashion, such as New York and Parisian styles. Her hair, purse, and shoes all had a feminine appearance, somewhere between the brazen plunging necklines and short hemlines of the flapper and the unflattering smocks of many pious Catholic women.[6]

Visual images help tell a story. Sofía del Valle appears in a photograph from the mid-1920s. It is undated, but the picture was probably taken in 1926. Sofía stands with four priests who taught in the Catholic liberal arts college she helped found that year, known as Cultura Femenina. Clerical garb had been outlawed in Mexico, part of the anticlerical articles of the 1917 Constitution. In public, priests wore dark, three-piece suits in the absence of collar and cassock. The spacing of the photograph is odd to the modern viewer. It too tells a story. One man stands to the right of Sofía, three to the left. More than a foot or two of space separates Father Luís Gómez from Sofía.

13. Elena Lascuráin de Silva (*seated far left*) and Clara Arce (*standing far left*), ca. 1925. Archivo Histórico de la Univeridad Iberoamericana Ciudad de México, Archivo de Acción Católica Mexicana, Fondo Unión Femenina, caja 15.

A bush separates Sofía from the other three. The picture tells a story of conscious modesty.

Sofía's clothing, fashionable yet modest, certainly appears different from many of her female Catholic contemporaries. Consider another photograph from the period, taken the year before in 1925. Two women in particular stand out: Elena Lascuráin de Silva and Clara Arce. Both were married, active laywomen. They helped lead the Damas Católicas for women thirty-five years and older. The two wear dark dresses, stockings, and shoes. Lascuráin de Silva wears a dowdy coat with rumpled lapels; Clara Arce wears a religious medal, and both wear close-fitting, bell-shaped cloche derby hats. Nuns often wore apparel similar to Lascuráin de Silva's and Arce's, as religious attire was also outlawed for consecrated women in Mexico at the time. In terms of color, style, and presentation, Sofía del Valle had a sense of Catholic couture lost on many of her female counterparts.[7]

On the surface both photographs seem to reinforce the conventional relationship between priest and laywoman. Men and women are not

Preparing the Future 71

touching. Adequate distance is given between the opposite sex, which provides a public avowal of decency and chastity. Lampooning the private sexual improprieties of horny priests and weak-willed lay parishioners happened quite regularly in the pulpy penny press.[8] Certainly the photographers and subjects of both pictures would have wanted to avoid such appearances. Yet apart from the issue of feminine style and public perception, the photographs also give the viewer a sense of Sofía's positioning in relation to both her female contemporaries and male clergy. Sofía stands at the center of her photograph. She is a single woman, around thirty-five years old when the image was taken. She had assumed quite an important role in the Catholic movement, especially as a woman. The priests pictured with her are all older than she, but all taught in the institute she had helped establish. In the other photograph, Lascuráin de Silva and Clara Arce also led an important women's association, but the clergyman is in the center, seated, the viewer drawn to him as the focal point of the photograph and the gendered story it tells.

Cultura Femenina faced immediate obstacles. Sofía had to recruit women to enroll in classes, committing to a course of four years. She recalled that convincing the parents of young women that their daughters would benefit from studies at the institute was a difficult prospect. At the time, there were no Catholic female institutions of higher learning in Mexico, and women were invited from various parts of the republic. Numerous meetings were held with parents of the new students, allaying their fears that Cultura Femenina would hinder their daughters' domestic responsibilities. Sofía remembered that one prominent member of the hierarchy, a bishop, was skeptical of the educational project. In order to win him over, Miranda and Sofía invited him to the final exams given at the end of a course of study. The bishop condescended: "My question is whether these wise ladies can cook a good meal?"[9] Sofía took this as a challenge, and at the next exam period invited this same bishop. The young women, in addition to the intellectual aspect of the final exams, prepared an elaborate meal for those in attendance. The bishop was convinced. She recalled that her goal was "to demonstrate that there was compatibility between

14. Sofía del Valle, ca. 1926. Photograph, Archivo Histórico del Arzobispado de México, base Miguel Darío Miranda, caja 8a.

knowledge and being a good housewife."[10] Although the first class of Cultura Femenina included a mere eight students, over the next several decades approximately five hundred young women would complete the four-year course of study.

Overcoming sexist attitudes was the least of Miranda's and Sofía's worries for the time being. The official opening of Cultura Femenina came in June 1926. By August a church strike had gone into effect. Mexico's bishops declared that until the religious articles of the Constitution were changed, priests would no longer give the sacraments in the churches. Police authorities had begun to inventory houses of worship, as they were now officially state property. Unregistered priests who performed their duties in secret were subject to arrest. Still, Cultura Femenina and the Social Secretariat continued to operate, not yet a target of police inspection. By the fall of 1926 Catholic rebels in the countryside began taking up arms.

A photograph of Sofía del Valle, taken around the beginning of the Cristero War, shows a woman of thirty-five. Sofía's pose and her setting

Preparing the Future 73

provide some clues as to where she sits at this point in our story. Memories of childhood and the safety of her family often were situated in gardens like the one pictured. Her family home, Quinta Sofía, always had a garden in bloom in its proper season. More than once, Sofía spoke about the meaning her family's garden held for her. It evoked serenity, as though the world was at peace. It was a life she would return to, the safety of her family, but one that she had the occasion and the necessity to leave more often and for longer stretches of time. The photograph proceeds from rich garden to concrete, a world hidden from view by the picture's frame. Unlike the garden, it lay outside the agency of her tending. Soon enough, travel would bring her to new geographies, primarily the United States and Europe. In those places there was much she couldn't control, much that disturbed the serenity she held dear. She encountered new challenges: prejudices against women, against Mexicans, against Catholics—a world outside her domination but one she would have to apply all her facilities to navigate in. The photograph reveals a wall between the garden and the receding concrete outside the frame. Mexico's religious conflict, like the wall, marked a boundary between two worlds for Sofía: an old world of the familiar, a new world of the unknown.

Sofía's call to the new world came early one morning, sometime late in 1926. Miranda was already at work at the secretariat offices that early morning. Four years younger than Sofía, Miranda was just over thirty years old. He kept his jet-black hair combed straight back, which made his dark expressive eyes, shaded by a pronounced brow, all the more striking. In the aftermath of the Cristero War he was made a bishop in 1937, then named the highest ranking clergyman in Mexico in 1956, and finally a cardinal of the church in 1969. But on that morning, in 1926, he was a simple priest who was about to receive a new mission.[11]

The man who came calling that morning was Bishop Pascual Díaz, and he needed Miranda's advice. Pascual Díaz was a former Jesuit priest whose rise in the ecclesiastical ranks had been swift. In his younger years, Díaz had been superior of the Sacred Family Jesuit residence in the del Valle family's old neighborhood in Mexico City. There he had

15. Miguel Darío Miranda in the Social Secretariat, ca. 1926. Personal collection of María Eugenia Díaz Gastine de Pfennich.

made fast friends with Alfredo Méndez Medina. They would "drink beer and fix the world" together in Diaz's quarters, as one superior wrote disapprovingly.[12] Jesuits are not supposed to seek higher ecclesiastical office. But their vow of obedience to the pope includes the proviso to accept a position in the hierarchy if the pope deems it necessary. In 1922 Díaz was named bishop of Tabasco, in Mexico's tropical southeast. Díaz's talent and charisma propelled him into the bishop's purple.

In Tabasco, where Diaz was bishop, the anticlerical storm that swept Mexico began to rumble and blow earlier there than in other states. Under strongman—only sometimes elected governor—Tomás Garrido Canabal (1922–35) the state of Tabasco implemented severe restrictions on the Catholic Church before similar, though somewhat less draconian, mandates came into force nationwide in 1926 under President Calles. Garrido Canabal's government limited the number of priests allowed to minister in the state, forced all priests to marry, closed and pillaged churches, destroyed religious images, and even outlawed the Spanish phrase for goodbye—"adios" (to God). Garrido Canabal also sought to impose the schismatical Catholic Church (Iglesia Católica Apostólica Mexicana) in Tabasco. Founded in February 1925, the schismatical movement received government backing for its synthesis of

Preparing the Future 75

revolutionary ideals with the Catholic faith. It had a small, but robust, following and absolutely terrified Vatican officials and Mexican bishops for what it threatened: a revolutionary church with no ties to the pope. It held the threat, many believed, of becoming like Bolshevik Russia. And in Tabasco that wasn't far from the mark. Garrido Canabal crowned a rogue priest in the state as the "Red Bishop." Garrido Canabal had a son named Lenin and a daughter named Zoila Libertad. The Tabascan strongman created a vision of a future agrarian socialist utopia on a model farm called La Florida; there he named his livestock and pigs after God, the Virgin of Guadalupe, and the pope. Graham Greene's 1940 novel *The Power and the Glory* is set in a fictionalized version of Garrido Canabal's Tabasco.[13]

Díaz was thus forced to the capital in exile—an internal castaway portending more severe exiles to come. He was of more "plebeian" origins than his fellow Mexican bishops, of a family with indigenous heritage. Díaz was heavy-set, barrel-chested, with a broad face, jowly in many respects. In the fallout from the Cristero Rebellion he would become the next archbishop of Mexico (1929–36). On that morning in late 1926 he was fifty-one.[14]

Miranda received his visitor warmly. Pascual Díaz began their conversation: "Padre Miranda, I've come on behalf of the Episcopal Committee. We the bishops have confidence in you; we would like to hear your point of view regarding what is happening in Mexico."[15]

Enormous complexity lay behind Díaz's request for advice. Much indeed was weighing on Díaz and the other bishops of the Episcopal Committee, a select group of senior Mexican clergymen chosen to lead in a time of crisis. The growing anticlericalism of the Calles government forced the bishops to make hard decisions that affected the present and future fortunes of the church. The bishops, at the urging of the Vatican's emissary, formed this committee to bring "unity of vision" among them. But bringing unity to the thirty-eight bishops in the Mexican hierarchy was not an easy job. José Mora y del Río, the archbishop of Mexico (1909–28), was the de-facto leader of the Mexican bishops. Deeply pious, Mora y del Río had presided over the Catholic renewal of the late 1900s and had weathered the revolution. He focused on social initiatives, including Méndez Medina's Social Secretariat. But Mora y del Río was quite old. He had become increasingly gaffe-prone. A statement he made to the press in February 1926—remarking to a journalist that the Mexican church rejected the 1917 Constitution—was an indicator of his declining tact. The incident set off Calles's Jacobins and duly set in motion the energies of police inspector General Roberto Cruz. Under Mora y del Rio's largely symbolic leadership, younger, more robust personalities made up the real force of the Episcopal Committee. Leopoldo Ruiz y Flores, then archbishop of Morelia, was named vice president and second-in-charge. Pascual Díaz was elected secretary of the committee: quite startling for a man who had been appointed bishop only a few years previous. Thirty-eight bishops in Mexico were divided between a handful of hawks set on fierce resistance, a handful of doves open to negotiation, and the vast majority of moderates somewhere in the middle.[16]

As secretary and main public relations official of the Episcopal Committee, Pascual Díaz was handed quite a responsibility. And the committee's first decision would prove to be a disaster: they suspended all public worship throughout Mexico. The bishops used interdict to protest President Calles's religious laws. Interdict meant the sacraments would no longer be provided to the Catholic faithful in churches; that is, until the laws changed. The decision allowed Catholics to practice the sacraments in private homes, under priestly administration, in order to protect the faithful from unreasonable legal restrictions on religious practices.[17] But interdict was a tactic used by bishops since the Middle Ages to cajole kings and princes to submit to the authority of the church. President Calles would prove not to be cowed so easily.

Calles's reform of the penal code had outraged the bishops and laity alike. The Calles Law, as it was known, was passed in June 1926. It was essentially a series of legal consequences for breaking the religious articles of the Constitution. Priests had to be registered with civil authorities or would be punished, often with two weeks in jail or fined 500 pesos or both. Similar consequences followed other infractions, such as wearing religious garb in public, clandestine cloisters, and religious schools. The state no longer recognized the consecrated life of monks and nuns, and their communities would be disbanded when found.[18] The bishops debated the drastic course of action involved in a church strike, but decided unanimously that, if the government presumed to control the church, the church would go on strike. The Vatican backed the bishops in their decision.[19] An economic boycott was implemented to parallel the sacramental one. The lay-run League for the Defense of Religious Liberty, known simply as the League, took charge of propaganda, publicity, and coordination of the economic protest. It all went into force on August 1, 1926, the same day the Calles Law went operational.

Soon enough, options for a peaceful resolution ran out. Ruiz y Flores and Díaz made overtures to Calles for a truce. A meeting held between the parties only revealed the hardening of positions on both sides. Calles reportedly said the bishops had two choices: "an appeal to congress or an appeal to arms."[20] Congress was tried first. A petition signed by one million Catholics for the laws to be changed, or at the very least a referendum on the issue to go to the legislature, was rejected. Lay Catholics in the countryside seemed to be making their decision clear. Many towns were appealing to force in an effort to defend religion—and their communities—against government intrusion. Catholic towns and hamlets dotted around the center-west heartland of the nation were in rebellion.

For the bishops protest and boycott were one thing, to sanction violence, quite another. In late November leaders of the Catholic Defense League came to Díaz and the Episcopal Committee asking the hierarchy to support armed defense; in essence, a general church-backed insurrection against the Mexican government. The League requested three things: bishops' support for the rebellion, commission chaplains to serve rebels in the field, and funds from wealthy Catholics to pay for war materiel. Díaz and the committee could not give the League what they wanted. However, they granted that Catholics were within their rights as citizens and as believers to defend themselves and their religion.[21] That was as close as Díaz came to being a cristero. The League went ahead without the bishops and called for a general rebellion, to begin January 1927. The Calles government responded by exiling Bishop Díaz to the United States. As a leader and mouthpiece of the hierarchy, he was branded a clerical mastermind of the rebellion. Díaz faced a long exile in the United States. From there he came to a clear stance on the cristero uprising, a conclusion shared by Leopoldo Ruiz y Flores: a religious war had no chance of success. The potential consequences—the threat of losing Catholic Mexico altogether—moved Díaz toward conciliation, a realist position.[22] He and Ruiz y Flores helped broker a cease-fire agreement in 1929. They were both painted as traitors to the cause of the cristeros, viewed as selling out to gain ecclesiastical promotion. Cristero expectations were this: the protest and fight were to continue until the laws were changed or the Calles government toppled. Neither occurred, but a peace was struck nonetheless. Díaz and Ruiz y Flores would be blamed for giving up before the holy war could be won.

But all of that would come later. The label of traitor was not yet something that weighed on the mind of Bishop Díaz on his early morning visit to see Miranda in late 1926. Díaz came to ask for Miranda's advice. Miranda, the young director of the secretariat, was indeed a simple priest, but one put in charge of a very important institution. Miranda helped direct much Catholic energy into significant activities. Díaz knew that whatever course of action the bishops chose, they would need the support of Miguel Miranda. And so Díaz put the question to him: How should Catholics proceed in these dire circumstances?

Miranda, for his part, had asked himself the same question. "We are faced with a difficult phenomenon to diagnose," came Miranda's calm reply, with an almost clinical detachment. "The state of violence against the church and against the Catholic faith goes against the soul and the foundational values of our people."[23]

The secretariat's director then laid out two directions for action: "On the one hand we have to attend to what is happening here and now: to follow the development of events and continue making appropriate decisions in view of present circumstances, with the conviction that this will pass, while the church is eternal." Miranda's first course of action was leadership through the current maelstrom. But there was a second as well. He believed this route was perhaps even more crucial: "On the other hand, it is very important, I'd almost say more important, to foresee and prepare the future."[24]

Pascual Díaz listened intently. He was silent for more than a few moments, his reply slow and measured. He felt the weight of his responsibility. "And you, Padre Miranda, how might you help us, from your position as director of the Mexican Social Secretariat?"[25]

The thirty-year-old Miranda, self-aware enough to understand that the secretary of the bishops' committee was asking for advice, made sure to give a caveat for what he was about to say. The young priest emphasized his adhesion and obedience to the bishops, adding: "One thing that I'd like to observe, with all due respect, and this is that the work of attending to the present requires one head, and the work of preparing for the future requires another head. I, as you can see, Monseñor, have but one head."[26]

A big smile stretched the vastness of Diaz's broad face. "Very well, Padre Miranda, I'll consult with the Episcopal Committee and tomorrow I'll return and tell you what we decide."

Twenty-four hours passed and Díaz returned with the bishops' deliberations: "Padre Miranda, we've considered your interesting reflections, which we believe are sound and we've decided to entrust you with preparing the future of the church, so that once this persecution passes, the current trajectory of the Mexican Social Secretariat will continue and be strengthened. We the bishops of the Episcopal Committee will dedicate ourselves to face the present situation."

Miranda's mission had been decided—preparing the future. The work of Cultura Femenina, and Sofía's role in that work, had suddenly become crucial to Mexican Catholicism's future. Preparing the future meant education and training, especially with the next generation in mind. Sofía del Valle was Miranda's most important collaborator and confidant in this work. The call to the new world had come.

Before leaving the offices of the Social Secretariat, Pascual Díaz turned to say one last thing. "Perhaps we will be chosen to be martyrs," Díaz remarked, "or at the very least misunderstood."[27]

Interlude

FAMILY ALBUMS

Recently
Sanborns, Mexico City, 9:13 a.m.

Strong saxophone Muzak plays in the Sanborns restaurant dining room. I fumble with my brand-new Olympus ws-852 digital voice recorder. I've never used it before. Mostly I deal with dead people, subjects who might have a lot to say, but whose words I can read in letters, diaries, and official documents.

Our search for some suitable place for Tere Huidobro, Héctor, and me to talk took us to Sanborns. It's Mexico's most iconic retail chain that features restaurant, café, gift shop, pharmacy, and department store. It's something of an institution, Sanborns, at least in Mexico City.

At the turn of the twentieth century Walter and Frank Sanborn, two American immigrants to Mexico, set up the capital's first soda fountain. In 1903 they opened a lunch counter, located next to the city's main post office. They had a knack for marketing, if only because they smartly decided to leave off the possessive apostrophe unknown in Spanish and simply went with *Sanborns* as a name for their establishment.

Just a decade after it opened Sanborns became famous. The Mexican Revolution came to luncheon at the restaurant. When the army of Emiliano Zapata descended on Mexico City in the late fall of 1914, the various Zapatista leaders chose Sanborns as a place of rendezvous. Several photographs from the time show two Zapatistas awkwardly perched at the Sanborns lunch counter. A bit of bread on dainty plates and porcelain cups and saucers are laid out before them. They wear bandoliers. One has an intimidating facial scar stretching from eye to mouth; his companion wears a gigantic sombrero that's somehow rolled upward, sitting like a cone basket atop his head. Even then Sanborns was an odd mix of traditional and modern.

In the 1940s Frank Sanborn sold his business to Chicago-based Charles Walgreen Jr. of the Walgreens drugstore chain. And Sanborns remained Walgreens' property for the next forty years. Locations sprang up throughout Mexico. Merchandising expanded. In 1985 Sanborns was sold again, this time to Mexican-based Grupo Carso, owned by Carlos Slim. In 2016 *Forbes* listed Slim as the fourth-richest man in the world. His estimated fortune is $50 billion.

Sanborns is *muy mexicano* and also not so much.

"*¿Algo más?*" Anything else? the waitress asks. We ask for refills on coffee.

The waitress is all business, which seems strange considering her extremely colorful, billowy skirt and lace-trimmed blouse. The nylon flower clipped above her ear—hair pulled back in a tightly braided bun—paired with the dress ensemble suggest that someone wants the wait staff to affect something akin to a clichéd Mexican fiesta. That mariachi might break out in song at literally any moment seems to be the aesthetic they're going for.[1]

"Anything else?" the waitress asks again after pouring the coffee.

We signal no and smile. Our smiles go unreturned. As the waitress's skirt twirls away from the table, I finally get my digital voice recorder turned on. It's running.

Later, I will listen to the recording I download on my computer. I will cringe at my ill-formed questions posed in Spanish. Just let them talk! I scold myself later.

The conversation begins. But not where I expect. Tere, and especially Héctor, are interested to know why I'm doing this. How did I come to know about Tía Popi?

"What's in it for you?" Héctor asks between a glance at me and a bite of enchilada.

"It's a great question," *buena pregunta*, I tell him. I begin in the Vatican. I begin with the folder I found with Sofía del Valle's name on it. I try to convey how Sofía's life is an interesting window into what it meant to be a Catholic woman in the twentieth century. I tell Héctor, as a historian, I don't plan on amazing royalties for my book. But I want to tell a story that's accessible. We laugh, or chuckle really. He seems satisfied. He warms up to me. I'd like to think Héctor and Tere can see I don't take my responsibility lightly.

But they want to know more. They ask whether I'm Catholic.

"No, I'm actually a Protestant. Most recently, a Presbyterian."

I'm a little reticent about this fact. Will they doubt my ability to tell Sofía's biography? I'm white, male, and American—and a Protestant to boot. What right do I have to narrate Sofía's story?

My background intrigues them. And I'm not sure what interests them more, that I'm an American, Protestant man studying a Mexican, Catholic woman . . . or the part about being a Presbyterian. It's hard to say, as both come with an assortment of odd baggage.

We're getting personal now. Vulnerable. I've let them see me and now Tere and Héctor let me see a little about them. Maybe trust is built when people choose to hear one another's stories? I take another bite of my pan dulce. I listen.

Héctor tells me about their journey of faith. How over the last ten years they've returned to a more committed Catholicism, how they've experienced hardship. Héctor has been kidnapped and held for ransom twice in the last ten years. They've been victims of Mexico's spiraling drug violence. As the cartels have positioned for more territory, there's been a rippling effect of organized crime. Drugs are the big game. But extortion, bribery, kidnapping, these have been the widening circles of the transnational drug trade. Mexican civil society, as represented by Héctor's personal experience, is exhausted. Violence caused Tere and Héctor to leave their home in Michoacán where groups like La Familia Michoacana have spread their network of corruption and impunity. They moved to Toluca, a ninety-minute drive from Mexico City. Even now they're in the process of returning to their Michoacán home. It's a courageous move. Tere and Héctor feel God at work in the process, painful as it's been.

"*Cosa divinas*," Héctor says, divine things. "I don't believe in coincidences. I believe in miracles."

Tere and Héctor see a divine hand at work in their lives, Providence guiding situations outside their control. They see it even in the special way events have orchestrated our meeting.

Tere wrote to me via Facebook Messenger a few months ago. She wanted to share the story of how she inherited so many of her aunt's possessions. For instance, she has Sofía's light blue Samsonite luggage, with engraved initials. She also keeps the cape given to Sofía when the Vatican bestowed on Sofía a special recognition: Dama de la Santa Sepulcro. Lady of the Holy Sepulchre. Tere maintains most of the family photos, dating from the late 1800s to the 1970s. Behind these things, these material remains, lies a story about family, an intimate history. Tere wrote me:

Facebook Messenger: 1:06 p.m.

Hi Steve! I had the chance to know aunt Popi when she was already getting on in years. We played pirinola (it's a table game I can explain to you at some point). We visited her in her little home to give her company as she really didn't get out much anymore. My parents separated when I was 5 years old and my sister almost 3. Perhaps because of this the women in the family pitched in, trying to compensate for the absence of my mom as we lived with my dad. It was aunt Popi who gave me my first stockings, my first pearl necklace, which had been hers. Anyway, she loved me and took good care of me.

For Tere, the things she keeps of Sofía del Valle are parts of her own past. Tere recounts to me that everyone always told her father that he was living in the past, keeping all the mementos he did. But now Tere sees it as providential. Something divine. These things her father kept, that she now keeps, might be useful to me to tell the story of her Tía Popi—that's special for Tere.

"I've already asked my Tía Sofía to help me bring you everything you may need," Tere tells me.

Sofía del Valle remains a presence for Tere. Tere's Catholic beliefs aside, the idea that those we love remain with us, are not lost to us, strikes me as completely and utterly natural. Historians are always closer to the Hereafter than we are led to believe in grad school.

Tere reaches for the brightly colored handbag. We make room on the laminate inlaid table. She lays out several family photo albums. We leaf through the aged pictures, glued onto red construction paper; some have notes, others do not. Tere knows Sofía del Valle was a relatively well-known, well-traveled, before-her-time sort of Catholic woman. But Tere's introducing me to Tía Popi. We talk about pirinola, that children's game she mentioned in her Facebook message, which uses a six-sided spinning top. We talk also of Christmas dinners with Tía Popi making her special turkey recipe (it included raisins). We laugh about Tía Popi ordering the children around, the forays she organized for the kids in the garden hunting for slugs, the appearances Miranda would make at family gatherings, patting the children on the head, telling them they're growing too fast. Sofía even gave Tere her pearl necklace.

I decide not to ask about what happened between Tere's father and mother. It doesn't feel right. But the gift of the pearl necklace is something that strikes me as we talk. Sofía in later years always had a string of pearls. You can see them in the photographs. No piece of paper could've conveyed what Tere is telling me. She's explaining the Sofía del Valle that's also her Tía Popi: the great aunt who loved her niece, who had a special affection for her, Tere, this girl without a mother. It's as if I'm tapping into a different kind of knowing, a source of knowledge that, for the historian, is often out of reach.

Later I will think about this constantly. I will reflect on how the historian's craft, with its reliance on sources, gets the story more right on a factual level than do oral sources, memories, and anecdotes. But does exactitude equal truth? Whatever I write about Sofía del Valle, for whatever acuity I might show in revealing her life—and through it the lives of others in the past—I will be convinced that I will have failed if I don't convey the truth of that gift of a pearl necklace.

We continue to turn the pages of the photo albums in the restaurant dining room. We stop at one picture where Sofía is young and beautiful. It's a striking photo.

"But why didn't she ever marry?" Héctor asks with a bit of curiosity.

"*Pues, fue consagrada,*" Tere immediately replies. She committed herself to God.

Tere says this with force, as if Sofía's choice never to marry was obvious to everyone.

"Surely she would've at least had a boyfriend at some point?" Héctor presses.

"I don't think so," says Tere.

Tere's mind is clearly made up about her aunt. The story she believes about her Tía Popi is fixed. Tere has all but stated earlier that Sofía del Valle is, to her, akin to the family saint. It's clear Tere wants to maintain Sofía's sanctity. A boyfriend could call that into question. I realize that, even in death, and perhaps in death all the more so, it's hard to separate Sofía's ideal—an ideal of consecration she herself performed for others—from the flesh-and-blood woman who lived with contradictions. Some truths, like the pearl necklace, only emerge when felt. Other truths need sources.

I explain what I know about Sofía's love life, her friendship with Miranda especially. Apparently everyone in the family is aware of their friendship. But they haven't seen the letters I have. Yet, the letters are hard to interpret. They reveal a deeper connection than perhaps anyone realizes, but nothing that contradicts Tere's assertions about Sofía. It's quite likely Sofía never had a boyfriend.

"Your Tía Sofía," I tell Tere, "said in one interview that she never felt a call to become a nun. But neither did she feel a call to get married."

"She remained in the middle, then," Héctor comments.

"She wanted to have freedom," Tere says with perhaps more conviction than she intends.

The idea hangs between us only a moment. It's as if, Tere realizes, the notion of Sofía wanting freedom from marriage smacks too much of feminism.

"Well...no...it's like"—Tere collects her thoughts, continues—"what I think is she wouldn't have been able to do the things she did with a man at her side."

"And more so in that era..." I begin.

86   Interlude: Family Albums

"Even more difficult back then," Tere agrees with me and adds: "I believe she needed freedom for what was destined for her."

As the pages of the albums turn, we drink further cups of coffee. I ask arcane details. Birth dates. Dates of death. About other surviving del Valle descendants. Tere doesn't know all the details. We can ask Tía Babi, she tells me, another family member we're scheduled to meet later that day. I ask about Sofía's brother, Francisco, who died in an accident in 1921. I'm still searching for details about his death, I explain.

"A very painful blow for the family." Tere only knows this for sure.

We're running late for our next appointment. I'll have to take photos of the albums later. But I assure Tere that I want to document everything.

The family albums return to Tere's colored handbag. She reassures me there'll be time for photos later. We dash out of Sanborns toward Reforma Boulevard, back past the Independence Angel. We're late for our meeting with *las viejitas*: four little old women who were young when they knew Sofía del Valle.

PART 3

~

Mexican Odyssey

Athena speaks. Dearest of the gods to me.
I don't know where you are, can't see you,
but I hear your voice, it lifts my heart—
no war cry, no trumpet, ever sounds so clear.

Odysseus speaks to Athena,
Sophocles, *Ajax*

10

The Catacombs

During the Cristero War, despite the church strike and despite the threat of police inspection, sacramental life continued in Mexico. It went underground, especially in Mexico City, where many priest refugees had settled. For Sofía, the work of Cultura Femenina proceeded as well. The project of education consumed her activities. Larger forces, those of church-state politics, were out of her control. Her response was to focus on the mission before her, training the forty or so women studying at Cultura Femenina.

Many Catholics didn't see it that way. What room for action that had been open for Catholics in the public sphere in the early part of the 1920s had now closed. Catholic schools had been shuttered; large numbers of male and female religious—the nuns, monks, brothers, and sisters of the consecrated life—had either left Mexico willingly or were forcibly exiled, especially the foreign born. Those that remained, like the Jesuits, operated in secret. The organized work of the social Catholic movement, the labor unionization, the savings and loan programs, the constructive project of building a Catholic alternative, appeared discarded for militant opposition. Sofía's work with the Social Secretariat remained an exception, but it too was raided, shuttered, and its work stunted. As with the early church, many Mexican Catholics believed these were the days of the tyrants. And like their early Christian forebears, the faith for them would survive in the catacombs.[1] Modern catacombs were private homes, often of the well-to-do, where priests could hide, Masses could be held in secret, and devotion to and consumption of the Eucharist could persist.[2] Sofía del Valle carried on in these catacombs with the vision of giving Mexican Catholic women a liberal arts education.

Even so, Mexico's religious conflict only compounded the difficulties in establishing the women's college. Catholic propaganda efforts continued, and the police began searching for mimeograph machines where antigovernment flyers were being printed. That search led police to Miguel Miranda and the offices of the Mexican Social Secretariat.

On November 6, 1926, Father Miranda was at work in the Motolinía offices of the secretariat when police officers arrived.

"You are being arrested," the agent in charge told Miranda.

"Why? I believe you are mistaken . . ." he protested.[3]

But police arrested Miranda, Rafael Dávila Vilchis (the secretariat's subdirector), and twenty-two other members of the diverse organizations working out of the office. It's quite possible that Sofía was among them. She constantly worked from the office. For the next twelve hours the group underwent a confusing ordeal. While there might have been no mistake in their arrest, the purpose for holding the Catholics seemed unclear to the officials in charge. In the morning, with no charges leveled, and the police unwilling to pursue the case, Miranda and his group were released.[4]

The raid, arrest, and detention were unorganized and haphazard. It very likely came as a result of a tip or on the orders of police leadership. Perhaps it was simply meant to intimidate Miranda and his Catholic workers. Without anyone being formally charged, the secretariat's work continued. However, this was only the beginning of a mounting campaign to destroy the organizational apparatus of the Catholic movement in Mexico City. All Catholic groups became colored by the decision of the Catholic Defense League to take up arms against the government and support the growing ranks of cristero rebels in the countryside.

In the waning days of 1926, after the police raid, Sofía received an invitation to visit an underground convent. It was located in the southern reaches of the capital, in Tlalpan, not far from Sofía's home in Tlacopac. There a group of cloistered nuns had lived since 1923. The abbess in charge was Sor María Concepción Acevedo y de la Llata, better known simply as Madre Conchita. Madre Conchita had stood her ground against police intrusion. The mayor of the municipality had looked the other way when other convents and Catholic schools were being closed down by government order. Madre Conchita had sent numerous invitations to Sofía to come to the convent, to see firsthand the work of prayer, penance, and piety that they were carrying on there, despite the religious restrictions. Sofía finally accepted.[5]

Inside the residence Sofía encountered Madre Conchita and approximately twenty nuns. They had turned their house into a cloister. Away from the prying eyes of police inspectors, cocooned there within the walls that kept out the capital's chaos, they could live out their vows of poverty, chastity, and obedience—sixteenth-century contemplatives in the 1920s. They wore full habits within those walls and devoted their lives to the adoration of the consecrated Eucharist—el Santísimo Sacramento.

But they couldn't keep the world outside the walls from seeping in. They had to be on constant watch. A nun stood guard at the door, vetting those who sought entrance. Madre Conchita had numerous contacts on the outside; the wife of the municipal mayor was a devoted Catholic who attended services there. The nuns received tips when the police did random sweeps, seeking to root out clandestine religious communities. When the tips came, the women would change out of their habits into plain clothes and leave the residence, making sure to remove, or hide, incriminating religious paraphernalia.[6]

Madre Conchita was delighted to give Sofía a tour, for her to meet the women there, and to show Sofía their chapel. A woman with intelligent eyes set above high cheekbones, a pug nose, and thin drawn lips, Madre Conchita led Sofía through the secret convent. It contained a makeshift altar; the centerpiece was a tabernacle where the consecrated Host was deposited each day, brought by a Jesuit priest who served as the community's chaplain. Sofía noticed something unusual. On each side of the tabernacle was a small wax figurine, one on the right, the other on the left. Adornments such as these were common enough. They were often saints, angels, or holy figures that inspired devotion and focused the prayers of the faithful. But these wax figures were different: one was a tarantula; the other was a scorpion.

Noticing Sofía's alarm, Madre Conchita explained that they symbolized two of Mexico's presidents—Obregón and Calles. Like their human counterparts, she warned, "they can kill you, if you don't kill them."[7]

Before she was the nun called Madre Conchita, her name was María Concepción Acevedo y de la Llata. María Concepción's childhood looked much like Sofía's. Both were born in 1891—in fact, just days apart: Sofía on October 18 and Madre Conchita on November 2, All Souls' Day, the day after All Saints. In the Catholic calendar All Souls' Day commemorates not saints and martyrs, but the ordinary departed faithful, that they too might find a path to heaven. Madre Conchita's lifelong wish was to be among the saints. But history would not be so kind as to fulfill that wish.

Saints and martyrs seemed to be calling to María Concepción from an early age. Born into a loving family—traditional and pious—they made a home in Querétaro, a few hours outside Mexico City by train. Despite the blessings of childhood, life in the world lacked something for María Concepción. "Inside me all of that felt nonessential," she remembered, "and somehow unimportant." A call to something greater was urging her to escape the world, to leave things of transitory value. "My vocation was already taking root in the form of rejecting the pleasant and easy life, growing, over time, into a positive eagerness to transform my tranquil existence into another more austere, more simple, because I wanted to imitate the saints whose lives I had read about."[8]

The paths taken by María Concepcion and Sofía del Valle diverged ever farther at this point. María Concepción desired the traditional saintliness of cloister, cowl, and habit, a mysticism of intimate union, closer to Terésa of Avila than Thérèse of Lisieux. Sofía chose a path closer to the latter: the holiness of a mundane, this-worldly variety, the daily pursuit of God in the contemporary world.

At the age of twenty, María Concepción entered the Capuchin order in Querétaro as a postulant. It was May 1911. The old regime of Porfirio Díaz was crumbling; revolutionaries in the north had taken control of Ciudad Juárez. In Querétaro, María Concepción was in retreat from that world, desiring a life more medieval than modern, dominated by the lives of the saints, whose story of mysticism and martyrdom she desired to enact in the present. Six months later María Concepción passed from postulant to novice. With examinations complete, María Concepción had her ceremony of dedication, where the novice takes simple vows of poverty, chastity, and obedience. It was December 8, 1911, the day the Catholic Church venerates the miracle of the Immaculate Conception. The bride was María Concepción, dressed in white, a long train following behind. Adorned in glittering jewelry, orange blossoms crowning her hair, she walked to the altar. An organ softly played and the nuns gathered there intoned a Gregorian call and response: "Come, Bride of Christ," they began.[9] Her marriage was not to an earthly husband, but to the Savior. María Concepción recalled feeling embarrassed that she wasn't crying like the rest, that she wasn't providing an outward show of feeling. She was conserving her emotion for an interior experience. All her energy was directed inside her soul. She remembered it as a "blue and pink daybreak of divine and mystical ideals."[10]

A year later María Concepción was fully admitted into the Capuchin order. Keeping the world out proved difficult. In July 1914 revolutionary troops entered Querétaro. Soldiers converted churches and convents into barracks. Anticlerical fervor had been added to the revolutionary project. Carrancista troops, directed by up-and-coming leaders such as Obregón and Calles, with young officers like the future police inspector Roberto Cruz in tow, began taking their fight to the church. The church's crime, according to the Carrancistas, was complicity with the forces of reaction—support for Victoriano Huerta, who had seen to it that President Madero was assassinated. Almost all of Mexico's bishops were exiled in July 1914. Rumors of executions, the burning of sacred icons, and even the rape of nuns traveled quickly around the nation. Foreign-born priests fled. Carranza's revolutionary armies moved from north to south, in what one historian has called a "reconquest of Mexican territory." Priests and nuns were reduced to the status of ordinary men and women, themselves "pillaged alongside the rest of the devotional landscape."[11] The Catholic press and the National Catholic Party folded.

And in Querétaro, the mother superior of the Capuchin order told her small community to flee. María Concepción and her fellow nuns changed out of their habits and put on plain clothes. Eventually the nuns regrouped. A girls' home run by the Servants of the Sacred Heart had room for them. Over the next year and a half María Concepción took care of the young orphans of revolution. Almost all were sick, malnourished, covered in parasites. For María Concepción it was a trauma. Her mystical ideal had been shattered. She was being yanked from the security of the cloister back into the damaged world beyond. The revolution, led by men such as Obregón and Calles, had come between her and a life alone with Christ. "My gentle and bright horizons turned gray. And my heart, which seemed born to be resoundingly happy, began to discover in its deep folds the seed of bitterness," she wrote of the experience.[12]

María Concepción became Madre Conchita in 1922. Her spiritual director informed her that she would be moving to Mexico City. She was being promoted to mother superior of the Mexico City convent. The group settled in Tlalpan, where she opened up a novitiate for the order. Young women, despite the clandestine nature of the convent, began making a decision to join their new mother superior in adoration of the Holy Sacrament. Conventual rules mandated that the nuns were not supposed to have contact with the outside world. But these were extraordinary times. Madre Conchita opened up the convent for priest refugees, laymen and laywomen, and all that might want to continue receiving Communion in secret.[13] It was then that Sofía del Valle visited the convent in Tlalpan, disturbed by Madre Conchita's improvised spiritual militancy.

In Madre Conchita's convent, Sofía del Valle stood before the chapel's altar. Obregón and Calles sat ensconced as objects of wrath: a tarantula and a scorpion.

"They can kill you, if you don't kill them," Madre Conchita said.

The meaning was clear, at least to Sofía. Madre Conchita seemed to be suggesting tyrannicide, the killing of the tyrant. Had it become a possibility, a dire remedy compelled by the times they lived in? The thought horrified Sofía. Her work with Miranda had such a different focus. Education. Training for the future.

Sofía was an invited guest at Madre Conchita's underground convent. She risked sounding rude, but she had to speak her mind.

"They are souls," Sofía objected, "and this is not my way of prayer."[14]

Sofía didn't record Madre Conchita's reaction. It's quite possible the moment became awkward, the nun surprised that Sofía didn't see the world as she did. Perhaps Madre Conchita simply shrugged off the apparent rebuff, not wanting to sour the visit further. Whatever transpired after the exchange, Sofía was bothered by what she had seen at Conchita's chapel. She vowed never to return. And regarding Madre Conchita, Sofía had only this to say in later years: she felt that Madre Conchita was a good nun, but admitted "there was something not normal about her."[15] It's hard to know if Sofía felt that way about Conchita at the time or, like many Catholics, increasingly rejected Conchita after the nun's arrest for conspiring to assassinate President Obregón.

Sofía also had relatively little to say about the route of violence taken by cristeros. Her surviving letters from the era only briefly mention her efforts to keep Cultura Femenina from involvement in rebel activities. Her clearest recorded statements on the subject came only decades after the rebellion. The first came in historian Alicia Olivera's 1972 interview with Sofía. The exchange is brief, but telling.

"Were you in agreement with the resistance movement of the cristeros?" asked Alicia Olivera, the interviewer.

"Look, I didn't involve myself," Sofía replied. "I've always been a pacifist and always . . ."

Here Sofía paused a moment. She collected her thoughts and continued: "What most interested me is education, because I consider that the biggest problem in Mexico then and now is the education problem."[16]

In a subsequent interview given a few years later, Sofía admitted her respect for those who felt called to the uprising. "I thought they were very courageous," Sofía said of the cristeros. "They were right, absolutely right, to do it." But for herself, Sofía continued, "I have never been a fighting woman because that's not my line in life." Her call was different. "I understood the value of women, the needs of women, when I came from Europe—to be active in government affairs—according to their capabilities, naturally."[17]

Sofía's answers are unsurprising. She had a personal aversion to violence. She had seen the destruction of war firsthand in Europe—the war-wounded on the trains of that continent during her youth. She had also seen the destruction wrought by revolution in her own country after her return. Her mission for education was about the future, when there would be a Catholic voice in the public square. Her concern was not the high politics of church and state; her worry was the lack of women who knew how to stand on their own as educated Catholics in a nation beset by troubles. "To strengthen them in their principles and their foundations, this was our labor," she explained. "If the whole world is set on fighting, then what happens when we are at peace? What happens if there is no one to work?"[18]

Even in the dark days of government persecution and the fight for Christ the King, Sofía's fight was spiritual, educational, and incremental.

11

The Voyage

Sofía del Valle's flight from Madre Conchita's convent, where she was horrified by the scorpion and tarantula on the altar, took her to a community of Catholics in Mexico City busy preparing for the future. Sofía was daily at work in the offices of the Mexican Social Secretariat. Father Miguel Miranda, the director of the secretariat, was the nominal head of Cultura Femenina, the new school for women. But Miranda oversaw all the ministries headquartered at the Motolinía residence. The JCFM—the Mexican Young Women's Catholic Association—was also housed there. What remained of the vastly diminished Catholic Workers Confederation, picked apart by competition with government and radical unions, still operated out of the secretariat as well. Preparing for the future meant educating for the future. Miranda actively promoted small classes for women, workers, and priests. The subject of these study groups was Catholic doctrine on social issues. The goal was providing a solid base for the individual Catholic to begin outreach.[1]

During the first year and a half of Cultura Femenina, Sofía's role was not unlike her function at Ericsson Telephones: a man was her boss; it was her job to see that his directives were properly implemented. But that was about to change. Sofía del Valle's apprenticeship was nearing its end.

Staying afloat amid the increasing floodwaters of persecution meant finding the proper life raft. Money had provided that buoyancy, but now financial resources began to deflate as well. The savings and loan bank established by the secretariat had at least provided small sums to fund operations. At the start of the Cristero War the bank, the Caja de Ahorros León XIII, had deposits of over 60,000 pesos and outstanding loans of slightly under that amount. In an effort to protect some of its assets in the mounting conflict, the secretariat's financial committee (of which Sofía's father was a mainstay) loaned 10,000 pesos to the conservative newspaper, *El País*. When the daily folded under government pressure, the loan was then assumed by the Mexican bishops, with Pascual Díaz acting as guarantor.[2] The loan proved well-timed as it allowed some of the bank's assets to be shielded from the government. But with the onset of civil war came economic slowdown; interest payments on loans halted. Depositors withdrew investments. The secretariat's cash flow trickled to almost nothing.[3] The Mexican dioceses had provided some monthly contributions for the secretariat, but now with church worship halted, these tithes also disappeared.

Sofía's Catholic community, like Madre Conchita's convent, was struggling to continue. Madre Conchita's community had, for a time, received protection from the municipal mayor. But then the mayor left office in 1927. Soon after, Madre Conchita and her convent were raided by police, the nuns marched out in the street and taken into detention. They weren't held long, and after their release, Madre Conchita reassembled her convent in several new underground locations: residences on Mesones Street, Zaragoza Street, and Chopo Street. As before, Madre Conchita opened her doors to lay Catholics, many of them young, mobilized in organizations like the Young Men's Catholic Association and the Catholic Defense League. As mother superior, it was she who dealt with the Catholic faithful who visited her community for counsel, sacrament, and solidarity. It was a job she loathed. "I confess," she wrote in her memoirs, "that returning to interact with a world that I had left with so much joy, assisting the counsel of as many people as might be drawn to our humble and silent gate, disgusted me very much."[4]

Madre Conchita's clandestine gatherings became a crossroads for counterrevolutionary spirituality. Her reputation grew as a saint in the making, known for her desire to die a martyr. Among the many who attended for spiritual relief were those planning violent resistance. There were makeshift bomb makers who supplied weapons to cristero rebels; one went off in the Mexico City Chamber of Deputies without loss of life. Another plot consisted of filling a hypodermic needle with poison. A young woman was supposed to dance with Obregón and inject him with the liquid. The plot failed. Madre Conchita always denied knowing the details of these plans, but she knew the conspirators. She maintained enough critical distance from these incidents to maintain a plausible defense.[5]

In early 1927 Madre Conchita met a young Jesuit priest: Miguel Agustín Pro. An unnamed mutual acquaintance introduced the two one day.[6] They talked "half-jokingly" for half an hour. Madre Conchita remembered that Pro didn't leave a profound impression. "I recognized him to be a priest who fought for the Glory of God, for the salvation of souls, and one who was unafraid of prison or death." But this was natural enough to Madre Conchita. She had met others like him.

In September 1927 their relationship changed, two souls who shared a special dedication to die as martyrs. Madre Conchita maintained in her memoirs that it was Pro, not her, who insisted they consecrate themselves as victim souls and martyrs. Conchita encountered Father Pro on one of her visits to the home of a Catholic woman who often held clandestine services.

"Look, *hija*," the priest told Conchita, "you and I are going to offer ourselves as victims to Divine Justice, for the salvation of the faith in Mexico, for the peace of the church and for the conversion of its persecutors."

Madre Conchita said no. She resisted. Pro told her not to be afraid, not to be a coward. Conchita finally relented, but first she had to confer with her spiritual director. Father Jesús Rougier, her spiritual guide, gave her permission. On September 23, 1927, a special Mass was held in Conchita's convent. Pro wept from the beginning. It was a spiritual reckoning. Here was the consecration and elevation of the Holy Bread; here were the flowers, the resolute prayers; and then the dedication of the sacrifice—their own lives—as victims for God. Afterward Pro told Madre Conchita that he heard a voice in his ears: "the sacrifice is accepted."

On the morning of November 23, 1927, a tightly packed multitude gathered outside the police inspection yard in downtown Mexico City. Onlookers gazed from surrounding gardens, rooftops, and awnings.

Photographers and journalists hurried into position. Amid the crowd of witnesses Alfredo Méndez Medina watched, helpless as armed officers led one of his spiritual disciples—his fellow Jesuit, his friend, Miguel Agustín Pro—to be executed. Méndez Medina later described Pro's "coolness and presence of mind" while facing his imminent death. Father Pro had no idea he would be executed until troops lined up in the shooting gallery of the inspection yard. When he heard his name called, the young Jesuit smoothed his rumpled clothes, straightened his tie, and said goodbye to his companion prisoners, two of whom included his younger brothers, Humberto and Roberto: "*Hasta luego muchachos*," see you later guys, he said simply and directly.

The subsequent details of the modern-day crucifixion scene vary little from Méndez Medina's account, written days after the event: Pro is led out by armed troops; police inspector Roberto Cruz oversees, calmly smoking a faro cigarette. Pro's guard, before leaving the priest at one end of the shooting gallery, asks for forgiveness: "Not only do I forgive you, I thank you," replies the Jesuit. He rejects the blindfold and, calmly, asks for just a minute. He kneels, crosses himself, makes his act of contrition, commending his soul to God; he rises and kisses the crucifix around his neck. The rosary clenched in one hand, he holds out his arms in the form of a cross. In a "measured tone," not a yell, he pronounces "*¡Viva Cristo Rey!*" ("Long live Christ the King!"); moments later, shots are fired. Then he falls lifeless, his arms still outstretched; an officer delivers the coup de grâce.[7]

Several days before, on November 17, 1927, Pro had been arrested. He was accused of serving as the "intellectual director" of a foiled plot to dynamite ex-president Álvaro Obregón's Cadillac as Obregón drove around Chapultepec Park on a Sunday afternoon with friends. While it is certain that Miguel Pro knew the conspirators, he probably had no role in the assassination attempt. Pro's brother Humberto was indeed the former owner of the Essex automobile used in the attack, yet based on this evidence—circumstantial at best—and without trial President Calles ordered Roberto Cruz to carry out the Jesuit's execution along with that of Humberto. Two others, Luis Segura Vilchis and Juan Tirado, who had without doubt been involved in the plot, were also executed. But Father Pro's death outstripped the others in terms of notoriety; perhaps his well-known apostolate in the capital, where he performed clandestine marriages and baptisms, impromptu masses, and Eucharistic gatherings in private homes, activities appreciated and lauded by cristero sympathizers, only heightened their sense of injustice in his summary execution. The church hierarchy, supported by testimonies of lay Catholics and other Jesuits who knew him, made sure to emphasize Father Pro's innocence in the affair. Still, even if subsequent research has been unable to completely exonerate him, Pro became the epic symbol, the "iconic" innocent sacrificial lamb slaughtered to wash away Mexico's sins, as well as the godlessness of the tyrant Calles and his revolutionary henchmen. Pro's status as a popular martyr was instantaneous.[8]

After the execution, the bodies of Father Pro and his brother Humberto were then transferred to the home of their father. Multitudes gathered outside—traffic police had to monitor the entrance because of the crush of the crowd—while Méndez Medina and another Jesuit prayed the rosary; they sat in vigil nearly the whole night. Sermons were given, and a consecrated Host was placed on top of Father Pro's coffin while the faithful took part in an Hora Santa (or "Holy Hour" focused on prayer and petition). Devotees touched crucifixes, rosaries, and flowers to Pro's body, immediately considered relics of the popular "martyrs." Méndez Medina recounted that one woman, her ten-year-old son in hand, admonished the boy, saying: "My son, look at these martyrs, it is for this reason I brought you, so engrave well in your mind what you're looking at, for when you grow up you'll know how to give your life defending the faith of Christ and die like them, innocent, and with great valor." Thousands joined the funeral procession from the Pro family home to the Panteón de Dolores, and upon their arrival, shouts of "Long live Christ the King" resounded.[9] As the casket was lowered into the crypt, the refrain began again, but this time it went: "Long live the first Jesuit martyr of Christ the King."[10]

Saints and martyrs are made by a community who venerates them. Pro's story helped Catholics make sense of persecution. It upheld their belief in sacrifice, honor, and suffering for a purpose. Pro's death confirmed that society suffered for the sins of a wayward government—for revolutionary sins against God's established order. Pro had stepped in as the required expiation—purging the blemish of apostasy on the part of Mexico's rulers. It was for the church to take on this role of punishment—hence the prayers, vigils, devotions, and pilgrimages to Christ the King. Christ had become king not by killing the tyrant, but by being killed by him. This was the Mexican theodicy of the day. Why did God let this happen? Answer: the sins of prodigal humanity. And so the solution: victim souls must bear the punishment that others deserved. Father Pro, Madre Conchita, and many cristeros viewed themselves as these victim souls. They were those who committed themselves to die "for the salvation of Mexico."[11]

Saints and martyrs can be unmade as well. Thus was Madre Conchita's path to martyrdom blocked. Madre Conchita claimed to have been too late to witness Pro's execution. But she found her way to the morgue where the bodies were taken. To gain access, she had persuaded the guards that she was part of the family. There, next to Pro's cadaver, Madre Conchita leaned down and whispered in Miguel Pro's lifeless ear that he must remember their commitment: that they both die as martyrs. Madre Conchita met Pro's family the day of the funeral. Her ministry began to shift direction: from convent counselor to Eucharist smuggler. Pro's younger brother, Roberto, was still in jail at the police inspection yard. From his cell, Roberto had watched in horror the deaths of his brothers. He figured he would be next, but the executions stopped before his name was called. It was President Calles who commuted the death sentence for Roberto: "Let that one live, we'll send him into exile," came the president's order to Roberto Cruz overseeing the executions. Madre Conchita volunteered to smuggle Communion bread to Roberto.[12] A priest consecrated the wafers and permitted Conchita to take them. She hid the Hosts in a jar of sugar, which accompanied the food she took to Roberto.[13]

Madre Conchita had a remarkable ability to charm her way into the good graces of police guards and officials of all sorts. She had a certain charisma and directness; perhaps her boldness allowed her entrance and access where others had no such luck.[14] Her ability to enter the prison soon became a matter of gossip. Madre Conchita wrote that other Catholic women, especially members of the upper-class Damas Católicas, had begun to spread rumors. Why had Conchita gained access when they had not? Madre Conchita seemed on good terms with the prison guards, which opened the nun to an implicit accusation: sexual favors were being traded for entrance to the jail. Conchita wrote she simply ignored these accusations for the most part. She chalked up her success to God's favor. But then accusations came from another source. Mexican clergymen began to accuse her of unlawfully administering the Eucharist, an action permitted by only a priest. She countered she was simply an intermediary, rising to an extraordinary occasion. The incident began to tarnish her name among Catholics in the capital.[15] The audience of the faithful had already begun to turn against her.

In the coming months another would-be victim soul happened into Madre Conchita's convent. His name was José de León Toral. It would be he who decided to crush the tarantula and the scorpion before they could strike.

Life was not at all easy in the Mexican catacombs. Sofía del Valle, like many other Catholics in the capital, had to worship in secret. For Sofía, the Cristero Rebellion of 1926 to 1929 didn't mean criminal trial, prison, or public scorn as it did for Madre Conchita. She didn't face the firing squad of Father Miguel Pro. Her experience of the religious conflict—secret worship, evading detection, simply carrying on—was probably closer to the norm. Relatively few underwent trials and tribulations matching the most notorious cases.[16] Still, fear pervaded life for many Catholics during those years—of police raids, harassment, and the possible destruction of all the Catholic movement had worked hard to build. Soon some of those fears became a reality for Sofía.

On the night of January 25, 1928, fifteen secret agents of the police inspection raided the offices of the Social Secretariat on Motolinía Street. Father Miguel Miranda was arrested. The women present, Sofía among them, had their purses and belongings searched, but were not detained. The reason why the women were not jailed was not immediately clear. Sofía later heard that police inspector Roberto Cruz had given an order to his subordinates: "We don't want any more old women, they put up too much of a fight, so don't bring in anymore old women, simply search them and if they don't have anything, let them go; just bring me the men."[17] Only Miranda was kept in jail. For three days he was held "without being able to sleep." The memory of Father Pro was on his mind while he was kept in a "fetid and flooded" cell. The fact that just a matter of weeks before Pro had been taken out of the "same dungeon" to "be martyred" was a constant reminder of the "possibility of my own death," Miranda recalled of the incident.[18] On a few occasions guards threatened Miranda with execution if his criminal fine was not paid—500 pesos, the penalty for directing an unregistered, and therefore illegal, religious institute.[19]

The police raid on the secretariat was part of a larger coordinated effort. Inspector Cruz organized a series of crackdowns that same week. A "heavy squad of mounted police" arrested 225 teachers and students from the Seminario Colegiar; another twenty nuns were arrested at the Josefina College. Both schools were accused of teaching the Catholic faith to children, in violation of the new penal code. Inspector Cruz stated to the press: "We have ample proofs in recent days that Catholic elements have begun to renew their seditious propaganda and that many have actually issued subversive proclamations to excite fanatics against the government." It didn't help that the secretariat used a mimeograph machine to make copies for its teaching materials. It appeared to the police that the "subversive proclamations" originated at the Social Secretariat. And although the Catholic institute run by Miranda did not directly provide education to children, it did support catechism initiatives then underway by Catholic activists in the capital. "Under the guise of cultural institutions," Cruz told reporters, "these places have committed violations of the legal dispositions affecting religious practices."[20] On these grounds, Cruz and the police moved forward with the raids. Sofía and the rest of the secretariat staff feared for Miranda's safety and provided the money for the fine. The ransom paid, Miranda was released unharmed, though shaken by the experience.

Miranda's personal trials didn't end with his brief imprisonment. He passed from one painful ordeal to the next. Miranda's father died just days after his release. A small comfort he took was that his father passed away "without him knowing of my imprisonment," he later remembered.²¹ Miranda's now widowed mother received spiritual aid from a family friend, Alfredo Méndez Medina, the former director of the secretariat who was back again in Mexico City during the rebellion. Méndez Medina had acted as a mentor to Miranda in the transition of the leadership duties of the Social Secretariat. Sofía and the del Valle family also supported Miranda during this period of grief. Miranda had been a frequent visitor to Quinta Sofía (the del Valle family home) in recent years, and it was there that he received comfort and strength while he "wept for" his father.²²

The intensity of life in 1928 deepened Sofía and Miranda's relationship. In the midst of the Mexican catacombs, emerging from the trials of carrying on the work for the future of the church—a task delegated to Miranda by the bishops back in 1926—Sofía and Miranda developed a lasting kinship. Their relationship was chaste. Nothing in their long and frequent correspondence, stretching from 1928 to 1981, indicates otherwise. But it was nevertheless an intimate connection. A mutual respect was clear between them, as was a palpable admiration for each other's unique qualities. Their common vision of seeing the Mexican church flourish after civil war cemented their bond. They began a quest together, and they shared their doubts about its outcome with one another. A growing vulnerability between them nurtured empathy and intimacy.²³

Distance also seemed to deepen their intimacy. The police raid and temporary closure of the secretariat offices forced Miranda to travel. The quest for the future in Mexico had to be pursued outside Mexico for the time being. Just a month after the shuttering of the Motolinía Street location, Miranda, with Sofía's assistance, managed to relocate the institute to a new locale—12 Eliseo Street. Sofía claimed they would carry on "even on the benches of Alameda [Park]."²⁴ Despite that determination, funds were drying up. Eleven professors taught classes for some forty students at Cultura Femenina. It had been just eight students a year and a half earlier. The school was growing, despite the religious troubles. The police raid left the secretariat and Cultura Femenina virtually penniless. Just 300 pesos remained in school coffers. The library and furniture had been confiscated, and what little was left the agents destroyed.

Something had to be done. Miranda made a plan in consultation with Sofía, Rafael Dávila Vilchis (the Social Secretariat's deputy director), and the remnant of Catholic activists still willing to partner with them. Miranda would travel to meet Mexican bishops in exile. He would seek assistance from American clergy and, from there, go on to Europe. The plan was to gain moral and spiritual support, but also money. If the time was not right at present for their Catholic works, at least a plan for the future should be developed. Reorganization of the Catholic movement, they argued, had to begin in earnest, and now, even before the end of the religious conflict.[25]

The decision made, Miranda left Mexico in March 1928. The death of Miranda's father still heavy on his mind, he had to tell his mother and sisters he was leaving.

"God bless you, son, don't stay away too long," she told him.

"No, *mamá*. I think it is only a question of a month or so."[26]

Sofía remained—a single laywoman—to run their still very new association, the JCFM. Just as important, perhaps more so, she directed Cultura Femenina, the nascent liberal arts college. Father Davila Vilchis took charge of the other activities of the Social Secretariat. But it was Sofía, for all intents and purposes, who became the person Miranda leaned on during his long hiatus. Separated in geography but united in a joint mission, their bond drew closer.

Miranda's estimation of a month of travel strayed far from that mark. He returned to Mexico in February 1929—eleven months later. But his return was brief; only a week or two later he was off yet again, back to the United States. He then reentered Mexico in July 1929, after the rebellion ended. Throughout his journey—on boats, ocean liners, and trains—he wrote Sofía. And in all the places he passed through—Havana, New Orleans, San Antonio, Philadelphia, Washington DC, Paris, Barcelona, Milan, Rome, and others—letters awaited him from Sofía del Valle.

Two lifelong celibates found in each other a needed friend, confidant, and partner in mission. Romantic love it was not, in terms of sexual consummation. Yet the celibate life, for Sofía and Miranda, was lived on the boundaries between romantic longing and spiritual calling.

Fortunately for Father Miguel Miranda, he didn't have to make the initial departure from Mexico City alone. Sofía, Francisco del Valle (Sofía's father), and at least one of Miranda's sisters traveled with him on the train to Veracruz. At the port of Veracruz, they watched Miranda board his ship bound for Havana, and the next leg of his trip. It was March 10. There was sadness in the parting. For Miranda, a lonely journey lay ahead. For Sofía, a "faithful waiting" impended—a phrase she expressed in one of her letters, and by which she meant perseverance in the task at hand, without knowing what the future held. The sadness of the farewell was punctuated by other emotions. Once on board, Miranda began to write Sofía, recounting that he felt "a great satisfaction in being able to enjoy [the company of] my sister and you at the port." Seasickness put Miranda in bed all the next day. In a somber mood he reflected on the past few months: "I've just begun to recognize the providential in being held up in Mexico; it gave us one more week to talk in Veracruz about the plans [we had made]." Miranda felt confident that the journey he was on, that began with the raid on the secretariat, had instigated the need to form a solid vision for the future mission of social action in Mexico. Doubts remained: "What will be, who can say?" he confided to Sofía. But Miranda could see the hand of Providence at work. And part of his realization was credited to Sofía and their talks in Veracruz before his departure. Before signing off, he remembered to give his regards to "Don Pancho," Sofía's father, and "Doña Chofi," her mother, with whom Sofía shared a nickname. "Hasta La Habana," he wrote—until the next letter in Cuba.[27]

Four days after arriving in Havana, Miranda wrote from a hospital bed at the Sanitarium of the Milagrosa. His news was tinged with embarrassment. He hadn't hit the ground running. Two days of seasickness during his boat journey meant virtually two days without eating. His first meal in Havana consisted of *mariscos*—seafood; in retrospect, a bad idea, he admitted, as the meal gave him food poisoning. The forced time in bed increased his doubts about his mission. Long hours, drinking only orange juice, left his mind to wander, "firmly fixed" on "the work of Cultura" in Mexico City. "Comfort me in the thought that the time here won't be lost," he pleaded with Sofía for encouragement.[28]

The food poisoning passed and Miranda's prospects improved. He wasn't completely alone in Havana. His uncle lived there, a man grieving like Miranda. He had lost a brother; Miranda, a father. Miranda had various other acquaintances in Cuba as well. Prominent Mexican bishops in exile had taken up residence on the island. But these were not permanent embraces. The transitory nature of these interactions made any comfort he took from them only momentary.

Havana was not a failure in at least one respect. The aged archbishop of Mexico, José Mora y del Río, lived in Havana after he had been exiled by the Mexican government in 1927. Despite losing control over Mexico's clergy and its lay rebels, Mora y del Río was still the highest-ranking Mexican bishop. Mora gave Miranda a personal letter of recommendation. It was timely encouragement, especially as Mora y del Río died just weeks later. The letter and the support it represented was a crucial first step to drumming up assistance for Cultura Femenina and the Social Secretariat among clergy in the United States and Europe.

In Havana, Miranda's thoughts continued to drift toward Mexico and Sofía at the helm of operations on Eliseo Street. "I received your letters from the 11 and 13 [of March]," he let Sofía know. "Don't forget that the fears that the heart occasionally experiences are always [sources of] abundant goodness as well." It appears that when news of seasickness and homesickness reached Sofía her letters expressed deep concern, even fear for Miranda's well-being. Miranda eased Sofía's anxiety. He joked about his bout of incontinence in the sanitarium. "Sooner or later," he wrote optimistically, "the full reason for these mysteries of opportunity will be revealed." He couldn't help confiding that "I think about you, very industrious, fully devoted to your daily work." Miranda assured her that he understood her "difficulties" and "I foresee the prudent and timely solution."[29]

A United Fruit Company vessel called *Gatun* carried Miranda from Havana to New Orleans. Some two weeks were spent in the Crescent City. His itinerary then quickened. From there he went to San Antonio to receive further recommendations from the Mexican bishops there, including Leopoldo Ruiz y Flores. Then Miranda began the most pressing phase of his journey: capturing the imagination and support of American Catholic bishops. From Texas he traveled by train to Washington DC, and then on to New York, with brief visits to Philadelphia. By the middle of May he had received at least half a dozen letters from bishops. The Vatican diplomat to the United States sent a personal recommendation directly to Cardinal Gasparri in Rome. Gasparri was the Vatican secretary of state, second in charge of church governance after the pope. Gasparri would be an important ally to win. By the middle of May 1928, Miranda boarded a steamship called the SS *Île-de-France* and crossed the ocean.[30] The groundwork in Cuba and North America was fundamental for the real goal: the backing of the Vatican for Miranda's plan for Mexico's future after the Cristero War ended. In Rome he hoped to present the plan to the pope. Many cristeros believed they had the moral support of the pontiff for their rebellion. There was no guarantee that the Vatican would support the work of Miranda, let alone see it as a blueprint for Mexico's Catholic future. Miranda and Sofía had a lot riding on the success of the mission.

Miranda spent a month or so in the United States before leaving for Europe. A simple summary of his itinerary and the letters of recommendation he received do little justice to the story of that month. Between Miranda's arrival in New Orleans in April, to his departure from New York on the SS *Île-de-France* bound for Europe in May, Sofía del Valle was his constant correspondent. Their letters reveal much of Sofía's life in Mexico, as well as the growing bond between them.

12

The Test

Life on the road for Miranda was made easier because of the del Valle family. After leaving Havana, heavy with sickness and loneliness, New Orleans was a respite. Anxiety eased into "peace and tranquility," he wrote Sofía happily. "Rest, tranquility, and air to breathe" were found in the home of Sofía's sister Clara and her husband, Alfonso del Marmol. Clara had married in the city, remaining there while the rest of the family moved back to Mexico in 1922. Clara's young son Panchito, "gracious and reflective," followed Miranda around wherever he went. With the del Valle family home open to him, no expensive hotel stays would be required. The Jesuits at Loyola University were a prime contact. So too was Newcomb College, a school run by Protestants. Part of Miranda's journey was seeing firsthand the inner workings of liberal arts institutions with religious curricula. Miranda's spirits were starting to lift.[1]

New Orleans provided Miranda with his own education into Sofía's life in the city. "I have often thought of you while walking these Streets of God in this city," he mentioned in one letter. "In it you spent so much time. Clarita continually helps me relive your memories." Miranda spent several afternoons with Clara. He found her to be a kind and gracious host. But Clara was homesick. She'd been the first del Valle daughter to marry. She was the talented one in the family—in Europe Francisco del Valle had paid scores of piano and voice teachers to hone Clara's skills.[2] New Orleans newspapers published announcements for her concerts; her wedding was a society event, as Alfonso del Marmol had links to Spanish royalty. But now Clara simply taught lessons at Tulane and gave recitals only rarely. Hopes of becoming a well-known opera singer had faded under the weight of everyday life. She'd settled into domesticity. Miranda couldn't help but notice Clara's jealousy when it came to talk of Quinta Sofía—how Clara wanted her family to visit more, how Francisco del Valle had made a business trip to Europe and failed to divert his itinerary long enough to spend time with his grandchildren. Clara loved her big sister Sofía, but she also felt the want of attention she'd always known as a child. "In my enjoyable and pleasant conversations with [Alfonso and Clara]," Miranda wrote, "I noticed they harbor hurt feelings toward [your father] for not visiting them on his return from Spain." Miranda realized he'd only made it worse when he told them Francisco del Valle had accompanied he and Sofía to Veracruz. "I encouraged her," Miranda wrote Sofía, "to resolve her most obvious difficulties." Miranda also encouraged Sofía to write Clara and clear the air.[3] Perhaps, for Clara, Miranda's constant questions about Sofía—Sofía's memories, Sofía's childhood, Sofía's attributes—stoked her fear of not being the most favored del Valle daughter.

Between Miranda's talks with Clara and his visits with Loyola's Jesuits and Newcomb's Protestants, he toured some of Sofía's past. He visited Hibernia Bank where Sofía had worked while living in New Orleans, "the actual building where you walked," he reported to Sofía.[4] Employees of the bank had "rich memories" of Sofía. "So, you see, it's been difficult to erase your memory from this place."[5] Sofía's colleagues remembered her, and it was also hard for Miranda to forget her.

An overnight train to San Antonio carried Miranda away from New Orleans and from his tranquility. It was a Saturday, the day before Easter 1928. Amid the jostling of the train, he struggled to type to Sofía his vision for Cultura Femenina, which was "called to be a light that shines and heats, at the same time." He saw intelligence *and* passion. "We need a generation more Christian in intelligence and in heart." Yet he moved from his vision for the future to his loneliness at the present. Missing Easter was a sacrifice; a "day that I would have liked to spend with you and with all of mine" back in Mexico City. Miranda had heard that a small earthquake had hit Mexico's capital. He had been worried about his sisters, who lived in an affected zone. Sofía had visited them and assured Miranda they were fine. Now, while the train jerked erratically, he typed out a few phrases of heartfelt thanks to Sofía for looking after his family in his absence.[6]

The train to San Antonio also carried Miranda's worries for Sofía. She had been sick with another bout of "hepatitis"—the first mention of this condition in their correspondence. The Spanish word Miranda used was *higadítis*, today commonly understood as hepatitis. But its literal translation simply means "liver inflammation." In 1928 medical knowledge of liver ailments was ill defined. It could be that it was bacterial, borne in contaminated food or water. Yet it appears more chronic than most bacterial strains, especially as Miranda referred to it on multiple occasions. "I have been very worried about your little sickness of the liver," he wrote. "I remember well that your '*higadítis*' is not content to molest you for a few days, but periodically" and often acutely.[7] Possibly it was a form of autoimmune hepatitis. The disease affects women under the age of forty—Sofía was thirty-seven at the time—and causes chronic fatigue, abdominal pain, aching joints, nausea, ulcerative colitis, even loss of menstruation, among other symptoms. Sofía described many of these issues, especially bouts of fatigue and stomach problems. Weight loss can also occur with autoimmune hepatitis, which Miranda alluded to in a letter: "Please get better, battle the famous '*higadítis*' and dedicate yourself to gaining weight, for which you are in much need."[8]

Sofía's life was increasingly fraught by illness. Usually it went unnamed. But Miranda's comments leave little doubt. Sofía suffered from a chronic form of liver ailment, very likely hepatitis. The stress of carrying out the work in Mexico without Miranda became clear throughout 1928. Miranda frequently reprimanded Sofía for taking on new assignments, whether teaching new courses or increasing her activities in the underground Catholic movement. Sofía was resilient, but wearing out. While Miranda experienced his own trials, loneliness, and doubt, Sofía was trying to hold Cultura Femenina together back in Mexico.

Sofía too had a vision for Mexico when the religious strife subsided. But what was left for her at present was a very narrow field indeed. Cultura Femenina's location in Mexico City put the whole operation in jeopardy. The school had moved from Motolinía Street to Eliseo Street, only a twenty-minute walk to the west of Alameda Park. Twelve Eliseo Street was a few minutes by foot from many government buildings in the Plaza of the Republic. The private home Sofía rented on Eliseo Street sat just a block or so away from police headquarters, where Father Pro had been executed and Miranda had briefly been imprisoned. And Cultura Femenina had potentially unwelcoming neighbors. In March 1928 the Soviet Embassy in Mexico relocated to 19 Eliseo Street. The Soviet ambassador, Alexandr Makar, tried to keep a low profile. Mexico and the Soviets had a tense relationship, which ruptured in 1930. Still, the Eliseo Street embassy received Pascual Ortiz Rubio (Mexican President, 1930–32) and Genaro Estrada, then the minister of foreign relations. Mexican Communist Party members and American radicals such as Carleton Beals visited on occasion. The embassy showed Soviet propaganda films.[9] As a private institution of Catholic education, Cultura Femenina operated on the margins of the law then in force. Sofía's school was located in the heart of Mexico City's anticlerical culture.

Sofía posted one of the students at the door of Cultura Femenina at all times. The women arrived one at a time, never in groups. The outer door was always locked. A priest from Huajuapan de León, exiled from his parish and living in Mexico City, brought the consecrated Host to the house every morning. He would come disguised differently each day. At 8:00 a.m. he deposited the Eucharist in a small *sagrario*, a tabernacle, manufactured by the women. After classes had ended for the morning, the priest would return at 1:00 p.m. to celebrate Mass and distribute Communion to the women.[10]

Despite fear of police raids and the school's penury, the spring semester of 1928 went ahead as planned. In the United States Miranda managed to scrape together a "few pennies" to alleviate the financial pressure that spring. Small donations came from U.S. Catholic bishops. Archbishop Curley of Baltimore paid Miranda's ticket to Europe in May. Registration fees and tuition were small—ten pesos to register, twenty pesos monthly tuition, and five pesos for each isolated class.[11] Furniture had to be borrowed for the Eliseo Street residence; so too were the typewriters. Books for the students' classes were scarce. Many young women had to learn solely from the oral lectures of the professors, without aid of their own textbooks. At times the students even lacked notebooks. The class for first year mathematics was left without an instructor. Sofía had no choice but to fill in, on top of her duties of administration.

"Problems with professors," the precarious "economic situation" of the students, and the "penury" that made "paying the rent difficult" consumed Sofía's days, weeks, and months while Miranda traveled abroad.[12] Part of the trouble with the professors was a personnel issue. In the majority, Cultura Femenina's professors were priests. Sofía had a difficult time assigning these priests to the subjects they "knew" best and to the courses they "most" wanted to teach. But scheduling was less of a problem than ego. When one prominent clergyman wanted to teach a class, Sofía had to turn him down because she had already made "arrangements" with a lower-ranking priest to teach it. The potentially mundane issue of scheduling became an issue of status. Sofía proceeded with caution. "God speaks for him who stays quiet," she wrote Miranda. She stuck by her decision, but made sure to suggest an alternative course in the Normal School for Catechism that the secretariat was in the process of initiating. "We will see if he gets mad!" Sofía wrote in a report to Miranda.[13]

For all the many challenges she faced, Sofía proved to be a demanding and intense director of Cultura Femenina. At the May convocation, when the students received their grades for the semester, Sofía didn't give glowing praise. You have been "called" to play "a providential role," she told the several dozen young women. Therefore, they had "an obligation" to prepare themselves "with complete dedication to be suitable instruments in the hands of Providence." Sofía assured her listeners that this wouldn't come easily. "There is no comparable pain in life than feeling inferior to the work entrusted to you," she pointed out, especially "when this inferiority or disability is due to a lack of diligence in taking advantage of the opportunities Our Lord gives us along the way!"[14] It was not a rebuke of the first order, but the speech was clear evidence that she, as the prefect of Cultura Femenina, had perceived an inexcusable lack of dedication on behalf of the fledgling student body. She decided to meet with each of the girls individually, to encourage a "higher performance" in the future.

Part of Sofía's worry during the spring of 1928 concerned her own ability to keep Cultura Femenina going while Miranda was absent. "I am making decisions on this and that, as the general situation depends on it," she wrote Miranda. But, she continued, "please make suggestions, because sometimes it seems that the spark is lacking here."[15] Miranda had provided a level of stability for Sofía. She was used to taking charge, but always under a covering that had been provided by men, whether her father, former male employers, or priests. With Miranda gone and the chaos of the rebellion upending the regular rhythms of Catholic life, she found herself in new territory. The students of Cultura Femenina looked to her, and so too did its priest-professors. Miranda did not return by that May. His absence gave her an education about her own resilience. Did she have what it took to lead Cultura Femenina?

While Sofía felt the spark to be lacking in Mexico, Miranda was starting to feel the warmth of some small fires just beginning to flame. Traveling back and forth between Washington DC and New York, Miranda could see the vision of what he was trying to accomplish more clearly. He was finding his stride in the political hub of American Catholicism located on the Eastern seaboard. Cultura Femenina, Miranda believed, was not just a school to educate women, but a tool to train well-prepared Catholic women in both heart and mind for the work of Catholic reconstruction. They were training to be the rank and file of a church in action. Cultura Femenina would be a pipeline, according to Miranda, envisioned to train an "elite" cadre of women who would then take up their places in the JCFM and other Catholic groups in Mexico. It was the fulfillment of Miranda's comment to Sofía back in 1925 that she must "multiply Sofías" in order to build something that would last. Already in Mexico, several "Sofías" were in training. Isabel Gibbon, Juana Arguinzóniz, and Aurora de la Lama—women who all became presidents of the JCFM in the 1930s and 1940s—were then completing their studies, or had done so, at Cultura Femenina.

In Washington and New York, Miranda promoted Sofía and Cultura Femenina as the model of the future church in Mexico.

Bishop Pascual Díaz took Miranda under his wing. He was the man who had visited Miranda that early morning in late 1926, when Miranda had received the call to prepare the future. The Mexican government exiled Díaz in early 1927. Since that time Díaz had emerged as the bête noir of cristeros and their supporters—the man who stood in the way of armed rebellion. Díaz established himself in New York, ingratiated himself with prominent American bishops, traveled to Rome frequently, and there gained the ear of Cardinal Gasparri. All of these endeavors had helped him stand out as the most reasonable Mexican churchmen with whom the Vatican could deal on the issue of the uprising. By January 1928 Díaz obtained a written authorization from the apostolic delegate in the United States for this role. He became *the* intermediary between Rome and the Mexican Catholic leadership.[16] All parties of various stripes would have to go through Díaz to get a hearing with Rome. Working in tandem with Díaz was Leopoldo Ruiz y Flores, who resided in San Antonio. Both Díaz and Ruiz y Flores pushed for the acceptance of Miranda's plan for Mexico's future, which decidedly rejected violence and armed uprising. The arrival of Miranda in Washington and New York in the spring of 1928 was fortuitous. Here was a priest who had begun to construct something for the future, they realized—something they could throw their full weight behind. Here too was a plan that could be offered to the Vatican as a way forward, as a clear alternative to the present rebellion. It was evident to Díaz that his intuition in trusting Miranda with the work of the future was paying off. Miranda received letters of recommendation from Rome's diplomat in Washington. The archbishop of Baltimore, Michael J. Curley, seconded the recommendation: "I have no hesitation in recommending you and your work to His Eminence the Cardinal Secretary of State. . . . I believe," he reiterated, "that the program you have mapped out will be of very considerable help in strengthening the Church of the future in Mexico."[17] The doors were opening for Miranda, and he could sense momentum increasing for his mission.

Still, there were moments of loneliness for Miranda. He was ravenous for news from Mexico, for some word from Sofía and the "girls" at Cultural Femenina. "I can fast from many things," but not from a lack of news and letters. "You know that very well." And when a big stack of letters finally arrived, many having been sent to various cities and finally forwarded to him, Miranda joked that "after a rigorous fast I received two packets of letters and one of photographs." Immediately he took them outside to the street and there lingered over the "exquisite letters," in large part from Sofía. "I devoured all the packages."[18]

The letters managed to satiate Miranda for a time. Yet he found further sustenance, once again and not for the last time, in the del Valle family. Hortensia del Valle, another of Sofía's younger sisters, was an Assumptionist nun. She lived and taught at Ravenhill Academy, a convent school for girls in the Germantown neighborhood of Philadelphia. It was just a three-hour train ride from Washington. Sofía's father, Francisco, had asked Miranda to visit his "little nuns" at Ravenhill.[19] Miranda obliged, and on a day free from other responsibilities caught the 9:00 a.m. from the capital. He arrived shortly after midday.

Ravenhill was a large Victorian mansion that had been donated by a wealthy family to the archdiocese. The "imperious gray brick building" was "ringed by manicured grounds, speckled with trees and flowers," remembered one former altar boy from the neighborhood.[20] Its biggest contingent of nuns came from the Philippines. At Ravenhill, Hortensia helped educate the well-to-do daughters of an elite business, political, and social class. Good manners predominated. The girls wore "white gloves to and from school." Admission was "tightly controlled," and even at its peak only about fifty girls from first grade through high school attended. Grace Kelly, Hollywood starlet and the future princess of Monaco, began studies at Ravenhill at the tender age of five in 1935.[21] In 1940 Rosemary Kennedy, the mentally troubled daughter of Camelot, attended the school briefly. So too did the first female president of the Philippines, Maria Corazon Aquino.[22] The school's mission to train Catholic young women intrigued Miranda. It offered him another point of reference from which to judge Cultura Femenina—and to appreciate Sofía.

Spending the day at Ravenhill was a homecoming of sorts for Miranda. "Today a dream has been realized! A visit to Ravenhill!" he reported to Sofía. Meeting Hortensia for the first time was "a very great satisfaction." Miranda saw Sofía in the visage of Hortensia: she bears "so many similarities of stature and other things with you." While the physical similarities were apparent, the emotional and spiritual resemblances were evident as well. He noticed the "profound energy in her soul," which reminded him of Sofía. Yet Ravenhill lacked a Catholic social vision, a commitment to reaching out beyond the confines of the ornate Victorian mansion. It was something he lamented. "I think that some of [Hortensia's] energies might not have an application here," he observed. He considered Hortensia's work at Ravenhill very "narrow" compared to the "very effective participation of her sister Chofi," for which Miranda had a keen appreciation. After the visit concluded, when Miranda returned to Washington, he was eager to describe everything to Sofía, not allowing himself "to sleep without leaving on paper" his impressions.[23] Miranda had now spent time with two of the del Valle sisters on his trip. Sofía was again the model against which he judged the others.

As April turned to May the spark of optimism Miranda had received from his reception by "very eminent" men began to run out. "In assessing the time spent, even though I still don't see the benefit [of my journey], for the most part I have felt it." He saw the tension between the concerns of today and those of the future. "I think about tomorrow in order to take advantage of the present." Yet thinking too much about the future could cause anxiety, even "fear," he admitted to Sofía. He would soon set off from the "continent of Columbus," he wrote Sofía, and he felt anxious about what awaited him. Leaving for Europe also meant a further loss of control for Miranda. He realized that the success or failure of Cultura Femenina was not presently in his hands. But he trusted Sofía, he found "comfort" in that she knew her "place of action" and that her "persuasion" was to work for the good of Mexico's Catholic future. "I also think about you in relation to tomorrow," he wrote her. "You have given so much already to those around you but tomorrow you will have to give more; yes, even more." Miranda assured Sofía that he esteemed all of her "efforts" and her "good example," and that "God will take care of the rest." His separation from the work in Mexico City, from friends there, and from Sofía would be all the more acutely felt across the waters of the Atlantic. He wanted to leave "her soul" with whatever "comfort, orientation, and hope" that his words could provide. Because, he wrote, "these will probably be the last lines I write to you from this continent."[24]

Miranda's letter came at a time when Sofía was sincerely in need of relief. "I received your letter in very anguished moments," she replied.[25] A test of character and resolve had confronted Sofía. The Cristero War, although fought outside Mexico City, was now seeking to consume the students of Cultura Femenina. Women—some twenty-five thousand strong by the end of the uprising—provided intelligence and logistical support for cristeros in the field. This women's army had taken the name the Feminine Brigades of St. Joan of Arc (Brigadas Femeninas de Santa Juana de Arco). It emerged first in Jalisco state, where the cristero movement was strongest. The growing Brigadas Femeninas army had ranks: generals, colonels, lieutenants, sergeants. The women were required to take oaths of secrecy, promising not to reveal, even to their husbands if married, what they were doing. They had noms de guerre: the Brigades' founder, María Ernestina Gollaz Gallardo, went by the name Celia Gómez. They trafficked in food and clothing, but also in bullets, which they hid underneath their clothes in *chalecos*, or vests, secured unassumingly beneath modest loose-fitting attire. Over the next year, cells spread south and east of Guadalajara, to Colima and Guanajuato. The Brigades secured supply routes all along the Guadalajara-Mexico City road. Their network then spread north all the way to the U.S. border and beyond; funding even flowed from Mexican exile and emigrant communities in Los Angeles.[26]

Celia Gómez, leader of the Brigades, was arrested in 1927, but released soon after. She decided to go to Mexico City. Cutting her braids, bobbing her hair, and putting on makeup, she went undercover in the capital as a modern woman, *la chica moderna*. She recruited for the Brigades, hoping to use the city's resources for the cristero cause. Soon, Celia Gómez recruited students and professors from Cultura Femenina.[27]

When Sofía first discovered the Brigades' recruitment efforts she was not altogether surprised. Before Miranda's departure, he and Sofía came to agreement on the policy that should guide them. The decision to actively support the cristeros would be "left to each individual's conscience." Yet Miranda emphasized to Sofía that women who chose to work with the Brigades would have to withdraw from Cultura Femenina and the JCFM. The secretariat had just been raided, Miranda and others imprisoned; they reasoned that the only way to protect "an organism in development"—the phrase used for both the school and youth association—would be to demand a hard line on the issue.[28] Studying had to be the students' only focus, Miranda insisted.

But with Miranda gone, Sofía had to deal with the issue of the Feminine Brigades. One of Cultura Femenina's professors, Father Gregorio Aguilar, philosophy teacher, had taken up a position as the Mexico City priest-advisor for the Feminine Brigades. Over the course of a month during that spring of 1928, Sofía noticed several students had not been attending classes—two sisters, Carmen and Trinidad Vidal, as well as Dolores Ortega, a long-time collaborator in the night school for workingwomen before Cultura Femenina even opened. Sofía was worried, and she thought she knew the reason for their absences. Finally, she called a meeting with Father Goyo, as Gregorio Aguilar was nicknamed.[29]

As director of Cultura Femenina in Miranda's absence, Sofía made it clear to Father Goyo that if he worked with the Feminine Brigades he would have to withdraw from teaching. The priest, resolute, pushed back. You do not have the authority to decide that, Father Goyo told Sofía. "All the angels came to my aid to prevent my temper from flaring," Sofía later wrote to Miranda. She collected herself—"with the best words and manners"—and proceeded to invoke Miranda's authority on the issue. It was Father Miranda's orders, not her own, that Goyo needed to obey, she said confidently. Sofía described the interaction to Miranda: "I merely responded that I was no one as an authority, that I only spoke in your name and that it was not my custom to dispute the orders of my superiors, but rather abide by them and execute them." In the meeting she expressed regret to Father Goyo, because they couldn't come to some agreement on the issue of Cultura Femenina students joining the Brigades. Sofía stood her ground, continuing her description of the exchange to Miranda: "I had only the authority of [choosing] whom to obey and this was you; and therefore I would not vary one iota from what I had been ordered and I left to the conscience of every individual the fulfillment of their duty." That being so, Sofía continued, "I would not tolerate any indiscipline among the girls." If students chose to join Father Goyo and the other "dissidents"—that was Sofía's word for the Brigades—they would have to withdraw from both the school and the youth association run by the secretariat.[30]

The conversation was "long and painful" Sofía recalled. But Father Goyo agreed to stop teaching his philosophy classes. The Vidal sisters left Cultura Femenina. Trinidad, one of the sisters, cried when Sofía told her the news. Their mother was involved with the Brigades and insisted they continue working for the cristero cause. Señora Vidal wrote Sofía a "rude letter," to the effect that Sofía was "anticountry" in her attitudes and in the policies of Cultura Femenina.[31]

Soon after the situation with the Vidal sisters another student, Dolores Ortega, was also found to be part of the "dissidents." Ortega attended classes at Cultura Femenina and helped lead a group for workingwomen in Mexico City. Ortega had been out sick for several weeks. One day Sofía heard that the study groups for these workers, which were usually held at the Eliseo Street residence, were being moved to Ortega's own home. Sofía saw this as a bid to further enmesh Cultura Femenina with the Brigades. She also felt it was a personal threat to her authority as leader of the school. "I pardon the infant because she is very foolish," Sofía seethed. "I attribute her action to outside influence, and at any rate her manner of proceeding pains me, because exposing herself to intrigue of this type is a lack of loyalty."[32]

Sofía made sure to give notice to all the workingwomen that the meetings would continue at Eliseo Street. She also personally spoke with Ortega about the issue. In Sofía's mind, the incident had been resolved, and she reported as much to Miranda. Yet it appears that Ortega continued her activities secretly. Years later, Ortega gave an interview about her experiences during the rebellion and explained that she didn't quit working for the Brigades. Ortega even mentioned that the assistant director of the Social Secretariat, Father Dávila Vilchis, knew about Ortega's work with the Brigades and privately condoned it.[33]

In addition to keeping a lid on the "dissident" situation, Sofía dealt with a host of issues that spring. She barely kept current with the rent, which was borrowed from a wealthy Catholic. Then there was organizing the upcoming exams and finding new students to fill the vacancies left by the Vidal sisters. She wrote Miranda of "insubordination" from students, their periodic "tears" and emotional stress, then "explosions of gratitude" from them, but in the main a general atmosphere of "fatigue."[34]

Sofía, for her part, felt the fatigue as well. She left her house before seven each morning and returned late in the evening. She wrote about headaches that only abated in sleep and took some "narcotics" given to her from her physician. She wrote letters to Miranda, or tried to at least, but often had to postpone them as the typewriter she used at Cultura Femenina was borrowed; one of the students brought it to the Eliseo Street residence in the morning but had to take it back home with her after lunch. Sofía sent one letter to Miranda that spring half typewritten, the other half written by hand. "To everyone I am a happy woman and content; only two intimates, Our Lord and you, know the rest," Sofía confessed.[35]

Despite all of it, from more thorny issues to simple fatigue, Sofía expressed keen awareness, or at least she articulated this awareness in moments of reflection when she was able to write Miranda, that she was growing personally and as a leader. "Anyway," she reflected, "in seeing you leave it did not even cross my mind that, in addition to all the work that I expected, I would also be involved in all these affairs and messes." It was good that she didn't foresee the challenges, she told him, otherwise "I would not have had the courage to face them." Then she added: "that saying about the cold according to the blanket is a great truth," referring to an adage roughly equivalent to "God never gives us something we can't handle." All the difficult experiences she was having, she continued, "are making me develop abilities until now unknown to me, and which, because of the cold"—referring to the trying environment at present—"Our Lord is giving me [these abilities] as a blanket, because I do not recognize them as my own."[36]

What were these new abilities? More than anything they appear to be less about technical skills—multitasking, organization, budgeting—than about her newfound capacity to trust herself. Her competence in tackling a mountain of work was not a new realization for Sofía. What she discovered was her ability, with God's help she emphasized, to do the work when it counted most. With Miranda gone, it was her effort that had to make the difference. It was a risk, and taking risks did not come naturally to Sofía. Her life to that point had been marked by excellence—in education, in intelligence, in creativity. But control and order—like the gardens of her youth she tended and cared for—were comfortable. Now her life, in its complexity, in the disordered and chaotic present, demanded risk. Sofía del Valle was coming to understand that she had what it took to live outside of safe, orderly gardens.

There is another key to understanding Sofía's anguish during the spring of 1928. Beyond the troubles with Cultura Femenina and the Brigades, Sofía was saddened by Miranda's statement that his letter would be the last he would write from North America. Sofía, writing a week later, reasoned that surely he would "receive letters in New York [from her]" before leaving for Italy. "I hope to receive some further word" from you before "the great silence" caused by the voyage over the Atlantic. Several days later, on May 18, she still hadn't heard from him. "I have received nothing from you during these days and I am beginning to feel uneasy and, if nothing arrives soon, my uneasiness will keep increasing until I am all in knots and God knows how many days or weeks it will last!" A good part of her anguish was worry for Miranda. "In the end, let God's will be done, but my heart is already tightening with so much pain that sometimes it feels ready to explode!"[37]

The suffering Sofía experienced was useful; at least that's what she made sure to convey to Miranda. She saw pain—emotional, spiritual, physical pain—as effective. When properly understood, channeled through prayer and petition, it could be beneficial for others. There's a parallel here between Sofía's conception of useful suffering and the

Catholic practice of the "victim soul."[38] Suffering was vicarious. If the person who suffered identified both with Christ as the supreme sacrifice and likewise identified with one who needed aid, salvation, and redemption, some important spiritual good could be won on behalf of others. Victim souls perceived their offerings of personal pain as help for the salvation and sanctification of others, even for the salvation of Mexico as with Father Pro, many cristeros, and Madre Conchita. Yet Sofía's sacrifice was intensely personal, devoted solely to Miranda. Referring to her pain, she wrote: "Every day I offer it up to Our Lord… [and] I desire that this purified, sanctified pain be the daily holocaust for you and your work!"[39] When Catholics used the word "holocaust" it referred to the priest offering the sacrifice of the Mass, consecrating the Eucharist to be consumed by the faithful.[40] But she used the word in reference to her own suffering and pain, likening it to Christ's sacrifice that could be transformed into the Bread of Life for the partaker. Sofía's pain had an almost sacramental quality, a means of grace for Miranda. "May Our Lord daily transform," she continued, "[the] grief I offer into smiles, light, warmth, well-being, success, strength, comfort, into righteous and holy satisfactions! I believe there to be closer to you, shortening distances and challenging time! So I will hope everything necessary to hope!"[41]

In form and content, much of the correspondence between Sofía and Miranda fits into a well-established relationship common to Catholicism: spiritual direction.[42] In terms of form, spiritual direction existed in many arrangements. Male seminarians training for the priesthood usually were mentored by older, experienced clergy. But spiritual direction often happened outside of clerical orders, between the ordained and laypeople. Male and female religious—monks, brothers, nuns, sisters—led men and women, both young and old, as spiritual directors. Religious orders such as the Jesuits especially took on the role, given their emphasis on education and mission. A kind of spiritual direction can even be seen in the relationship between Madre Conchita and the infamous José de León Toral, the assassin of ex-president Álvaro Obregón.

Sofía's connection to Miranda often hinted at spiritual guidance. The confessional tone of many of her letters, her insistence on self-examination found there, evoke the spiritual exchange common between priestly advisors and their lay disciples. It was a practice very old in Christian tradition. St. Francis and St. Clare, Abelard and Heloise, St. Teresa of Ávila and St. John of the Cross—the list goes on of the intimate, even sometimes spiritually erotic language between priests and Catholic women, whether nuns or laywomen.[43] And it was a practice characteristic of modern Catholics as well: Pius XII and Pascalina Lehnert, Thomas Merton and Margaret Randall, John Paul II and Anna-Teresa Tymieniecka. In Mexico, too, there were other examples of intimate friendships, like Sofía's and Miranda's, forming between priests and laywomen. Father Félix de Jesús Rougier, for instance, co-founded the Missionaries of the Holy Spirit with Concepción Cabrera de Armida, a widow and mother of nine children. Cabrera de Armida became famous for her mystical writings describing Jesus and, because of her spiritual gravitas, inspired awe in men like Father Rougier. Like Sofía and Miranda, Cabrera and Rougier shared an intimate friendship and partnered in establishing an important religious institution in Mexico. A process for Cabrera de Armida's canonization began in 1959.[44] Sofía's relationship with Miranda stood well within an established practice of close spiritual guidance. From the perspective of the modern viewer many of these friendships may appear to be more than platonic. In the main, however, they were chaste—the intimacy of language shared between priest and laywoman was a vehicle for sharing with each other the mystical encounters experienced. It wasn't code for something else.

Often in relationships of spiritual direction, the female writer looked to the priest for strength and stability. Sofía's letter of May 14—the same where she spoke of her pain as a kind of redemptive prayer—spends long paragraphs listing her inadequacies for the "work" of Cultura Femenina. "More than anyone else you know my incapacity for it," she confessed to Miranda. In a searching and introspective examination of her aptitude, or lack thereof, she held herself to the same high standard she had set for the students of the school. She even used similar language to criticize herself. The problem, she believed, was not a "lack of willpower," of that there was an "overabundance," but rather Sofía despaired at her incompetence. "But my uselessness, my ignorance, how do I make up for these?" she probed. She had no choice but to trust, hoping that with "the grace of God, I will do as much as is possible with what is in my hands to gird myself daily, to be a more suitable instrument in the hands of God and to collaborate to the measure of my poor forces for the improvement of those that I have been given!" With words reminiscent of St. Thérèse of Lisieux, to whom she had dedicated her ministry, Sofía reminded Miranda: "Don't forget my smallness, my misery, and help me with all the efficacy of your prayers *to be* and *to do* what God and you would expect of me."[45]

Pleas for guidance, confessions of weakness, and reaffirmations of proper gendered and religious power dynamics—all elements often characteristic of spiritual direction—figured in the relationship between Sofía and Father Miranda.

Yet something beyond spiritual direction and the quest for sanctification, which was often the guiding goal of these relationships, motivated Sofía's vulnerability. It wasn't simply a relationship built on the quest for spiritual perfection. The line between spiritual direction and romantic intimacy was thin. And as with the cases of Thomas Merton and Margaret Randall, with John Paul II and Anna-Teresa Tymieniecka, so with Sofía and Miranda: spiritual intimacy and emotional commitment were clearly evident.[46] Sofía and Miranda, like other modern examples, freely chose each other. It wasn't forced, constrained to spiritual advice or to confession. Both partners looked to the other for strength and for intimacy. There was something different in Sofía's and Miranda's celibate relationship absent in traditional spiritual guidance arrangements.

Sofía's deep attachment to Miranda may perhaps be the starting point in trying to unravel where spiritual direction ended and their personal relationship began. Her letters spoke of pain caused by separation, a longing to have Miranda back again, not just so that the work of Cultura Femenina would be smoother, but so that a feeling of wholeness might return to her personally. There was a mutual affection, playfulness, and shared good opinion of each other's contributions. There was a vulnerability based on trust in the burdens they carried together. To whom else could Sofía and Miranda express the kinds of doubts they shared in their letters but to each other? Sofía at least allowed herself to write Miranda without the filter she commonly applied in communicating with others. In one letter she put it this way: "You already know my bad habit of pouring out my heart on the page, something that only happens to me with you."[47]

Vulnerability also grew out of Sofía's unique position. She remained under Miranda's authority, even in his absence. But in practice she was running Cultura Femenina, making decisions on a daily basis that could not be approved by Miranda because of his distance. Sofía was a natural leader with a strong personality. But this was a first for her. Now she was in charge. In all of her roles previously, she had shown up with energy and creativity, applying each to the project at hand. The necessity of the times put her in the role of decision maker. She arranged the class schedules, figured out how to pay the rent, and negotiated with the priests, bishops, and clergy who in essence had to let Cultura Femenina sink or swim based on her judgment. In theory, the men in her life maintained their spiritual and gendered control over her. It was something she herself constantly reiterated. The balancing of roles and responsibilities was difficult. But Sofía was making the school function amid persecution and government resistance. If that weren't enough, she had her personal battles with illness, the "famous," yet unclear, liver condition that she came to live with.[48] When the determination of her spirit was willing, her body could be knocked out in bed.

Miranda was a safe person to air these and other trials to. Sofía's family knew him. Sofía's sisters in New Orleans and Philadelphia had developed friendships with him. Miranda's vocation as a priest meant that part of his calling was to hear the confessions, the vulnerabilities of laypeople. That seemed to be the open door through which Sofía initially walked. And once past the threshold, a relationship beyond priest and parishioner developed.

For Miranda, as a priest, the question of vulnerability had a different calculation. How safe was Sofía as confidant? Certainly, his letters evidence trust in her capabilities, trust in her ability to keep confidences, trust in her compassion. But did Miranda experience conflict between his vocation as priest, called as he was to sexual celibacy, and his genuine affection for Sofía del Valle? It's a question that can never be fully answered by their many letters. But clues exist, and they would become more apparent once Miranda reached the Old World.

13

Gasparri's Parrots

> Sisyphos also I saw and his tedious task, as he held
> up a monstrous stone with both hands.
>
> Homer, *The Odyssey*

In Europe, past and future began to converge in Miguel Miranda's present. His first stop was not Rome but Paris, where he encountered old friends.[1] He stayed in Paris only a few days before taking a train that crossed Europe with Rome as its destination. On board he watched the mountains in the horizon grow larger, the train finally surrounded as it crossed the high elevation of the Alps in the middle of the night. He settled his mind by writing to Sofía, dedicating the letter to her: "my most faithful and inseparable CROWN."[2] The full measure of what Sofía meant to Miranda is perhaps unknowable, but his regard certainly went beyond a relationship dictated by virtue of circumstance alone: he as the priest and leader, she as laywoman and follower. They were partners, and acknowledging a bond that drew them together into something bigger than either of them could be separately seemed perfectly natural.

Miranda found Rome full of friends and acquaintances from his days as a seminarian at the Latin American College. Pius IX (1848–78) established the Colegio Pio Latino Americano in 1856 to instill "Roman virtues" in the training of clergy destined to serve in Latin America.[3] The Pio Latino was where the priestly elite received their training, imbibing the doctrine of papal authority that lay at the cornerstone of the Holy See's bid to do battle against secularization, against the many *isms* of the day (liberalism, socialism, etc.), as well as to promote Vatican power over and above national control over Catholicism. It was where the popes hoped to make Latin American Catholicism truly "Roman."

The Pio Latino provided the seminarians lodging in Rome; it was where these aspiring priests who found themselves far from home had their principal community, where they rubbed shoulders with other young men from around Latin America. While they lived at the Pio Latino they studied at the great Catholic universities of Rome—principally the Jesuit-run Gregorian University. Graduating priests, many of them future bishops, were steeped in the social teachings of the church associated with the papal encyclical *Rerum novarum* (1891), later expanded upon in a treatise by Pius XI, *Quadragesimo Anno* (1931). Miranda's vision for Mexico, and the implementation of a plan along Roman lines, was particularly influenced by his training at the Pio Latino.

When Miranda arrived in Rome in 1928 he boarded at the Pio Latino, located at 3 Gioacchino Belli Street. Miranda had returned to Rome as a missionary priest made good. Not only did he speak Italian, but he duly put his work in Mexico into an understandable vernacular they could appreciate and support. He knew how to translate Mexican Catholicism into Roman.

As Miranda readied his proposal to the pope, and as Sofía worried about the future in Mexico City, in the Vatican Cardinal Pietro Gasparri talked to his parrots. Gasparri had several of them, large green macaws from South America, which he kept in enormous cages in his private apartment in the Vatican.[4]

"*Non prevalebunt,*" he mumbled to them in Latin as he gave the birds their daily provisions: they shall not prevail.

It was only a matter of time before the parrots began to repeat the phrase.

A squat man, and round, Gasparri was known for informality, a trait perhaps gained in his youth, groomed as he was in the country at his family's Umbrian farm, northeast of Rome. There, he took his holidays, accompanied by members of his staff who would bring him stacks of official documents to work through as he sat under the eaves of one of the many spreading trees, "enjoying the shade, the fresh air, and the view."⁵ He often wore only a simple black cassock, augmented only by a large, wide-brimmed hat also made of cloth.

If Pietro Gasparri appeared to be merely an informal country priest, a humorous and kindly parish pastor, looks could be deceiving. The man was seventy-seven years old in 1928. He had served two popes as Vatican secretary of state, the Holy See's second-highest office after the pope himself. Gasparri's outward manner—"down-home" is the phrase used by one historian—disguised the inner workings of a shrewd diplomat.⁶ He had ample field experience: Gasparri was the apostolic delegate in charge of Rome's diplomatic mission to Peru, Bolivia, and Ecuador at the turn of twentieth century. In 1907 Gasparri received the red hat, designating him a cardinal. Even then, as a cardinal, the scholar and jurist defined his personality more than his status as a prince of the church. It was rumored he would remove his scarlet skull-cap and use it to wipe his messy ink pens. At the outbreak of the First World War he was made secretary of state. Gasparri was now in charge of Vatican foreign policy. He had reached the pinnacle of his career; only the office of pope remained outside his reach.⁷

During World War I, under Gasparri's administration, the papacy tried on a policy of official neutrality. Both the Allies and the Axis powers had Catholic sons on the fields of battle. The pope, as father to all, had ceased being a sovereign in the technical sense. The papal states had disappeared when Italy became a nation-state. The Holy See's spiritual legitimacy was its sole claim. Although both French and German mistrust of that neutrality was a constant, Gasparri forged a way out of the Vatican's irrelevance in international affairs. The strategy was diplomacy. Hemmed in by the Italian state, which the Vatican did not recognize, Rome looked to Europe-in-reconstruction for allies. Gasparri managed to sign new treaties in the aftermath of war, especially with the successor states to former Axis powers. Eastern Europe and Latin America also came increasingly within the orbit of papal diplomatic overtures. Each treaty, each recognized Vatican diplomat, became another tally in the Vatican's favor in the battle with Italy over papal legitimacy. Under Gasparri's pragmatic hand, Rome sought to cinch the ties that bound Catholics from Chile to Czechoslovakia.[8] And Gasparri was doing it through diplomacy.

After championing Achille Ratti's papal candidacy and eventual election as Pope Pius XI in 1922, Gasparri was rewarded in kind; the new pope renewed Gasparri as secretary of state. Papa Ratti, as Pius XI was known, had a severe temperament that only grew sharper and more unbending with age. But Gasparri was a faithful servant of Pius's vision of alignment and reconciliation with Italy. Mussolini emerged as the Vatican's "Man from Providence" who would restore a Catholic state to the Italian Peninsula. It was Gasparri's pen that would sign the Lateran Accords of February 1929, restoring a small autonomous state to the papacy. The price was an alliance with Fascism—a high price indeed as it cost the independence of the Italian Catholic lay movement, Catholic Action, drowned by Mussolini's *fascisti* cadres and black-shirted brigands.[9]

It would have been natural for an outsider to assume that Gasparri had the pope's confidence. It was Gasparri who had touted the pope's diplomatic overtures, Gasparri who was even in the summer of 1928 in negotiations with Mussolini's government. But appearances deceived here as well. As early as 1926, according to one historian of the papacy, Pius XI had lost confidence in his secretary of state. And in an effort to force Gasparri's resignation, the pope mounted a campaign of humiliation against him. Pius, ever the papal tyrant, made Gasparri "wait in the anteroom before seeing him" and subjected him to treatment "that not even a servant would tolerate."[10]

Taciturn and moody, Pius XI had chosen to support Mexico's church strike in 1926; and that, over the recommendation of Cardinal Gasparri, who argued for a more pragmatic tactic, urging his fellow policymakers in one meeting to allow priests to register with the Mexican government, as the law demanded. "Even with a bad law," Gasparri argued, "there can be a manner of action that does not imply approval of the law itself."[11] For Gasparri, preserving the faith meant keeping the Catholic sacraments available in churches. Legal maneuvers, though not ideal, would keep priests in their parishes. Gasparri continued: "If a bishop allows priests to inscribe in the civil registers"—a possibility then being put forward by none other than Leopoldo Ruiz y Flores at the time—"it does not imply acceptance of the law, but merely removes an obstacle unjustly placed to the exercise of a right."[12] Yes, argued Gasparri, the Mexican anticlerical laws (especially Article 130, essentially making priests functionaries of the state through forced registration) should be condemned. But some sort of compromise was surely possible, he believed.

For Gasparri, Mexico and Italy were not poles apart. In both a tentative, yet principled compromise could result in the survival of Catholicism, even the restoration of Catholic liberties. Not so for Pius XI. The pope trucked no compromise with Mexico in 1926. The church strike was approved, and the cristero insurgency followed soon after. To the pope, anticlerical Mexico was a world apart from Fascist Italy. There were sure signs of hope in Mussolini for Catholic restoration. Those hopes seemed to be borne out by the summer of 1928; conciliation was real and imminent.

And so Pietro Gasparri, no longer a trusted voice in the pope's ear, could be found talking to his parrots in his private apartment. A veteran American reporter in Rome, Thomas Morgan, visited Gasparri in his rooms one day. When the subject turned to Mexico's religious conflict, Gasparri spoke with assurance of the end he could foresee: throughout its history the church had "survived fierce and bloody tests but had overcome them all and grown stronger from them," he told Morgan. Gasparri pointed out that in Mexico the church was passing through just such a test at present. But Gasparri's faith was undaunted: "Calles and his bands could not suppress the Church." Then with a note of resolution, he said in Latin: "*Non prevalebunt.*" They shall not prevail. It was if Gasparri was "issuing an edict of defiance," Morgan later wrote. Several times Gasparri repeated the Latin dictum, speaking it more softly to his parrots as he fed the birds in their large cages. On seeing Morgan to the door, the parrots squawked behind him: "*Non prevalebunt, non prevalabunt.*"[13] The aged diplomat often ruminated over the phrase to his birds as he thought of Mexico's predicament and perhaps his own increasingly marginalized role in Pius XI's administration.

With Gasparri, appearances were deceiving. At the beginning of January 1928 he told the British ambassador to the Holy See, Sir Odo

Russell, that "he was at his wits' end to devise some means of relieving the sufferings of Christians" in Mexico. Russell found him "unusually perturbed" on that occasion. A few weeks later, Russell returned to Gasparri's private rooms and found the secretary of state more serene.[14] Gasparri, in fact, wasn't revealing all his cards to Russell. Even then, the American ambassador to Mexico, Dwight Morrow, was already in conversation with an American priest, John J. Burke of the National Catholic Welfare Conference (NCWC), who had previously been commissioned by the American apostolic delegate to do so. Movements toward a negotiated peace had already begun. One of Gasparri's nephews even served in the American apostolic delegation.[15] Although Gasparri appeared to bend to secular governments in seeking conciliation, his goal was the survival of the church. And while he had suffered with serene patience the bullying of his pope, seeming to bend to his boss's abuse and decisions, Gasparri's parrots told the truth of their master's inner resilience: *non prevalebunt*, they shall not prevail.

Two Mexicans, Miguel Miranda and Sofía del Valle, and their plan for Mexico's future, held a further key to Gasparri's victory. For conciliation to work in Mexico there had to be a plan ready for what came after the peace.

After a bit of waiting and much preparation, Miguel Miranda finally got his opportunity to present a plan for Mexico's future to the pope on June 18, 1928. The eight-page report, written in Italian, summarized seven years of work by the Mexican Social Secretariat. Miranda's visit was facilitated by Leopoldo Ruiz y Flores. Ruiz left nothing to chance. He traveled to Rome from his residence in San Antonio, Texas, for the occasion. Ushered by staff and Cardinal Gasparri, Ruiz presented Miranda to Pius XI.[16]

Miranda's audience with the pope was to the point. He didn't merely summarize his written report. What Miranda did was lay out a vision for Mexico's salvation in the present conflict. It was not a force of arms, he emphasized, but the force of minds that would prepare the future for Mexican Catholicism. Forming the Catholic conscience through education was the key to Miranda's appeal. "Creating an elite" among "our youth" would be, Miranda explained, "the principal instrument in this our noble work." Mexico's Catholic "elite" was already being formed in Cultura Femenina "in the midst of persecution," he told the pope. What was needed at present was to take the "strength of heart" of these young people and add it to an "intellectual base." Miranda was proposing an extension of the work, begun among the women of Cultura Femenina, to other groups—men, older women, youth, workers, and students. And all of these groups, Miranda urged, would begin that work within their own specifically formed organization under the umbrella of Catholic Action, duly regimented and led by the clergy.[17] Miranda seemed to promise, if the pope agreed, the reconquest of Mexico's cantankerous laity, many of whom were then in rebellion. Despite Pius XI's stubbornness to bend in the face of Mexican revolutionary fury, the pope had constantly recommended Catholic Action. Miranda's vision melded quite beautifully with the pope's.

The details were spelled out in the written document Miranda left with Gasparri and his staff. In it, Miranda asked for two things. First, he wanted letters of approval for his work, with signed recommendations addressed to the Catholic universities of Europe and the United States. With these he hoped to gain scholarships for Mexican activists to study abroad at the best Catholic institutions of the day. There they would be steeped, as he had been, in the social teachings of the church. Second, Miranda asked for money. The work in Mexico would not survive without financial assistance. With these two requests he laid out strategy. The report foresaw the establishment of Catholic Action along Roman lines: four regimented associations for lay Catholics (men, women, young men, young women). It recommended the development of the Catholic Labor Confederation, but duly modified to function within the Mexican anticlerical context. Next, the report envisioned a social service school like the one Miranda had observed at the Catholic University in Washington DC. And then, finally, the document called for Mexico's own Catholic university, to be developed at present for a future when such an institution might be established.[18]

The Vatican authorities were convinced. Just two days after the audience, Gasparri telegraphed the papal diplomat in Washington. As long as the activities under Miranda, and duly overseen by the bishops, were "outside of politics," Gasparri transmitted, His Holiness "was willing to approve it."[19] Money from a fund set up for Mexico, donated by many Catholics around Europe, was approved for transfer to Miranda's secretariat. The sum came to 10,000 USD. As requested, letters of introduction to Catholic universities were also provided.

Miranda, however, was kept in suspense. He didn't receive a formal reply from Gasparri until the fall of 1928, four months after his audience with the pope. Nonetheless, the future had been decided, even if Miranda and Sofía hadn't yet received the news.

The problem for Pius XI and Gasparri, as well as for Pascual Díaz and Leopoldo Ruiz y Flores, was how to solve the present. The pope continued to believe that "sufficient public guarantees" were necessary for an agreement to be reached with the Mexican government. For Pius, this meant protection for the bishops, some sort of amnesty for cristeros, and confidence that measurable progress could be had toward modifying the law. Gasparri, working toward a pragmatic compromise but one that would turn in the church's favor, duly communicated the pope's wishes on the issue several times during 1928. Negotiations ebbed and flowed through various intermediaries. But a shift was occurring. Despite the pope's continued stubbornness, Gasparri's approach toward settling the conflict was becoming more practicable. It was the moderate Ruiz who would ultimately receive the Vatican's approval as the clergyman enabled to say yes or no to the eventual agreement. Ruiz, like Gasparri, saw the Mexican situation similarly: a modification of the laws was not necessary to end the conflict, only an initial opening on the part of the Mexican government was essential. They required guarantees that the church's existence would be recognized, if not by law, at least in practice. Miranda's proposal for Mexico's future, which was then effectively being made operational in Mexico by Sofía del Valle, gave assurances to both Gasparri and Ruiz. If they could find the right opening with the government, at least they knew that the Catholic Church would not perish on the battlefield with the cristeros. Miranda and Sofía's proposal was proof that, when the fighting stopped, there would be someone left to work.

14

A Long, Hot Roman Summer

On June 19, the day after Miranda's portentous visit to the Vatican, he finally had time to write Sofía. It was his first letter since his arrival in Rome. He'd been too busy preparing his report to the pope and meeting with old acquaintances to write earlier. However, Miranda reported absolutely nothing about his meeting at the Vatican. He only hinted at it in veiled language. "My only sacrifice now," Miranda wrote, "and which I make with my whole heart, is having to wait until later to communicate the most beautiful results of my trip." Several weeks went by and Miranda was still spinning his wheels in Rome. The weather had turned unbearably hot. In one letter he described feeling like a roast cooking in an oven. Again, he made a veiled reference to the important news he was withholding. "I struggle violently with my will to not tell you anything until my work has been completed," he confessed. But, Miranda continued, it was better not to foretell the results of an exam before the student had taken it and then seen the grade achieved.[1]

Unsure of the future, a sense of anxiety began to set in regarding the work in Mexico. He had finally received letters from Sofía and others filling him in on the details of the present. Miranda acknowledged he was losing "control of the time in these days." The tenor of his letters switched from an intimate confidant to a kind of frustrated manager, desperately trying to make his will felt from across the ocean. "Any inclination to modify the plan of studies at present should not even be considered," he firmly wrote Sofía. "I believe one of the great mortifications that everyone has to make, and especially you," he scolded, "is to put faith in my poor words so that your energy will be used in the most advantageous manner." He continued sounding a note of male condescension: "Before being formed [intellectually and spiritually] a girl is of little value; formed partially she is worth a fourth [of a whole person]; but formed perfectly she is not only as valuable as one, but as three or four." Miranda feared that the needs of the present religious conflict were sapping Sofía's strength as well as that of the students of Cultura Femenina. He told Sofía not to concern herself with the constant requests from clergy and laity alike for assistance. Sofía needed to redouble her efforts on the goal of education, Miranda wrote, remembering that what they were aiming for was "the profound preparation ... of the 'elite,' and although [progress was] slower it was more secure." He belabored the point to Sofía, reminding her of her limitations caused by frequent bouts of illness. After long paragraphs he finally ended: "the sermon has finished."[2]

A similar tone of condescension, even emotional distance, returned in another letter from Rome. "I never would have thought that your imagination would be working so hard, [simply] for the lack of news during three weeks," Miranda wrote brusquely. "I thought I had made it clear in my earlier letter that I had lost control over time." Miranda could see that apparently Sofía had been "imagining a thousand and one things, which fortunately have not happened," he assured. "So calm yourself, and once I explain everything you will deem me reasonable." "Consider," he continued, "that sometimes I remember that I should send my greetings to everyone, and thus I post ten and twelve letters so that no one misses out on receiving a token of my esteem."[3]

But during that summer Miranda's sermonizing, even irritability, could turn softer. After he hadn't received news from Sofía for over a month he cabled her, inquiring solicitously about her health, asking for news of the school, and expressing concern that he hadn't heard from her in a month.[4] While Miranda waited on a reply, and while he waited on the decision from the Vatican, he complained in letters to Sofía of Rome's "enveloping sun" and the unfortunate choice he had to make daily between "pasta or fasting."

Then the headlines hit Rome: the Mexican president-elect, Álvaro Obregón, had been assassinated on July 17, 1928. Miranda immediately thought of Sofía and the danger she might face in Mexico City. "I have been very anxious, as you can imagine," Miranda wrote Sofía, "because of everything being said in the press."[5]

Obregón's assassin, José de León Toral, seemed like an ordinary young man to Madre Conchita.[6] They met through a mutual acquaintance; Toral was one of the many Catholics who frequented Conchita's Holy Hours and Masses. Toral was young—just twenty-eight—and the father of two small children. He had dark eyes and dark eyelashes; he was good-looking and a bit foppish. A small build, a sensitive temperament, and artistic talent—these characteristics conspired to make him appear effeminate to many. He too was on a mystical adventure, but his mysticism seemed to be leading him toward obsession and radical action. He'd been soccer buddies with Humberto Pro, a member of the ACJM, and leader of a small group in the Catholic Defense League. He was an art student but, when his prospects in business dried up, he supported himself and his young family as a professor of drawing. He spent much of his free time with other Catholics in the clandestine piety networks. He conversed with Conchita on occasion, perhaps once a week, sometimes more. Among the topics of discussion, some banal, Toral brought up the persecution in Mexico. In his testimony at trial he would say that his determination to kill Álvaro Obregón was influenced by Madre Conchita.[7]

Toral fixated on Obregón. But by all accounts his real motivations seemed to be known only to himself. He tended to act impulsively and made a kind of fetish of the president-elect. He stalked him. He fantasized about the act of tyrannicide. He followed Obregón, each time allowing himself to begin acting out the fantasy, but each time pulling up short. Obregón had been elected president earlier that summer, to take over for Calles in December 1928. When Obregón returned to the capital, Toral watched him arrive at the train station; he lurked outside Obregón's home. Toral couldn't get close enough, or get up his nerve enough to go through with his fantasy. Then, Obregón was at a restaurant on the outskirts of the capital—La Bombilla—hosted by political supporters. Obregón sat with advisers and aides at a raised table at one end of the large outdoor restaurant. Toral got close by doing a quick sketch of Obregón. He said he wanted to show it to the next president of Mexico. He made his way between the floral arrangements and the table with the seated guests—it was a tight squeeze. Obregón looked up and smiled slightly. Toral took out his gun and unloaded five shots at point blank range. Two fast, followed by three more. Álvaro Obregón slumped forward, dead.[8]

The restaurant immediately erupted in pandemonium. Toral was disarmed; pistols were drawn and the exits blocked. "Don't kill him!" shouted one of Obregón's aides. If they shot Toral on the spot, which many wanted to do, they feared not being able to find out the assassin's motive. Toral didn't flee. He didn't resist. But he received a beating nonetheless. Taken to police headquarters, Toral was tortured—hung by his toes, fingers, and genitalia—over the next several days. At first he refused to give his name. He said only that what he had done he had done for religious motives. Toral's captors didn't believe it. Many Obregónistas suspected the machinations of Calles or even Luis Morones, the labor leader who had also run for president, but who had lost to Obregón. Through markings on Toral's clothing, the police were able to track the assassin to a Chinese laundry. There, they discovered his name and arrested his family. Toral finally began talking when he was forced to hear what he thought to be his screaming family being tortured in the interrogation cell next to his own.[9] He insisted that he acted alone, and that he could bring them to someone who would corroborate his story. Toral made the police give assurances that the person would not be implicated. That person was Madre Conchita.

News of Obregón's assassination reached Conchita soon after it took place. A first hint that something was off came when the convent's chaplain arrived alone. Toral had been assisting the chaplain in Mass at Conchita's services. That same day, Conchita's sister told her that it was Pepe, Toral's nickname, who had been arrested for the crime. Moments later police arrived with Toral, and the authorities escorted him inside. The nuns were terrified, but Conchita stood unwavering.

"I've come to see if they will believe you," Toral told Conchita. "I've come to see if you want to die with me."

"Yes, with pleasure," Madre Conchita replied, resolute.[10]

A world away, in Rome, Miranda finally received relief from his worries in early September. Sofía wrote that Cultura Femenina had received the "patent protection" of God in the aftermath of Obregón's assassination. For Miranda, peace also came in the form of acceptance. He couldn't control events in Mexico. He had to relinquish it, looking to Sofía for "the continuation of the school and its related labors," he wrote. Anxiety had perhaps caused Miranda to exact his authority a little too strongly but, still, he trusted Sofía. "God has used you," he felt sure, "to offer me in my long absence the comfort of knowing that our nest has not only preserved its vitality, but that it is growing. May God reward you." Miranda's summer in Rome had taken him to the limit of his human efforts. He had to trust in help from outside. He could no longer control the outcome. His successes, he was sure, were linked to Sofía's prayers, her trials, and the daily offerings the students of Cultura Femenina made for him. "As many times as Our Lord deigns to let me take one beneficial step," he wrote Sofía, "or to see a door hidden from view or goodwill open for me, it is always then I think that it is due to your prayers and suffering and those of all the others there that are united in unceasing prayer for us."[11]

Once he had confirmation that the Vatican had approved the plan and that money would be included, he seemed to recoup his own vitality. The pieces began to come together. A short trip to Milan resulted in the full recommendation of Father Agostuno Gemelli, the director of the Federation of Catholic Universities. The relational pieces also aligned. Miranda's attitude toward Sofía had been disciplined. "I once again lament that you have had to go without news for more than two weeks," he wrote. "Patience. You will see that I have already corrected myself in this, at the very least."[12] By the end of September, Miranda was able to leave Milan and begin making contact with universities in Spain and Switzerland. The plan for the future was approved; the work in the present was putting it into practice.

As Miranda toured Europe with the backing of the Vatican—Milan, Padua, Lausanne, Fribourg, Paris, Madrid, and Barcelona—Sofía again suffered a recurrence of her liver ailment. After receiving a photograph of Sofía for his album, Miranda was shocked to see her "extreme thinness," which he wrote only confirmed to him Sofía's poor health.[13] Sofía didn't explain the severity of her condition to Miranda. Miranda had to receive details of Sofía's condition through her father, Francisco del Valle. "We make Sofía eat something at eleven and at six in the evening," Francisco wrote Miranda, "which has very much improved her state of being as she is better nourished, with her appetite returning at the right hours; may God assist this method as I believe it will very much amend her digestive difficulties."[14]

Despite Sofía's poor health, which recovered slowly under her parents' care, Quinta Sofía was a place of celebration. On September 30, Sofía commemorated her saint's day, called the *día onomástico* in Spanish. Choosing among many possible saints by that name, Sofía's parents named her after St. Sophia of the second century. Church tradition held this Sophia was the widowed mother of three virgin-martyrs—the aptly named Faith, Hope, and Charity—who suffered for Christ at the hands of Roman emperor Hadrian (117 AD–138 AD). A group of young women from Cultura Femenina gathered for a special dinner in honor of Sofía and the saint. The party seemed to lift her spirits.

Sofía's sole-remaining brother, Enrique, was soon to be married.[15] While the marriage was a happy prospect for the family, it also meant further financial responsibility for Sofía. Her siblings had, one by one, moved away. Matilde, her oldest sister, looked after their grandmother in Spain; Hortensia and Consuelo were nuns; Clara and Ana María were married. Now Enrique too was making his exit from Quinta Sofía. Sofía was the last remaining child at home. Francisco Sr.'s business endeavors had suffered during the religious conflict. He turned most of his efforts to small-scale agriculture, mostly planting alfalfa, as well as raising three cows, with whose newborn calves he hoped to turn a meager profit. Fortunately, the donation Miranda received from the Vatican provided some salary relief for Sofía and the other professors. But the administration of these funds was slow. Not until the spring of 1929 were the funds made available.

Miranda lay awake thinking of Sofía on the night of September 30. The news from Mexico was constantly troubling. There was Sofía's sickness and the news in the press about Madre Conchita and José de

León Toral. A plan began to form in Miranda's mind as he stared into the dark room. Maybe there was a way for Sofía to leave Mexico City, if just for a short vacation? In December, Cultura Femenina would have suspended classes for the Christmas holiday. Perhaps, he considered, Sofía could visit Clara and Alfonso in New Orleans, then visit Hortensia in Philadelphia, and after that they could meet in Washington. There they could plan together. Miranda could finally reveal all the details of his journey, without having to hold anything back, as he had had to do in his letters. He pitched the idea to Sofía. "You need to rest, to get out of that environment at least for a little while," Miranda argued. He tried to head off her misgivings: "I know you will say that the 'money' is lacking and even this I have thought about and the issue has been resolved."[16] Miranda asked Sofía to talk it over with her parents and to make the necessary arrangements so that her travel could be adequately planned.

Several days later, Sofía's sister Clara wrote Miranda that Sofía needed a vacation. Miranda wrote Sofía urging her to accept. The chance to leave Mexico for a brief trip couldn't come at a better time. Sofía was indeed eager to travel. The trip would coincide with Miranda's return from Europe. He felt he was close to wrapping up his work in Europe. He received the promise of scholarships at the University of Milan and at the Commercial University of Fribourg; even the cardinal archbishop of Spain donated a small, but symbolic, sum of sixty pesetas. To Miranda it was just another indication of God's providential protection over Cultura Femenina and the secretariat.[17]

Miranda's release from his days of waiting in Rome allowed for an opportunity he couldn't resist: a visit to Villaviciosa, the del Valle family's hometown in northwestern Spain. Matilde, Sofía's sister, still lived there, attending to Sofía's paternal grandmother. Matilde was the eldest del Valle child and, as Miranda described to Sofía in one letter, "she and you are the ones who most resemble one another among your siblings. . . . Physiognomic features, identical," his description continued, "common family vocabulary, similar gestures, equal tenacity, complementary aspirations, [and] among other aspects, great likeness." At times, he wrote Sofía, "I felt I was talking with you although in many respects there is a perfect distinction." Listening to Matilde, he laughed to himself, thinking of Sofía's manner of conversing and how, here with her sister, Miranda saw hints of Sofía. "She knows how to argue like some other people I know," Miranda noted, referring to Sofía's strong personality.[18]

Miranda felt certain that Matilde's talents were being underutilized. In Villaviciosa it was easy to "die of asphyxiation," he observed. All the more so, he believed, for a mature woman such as Matilde whom he felt would be better suited elsewhere. Miranda felt Matilde would increase the "warmth of Quinta Sofía" if she were released from her duties in Spain.[19]

Just a few days after Miranda's visit to Villaviciosa, preparations were underway in Mexico City for the trial of José de León Toral and Madre Conchita. It began on Conchita's birthday, November 2, 1928, All Souls' Day. It was the biggest media spectacle in Mexico City since the trial and execution of Emperor Maximilian in 1867.[20]

Why weren't they simply summarily executed? Father Pro and his three companions had not been tried for their alleged crimes. And, moreover, Obregón had not been assassinated by the attempted assault. Now the president-elect was dead, and a crowd had witnessed Toral carrying out the murder. No one doubted that Toral had pulled the trigger. The answer was politics. A widening division had grown between the followers of Obregón and the followers of Calles. Obregón was elected as the next president. Many Obregónistas suspected that Calles or his associates were behind Obregón's death—that Toral was just a fall guy for the machinations of unseen forces in the shadows. A trial had to be carried out to avoid further rebellion and chaos. Calles knew the political landscape was fraught and made sure to announce he would be stepping down from the presidency as expected. An interim president would take office: Emilio Portes Gil, an Obregónista who was expected to carry on the caudillo's vision and legacy.

Toral maintained his motives had been religious. But religion was a tricky, and indeed fraught, subject at the moment. Putting Toral on trial for a religiously motivated political assassination raised two problems. First, the Constitution stated that political crimes didn't carry a capital punishment. Criminal charges were another matter. Criminal murderers, if convicted, could be put to death. Making a criminal conviction stick was imperative for Calles and the revolutionary politicos supportive of justice for Obregón. Second, putting Toral on trial for what was tantamount to sedition for religious reasons would be like putting thousands of Catholics on trial for the same thing. It was bad press. While not every faithful practicing Catholic agreed with Toral's ultimate solution, many abhorred the regime and could sympathize with his motivation. Standing up for one's religious beliefs to the point of sacrifice was a constant trope of the era. Civil disobedience was commonplace. Going to Mass in a clandestine location, supporting cristero forces, or at the very least providing material support for the Catholic Defense League in Mexico City were crimes punishable by fines and imprisonment. The revolutionary state might find it necessary to fight rebels in the field. But there was little cachet for a media spectacle in the courts pitting the government against the religious beliefs of ordinary Catholics.[21] If religion was made an issue, it had to be framed as the religion of a corrupt clergy, whose long fight against order and progress stretched back to the nineteenth century.[22]

And then there was the issue of noticeable, though slow, progress in the realm of diplomacy. High-level talks had begun between Calles and the Reverend John J. Burke of the American NCWC. The tentative agreement worked out had stalled awaiting Vatican approval. Nevertheless, both the Calles government and Catholic leaders showed a remarkable amount of restraint throughout the trial. Public condemnations were mainly reserved for the fanaticism of Toral and the so-called intellectual author of the assassination—Madre Conchita.

Gender and sexuality became the escape route from the politically fraught issue of the religious conflict.[23] The government built a criminal case against the two defendants by diverting attention from religion and by instead focusing on Conchita's gender. Of course, this was mostly a subtext to the trial. It's not as though journalists provided profound gender analyses of the affair. But Toral and Conchita were pigeonholed into a set of existing stereotypes: a strong-willed, intelli-

16. A view of the trial, 1928. Madre Conchita sits with hands folded. Toral stares blankly. SINAFO, INAH, Fototeca Nacional, Archivo Casasola, "Concepción Acevedo de la Llata y José de León Toral, durante un juicio," num. inv: 45237.

gent older woman who used her feminine wiles to seduce a weak-willed and sexually inexperienced man to do ghastly things.[24]

Inside the small courthouse the crowd competed for seats. Some fifty congressmen attended the trial. One representative even shouted at the jury, "If you will not do justice, then we shall punish them!"[25] The crowd hissed during the defense attorneys' questioning of the defendants; they applauded during the prosecution's cross-examination. Toral's testimony went on endlessly, admitting that if Conchita had told him not to kill Obregón, he probably would've thought better of it. He told the jury that Madre Conchita had said that the religious conflict would only end when Calles, Obregón, and the schismatic leader Patriarch Pérez were dead. But did this amount to being the "intellectual author" of the crime? Conchita and her lawyers argued no; the prosecution sought to build a case that Conchita had so much influence over Toral and others that she used her age, intellect, and even sexual charisma to persuade the fanatical and weak-willed Toral to do her bidding.

Innuendo and image persuaded many Mexicans of Conchita's guilt in acting as puppeteer to Toral's pliable marionette. One reporter described Conchita's appearance. She had "a hairstyle not exactly like a 'bob' nor like a 'flapper' but instead quite unkempt, as if she had just cut off her braids with a pair of scissors, without taking care to give it the necessary touch-ups."[26] Female murderesses were often described as homely in the press. Conchita seemed to fit the description. The crowd had no problem interjecting its belief: death to Toral and the "prostitute Concha," one attendee shouted. Juan Correa Nieto, the district attorney, seized on Toral's statements of their intimate friendship: "I have my spiritual director, but there are times when two hearts, although they are laypeople, understand one another better than the director."[27]

If religion entered into the prosecution's strategy, it was bad religion. Correa Nieto brought up the fact that Conchita had used a branding iron to tattoo the name of Christ—JHS—over her breast. He then highlighted that other alleged Catholic criminals had similar markings. Conchita was painted as practicing a faith that was odd, masochistic. Politicos at the time said they had heard rumors of orgies in her convent. Toral's wife was quoted as being disgusted at her husband's relationship with the nun. Conchita's use of the familiar nickname "Pepe" was mentioned; so too was Conchita allowing men into her quarters. All this seemed to imply that Conchita was far from the pure "iris" the defense made her out to be.[28]

The defense countered. Demetrio Sodi led a team of five attorneys. Sodi had served under Porfirio Diaz as a minister of justice and for a time as president of the Supreme Court. He had taken the case as a gesture toward Obregón's widow, who had written the jury asking for clemency toward Conchita and Toral. Sodi confronted the religious persecution head on. This was a political act, he reasoned, and therefore not punishable by execution. Sodi likened Conchita's branding herself to the corporeal sanctity of St. Francis and St. Teresa of Ávila—mortification was part of the pure Catholic faith, according to Sodi. Conchita was merely following in a long tradition of penitential spirituality, he maintained.[29]

As the case dragged on, President Calles intervened. The president was afraid that despite the prosecution's avoidance of the religious issue, it was beginning to seem like his own government's actions in the Cristero War were being adjudicated. He asked the attorney general, Ezequiel Padilla, to make the closing arguments for the prosecution. Padilla, a former student of Sodi's, agreed.

Padilla confronted the issue of religion directly. He argued that Toral and Conchita had indeed committed a crime against the Republic, against society, and against the law. "But it is also a crime against their own religion," Padilla asserted. Madre Conchita, as a consecrated woman, was part of the clerical problem in Mexico, Padilla thundered. And it was the clergy who the government was trying to stop, not the humble majority of the Catholic faithful in Mexico. Padilla endeavored to separate the noble character of Catholic Mexico from the ignoble scheming of a political clerical class. Catholic Mexico, argued Padilla, was made "of Catholics who have found it their Christian duty to resist the worldly tendencies of the clergy and defend the doctrines of Christ." Padilla then made Obregón out to be the true martyr. "The figure of Obregón was not that of a politician, nor that of a military leader; it was that of a man who carried in his bosom precisely Christ's socialistic virtue; who had as his mission on earth to reject what is called aristocracy in the clergy, or what is called aristocracy in capital, and descend to what is called democracy in religion, to what is called democracy in the division of wealth."[30]

The audience erupted in applause. When Sodi tried to give his closing remarks for the defense he was shouted down. "I have finished, Your Honor," he finally gave in. But the trial and verdict were basically predetermined. Padilla, who greatly respected his old mentor, took him by the arm and walked out of the courtroom accompanied by an armed guard.

The jury, who had been threatened, quickly returned with the verdict: death for Toral, twenty years in prison for Madre Conchita.[31] Thousands of Catholics attended Toral's funeral, though not nearly as many as had come out for Father Pro's. Conchita spent the next decade on the Islas Marías penal colony. Neither the Catholic hierarchy nor the laity protested Conchita's sentence.

In November 1928 Miranda's time in Europe was coming to an end. The mission had been a resounding success. Sofía had proved herself a capable caretaker of Cultura Femenina. She grew in his estimation during his long absence. Yet, at a time when Miranda should've been rejoicing at his success, despair was once again not far from his thoughts. His mother was ill. On November 22 Miranda wrote Sofía of his hopes to return soon. Yet a sinking feeling blunted his optimism: "I am shocked by the very disheartening news of my mother, which I received from home. It weighs heavily on my soul, as she is the most precious treasure Providence keeps for me after the death of my late father."[32] A few days later, Miranda learned that his mother had died on November 22. Leaving Mexico he'd taken with him the pain of a lost father; on his return trip he carried the loss of his mother. "Our Lord has just sent me the most painful trial in depriving me of my beloved mother," Miranda wrote Pascual Díaz. "I have found myself alone, completely alone in a very painful trance," he continued. "Only Our Lord has accompanied me in my desolation. God be praised."[33] On December 9, as he grieved alone, Miranda boarded the ss *Paris* for the journey back to the United States.

15

The Return

The ss *Paris* bellowed black smoke as the ocean liner slipped through the mouth of the Narrows and then steamed straight into the belly of the Upper Bay of New York Harbor. It was high tide on the morning of December 16, 1928.[1] Miguel Miranda was one of the passengers.[2] It had been a long voyage. He wrote in one letter that his thoughts and prayers had constantly gone to Mexico, while his body was presently so far away.

Miranda stepped off the gangway of the ss *Paris* into a New York hoarse with the last flush-faced toast of the Roaring Twenties. The luxury ocean liners all docked at the Chelsea piers, located between Twelfth and Twenty-Second Streets. Bootleggers often smuggled copious amounts of champagne and liquor off the ships.[3] The docks and the well-heeled travelers were a symbol of rum-filled, Prohibition-era opulence. One twelve-hour fete held aboard a ship docked at the Chelsea piers that year brought thousands of partygoers.[4] More than one million travelers for foreign ports departed and arrived on the ocean liners each year in the late 1920s. The luxury boats, although giving way to new "classless" cabin ships, were still a floating microcosm of America's haves and have-nots. Ellis Island received its "huddled masses," the Chelsea piers its suits and mink furs.

Miranda had no idea someone waited for him. Then, a familiar face: Alberto María Carreño, a former Cultura Femenina professor, was smiling at him from the crowd. Carreño, now the personal secretary of Pascual Díaz, was sent to escort Miranda to the College of St. Francis Xavier in Brooklyn. Díaz would host the tired traveler there. After recognizing Carreño on the pier, Miranda rushed to embrace him.

"I have a surprise for you," Carreño said, pulling back after a moment to observe the haggard-looking Miranda.[5]

Miranda had had enough surprises of late, devastating ones, which made him instantly think the worst. "Let it be whatever God wills," he told Carreño.

"You won't believe who is waiting for you," Carreño baited.

The form of a woman slipped up behind them, and then Miranda turned and recognized the face. It was not Sofía. Her trip was still several weeks away. The woman was Juana Arguinzóniz, one of the "girls" of Cultura Femenina, who had helped Sofía run the school in Miranda's absence. Juana was in New York on her own holiday. Miranda's face clouded with emotion, feeling the joy of seeing two people who knew him and cared for him. Juana brought greetings from Sofía and the rest of Cultura Femenina. He was especially grateful for the reception, even as the memory of his mother's death still weighed heavily.[6]

It's tempting to imagine Miranda disappointed that Carreño's surprise visitor was not Sofía del Valle. Juana Arguinzóniz, her sister Luisa, and their mother appear sporadically in the letters between Miranda and Sofía. They were Miranda's friends to be sure—friends also of Sofía's—and important collaborators in Cultura Femenina and early leaders of the JCFM. Still, Sofía alone shared a special bond with Miranda. Carreño acknowledged as much. In one letter to Sofía he highlighted the distinction Sofía held in relation to Miranda. "It is you," Carreño wrote, "who is the worthy companion of my friend and you deserve complete happiness."[7] Sofía was charged by Miranda as caretaker, the one chiefly responsible for Cultura Femenina in his absence. And it was Sofía whom Miranda let into his confidence, who became more than a trusted fellow worker in their mission. Their intimate letters, leaning on one another throughout their separation, again and again asking for prayers, confessing their weakness and expressing their needs—for news, for hope, for empathy—all these reasons point to the possibility that Miranda desired to see Sofía's face among the crowd on the dock of New York Harbor.

But if Miranda held any disappointment he kept it to himself. His reception by Carreño and Arguinzóniz was comforting, even without Sofía present. He wrote to Sofía of his experience at the dock: "I found it difficult to talk and my vision clouded each time I looked at those two friends who were only there to surround me, in their own name and for those they represented, with grace and comfort, all of which I have lacked for some time.... I will tell you everything else when we see each other," Miranda concluded. Although absent in body, Sofía and everyone else Miranda loved was present in Carreño and Arguinzóniz. They were two representatives from the "nest"—Miranda's nickname for Cultura Femenina—back in Mexico City. A piece of home came to greet Miranda at the dock and, although Sofía was not there, he was overjoyed to feel closer now than before to the end of his journey.[8]

Miranda, perhaps, was not so much disappointed that Sofía was absent at the dock. He was disappointed that Sofía took longer to arrive in the northeastern United States than he would've hoped. Anticipation, anxiety, desire—all these emotions poured through Miranda's letters in the weeks before they were reunited. He imagined what his and Sofía's conversation would be like, having been able to communicate only through letters up until that point. "Because of all the time I've spent almost alone," he wrote, "I think the day when I can chat in the nest, we will have to remain there quite long, even if I was able to imitate certain people I know"—Miranda of course meant Sofía—"at the maximum velocity of two thousand words per minute!"[9] After his return to New York, and after a brief trip to Washington DC, he hoped to spend Christmas with Sofía. "You cannot imagine the joy I felt at your departure from Mexico to New Orleans," he told Sofía.[10] But Christmas together was not to be. Sofía had been delayed and decided to stay in New Orleans for a few days before then going to see her sister Hortensia in Philadelphia. "How I would have loved to spend Christmas in New Orleans," Miranda wrote. He wanted Sofía to leave her visit with Clara till later, to come to Philadelphia "as soon as possible" so that she would be closer to Washington.[11]

Miranda's desire to see Sofía was personal, but it was also wrapped up in Sofía's value to the plans he was making. Miranda wanted to make a presentation to the Catholic University of America about scholarships for Mexican students. He needed Sofía's expertise in English to overcome his own "difficulty with the language." Miranda's English was improving, but it was still far inferior to Sofía's. He called himself

Sofía's "pupil," and, in quite choppy English sentences, he wrote to Sofía: "But now this short letter will show you, your pupils progresses, and his will progressing continually."[12] Miranda expressed his desire for Sofía to come to Washington so that "you yourself can take charge of the presentation."[13] Miranda's impatience didn't hasten Sofía's arrival. Their reunion had to wait until January.

A new year brought new beginnings and new hopes for Miranda, Sofía, and Cultura Femenina. With the close of 1928, perhaps a bit of distance could grow between the present and what was, for both Miranda and Sofía, a truly difficult year. Almost a year had passed since Miranda's arrest, the raid on the secretariat, and the death of Miranda's father. Then there was Sofía's sickness, her difficulties learning to lead Cultura Femenina in Miranda's absence, the fear of discovery, the assassination of Mexico's president-elect at the hands of a Catholic, the death of Miranda's mother, long journeys, solitude for them both, many partings and long silences—these had been the marrow of the year 1928. If New Year's 1929 had not rent every tie to the painful memories of the previous year, at least Sofía and Miranda faced the new year ahead together.

The first week of January 1929 Sofía took the train from Philadelphia. She sent Miranda a telegram announcing her arrival time in Washington. Miranda wanted to be there waiting at the station. He arranged for Sofía to stay at the Convent of the Josephine Sisters, many of them Mexican nuns, their house just "a few steps from the university." Miranda looked forward to telling Sofía all the details of what he had accomplished on his mission—Vatican support, the backing of bishops and schools from Rome to Fribourg to Madrid—and then there was the money. Indeed finances were a key victory, if at least to alleviate some of the pressure of rent, salaries, materials, and debt. "I am comforted," he wrote, "to see a tomorrow coming without this anxiety the secretariat has had to experience until now."[14] The $10,000 from the Vatican was not enough to calm that anxiety completely, but it was good tidings for a new year.[15]

These are all the facts that are known of Miranda and Sofía's reunion that January. No trace of the details of their reunion shows up in the

The Return   155

many letters between them. This isn't surprising. The need for detailing the reunion once they were together was less pressing.

A blank page exists in their history; not empty for Miranda and Sofía, but blank for the historian. The novelist might truly let imagination fill that blank page: their nervous anticipation, searching looks out train windows, embraces (perhaps awkward at first), maybe lingering hand in hand for a few moments, then a stream of unconnected exchanges until finally, when adjusted to the new reality of one another's presence, they fulfilled Miranda's vision of speaking at two thousand words per minute, filling in every gap more easily with voice and tone than had been possible by handwritten or typewritten words. Filling blank spaces comes more easily for novelists than for historians. And perhaps the reunion was underwhelming, showing no sign of the intimacy expressed in their letters. History is full of silences, and the story of Miranda and Sofía's reunion in January, much longed for according to the record—that much we do know—must remain untold.

The documentary trail resumes shortly after their January reunion. Bishop Pascual Díaz, exiled in New York, was also glad to see Sofía. Díaz, as the official liaison between the apostolic delegation in Washington and the Mexican bishops, was in sore need of reliable information from Mexico. Most Mexican bishops had been forced out of the country—some to Europe, others scattered throughout the United States to San Antonio, Los Angeles, and Chicago mainly—and few remained south of the Rio Grande. From where Díaz sat in New York, he and his colleague Ruiz y Flores had access to influence in Washington and, from there, had also gained the best hearing at the Vatican. What Díaz and Ruiz needed were reports from Mexico City itself.[16]

If 1928 had been a year of difficult quest for Sofía and Miranda, it was also a long, arduous year for Díaz and Ruiz. Several Mexican bishops were unwilling to back down unless the laws themselves were changed—that had been the criterion put forward by the pope in 1926. On that basis the church strike had begun. But Ruiz had made progress on the Mexican bishops. After he returned from Rome in October 1928, Ruiz spent the month of November in Los Angeles and San Antonio consensus-building among his exiled fellow bishops. The

San Antonio meeting in particular produced a resolution favorable to peace. The bishops there, under Ruiz's leadership, wrote a letter to Pius XI. Signed by just under half of Mexico's bishops, the letter acknowledged "that Your Holiness is prepared to enter into conference with the Mexican government." It continued that the prelates understood that "for the bishops to return to their diocese and for the priests to reestablish public worship, it shall be sufficient to have securities on the part of the government, but securities sufficient in judgment of the Holy See—which securities may be obtained even while the conferences are in progress without it being necessary to await the conclusion of such conferences."[17] Ruiz had gotten the bishops, at least a good number, on board with a settled agreement. Public worship would start, as long as the agreement was strong enough to assure that the government would initiate talks leading to a modification of the laws. Yet Obregón's assassination had brought any talks of peace to a halt. With Conchita's and Toral's trials over—prison for the first, execution for the second—a new opening seemed possible.

Díaz and Ruiz were hoping for that opening. And information from Sofía on the status of Catholic life in the capital was an important part of feeling whether or not the time had come for a new approach toward a peace settlement. Carreño, on Díaz's behalf, wrote Miranda asking if he would have "the kindness to authorize Sofía to give [Díaz] a detailed account of all the events that she reported to [Miranda]."[18] This was crucial, Carreño continued, "because [Díaz] needs to [be apprised of] all the various threads of the affair." Pascual Díaz managed not to be shut out of the complex web of diplomacy of 1928. He carried on direct and indirect communication with the U.S. ambassador to Mexico, Dwight Morrow.[19] President Calles left office in December 1928. The interim chief executive, Emilio Portes Gil, intimated to Morrow his willingness to talk.[20]

When Díaz summoned Sofía and Miranda to New York, they went. The details of Sofía's meeting with Díaz are not in the archive, and whether the bishop found anything of value for his task at hand is not clear. It seems likely that the mere fact that Sofía had kept Cultura Femenina and the JCFM alive during the conflict was important to

Díaz. If peace came, at least he knew that there were those like Sofía and Miranda, and the students of Cultura Femenina—all the classes and preparation happening in the secretariat—ready to help rebuild. And if peace came, Díaz could be sure that Sofía and Miranda were ready to work under the bishops' authority.

The money from the Vatican finally came in early January 1929. The American apostolic delegate, Fumasoni Biondi, issued a check for 10,000 USD made out to Miranda and Ruiz. They deposited it in a new account opened at the Riggs National Bank, New York.[21] The money didn't remain there long. They immediately deposited 5,000 USD in the savings and loan bank established by the secretariat in 1924 to keep it from being liquidated.[22] The financial committee, including Francisco del Valle, had kept it alive, just barely, during the Cristero Rebellion. Another 3,000 USD was made out to Pedro Lascuráin, prominent Catholic lawyer and former interim Mexican president in the dark aftermath of Madero's assassination. Lascuráin then was to dole out a monthly sum to the secretariat for operations and salaries. Sofía reported to Miranda that by March, Cultura Femenina still hadn't seen the money.[23] While slow in coming, Vatican money enabled the secretariat to oversee the post-cristero reconstruction.

Just days after Miranda and Ruiz deposited the money in New York, Fumasoni Biondi presented Miranda with a communiqué from the Vatican. The money didn't come without strings attached. One of those strings was that the secretariat remain nonpolitical. "The secretariat," the communiqué stated, "should abstain from all participation in armed or political parties." It was important that the secretariat "not give its name" to any movements such as these, the memo stated, which of course included the League and the cristeros.[24]

The document was couched in typical Vatican ambiguity. It made a distinction between the policy of Catholic associations, attached to the bishops, and Catholics as private citizens, who "were free to exercise their rights as citizens."[25] The arrhythmic dance around Catholic politics—Catholic institutions must remain outside politics, but Catholics had a duty to vote and lobby their governments—would increasingly be the awkward soft-shoe of Vatican directives for decades to come. It was a dance choreographed not just for Mexico, but for Catholics worldwide; in each national context, the Vatican pushed a nonpolitical Catholic action to insulate the church from troubles like those in Mexico.

Miranda's secretariat, Sofía as well, was being tasked with the work of reorganizing the post-cristero Catholic Church. Miranda and Sofía's "nest" was to be the model for the Catholic Church in Mexico as a whole. The Vatican, and bishops like Díaz and Ruiz, wanted to be sure that this model for the future wouldn't cause problems when the peace came. Miranda and Sofía's vision—educative, incremental, peaceful—matched the future desired by Rome; that was a principal reason Miranda's presentation had been so enthusiastically supported and promoted by the Vatican. And it was why money had been given to promote and sustain it at this critical moment.

All told, Sofía's stay in the United States was brief. Her presentation of the work of Cultura Femenina to Catholic University and the NCWC yielded several scholarships for students from Mexico to study in Washington. Sofía left an impression on the Reverend John J. Burke and the leadership of the National Council of Catholic Women. She also impressed the Josephine Sisters, with whom she stayed while working with Miranda in Washington. Four weeks after she left, Miranda wrote Sofía that the nuns there could speak of nothing but "Sofía" whenever Miranda ate with the women in the convent rectory.[26]

Sofía was back in the Mexican capital for the new term of Cultura Femenina. Miranda too had briefly returned to Mexico City, but the details of his visit are murky. However much he wanted to stay in Mexico, it soon became clear that a return trip to the United States would be necessary. The work of the Social Secretariat needed more funding. By April 1929, although much had been accomplished, Miranda still had to meet with American bishops; perhaps, he thought, the secretariat's funds could be increased even a little. He sent out one hundred letters to bishops across the United States—signing each, sealing every envelope, writing Sofía that his skill at the job would've outdone even her own efficiency, then joking that in truth he couldn't take the credit, it belonged to the "sponge" he'd used.[27] The results were paltry: just 500 USD from the U.S. bishops. It was a bit perplexing to Miranda. The Knights of Columbus, an influential lay Catholic organization in the United States, had raised one million dollars for Catholic propaganda efforts in educating the American people about Mexico's religious troubles. A mere fraction of that amount would sustain Miranda and Sofía's efforts.

Miranda's friend, Bishop Curley of Baltimore, bluntly told him that the American hierarchy viewed Mexican Catholics with a certain suspicion. Miranda was at a loss to understand the roots of this mentality. He wrote Sofía that unfortunately "very little had been done to illustrate the good that we have [accomplished]" to the Americans. "Selfish interests," he continued, people "who obey in their actions means that cannot easily be aligned with good faith and with truth"—these were the bad examples that Miranda felt had put off American Catholic leaders.[28] It's unclear who Miranda believed these "selfish interests" belonged to. But from the beginning of the rebellion, League leaders, dissident exiles, and even militant bishops like Jesús Manríquez y Zárate (exiled in Los Angeles), had sought the backing of U.S. Catholics, especially American dollars, to fund the civil war. It's likely Miranda referred to these militant attempts at fundraising. Miranda saw that the quest for the future in Mexico had to be a quest for friendship with the Americans. "A firm foundation will only be built on the basis of friendship," he expressed to Sofía, "which will result in a measurable harvest for our educational endeavors."[29] Understanding came through relationships, Miranda had come to believe, and that took time and, with it, the talents of language, grace, and tact. After all his time away, he had come to realize that the mission was really just beginning, even when he wanted it to be over. At the very least he had to tie up loose ends, and for that, he wrote Sofía, he would remain in the United States another couple of months.

Sofía took the news of Miranda's delay with resilience tinged with sadness. "For my part," Sofía responded, "although it means an enormous sacrifice to me to think of one or two more months without you here, I feel it is justified." She promised to increase her letters. "So your absence is less burdensome, I promise to send you letters daily," Sofía committed, "naturally hoping to receive in exchange, not daily, but every third day or at least two times a week."[30]

In the spring of 1929 Sofía had come to understand something about her relationship with Miranda. She was his "complement," a supporting feature, Sofía wrote in one letter. It wasn't a begrudging acknowledgement, as if she had no other value than to be the woman behind the man, chafing under subservience. Sofía wrote about their complementary relationship with pride. But in putting the sentiment on paper, making it so plain, sending it to him in a letter, she worried it might be misunderstood. She took a risk in doing so. Perhaps "complement," she realized, made her sound like she undervalued her role. And although it went unsaid in their letters, maybe the word "complement" sounded too much like language used for marriage partners. Their relationship was already under some scrutiny. When she visited Miranda in Washington in December 1928, she wrote him that she wasn't going to let the students know, as it might give rise to rumors.[31]

Catholic thinking on marriage emphasized complementarity; hence, Sofía's awareness that the term could be misunderstood. God created men and women equally, church doctrine said, but men and women had distinct roles. Men were given the responsibility of leadership—of the family and of society. Women, like the first woman Eve, had been given the role of helper and companion. When confronted by the independent modern woman, many Catholics chafed, not against the notion of men's and women's equal value, but against the supposed "sameness" of the sexes. Certainly, the argument for gender complementarity within the church had been abused—Sofía herself acknowledged as much; that men had the duty to rule with an iron hand was absurd to Sofía. But, Sofía asserted, when properly understood, complementarity between men and women was a relationship of equal value but of distinct roles. The question for Sofía was not the "sameness" of men and women, which she rejected. Rather, the question was what these distinct roles consisted of in a changing world. Sofía's own role as director of Cultura Femenina, in Miranda's absence, called into question the boundaries acceptable for women. The necessities of the present religious conflict had propelled her into a leadership role usually given to a man. The distinct roles laid out for Catholic men and women, for priests and for laity, were blurring.

Whether "complement" evoked too much the language of Catholic marriage, or because she sensed her own leadership pushed against distinct roles guiding gender relations, Sofía was concerned that she had been misunderstood. In a subsequent letter, she tried to explain herself, to disabuse Miranda of any wrong conclusions. "Regarding [my] letter of [April 6]," she began, "I wished, after it was sent, to make clarifications, as it could be interpreted differently from what inspired it.... Also," she continued, "you know how my life is at the moment and [that] I was not able to return to [address] it, but now I have thought of it again." Defending her earlier letter, she wrote "I would not think it lowers one's own estimation in speaking of 'complements.'" On the contrary, Sofía continued, "in relation to you I find myself functioning as a complement, as the cork is to the bottle, as the stem to the flower itself." Extending the metaphor to clothing, Sofía understood her role not as simple adornment, but as a vital piece holding everything in place. "Keep in mind," she suggested, "I am the button on your jacket—my complementarity even goes there. Imagine how *proud* the button is feeling to be part of such an important outfit!" She underlined the word "proud" in her original letter, as if to emphasize her enthusiasm for her position in their relationship. "So that is what I am," Sofía asserted, "on my own I am worthless, but joined to you I feel myself *something*." Sofía didn't speak this way with other men. "[My] bad habit of pouring my heart out on the page" was "a thing that only happens to me with you," she wrote.[32]

Letters are not windows on the soul. But they can offer a unique, though not perfectly clear, view into an otherwise interior world. What might Sofía have been trying to clarify in her letter to Miranda? To be sure, it was a reassertion of proper gender boundaries. In using the word "complement" Sofía emphasized her dependent role in their relationship. And this was in line with Catholic doctrine at the time. A cork, a flower stem, a jacket's button—these were all items that support the function of the object as a whole. But the letter hinted at something else. Sofía understood her *unique* role in relation to Miranda. Their relationship was both special and essential. Sofía and Miranda made one another whole. Yet Sofía was at pains to make sure their relationship was controlled and correctly ordered, in line with Catholic doctrine. Control and order were two things she felt comfortable with. But again, just as with her risk in running Cultura Femenina without Miranda, there was risk in a special and unique relationship with Miranda. Sofía wanted reciprocation, even validation, for her uniqueness, evidenced by her desire to receive Miranda's letters at constant intervals. The risk was that her unique complement to Miranda could be construed—by him, by the Catholic community—as too intimate, of having overstepped the acceptable boundaries for a celibate priest and laywoman. Sofía was surely aware of the accusations against Madre Conchita in the press. It's quite likely Sofía was at pains to stress appropriate boundaries in order not to appear like Conchita.

There's no evidence that a romance was in the offing between Sofía and Miranda. Nor is there evidence that such a relationship was imagined by either. It was not a possibility within the boundaries they both accepted and sought to live within. Yet Sofía, in writing Miranda, was aware that boundaries were shifting everywhere and she took the risk to tell him that she considered their relationship something special, in need of clarification.

If Miranda responded in kind to Sofía's letter, it wasn't preserved among their correspondence. His letters during the spring of 1929 focus on his task at hand: fundraising and making inroads among American Catholics. And in those endeavors, he was discouraged. "What [little] has been acquired reflects the limit of goodwill," he wrote.[33] He felt it impossible to cover, at least for the present, what the Social Secretariat lacked in terms of finances. As April turned to May and then to June, Miranda began sensing that the religious conflict was nearing an end. It's not clear if he had any inside information. Nevertheless, what he read in the newspapers seemed encouraging. Miranda wrote Sofía on May 9: "The recent news in the press regarding our matters have today been full of comfort. Might we be close to the end of so many bitter pains?"[34] For Miranda and Sofía, the peace could not come soon enough.

16

The Peace

The peace had come. The bells tolled and had been ever since the church and the state had decided to end the fighting. It was a week after the peace, June 29, a Saturday—St. Peter's and St. Paul's Day in Roman Catholic reckoning. Thanks were to be made publicly at the Basilica of Our Lady of Guadalupe, Mexico's national shrine.

And out in front strode the man who had decided for peace, Archbishop Leopoldo Ruiz y Flores—that bookish, balding, Ruiz—oval-spectacled, unassuming, described even at one time as "Pickwickian." Once undervalued and underestimated, this Ruiz marched resolute, chalice in hand, flowers stuck between breast and cup from where they'd been thrown by innumerable hands, the onlookers stretching forth in the thousands. The crowds sprawled out and around Ruiz, finally giving way to an aisle as Ruiz proceeded onward with Host under lamb's wool, onward as a veiled woman grabbed Ruiz, kissing him as he passed, onward as others, on penitent knees, touched the hem of his robe. Ruiz stopped briefly before entering the church, turning back toward the City of Mexico, signing three large crosses in the air with the Bread of God over the faithful and the city beyond. Onward once more, Ruiz made one last valiant push through the nave of Guadalupe's church before depositing the exiled Host back to its home on the high altar underneath the serene gaze of the Mother of God, her image miraculously painted there, it was believed, on the mantle of the Indian Juan Diego. The painted mantle hung above the church's altar as the long-venerated sign of God's favor for Mexico, the *pueblo amado de Dios*.[1]

The Mexican people had now returned to public worship.

The church had made peace with the Mexican government. And it was Ruiz who had made it happen. The rest of his days, until his death in 1941, Ruiz would have to defend that decision. For better or worse, here was the man who had made Mexico's bells toll.

At the moment of decision Leopoldo Ruiz y Flores didn't hesitate. Early in the month of May 1929, intermediaries made it clear that the administration of Mexican president Emilio Portes Gil was open to once again negotiating with the church. After Obregón's assassination, Calles stepped aside. Portes Gil was elected interim president. The Vatican, for its part, named Ruiz apostolic delegate to Mexico, ad referendum, meaning that the appointment was specific for the task at hand: negotiating the peace. Ruiz would have the final *yes* or *no* in the negotiations. Ruiz chose Pascual Díaz as his companion for the mission. Before the train from Washington DC to St. Louis, and then down to the border where they met in secret with Morrow on the ambassador's personal Pullman, Ruiz telegrammed Gasparri, asking just how much latitude he would have in negotiating the peace.[2] He needed to find out the mind of Rome.

On June 3, 1929, Ruiz petitioned Cardinal Gasparri via telegram:

After conferences held Washington with Señor Legorreta regarding dispositions president Mexico, may I ask whether the Holy Father would authorize resumption worship, if I obtain from president official decree that recognizes the right of the church to its existence and freedom, declaring that conferences have begun to study application, interpretation, and also modification of the laws in accordance with the above principle and giving every guarantee for all priests who are registered by their respective bishops. This seems best that can be obtained right away; the rest will depend on the conference and good will. In my opinion it seems best hasten resumption worship to avoid excitement tempers on both sides.[3]

Gasparri's reply, June 4, reached Ruiz through a series of intermediaries: "Received telegram Monsignor Fumasoni, Holy See informs Archbishop Monsignor Ruiz that Ruiz has full confidence of Holy

See, therefore do what seems best suited to glory of God, honor Holy See, good of souls."[4]

Gasparri had given authorization. It would be Ruiz's call to make. On the afternoon of June 21, Ruiz struck a deal with Mexican president Portes Gil. All involved—especially Morrow—looked on the prospects for peace with skepticism. The laws weren't changed, but worship would be reinitiated in Mexico. The notes published later that evening by both the government and the church agreed on a cease-fire. With Ruiz's consent, the church's crusade had ended, although many of the crusaders were unwilling to accept it.

As evening came on in the Mexican capital, Ruiz and Díaz left Chapultepec Castle where the negotiations took place. They told their driver to take them to Guadalupe's basilica. Word had not yet spread of the peace. No one recognized the two dark-suited priests as they made their way through the church. There, at the altar in the basilica, they took a few minutes for themselves, emotion welling in Ruiz; prayers flowed that God might accept the decision made. Ruiz's knotted throat prohibited speech for a few moments. He composed himself, giving a brief sign of the cross—forehead, shoulder to shoulder, breast—then he looked at Díaz and said: "*Señor*, here before Most Holy Mary, I must inform you that you, Illustrious Sir, are the archbishop of Mexico."[5]

Pascual Díaz, understanding the enormity of responsibility now placed on his shoulders, replied: "*¡Hombre, qué barbaridad!*" (How barbarous!) As Díaz had said to Miranda back in 1926—"perhaps we will chosen to be martyrs, or at least misunderstood"—the new archbishop of Mexico could see what role had been laid out for him.

The two priests in plainclothes remained a few minutes longer under Guadalupe's gaze.

When the bells began tolling early on Saturday, June 22, propelled by eager lay Catholics throughout the city, Sofía del Valle had not yet arrived at the Eliseo Street residence of Cultura Femenina.[6] As director of the school, she knew Saturdays were workdays. Cultura Femenina was in session on Saturdays, but not on Thursdays and Sundays. When Sofía left her house before seven on June 22 she prepared herself for her normal commute via train and streetcar. The news of the peace had broken the night before. On Saturday the notes by Portes Gil and Ruiz were published side by side in the daily newspapers. Soon after Sofía's arrival at Eliseo Street she decided to suspend classes for the day. It still wasn't known when the priests would return to say Mass. But that didn't stop the Catholic faithful of the city, Sofía and the students of Cultura Femenina included, from giving thanks.[7]

Throughout the Mexican capital, from the well-to-do colonias to the humble shanty neighborhoods far from the fashionable Reforma Boulevard, they began to make their pilgrimage, young and old, rich and poor, toward Guadalupe's basilica. With classes canceled, Sofía joined the three-mile trek from downtown to the outskirts of the city where the basilica stood. What seemed an unending stream of the city's people made their way during Saturday and Sunday to the national shrine, where the miraculous painted image was hung, and also to the Little Hill above the basilica, the site of Juan Diego's reported vision of the Virgin almost four centuries before. In automobiles, buses, streetcars, on foot, and on their knees, the crowds reached some one hundred thousand. "The constant stream paralyzed traffic in the vicinity for hours," recounted the *New York Times* reporter on site.[8] The impromptu pilgrimage was entirely led by the laity. No priests were seen in collars, though many of the city's eight hundred or so clerics, many of them resident exiles during the conflict, filtered through the crowds inside the shrine. No benches or pews were in place. The worshippers came in through the central doors, which had never been closed to lay Catholics during the interdict, only closed to the ministrations of priests. The liturgy had often been said by the laity, Masses without the sacramental consecration of the Eucharist. Now there was hope that the Bread of God would soon return. As the worshippers filed in, a "low steady hum" of prayer and supplication vibrated in the basilica, "whispered prayers" magnified by the church's cavernous ceiling. The crowd slowly advanced toward Guadalupe, all on penitent knees at this point, "each to bring his candle and entreaty before the shrine of the Virgin." The drips of tallow from thousands of flickering candles "fell unnoticed upon the advancing tide of worshippers, whose thoughts were outside the worldly sphere," wrote one news correspondent. Here, a prayer for peace was said; and here also men came without hats, head bared, and women with mantillas, the traditional head covering, black and somber. "Men with their wives and with children in arms formed separate groups," the reporter described, "in many instances the heads of families reading prayers to their children." "Lay workers," women like Sofía and the students from Cultura Femenina, led prayers "in obscure corners" for "illiterate folk."[9]

Sofía del Valle, amid these worshippers of all classes, ages, and sexes—Mexicans all—gave thanks as well.

After the accords had been signed and his official business done for the day, American ambassador Dwight Morrow quickly retreated to his small home in Cuernavaca, where his wife, Betty, waited for him. Exhausted, he went to bed. The next morning, Saturday, June 22, he heard the bells ringing loudly outside his home. Morrow laughed.

"Betty, I have opened the churches," he said groggily. "Now perhaps you will wish me to close them again."[10]

While Morrow joked with his wife, Ruiz spent the next week arranging for it to happen. He and Díaz conversed with Morrow, but also Portes Gil and members of his administration in efforts to make sure that registered priests could once again say Mass.[11] Ruiz also planned the official opening of worship for June 29, that resolute day when he symbolically returned the Bread of God to the Mexican people at Guadalupe's basilica. Amnesty letters were sent out to Mexican army field commanders, but not all reached their destination.[12] Nor were all cristeros willing to lay down their arms. The peace, like the sacred wafer of Communion that supported the presence of Christ, dissolved quickly over the next two years. Ruiz, the decision maker, had opened Mexico's churches—but he also had to work to keep them that way.

Miranda returned from the United States to Mexico in the summer of 1929. Pascual Díaz, now archbishop, named Miranda the man in charge of the post-peace reconstruction. Miranda headed a team of priests, Sofía assisting, to draft the new statutes for Catholic Action.[13] By the fall of 1929, four fundamental associations had been created.

Sofía put her efforts into expanding Cultura Femenina and in growing the group for young women, the JCFM.

Throughout 1930, Miranda was once again in the United States asking the NCWC for money. Miranda envisaged a permanent fund from the American church for Mexican Catholic Action. William Montavon, a lawyer working for the NCWC, rejected the idea, arguing instead that the education of secular clergy and catechism for children were more pressing needs than Catholic Action. He wrote to Rev. Burke that the idea put forward by Miranda, in its present form, was "very crude, even offensive."[14] The NCWC had its own ideas, suggesting that a "Mexican Sunday" be held to raise funds. As Miranda had said to Sofía in one letter, cementing the bonds of friendship and understanding with the Americans was a work left undone. The Mexican Church had its vision of the peace; the Americans their own.

Ironically, Miranda and Sofía did receive another donation from the NCWC in 1930 after all. However, it didn't come from American Catholics. Rather, former American ambassador Dwight Morrow, a Presbyterian and former J. P. Morgan associate, much maligned by cristeros for his role in settling the religious conflict, gave 12,500 USD to the NCWC, to be given to Archbishop Orozco y Jiménez in Jalisco and to other ministries in Mexico City. Morrow's money helped pay for two courses at Cultura Femenina that year.[15]

Sofía del Valle soon joined Miranda's travels. Although the present and future seemed to coincide with the establishment of their plan, much remained to be done. Winning the friendship of the Americans was a clear necessity. So too was their exit from the catacombs of persecution.

Interlude

LAS VIEJITAS

Recently
Headquarters of the Mexican Catholic Women's
Union, Mexico City, 11:17 a.m.

I've kept four old ladies (*viejitas*) waiting. There's a basket of untouched cinnamon-sugar donut holes on the conference table where the women sit. Everything's been set out in proper order: porcelain cups, lace doilies, and pristine tablecloth. I suspect my late arrival has held up the coffee and donuts.

I glance at the four ladies seated at the long conference table. I catch their eyes and smile as I quickly take out a notebook, set up the ws-852 digital recorder, and try to look professional.

I'm tempted to stuff a donut hole in my mouth.

We just arrived moments ago—Tere, Héctor, and I—after a mad dash from Sanborns. Our next appointment, Tere tells me, will be a surprise. I know I'm interviewing several women who knew Sofía del Valle. I don't know exactly *who* in particular.

Tere recognizes we've arrived at our destination: Headquarters of the Mexican Catholic Women's Union. The Spanish acronym is UFCM, Unión Femenina Católica Mexicana. This has been the central office of the UFCM since the 1950s.

Sofía del Valle worked for the UFCM in later years and spent time in this office. She eventually aged out of the JCFM, the group for young women she established.

The headquarters of the Mexican Catholic Women's Union hardly looks changed from when the office was established in the 1950s. There are portraits on the walls of all the popes for the last eighty years.

Tere leads us to a large meeting room. One wall is occupied by an old bookshelf filled with sacramental paraphernalia, bound volumes of the organization's magazine—*Acción Femenina* (Feminine action) it's called, which began in 1933 and is still being published today—and old manuals of Catholic doctrine. Another wall has a rollaway door behind which is an altar. Nuncios and cardinals have celebrated Mass here. Sofía at one time sat in attendance. In one corner a glass case contains what seem to be relics of some kind.

Later I'll realize that Pius XI, the pope in the 1920s and 1930s, sent the Mexican Catholic Women's Union a pair of his oval spectacles as a gift. That's what's displayed in the glass case. After a bit of jiggling, one of the women will pry the glass case open so I can examine the glasses. Pictures of Pius XI with furrowed brow will take on a whole new meaning for me after I see those thick lenses.

The women smiling across the conference table at me are the special present Tere has prepared in advance.

Surprise!

Tere told me only that she'd contacted some of the women involved in preserving the history of the UFCM. These four women are in their seventies, eighties, and nineties. In 2009 they financed the publication of an unfinished memoir Sofía dictated to a friend back in 1976. I'm hoping they have the original. The published book seems incomplete to me. It's not the full text. A priest, who also happens to be a historian, edited the original and quoted extensively from it. The memoir is the only work of life writing Sofía attempted. The other document that comes close is Sofía's interview with Alicia Olivera in 1972.

A conversation with these four women seems like a crucial step in discovering more about Sofía del Valle.

I'm way out of my league, I suddenly realize, as the four women include:

María Elena Álvarez de Vicencio, a former Mexican legislator.
Guadalupe Aguilar Fernández, a former student of Cultura Femenina.

Mercedes Gómez del Campo de Zavala, the mother-in-law to Mexico's former president, Felipe Calderón (2006–12).

María Eugenia Díaz Gastine de Pfennich, a former president of the World Union of Catholic Women's Organizations or WUCWO. (It turns out she also just so happens to be the great-granddaughter of none other than Porfirio Díaz, Mexican dictator [1876–1911].)

All of them are here to tell me about Sofía del Valle.

For a fleeting moment, a whole imagined world passes through my mind. The four women's résumés read like an imaginary wish list dreamed up by Sofía del Valle in the 1920s. And so, in this brief moment, I picture Sofía in the twenties just starting her new school, Cultura Femenina. She's got a handful of students. Another dozen or so are in the JCFM, the Catholic group she started for young women.

She has formidable obstacles.

There's the incomprehension of some of the Mexican bishops to deal with, and for that matter, the resistance of many Mexican men. The idea of educating women past primary school is not normal in that era. A woman's place is in the home, Sofía often hears repeated. There's even a proverb bandied about quite a bit in Mexico at the time: "A woman who knows Latin will never find a husband nor come to a good end." Sofía hears it said frequently. She's up against cultural norms and she's battling religious traditions. If that weren't enough, there's the Cristero War, there's hiding from government inspectors, there's a lack of money and resources.

And women in Mexico didn't even have the right to vote!

Sofía dreams anyway.

For this brief moment—before the interview begins—I picture Sofía in the twenties preparing for the future. She has a conviction about what she's doing: "If the whole world is set on fighting, then what happens when we are at peace? What happens if there is no one to work?" Sofía is convinced that she has to make sure there'll be intelligent Catholic women ready when the time is right.

Sofía's aspirations do come true in the four women sitting across from me.

The Legislator: María Elena Álvarez de Vicencio[1]
   Born: 1930
   Education: Teaching certificate (until 1980); licentiate, masters, and doctorate in political science, UNAM (1989).
   Career: Diocesan president, JCFM (1945–57); Executive Committee of Partido Acción Nacional or PAN (National Action Party) (1958–present); elected federal deputy (four terms); Mexican Senate (one term); president of the House of Deputies (Mexico's lower house of congress).
   Family: Married thirty-four years to Abel Vicencio (deceased); PAN activist; former president of ACJM; five children and fourteen grandchildren.

The Social Worker: Guadalupe Aguilar Fernández
   Born: 1924
   Education: Instituto Superior de Cultura Femenina (1945); master's degree in social work; studies in the United States observing social work.
   Career: Founded JCFM branch in Coyoacán, Mexico City; National Committee of UFCM (1961–65); director, School of Social Work, Vasco de Quiroga, Mexico City; UNESCO worker in Paraguay.
   Family: Single.

The Mother-in-Law: Mercedes Gómez del Campo de Zavala
   Born: 1932
   Education: Escuela Libre de Derecho, Mexico City (attorney).
   Career: JCFM member (Chihuahua); national counsel of PAN (1962–68); teacher at Assumption Academy, Mexico City.
   Family: Married to Diego Zavala Pérez (judge, deceased); seven children. (Her daughter, Margarita Zavala, married Felipe Calderón, Mexican president. Margarita ran for president in 2018. She didn't win, but she put up a valiant campaign.)

The Ringleader: María Eugenia Díaz Gastine de Pfennich
Born: 1940
Education: Master's degree in teaching.
Career: National president of UFCM (1989–96); president of WUCWO (1996–2006)
Family: Great-granddaughter of Porfirio Díaz. Her father was Manuel Díaz Raigosa, grandson of Porfirio Díaz.
Note: Díaz Gastine's mother transcribed Sofía's unfinished memoir.

The women begin their memories of Sofía. They speak in turn; first one at a time, then all together. I notice their stories about Sofía are stories about themselves. The women they've become find echoes in the Sofía they remember.

María Elena Álvarez de Vicencio, the legislator, describes a Sofía of ample soul, of foresight, a visionary.

"*Bueno*," Álvarez de Vicencio tells me, "I joined Catholic Action at sixteen years old."

The four-time congresswoman and senator is all of about ninety pounds. She wears her hair back in a tight bun. Her voice warbles a bit, but she speaks with conviction.

"I heard all the leaders speak about Sofía del Valle," she continues. "I formed a conception of her as a very active and hard-working woman who always thought about what lay ahead." Álvarez de Vicencio sees Sofía as a forerunner. "For having founded her groups"—the JCFM and Cultura Femenina—"I thought she was a visionary."

Álvarez de Vicencio explains how, on two occasions, she visited Sofía with a group of JCFM members. She remembers how Sofía spoke to the young women—not the content, but the manner—that Sofía had "an impressive personality." She was a woman "who had given her life to this organization that I was enchanted with," the former legislator recounts. Sofía's example helped convince Álvarez de Vicencio she could serve the church without becoming a nun. She considered it, she tells me. Instead she devoted her life to the PAN and Catholic political activism. She admits with pride that she served the party "for which Margarita is candidate for the presidency."

Later, I will find out that party politics conspired to exclude Margarita Zavala from the PAN nomination. Margarita Zavala didn't take no for an answer and will run as an independent. She will, however, drop out of the race before the general election.

Álvarez de Vicencio admires Sofía as a visionary who thought about what lay ahead, about the future. She interprets her work, like Sofía's, as one of preparation. Perhaps Álvarez de Vicencio too daydreamed at the beginning of her career of a time when a Catholic woman would run for president.

Guadalupe Aguilar Fernández, by profession a social worker, describes a fearless Sofía. She knew Sofía principally as dean of Cultura Femenina. She remembers Sofía's weekly talks to the students, recalls Sofía's confidence and her constant trips abroad, how Sofía had to raise money for the school through donations drummed up across the length and breadth of the United States. It was Sofía, remembers Aguilar Fernández, who first prodded her to visit the United States. She also mentions Sofía's friendship with a prominent feminist, Aurora Arrayales. Sofía was unafraid to sit on the committee of the organization founded by Arrayales, El Instituto de Seguridad y Servicios Sociales (the Institute of Assurance and Social Services). Aguilar Fernández recounts how she visited Sofía several months before Sofía's death. They sat together all afternoon; "her memory very good," she says. "Although at times she remembered more of the older stuff than the new."

The four women laugh. They too have discovered memory's ironies. The more distant past remains clear because of its essential role in the women they've become.

Aguilar Fernández tells me she went to Sofía's funeral. And a year ago, she attended a memorial service for Sofía held at the Metropolitan Cathedral. They installed a plaque commemorating Sofía on the niche containing her ashes. Aguilar Fernández was the only Cultura Femenina graduate to attend the memorial. The others, she says, were too afraid to travel to chaotic downtown Mexico City.

"It doesn't make me afraid," emphasizes the former social worker. "I took a taxi, arranged by telephone, and it left me at the Palacio [de] Bellas Artes."

At the other end of the table, Tere Huidobro gasps. Aguilar Fernández is ninety-three years old. It's about a mile between where the taxi left her and the Metropolitan Cathedral. The city center is clogged with traffic. And to Tere, downtown is a dangerous place for a ninety-year-old woman to walk alone.

Aguilar Fernández smiles. "I was completely happy with life."

"Notice how she is," one of the women motions at Aguilar Fernández. "That's how Sofía was."

Laughter in the room again.

Sofía: the woman unafraid to do what's necessary. Guadalupe Aguilar Fernández keeps that Sofía with her.

Mercedes Gómez del Campo de Zavala, the mother-in-law of Mexico's former president, and the mother of Margarita Zavala, the presumptive presidential candidate, remembers a different Sofía. The "visionary" and the "fearless woman" don't contradict Gómez del Campo's version. But it's still a slightly different picture. Gómez del Campo knew a Sofía who didn't justify her value to society as a mother or as a wife. "It's the most absurd notion," says the mother-in-law of a Mexican president. Sofía's value was in being human, she asserts. And so too with Gómez del Campo. She's proud of her son-in-law, proud also of her daughter. But Gómez del Campo is her own woman. She makes this clear. For instance, when she introduces herself to me it takes exactly one minute and thirty-three seconds for her to tell me her name. (I will verify this later.) Mercedes Gómez del Campo, she says; that's her name. By custom, she explains, she puts the name of her husband, *de Zavala*.

"But *de* can mean many things." She has a glimmer in her eye as she says this.

I know what she's talking about. In Spanish, *de* can mean "of" or "from." Gómez del Campo is criticizing the use of *de* for married women. It signifies property ownership.

"I'm not only his property," she quips, "but I'm also his proprietor."

She says this in a pithy way. I'm sure she's used it before. What she's describing is marriage as joint-ownership, a partnership.

Gómez del Campo is her own woman. She's been accustomed to making decisions on her own. For instance, I learn that she was kicked out of law school in San Luis Potosí. The governor of the state, Gonzalo N. Santos, claimed the entire university had signed a petition of political support in his favor. Mercedes Gómez del Campo, a young law student at the time, visited the school paper the next morning. She told the editors she hadn't signed. She demanded they print a clarification stipulating as much. By the end of the week the law faculty informed her that she wouldn't be allowed to finish her studies. She moved to Mexico City and completed law school there. She joined the PAN; she married, but continued her partisan activism.

It's unsurprising, I think to myself, that this woman's daughter, Margarita Zavala, made waves as the first First Lady to have a political career of her own before her husband was elected president. Gómez del Campo taught her daughter to be her own woman as well.

And so she tells me how Sofía was "one of the greatest examples of female celibacy": a celibate laywoman who developed a career on her own. Sofía had "an enormous impact on my life," she asserts. The character of the JCFM—"strong, decided"—came from its founder, she explains. A woman who could stand alone. The Sofía that Gómez del Campo keeps close is the Sofía who recommended women wear pants before it was culturally acceptable to do so. She tells me that's exactly what she remembers Sofía saying in the room we're sitting in.

The four women laugh at the thought of Sofía recommending pants to Catholic ladies.

Tere, from the other end of the table, interjects. "In the era that we're talking about, the women . . ." She hesitates. She's trying to formulate her thoughts. "The women didn't have what she had."

The four women agree. But to me it seems that their lives should qualify them to be on the list with Sofía.

Saints are made by the community that venerates them. It's not that the Sofías these women imagine are fictions. They're just not the whole truth. Sofía wasn't always visionary, wasn't always fearless, wasn't always independent.

I think about Sofía del Valle, the complex woman I've discovered in the archives. What gets lost in memory and saint-making is change over time.

Sofía the visionary, the fearless woman, the independent woman—all these Sofías are materializing in the room.

Perhaps this is how saints are made?

Before I can redirect, the conversation moves forcefully to Sofía the saint. María Eugenia Díaz Gastine, the ringleader of our gathering, speaks. She's the great-granddaughter of Porfirio Díaz. She was president of WUCWO. I know that that organization was the vehicle for a lot of Sofía's international work in the 1930s and beyond. Díaz Gastine is the real force behind the project to document Sofía's life. It was Díaz Gastine's mother who knew Sofía well and she who transcribed Sofía's attempt at memoir.

Díaz Gastine describes a Sofía who wouldn't be ignored. And she's made it her mission to keep Sofía's memory from being ignored in the present.

As she speaks, Gómez del Campo pipes up. "Single, Mexican, and Catholic," she quips, "all the requirements to be ignored."

Díaz Gastine agrees. She tells me a story. She explains why she feels a personal obligation to keep Sofía's memory alive. When she was president of WUCWO—this was after Sofía's death—she remembers praying for Sofía's help and guidance. She recognized that, like Sofía, she too was a woman operating in an international sphere outside her control.

"Please, Sofía," Díaz Gastine remembers praying, "if you help me during this time, when I return to Mexico, when I finish my term as president, we will search for your history. I promise it."

Díaz Gastine's role as ringleader began soon after Sofía's death. Her mother had preserved Sofía's memoir. But Díaz Gastine's mother died just two years after Sofía. It was then that she inherited the job of preserving Sofía's memory. Díaz Gastine's mother told her to do it. Her term as WUCWO president and her promise to Sofía sped up the process.

The problem was she couldn't find the memoir.

It finally appeared, she tells me, after much searching. Díaz Gastine then contacted a priest who agreed to work the memoir into a publication. It came out in 2009. Though it added some context, much of it was out of sequence.

Díaz Gastine explains that the priest, after reading the unfinished memoir, declared: "Here is true sanctity."

"But who will pay?" she offers as an afterthought.

Laywomen aren't often made saints. That's what she means by the question. Making saints is often about money, because it's a long process of promoting a cause for sainthood in Rome. Priests and nuns have built-in backing because of their religious affiliation. Most laywomen don't.

Tere intervenes. She unzips her large cloth bag and takes out a black cape with scarlet embroidered crosses. It was the cape bestowed on Sofía when the Vatican honored her.

"As you said," Tere directs herself to Díaz Gastine, "laywomen can't be saints, but it's also said that the altars should be filled with their relics." She holds up Sofía's black cape as a relic.

The four old ladies hope that Sofía might one day be canonized. But, they say, it's the job of a younger generation.

I steer the conversation back to the unfinished memoir.

"Sofía always said the memoir made no sense," Díaz Gastine says.

"Do you have the folder?" I ask.

I really want to see what's in that folder.

She tells me yes.

I smile and stuff a cinnamon-sugar donut hole into my mouth.

What gets remembered? The thought whirs through my head in an endless loop. Once it plays, it stops, rewinds, and plays again.

What gets remembered? ... ka-tschkh ... scrrrdldldl ... ka-tschkh ... What gets remembered? ... ka-tschkh ... scrrrdldldl ... ka-tschkh ... What gets remembered?

I sit at a table in a large storage room. Lining the walls are wooden built-in shelves. Boxes of books fill them; boxes also of old photographs. In front of me on the table is a thick three-ring binder. It's one

Interlude: *Las viejitas* 179

of those standard white vinyl binders; clear plastic pockets allow for easy insertion of printed cover sheets. The labeled spine reads: *Life of Sofía del Valle.*

Ka-tschkh ... scrrrdldldl ... ka-tschkh ... What gets remembered? ...

I follow Díaz Gastine through the headquarters of the UFCM. She's hunting for photographs and for what amounts to Sofía's attempt to write her own life story.

We pass through the hallway toward the storage room. A piece of furniture catches her eye. It's a tall wooden pedestal with a plant on top. She grins at me. She says she almost forgot; this might be of some interest to me. She asks me to lift the plant off the top. She doesn't want to hurt her back, and since I'm young and strong, would I mind?

I lift the plant off the wood pedestal and place it on the floor next to the base. Díaz Gastine scurries forward and dislodges the pedestal with an easy tug. I look inside the shallow cavity revealed when the pedestal's removed.

"For hiding the consecrated wafers." Díaz Gastine smiles. "Sofía told my mother to keep this as a reminder of the days when they had to hide from police inspection."

I think about Cultura Femenina during the Cristero War. Holding Mass in private residences was illegal. Sofía concocted a ready-made hiding place for Communion wafers. If the police came looking for incriminating evidence, they could hide it here—in a shallow box inside the pedestal.

"Wow," is all I manage to respond. What else is hidden in these offices?

Díaz Gastine leaves me alone with Sofía's life story preserved in a three-ring binder. The four women, as well as Tere Huidobro and Héctor, are across the hallway in the conference room.

Inside the binder, the life story's in typescript. Of the three copies, one's clearly a computer version; someone's transcribed it recently. Another's a photocopy of the original. And so it's the original, with notes written in margins, with pen strokes through certain words and sentences, that draws my interest and attention.

The click-rewind-click-play starts in my head again. *What gets remembered?*

Memory is a funny thing. What gets remembered has more to do with the story one wants to tell than with the simple recall of facts from the past. What one remembers is not merely a product of functioning, or faulty, mental record keeping. Memory is performance. It's an argument about what mattered, what didn't matter, and what meaning can be drawn from those events selected for presentation. And when one's own life is the subject of presentation, it's an argument about the self. Identity. Memory constantly gets rewritten in the light of what one has become.

What gets remembered are those things that match with self-definition: here's who I am and here's how I got this way.

What strikes me about Sofía's memoir is that part of her identity is here.

The memoir in front of me is a record of some of Sofía's mental visits to the past. The same can be said of the 1972 interview with Alicia Olivera. They tell me about Sofía's internal world, her feelings, her experience. The memoir and the interview aren't careful historical practices. Sometimes memories are fictions—stories coated in sugar for easy consumption. Yet I can't get away from the idea that historians write fictions too. There is no history as it happened. The minute we select what goes in, what gets left out, and what we make of it, we're susceptible to the same foibles as memory.

History and memory need each other. History gives context. It aspires to precision. Memory, on the other hand, provides immediacy. It aspires to authenticity, individual experience. History and memory can both be painful. But history, if it's done right, tells a truth even when it hurts to tell it. Memory can hurt too, but its edges have a way of softening over time. It's hard to live with ambiguity, hard also to live with open wounds.

I make up my mind to put my history in conversation with Sofía's memories.

Her memoir sits on the table in front of me. It strikes me as funny that Sofía felt her memoir made no sense. True, it's out of sequence, but life can feel like that. The memoir starts in 1922 with her return to Mexico. Then it backtracks to her childhood and family. It ends in the 1940s, and abruptly, in the middle of a sentence. Was a page lost? I wonder. Or, perhaps she got tired of her trips to the past? Maybe she couldn't make those trips as often? Did her memory fade?

As for the precision of the memoir, it's sharp. It's the same with her interview with Alicia Olivera in 1972. Her omissions seem less to do with forgetting than a desire to withhold. Rarely does she forget important details. Some names are wrong, but not very often. At the end of the memoir is a single-page document, set off from the rest. It was written by Díaz Gastine's mother. She describes Sofía's declining health and her death in 1982.

I want to know more about that time. There's barely anything about her later years in the archives.

And then there's something else that grabs my attention. I realize that to get to the end, I'll have to finish the middle. Very early in Sofía's first-person memoir, she relates the story of her entrance into an international career. It's clearly important, taking up a large portion of the manuscript. It's a memory, I realize, of how Sofía learned to survive as a woman alone.

PART 4

A Woman Alone

17

Out of the Shadows

> The participation of the laity in the apostolate of the hierarchy.
> Definition of Catholic Action given by Pope Pius XI in 1927

The peace of June 1929 meant work for Sofía del Valle. *A lot* of work.

But it was work she didn't face alone. With Miranda's return to Mexico, Sofía didn't fade into the background of an expanding Catholic movement. The explosion of responsibilities that came with the peace—making the JCFM and the other branches of Catholic Action operational, for instance—required Miranda and Sofía to work in the same mission, but rarely in the same place at the same time. Miranda continued as the leader of the Social Secretariat and the man in charge of implementing Catholic Action. He was also still the nominal head of Cultura Femenina and the priest with ultimate authority over the JCFM. But his duties required attention to the Catholic movement writ large, on a national scale. As a kind of chief operations officer of Catholic Action, his focus was increasingly vision casting, training leaders, and fundraising. Sofía's sphere had grown with the peace.

Not only was Sofía the prefect, later dean, of Cultura Femenina, she was the national president of the JCFM. The work she put her hand to would be principally reinforced by a growing group of young women. Like her, they were single and educated, with ambitions to use professional expertise to assist in the Catholic reconstruction of Mexico.

The peace that brought a bit of distance between Miranda and Sofía on a day-to-day basis also brought a geographical spread of the Catholic movement. The Eliseo Street residence, where Sofía had weathered the persecution, was abandoned for a bigger house, at 25 Guillermo Prieto Street, southeast of downtown.[1] The Motolinía Street residence, confiscated in 1928, was reclaimed, and there Miranda had his offices. The central bureau of the four Catholic Action organizations set up at Motolinía Street. One house had grown to two.

From the house on Guillermo Prieto Street the JCFM and Cultural Femenina grew rapidly. Eight founding members of the JCFM quickly grew to twenty. By the spring of 1930, the JCFM had been established in nine parishes of the capital with 972 members.[2] Lay people were apostles; or, at least they had been given the freedom to participate with priests and bishops in apostolic work—and that was the tension. Were they apostles in their own right? Theologically, the answer was no—only the ordained were considered apostles. But Sofía and her lay disciples certainly began acting like ones. The theology of the laity was slow in forming. Lay people could *assist* in the apostolic work only, according to Catholic Action norms.[3] In practice, Sofía and the JCFM were doing the work that needed to be done—visitations, organization, outreach, counsel, meetings. They didn't say Mass or give the sacraments, but they were becoming the public face of post-cristero Catholicism.

If the peace of June 1929 brought expansion, growing pains were not far behind.

The plan envisioned by Miranda and implemented by Sofía—elite training first, action second—seemed to be bearing fruit. The young JCFM members held "Parish Days" throughout the capital. There, the rationale and spirit of Catholic Action was explained, new members were signed up, and parish councils were formed. The next three national presidents of the JCFM were already associated with Cultura Femenina at the time. Juana Arguinzóniz was then the subdirector of the liberal arts school. Aurora de la Lama, Eugenia Olivera, and Isabel Gibbon were then in the midst of studying at Cultura Femenina. A fourth JCFM president, Emma Ziegler, was in Puebla at the time. She and her sister Felícitas had been early promoters of the JCFM during the Cristero War. The Zieglers had helped build the organization to almost three hundred members in Puebla state. Young women in Zamora (Michoacán) and León (Guanajuato) also soon established groups. By the end of 1930 twenty-two dioceses, out of a total of thirty-eight, had JCFM branches—8,605 registered members in 133 parishes nationwide.[4] The JCFM made up almost 30 percent of Catholic Action in the first years of operation. The only branch with more members was the Damas Católicas, rechristened now as the Mexican Catholic Women's Union (Unión Femenina Católica Mexicana or UFCM).[5] The UFCM, however, had a head start of nearly two decades to build upon—the JCFM, for their part, had only been around less than five years. The expansion under Sofía del Valle's leadership was startling.

Internal feuds lingered over the accords Ruiz had consented to. By the government's accounting, dubious at best, some fourteen thousand cristero rebels were peacefully mustered out in the weeks after the peace came. One historian calculated that as many as fifty thousand cristeros were fighting at the time of the June 1929 peace. As the peace came, planes flew over the western states—Jalisco and Michoacán principally—dropping leaflets to unreached militants, informing them that the war they'd been fighting was over.[6] The cristeros mistrusted these assurances. Why would they now trust the government's paper assurances of safe conduct? Even among those who laid down their arms, many took them up again a few years later. Some fought on until the early 1940s. One historian estimates as many as five thousand cristeros died after the official "peace" of 1929.[7] Many were the target of personal vendettas, some fell outside the federal government's ability to protect them from local bosses hostile to the church, and still others suffered official retribution from the state.[8]

The survivors didn't emerge unscarred either. Thousands of emigrants—their homes demolished, their towns burned, ash and soot covering all—left Mexico's heartland for the United States. Mexico's Cristero War added to the pressures—demographic and economic—that drove a first Great Migration of Mexicans to the United States in the 1920s. At least 1.5 million Mexicans, from the newly arrived to those of ethnic heritage, resided in America by 1930.[9] War casualties reached almost one hundred thousand dead, while at least equal that amount perished from disease and hunger or were wounded and disabled because of the civil war for Christ the King.[10] The plan for Mexico's tomorrow seemed far too small a bandage for such wounds.

After the peace came, the chief task of the Mexican hierarchy was to implement an international model of Catholic Action. In theory, the movement was defined as the participation of the laity in the apostolic work of the hierarchy.[11] Thus imagined, Catholic activists built through this apostolate a parallel hierarchy of the laity. Just as bishops held the highest rank in the Catholic hierarchy, urban, hispanicized lay elites held the most power in the Catholic Action movement, at least in terms of the structural formation. International Catholic Action on the Roman model emanated from Europe, was received by the national bishops, and duly delegated to middle- and upper-class Catholics, who took their role seriously and often moved quickly to implement the organization first in the archdiocese, then in the parishes of the capital, and after to the auxiliary dioceses and parishes of the republic. The annual bishops' meetings debated how to organize Catholic Action within national contexts, setting up episcopal subcommittees with direct control of the organization, usually designating one or more bishops to be the national assessors of the movement. From there, four main branches were established through a series of directives agreed upon by the bishops: men, women, young men, and young women.[12]

If the Vatican secretariat of state thought it necessary, the process was assisted by a pontifical letter, drafted by the papal bureaucracy, but duly signed by Pius XI. Not all Latin American countries received such a letter. It was a mark of distinction when it could be solicited or urged by bishops and lay Catholics.[13] The letter provided legitimacy for the work of reorganization of the Catholic movements in Latin America—from a loose confederation of associations to a highly corporate structure—that naturally needed to take place and was often a strategy at eliminating the multiplicity of ideas about what Catholic Action meant. The letters were always received and interpreted through the lens of previous organizational attempts. But they lent an urgency to the work of establishing Catholic Action on a Roman model. The branches of women and young men had operated in many Latin American republics in some form for over two decades. The Roman model meant that the branches would be expanded, encompassing a national committee, often called a junta, of the presidents of the four main branches. The pattern was also to be established on the diocesan and parish levels. At each level the hierarchy was certainly present, from the national assessor of Catholic Action on down to the diocesan and parish ecclesiastical assistants. But lay Catholics established diocesan and parish centers for each branch—usually the elite lay Catholics of the capital, who received with their apostolic mandate a new authority and wide berth for action.[14]

For Sofía the burst of fast-paced growth was a coming out, a public entrée. On June 8, 1930, the JCFM celebrated the Feast of Pentecost at the Church of La Profesa in downtown Mexico City. For the last three years Sofía and the JCFM had celebrated Pentecost in secret, on a rural hacienda owned by a Catholic who'd donated space for the event. Now they could worship *inside* a church. And not just *any* church: La Profesa was located in the heart of the city. Pentecost celebrates the sending of the Holy Spirit on the original apostles of Jesus fifty days after his resurrection—tongues of fire descending upon them in irradiated spiritual power. Power to be witnesses. Power also to make a stand for the church of Christ. (The original Greek for "witness" is the root word for "martyr".) La Profesa was adorned with flowers. Some four hundred young female apostles—the word's literal meaning is "sent ones"—filled the sacred space. In place of tongues of fire, candlelight shimmered above their bowed heads.[15]

Miranda preached the sermon. Sofía sat with the women, overcome by emotion. Perhaps she recalled that it had been here, at La Profesa, where Alfredo Méndez Medina had invited her to join the Social Secretariat back in 1922. Back then, the mission to women had been just an idea, a desire. Now it was real. The gathering was a fulfillment, partial certainly, but still a realization of Sofía and Miranda's long work of preparation. Eucharist—Apostolate—Heroism: Miranda presented these three words as the pillars of the young women's movement. "Only in the Eucharist," he said, "can young women encounter the power necessary to obtain the goal of organization, which is nothing less than the apostolate"—in other words, the church's missionary outreach to the world—"and the measure of the apostolate should be, if necessary, heroism."[16] The Bread of God would sustain them. Their mission was

Christian restoration. They were to give all they had to accomplish their goal. Eucharist—Apostolate—Heroism was to be the JCFM's motto, its statement of value and of mission. These were the words printed on the association's journal, called *Juventud* (Youth), which first went to print in April 1930. The motto also adorned the shields and banners hung up around La Profesa as Miranda spoke. Mass was said, the Eucharist consecrated and then distributed by Archbishop Pascual Díaz.

Later that evening at the Motolinía Street residence, the JCFM leaders reported their accomplishments so far. Sofía, named the JCFM's first national president, presided. The JCFM "presents itself for the first time in public," she told those gathered, "full of hope, anxious to take up all its activities in fulfillment of its very important part in the work of the Christian restoration of Mexico."[17] In a later issue of *Juventud* Sofía likewise wrote of the experience of going public. "The last three [years] were spent in the catacombs and now for the first time [Cultura Femenina] presents itself publicly to society." It seemed to Sofía that the troubles of the past were finally receding. "During 1926, barely able to contain our impatience and [driven by] our irrepressible desire to labor for the church, we began the work of training the first young women that would be presented ready one day, that is to say today, in a tight phalanx in order to complete the apostolic mission for which they have been called with enthusiasm and generosity."[18] One day had become *today*. It felt like the future had arrived.

18

The New Woman

Sofía and the women around her—women like Juana Arguinzóniz, Aurora de la Lama, and a host of others—found in their mission, and in one another, meaning and purpose. One former graduate of Cultura Femenina and an early JCFM member put it this way: "That band of enthusiastic young women meeting at . . . 25 Guillermo Prieto Street felt that this organization had come to fill the emptiness in their lives. . . . We all need lives in common," she continued, "to have soul mates who understand us, to feel the stimulus of their example, to be warmed in the passion of their enthusiasm . . . all this we found in the organization. We understood that we needed to organize to stretch the large loop of sisterly love farther to all Catholic young women in Mexico." The young women felt it a "great and noble cause to which their energies were concecrated."[1]

Sofía stood at the center of a growing sisterhood. She was older, at almost forty, than the average JCFM member or Cultura Femenina student. The majority fell between fifteen and twenty-five, although thirty-five was the suggested cutoff for membership in the JCFM. Marriage also meant an exit from the group. Sofía was the older sister who was looked up to, admired.

A photograph from the early 1930s shows Sofía again in a garden scene. It hints at maturity and evolution. The light-colored cotton dress of earlier years—low-waisted, fitting in with 1920s style—has disappeared. In its place Sofía wears more serious attire. The change was at least in part due to shifting fashion ideals. The styles of the 1930s returned the waist to its natural place; calf-length dresses were common again, the upper body and bust were emphasized in cropped jackets and defined shoulders.[2] But the change in Sofía's style also came from her station. She was dean of a school, president of a national

17. Sofía del Valle, ca. 1930. Personal collection of María Teresa Ruiz de Huidobro Márquez.

association. Hairstyles in the 1930s changed as well. The boyish bob evolved into more voluminous demi-waves, finger curls, and perms. Sofía's hair reflects this shift. It's clipped back with a slight wave. Small adornments such as earrings can be seen in the photograph, and also a ring, a sign of her commitment to God and to celibacy. In coming years she would always wear a string of pearls. Owing to her status as a single woman she bore the title "señorita"—"Miss." But Sofía was a woman approaching middle age. She had the air of a professional.

The younger women in Sofía's circle took notice. María de la Luz Lazo, a student at Cultura Femenina in 1930, later described Sofía as a woman of rich "capacities," "culturally balanced, refined" and with "exquisite bearing." "She opened a large horizon for us," Lazo maintained. "For the first time we could see that a woman could consecrate her life entirely to God without being a nun, without having the depressing and forlorn aspect of many souls dedicated to religious activities, which are frequently confused with sanctity." Each day at Cultura Femenina, Lazo and the other students observed their dean. Sofía, Lazo recalled, "made us realize that it was possible to successfully combine a complete surrender to the Lord and continue being attractive, elegant, joyful: to travel, speak languages, be refined, sophisticated, interested always in the cultural and spiritual manifestations of her era." What they saw in her they wanted for themselves.[3]

As viewed by others, Sofía's life was becoming an ideal, an aspirational type, a model for Catholic women. Sofía's vision of womanhood was new in her public confidence, her cultural facility, her demand for intellectual equality with men—new in her professional ambition, even. Yet Sofía's vision was old in her acceptance of a male-dominated hierarchy, conservative in her commitment to chaste sexuality, traditional in adhering to complementary gender roles. Sofía wrote in the pages of *Juventud* that she desired the members of the JCFM to be "representatives of the 'Mexican Catholic Ideal.'"[4] She herself endeavored to embody it, balancing the new and the old in what like-minded Catholic contemporaries in the United States called True Womanhood. Sofía, like many women of her day who remained deeply pious and culturally engaged, was a "new woman of the old faith."[5]

Like all ideals, aspiration is one thing, reality another. In the early 1930s Sofía led a school that taught between thirty and seventy students each year. They were young, Sofía acknowledged; and in a sense, she considered their immaturity natural. They broke windows playing volleyball, they talked too loudly in the common rooms, yelled from the top

18. Students of Cultura Femenina on field day, ca. 1930–32. Photograph, Archivo Histórico del Arzobispado de México, base Miguel Darío Miranda, caja 8a.

of stairways to get the attention of their professors—an indiscretion particularly foul to Sofía since the professors were also priests.[6] The students distracted one another in classes. Luz Lazo, who wrote of her profound respect for Sofía, was reprimanded by one professor for "interrupting class with impertinent questions." Consuelo Barousse, who spearheaded her own parish branch of the JCFM, "was accustomed to passing the time drawing" in her Mexican history class. An early report from the prim professor of English, Miss Mary Hawkins Jones, stated: "the pupils have been unpunctual and inattentive to their duties."[7] The students wore tight-fitting, too-short skirts, very much in fashion. Some students never procured the books recommended by their professors, whether due to lack of funds or simple lack of interest is not clear. In short, they were regular, young college students.

For Sofía, lover of order and respectability, it was a challenge she meant to face. Each student was furnished with a copy of the *Regulation for the Students of Cultura Femenina*. Sofía's two assistants, Juana Arguinzóniz and Rafaela Elguero, operated as disciplinary prefects. Two-thirds of the classes had to be attended or the student would not be allowed to take the exam. "The entrance and exit from the classroom," stated the document, "will be done in orderly fashion." When a student was late, "they should enter in the back of the class." "Composure and silence" should be maintained during instruction, read the rules crafted by Sofía. "Due respect" should be given to teachers and superiors, and the students "will observe in their conduct, the dignity appropriate for a young Christian woman." Sofía's *Regulation* stated:

1) If one's skirt is narrow and short it should be covered by one's bag, or in its absence with a purse.
2) An appeal to all students: No speaking to professors from the top of the stairway.
3) If one forgets one's handkerchief in class, please do not interrupt, simply go to the library where they can be had wholesale.[8]

For Sofía, the dignity of a Christian woman meant modesty, proper decorum, and due respect. Some presence of mind didn't hurt, either.

As dean of Cultura Femenina, Sofía demanded a professional atmosphere. Even the most obvious was pointed out: notebooks should be purchased, preferably grid-lined. If needed, she wrote, "a magnifying glass" should be obtained "to facilitate the reading of pages of text." And as for the broken windows, Sofía stipulated that the guilty student "would be obliged to bring a sheet of newspaper to keep out the wind." Yet for all of Sofía's severe desire for discipline, there was humor. If a student unstuck a classroom desk from its place, she wrote, the culprit "should bring candy-coated chewing gum" to fix it. Sofía certainly knew this was an insufficient solution, but it highlighted the school's scarce resources; perhaps if they remembered Sofía's dry humor, it would help the students take better care not to break something in the first place. "But make sure it's Chiclet Adams!" Sofía joked, referring to a quality brand of the era.[9]

Sofía and Miranda courted numerous foreign visitors and potential donors throughout the 1930s. She wanted the students of Cultura Femenina to show off their "training" to these guests. "Due to the large number of foreign visitors that we are honored to receive," Sofía

19. Students at Cultura Femenina, ca. 1930. Photograph, Archivo Histórico del Arzobispado de México, base Miguel Darío Miranda, caja 175, exp. 24.

wrote to the young women, "in this very hour the students will learn to say 'Good by' [*sic*], 'Good morning,' 'Thank you,' Oh! yes. To smile placidly and nod with one's head although one would rather say no." Sofía's tone—"this very hour"—suggests that some Cultura Femenina students didn't much like giving placid smiles and nodding their heads for foreign visitors.[10] Courtesy was a must. Anything else was unacceptable to Sofía.

Sofía was outwardly pleasant and sophisticated. Underneath, she was emotional and passionate, as her relationship with Miranda suggests. But she could also be strict and unbending. She was a woman of demanding expectations.

The ideal was printed in school brochures. Miranda's scrapbook he collected during his travels—photos sent by Sofía—evolved into sleek advertising pamphlets. They distributed them in Mexico City; they mailed them to other dioceses in Mexico and to the United States. One showed up in the files of the NCWC at the Catholic University of America.[11] Order and respectability are pictured. In one photograph,

20. "Respectable" students in class at Cultura Femenina, ca. 1930. Photograph, Archivo Histórico del Arzobispado de México, base Miguel Darío Miranda, caja 175, exp. 24.

the students look with focus at the open books before them, the desks in ordered rows. Each dons a white smock, conferring a clinical lab-coat look.

Cultura Femenina wasn't just etiquette training. It wasn't a cotillion. Order and respectability had their ends. They were guards against contemporary dangers. "With every passing day," wrote Sofía in the school brochure, "it becomes apparent, in our current era, that women need to prepare for a life more difficult and painful than in times past." She recognized and embraced that the sphere of women's "activities are widening." "New obligations" also "assign new rights," she added. But there were also "new dangers" that "demand a more complete and more solid training." A "balance between economic necessities and aptitude and expertise in work" had to be struck, she continued. "You have been called"—appealing to her female audience—"to be an advocate of culture in our nation and a most effective civilizing factor in it, now influencing in the intimacy of the home, now outside of it

The New Woman 197

with many resources at your fingertips, preparing for such a momentous mission in the most opportune and effective manner possible."[12]

Order and respectability were guards against the dangers of the times. And though these dangers didn't get printed in the brochure, Sofía's readers would have understood them. There were dangers in fashion, in romance, in the work place; dangers that thrust women out of the home, away from maternal obligation and faith. Sofía rejected the New Woman in so far as she represented a rejection of tradition. She rejected what she saw as the fierce individualism of the feminist. She refused the idea of self-development without self-sacrifice. Sofía was under no illusion that women should—or could—inhabit submissive, voiceless, domestic obscurity. New rights she accepted. But for her, they came with obligation and responsibility. In Sofía's vision, neither family life nor the world outside could be abandoned. Hence, for her, this meant "a life more difficult and painful than in times past."[13]

The vision Sofía imparted at Cultura Femenina, and in the JCFM, was of a Catholic-inspired True Womanhood. This meant that women were equal with men, but not the same. There was a "feminine culture" distinct from male culture that Sofía endeavored to develop. True Womanhood, for Sofía, included maternity, but it could also extend to spiritual motherhood for celibate women. Equality with men meant self-development, education, but she balanced these with sacrifice and familial responsibility. Aptitude and ambition were necessary, Sofía believed, but only in the service of others—family, nation, church. Ambition, she felt, could lead to selfish individualism, which was at odds with Catholic True Womanhood.[14] In other words, Sofía affirmed, one's personal happiness was not the measure of a woman's success, nor should it be the chief end of a woman's life. Her vision of True Womanhood would've had much in common with the late nineteenth-century "woman movement" in Europe and the United States. Temperance societies and suffragettes upheld similar ideals.[15] By the 1930s, however, that was not the case. Sofía del Valle might have appeared hopelessly out of date to Margaret Sanger, a leading advocate of sex education, birth control, and the belief that feminism was grounded in a woman's right to control her own body.[16] But comparisons are always relative. Within the Catholic Church, Sofía was on the cutting edge. She affirmed higher education for women. She felt Catholic women should and could professionalize. She believed that all women should be concerned with protecting the home, yet not all women were called to marriage and birthing children.[17]

Soon attacks were directed at Sofía. But she encountered resistance not for her vision of educating women—at least not for the time being. Resistance came at first because Sofía was dead set against reigniting a war for Christ the King. It was from within the church that Sofía would experience the most resistance in the early 1930s.

19

Resistance

> "You've got it right there, Sully, but did you hear the other definition going round?"
> "The other one?"
> "Yes. 'Catholic Action is the interference of the laity in the inactivity of the hierarchy.'"
> Thomas K. Sullivan, *One Happy Old Priest*

Peace, organizational extension, mounting membership rolls—the first eighteen months of Catholic Action seemed a resounding success on paper. Yet paper told only part of the story. There was resistance, push back, within the Catholic movement in Mexico. Resistance to Miranda and Sofía's plan for the future came not from red-eyed revolutionaries but from Catholics.

Cristeros, as well as members of the Catholic Defense League and their sympathizers, made up the main ranks of the resistance to Catholic Action. Many Jesuits also put up a fierce battle of foot dragging, eye rolling, and noncompliance. Pascual Díaz, the new archbishop, was a Jesuit, so the anti–Catholic Action sentiment wasn't universal within the Society of Jesus. But prominent members of the order in Mexico had seconded armed resistance, men like Alfredo Méndez Medina. After all, it had been their religious brother, Miguel Pro, who had been martyred for the cause. It was not something easily forgotten, the execution of Pro—not something easily stomached to simply give up the fight and negotiate with the very government who had killed Pro.

Part of the resisters' critique had some merit. They felt Catholic Action was simply not up to the task of defending the Catholic faith against its enemies. "Our enemies in Mexico neither fear Pontifical

Masses, nor religious solemnities, nor the splendor of worship," wrote an incensed Méndez Medina to his Jesuit superiors in Rome.[1] The religious activities promoted by Catholic Action, he continued, had the consequence of "contenting the people, that is lulling them to sleep, distracting their attention, assuring that attention is not directed toward other more profound necessities, like liberty of education, political liberty, etc." What irked Jesuits like Méndez Medina was that attention to civil liberties *had* been part of the League's platform; civil liberties *had* been part of the Young Men's Catholic Association, the ACJM. But no longer. Miranda helped rewrite the goals, methods, and means of Mexico's Catholic organizations. Miranda stuck to the pope's idea that Catholic Action was not to be a surrogate political party. The problem Méndez Medina was acutely aware of was that, in Mexico, Catholics were denied the right to form *any* political parties at all. It was against the law. Now it appeared that the Catholic Church itself was doing likewise. The revolutionaries had banned Catholics from politics and so too had Catholic Action. It angered Méndez Medina that, after the peace came, Catholic Action seemed to strip away anything political from the Catholic movement. Catholic Action seemed too pious, too cordoned off into education, into training, and into formation, according to resisters like Méndez Medina. "Religious action, in itself, is always necessary," he wrote, "but not sufficient for the proposed end, that is to defend the faith combatted by the holders of public power."[2]

The resisters' critique of Catholic Action hinged also on personal antipathies. If they hated the peace accords of 1929, they came to loath Ruiz and Díaz who had brought about that peace. Another Jesuit, writing from Guadalajara, didn't mince words: "What is certain is the peace accords have been a horrible blunder and they have deceived those that form the Mafia that govern us, to wit, Ruiz . . . and Pascual Díaz, and through them the deceit has reached the pope."[3] Méndez Medina, for his part, expressed his dislike for Miranda in one tirade to Rome. "Catholic Action, according to the pope's thinking at least, is not so bad," the Jesuit wrote, "but as conceived by its callow director or 'dictator' Dr. Miranda, it is a complete bust, in addition to other reasons, for its complete economic breakdown. They are behind on the rent, on salaries for employees, light, telephones." Méndez Medina grumbled over Miranda's "lack of adaptation" of Catholic Action to Mexico's unique environment and for his "lack of tact" in implementing his plan.[4]

It's tempting to think resentment, at least in part, fueled Méndez Medina's fury. The Jesuit was approaching his mid-fifties in 1930. He was frequently ill, often writing letters from his sickbed. His dry wit and wry sense of humor began to tend toward the cynical and the bitter. The Social Secretariat had been Méndez Medina's creation. It was wrested away from him in its prime. Of course, this was partially his fault, considering the serious charges against him of sexual misconduct. Yet part of it wasn't Méndez Medina's doing. Jesuit policy had shifted under him—Society policy wanted to minimize the role members of the order played in economic projects like the Social Secretariat. Miranda, as the new director, had been Méndez Medina's protégé of sorts. During the transition of leadership, Miranda wrote constantly asking Méndez Medina's advice.[5] It had even been Méndez Medina who had been a comfort to Miranda after the death of Miranda's father in 1928. Over time, Méndez Medina watched as the Social Secretariat had become a tool for Catholic Action. His former Social Secretariat was now the administrator of Catholic Action. Two bishops—Ruiz and Díaz—had made it so. And Miranda was working with them. Méndez Medina's plan for the future had been organizing a Catholic labor movement. That plan seemed discarded now; in its place were four organizations that, to him, talked endlessly about educating for tomorrow. All of this was salt packed into still festering wounds. The idealistic, young, Jesuit labor organizer had become a middle-aged nonentity in terms of leadership. He didn't simply accept that fate. He raged against it. "There is no worse fight," he growled in one letter, "than the one not undertaken."[6]

As the jewels in the Catholic Action crown, the JCFM and Cultura Femenina came under attack as well. Sofía's own role was criticized. The exact nature of the criticism is unclear. But it seems Sofía—connected with Miranda, Ruiz, and Díaz as she was—became a target. One Jesuit wrote of the "holy women" who surrounded Díaz, who did nothing but "adulate" him.[7] Perhaps Sofía was cast as one of these. But whatever the content of the attacks, they felt real to Sofía. She mentioned in one letter to Miranda of "the great opposition to Catholic Action and to our ministries of Cultura Femenina and Juventud [the JCFM], and against myself and against you."[8] The pressure reached a point where Díaz and Miranda concluded that Sofía should travel to Europe. Ostensibly the trip was for training. She could attend conferences, take a course offered on Catholic Action in Paris, as well as make contacts with women leaders on the continent. Yet privately, there was another reason for the trip. Her health was declining again; there were troubles with her liver, which put strain on her digestive system. She complained of stomach problems and even bouts with what was probably colitis. Sofía was tired and depressed by late 1930. She left Mexico with doubts about her future with Catholic Action. Would she be replaced in her absence? The jubilation she'd felt at thinking the future had arrived faded. The future seemed once again to be out of reach.

20

Les femmes internationales

In her pilgrimages across borders Sofía would find a new place in the second half of her life. Much of her youth had been spent in Europe, while her early adulthood was lived in Mexico. Middle age would be spent bridging those worlds—Europe and Latin America—and connecting them through friendships and organizations. Her life would be a bridge across the seas.

Miranda's mission in 1928 and 1929 had been for the future. Sofía had remained at home, in "the nest," as she and Miranda called it. Now she was venturing abroad, and it was Miranda who stayed at home in Mexico, at least for the first part of her absence.

The letters between Sofía and Miranda began to multiply. During the Cristero War Sofía learned self-reliance and, when her efforts fell short, faith. Now she needed these in abundance. Facing new challenges— the worlds of international Catholicism—would require her to act on her own to an even greater degree. But the tether was not sundered. Her letters were a link, not only to Miranda, an intimate friend, but to a sense of control and order, one where she felt more comfortable carrying out orders than giving them. She feared failing in Europe. It was as if, to Sofía, following orders was a failsafe. If she acted in accordance with the demands and wishes of others, she could relieve herself from bearing full responsibility for the consequences if she failed.

The troubles of Mexico City receded from Sofía's mind as she was carried by train to the Laredo border crossing on November 17, 1930.[1] Rail brought her to New York and then a steamship, with a thrifty tourist third cabin ticket, ferried her to England. In London Sofía's youngest sister waited. Once again, and not for the last time, she found some peace in the embrace of her family.

Consuelo, the youngest del Valle sibling, was twenty-four in 1930, some fifteen years the junior of her big sister Sofía. Consuelo was born shortly before the del Valle's left Mexico for Europe in 1907. She joined the Assumptionist order and was on the cusp of making her final vows as a professed nun. Her training was at a large convent located near Kensington Square in London.

Sofía spent several weeks there, taking part in the nuns' celebration of the Feast of the Immaculate Conception, an important holiday dedicated to the Virgin Mary. She savored her "free moments with Mother Consuelo," Sofía wrote Miranda, "being with her and chatting about everything and everyone."[2] Two of their sisters, Ana María and Clara, had recently given birth to new nieces and nephews. They caught up on family news and gossip. Their oldest sister, Matilde, who still lived in Spain taking care of their grandmother, had told the family of *abuelita*'s failing health. Perhaps, Sofía thought, she could persuade Matilde to return to Mexico with her after their grandmother passed.

At the convent, Sofía sampled the life of a nun. It had purpose and felt ordered. "The women religious carry on a very complete liturgical life," she reported to Miranda, "the solemn vespers they sang . . . and the Mass and Offices with Gregorian chant have given me intense spiritual satisfaction."[3]

The nuns, for their part, peppered Sofía with questions. What was it like in Mexico under persecution? The nuns sat rapt as Sofía described her experiences, hiding from police inspection, the danger of life as a Catholic outlaw of sorts. Tales of the modern martyrs, Miguel Pro included, fueled the imaginations of nuns like Sofía encountered in London. They could live vicariously through Sofía, fantasizing about being persecuted for Jesus and remaining faithful through it all. Mexico was a powerful story in those days. Sofía found she had a talent for telling the story of Mexican persecution. She immediately was invited by the nuns of the Assumption to give several semipublic talks on the subject.

Was this to become part of her mission? Sofía wondered about the idea in a letter to Miranda. Perhaps she could speak about Mexico to those interested in assisting the work there?

Les femmes internationales

The two del Valle sisters, Sofía and Consuelo, left England a few days after the Feast of the Immaculate Conception. They were headed to Belgium, where the Mother House of the Assumptionist order awaited. It was the headquarters of the order of nuns Consuelo belonged to, and where novices like Consuelo professed their final vows. Sofía felt fortunate to be with her sister for such an important rite of passage. So they traded one convent in Kensington Square for another in Val Notre Dame, located in the Meuse Valley, not far from the town of Huy, and just a bit farther from Liege in southern Belgium.

The fog they left in London greeted them in the Meuse Valley. The weather patterns throughout Europe were dreadful in December 1930. Freezing weather at ground level met high-pressure systems, creating a temperature inversion; hence, fog was trapped under a closed ceiling of clouds. In the Meuse Valley, however, the fog turned deadly. The area along the River Meuse held the distinction of being one of the most industrialized regions in continental Europe. Steelworks, zinc smelters, glass manufacturers, fertilizer factories, even explosives plants crowded the river valley. As factory chimneys billowed their toxic breath—the tallest chimneys unfortunately couldn't reach above the atmospheric ceiling—the pollution hung heavy in the dense fog. Coughing fits, laryngeal irritation, respiratory complications—asthmatic symptoms in the main—but also nausea and vomiting, beset the people of the valley, not far from the Val Notre Dame convent. The aged, the infirm, and those with cardiac conditions suffered most. In a few short days approximately sixty people died. It was the first scientifically observable instance of lethal smog.[4] When Sofía and Consuelo arrived in Belgium, the worst of it had passed.

The convent at Val Notre Dame was nestled in rolling hills with neatly manicured fields and skirted by a thin layer of woods. A photograph from the period gives no indication that the pastoral serenity was just a few miles from the industrial heartland of Belgium. A dozen or so buildings made up the Assumption convent compound. Brick-and-stone-framed structures, sloping A-frames, an arched gatehouse—all evidence the unique Mosan Renaissance style of the Meuse Valley.[5]

Sofía supported her sister during and after Consuelo's profession of vows. She was to remain with Consuelo for Christmas. But Sofía had appointments in Belgium. Her escape from Mexico in 1930 and 1931—to recoup, to learn, to network—was an entrance to an international world of women's activism. Sofía's welcome to that world began in Belgium. A meeting with Mademoiselle Christine de Hemptinne, resident of Ghent and president of the Youth Section of the International Union of Catholic Women's Leagues—the largest international Catholic women's association in the world—was the first item on Sofía's agenda. And so while Consuelo remained at Val Notre Dame, Sofía set out alone. She told Consuelo and the nuns at the convent she would return by Christmas Eve.

Sofía said goodbye to her sister at Val Notre Dame and arrived first in Brussels, capital of Belgium, and then immediately took a train to Ghent, a Dutch-speaking region in Flanders where the de Hemptinne family lived.

In 1930 a single woman traveling alone was not unheard of. Women, from poor immigrants to rich socialites, had regularly traveled unaccompanied since the late nineteenth century. But certainly single women traveling alone could, and did, raise questions. Male headship of the home and the given religious sensibilities of a family often dictated whether a single woman was permitted to travel. In the main, society, at least in western Europe and the Americas, no longer prohibited women from traveling alone. In the early twentieth century, etiquette guides, published by the likes of Lady Trowbridge or by *Vogue* magazine, included the norms expected of respectable young women on solo journeys.[6] The central advice always had to do with women guarding their interactions with men in public and in private. The onus was always on women to behave properly—for women to avoid "unwise" acquaintances with men while traveling, whether by rail or by sea. The existence of etiquette manuals shows some anxiety over travel. It mattered to someone somewhere *how* women traveled. One historian notes "the fact that writers still felt it was necessary to advise these women in the interwar years does suggest . . . that there was lingering unease about such journeys, even while it was accepted that women would not be prevented from undertaking them."[7] For Sofía, whose Catholic work required her to travel alone, the male authorities in her life did not prohibit her from traveling. Yet it was always clear that Sofía, as a representative of a Catholic ideal—chastity, respectability, virtue—assumed there was a right way to travel.

Sofía's journey to Ghent proceeded without incident. As she made her way to Christine de Hemptinne's home, Sofía could feel her nerves rising. Christine was the daughter of Belgian nobles, her father a count, her mother a countess. They were extraordinarily rich and extremely Catholic. Her father was a major donor to Catholic Action in the 1930s.[8] Her mother operated a school for Catholic girls. Like other members of the Belgian nobility, they spoke French, although they lived in Dutch-speaking Flanders. Christine, born in 1895, was a few years younger than Sofía. But like Sofía, Christine was a lifelong celibate—single, never a nun, she devoted her time exclusively to organizing Catholic women. She had frequent dealings with the pope. Sofía was apprehensive to meet Christine, a woman in charge on an international level.

Catholic Action had its parish groups, the most local expression; it had its diocesan committees and its national directors. Sofía knew these aspects well. They were the tiered structures she'd been struggling to form for the last year. Catholic Action also had an international character, led by an elite class of women.[9] This level, the international, was what Sofía desired to learn more about. And Christine de Hemptinne was one of the most important figures in Catholic Action for young women.

The organization of a separate branch of Catholic Action for young women was somewhat new. Catholic laywomen had been organizing in substantial ways for almost a century by 1930. For instance one group, called the Association of Ladies of Charity of Saint Vincent de Paul, established an international presence in Europe and the Americas in the 1800s. Lay female volunteers devoted their time to social welfare, in-home nursing, and care for the poor. These sorts of associations proliferated by the early twentieth century.[10] But an evolution in organization occurred around the outbreak of World War I. Groups like the Ladies of Charity were connected to religious orders. The new

Catholic Action groups didn't have that same connection. They were directly under the authority of the bishops. The first of these new types of women's organizations mirrored more secular female associations, temperance leagues, especially. The Catholic laywomen's groups were populated mainly by mature, married women: hence, associations like Mexico's Damas Católicas. At the time unmarried, younger women often joined as aspirants, if they joined at all.

In 1910 a first step was made toward international organization. In that year, the International Union of Catholic Women's Leagues (IUCWL) was founded. Its married, female president was appointed by the pope. In 1930 Madame Florentine Steenberghe-Engerin, from the Netherlands, was president. The IUCWL, as it was known, gathered national women's groups under the covering of its spreading wings. It became *the* main counterpart—opposition might be more appropriate—to international feminist groups. The International Council of Women and the International Alliance of Women campaigned for the female vote, for an Equal Rights Amendment and, to some extent, for birth control. The IUCWL opposed these issues.[11] Their disapproval of equal rights legislation stemmed from a fear that these laws might actually remove protection for women in the workplace. If laws cast men and women as the same, they argued, this would be a danger to women who might have a family to care for.[12] Women, in other words, needed special protection because of their God-given role as mothers. Catholic women of the era perceived birth control as plainly against Catholic teaching. Yet their opposition extended to all areas that tinkered with fertility, resisting sterilization laws, and the like. Catholic views on female suffrage, however, were a bit more nuanced. After the female vote became more common, the IUCWL accepted it as a given. Catholic women were directed to use their vote to protect the family, which often meant advocating a "family wage"—men, in short, should receive enough salary to take care of their families without the wife having to resort to paid work.[13] And so, the IUCWL promoted social welfare, care for immigrant families, catechism, international peace initiatives, and the education of women.[14] Many of Sofía's views—that self-development should be balanced with self-sacrifice, that a

Les femmes internationales

woman's public voice was needed to protect the home, that men and women were not the same, but complementary—were part of the IUCWL's platform. She felt at home with the ideology she found in the International Union of Catholic Women's Leagues.

After World War I it became clear that one large women's association couldn't adequately represent the needs and special challenges associated with young women. Italy, France, Holland, and Belgium were among the first countries to establish a separate organization for young Catholic women. Pope Benedict XV (1914–22) reportedly pleaded with Signorina Armida Barelli to start a young women's branch of Catholic Action in Italy. "I have never traveled alone," Barelli told the pope, "I've never been without my mother, I've never spoken in public."[15] Barelli was being modest. She spoke three languages, had been trained at the best schools, and was a powerful speaker. While she might very well have conformed to the prevailing norms of Catholic respectability, the work of organization required bending those norms. She learned to travel alone. Whistle-stop tours of Italy brought thousands of young women out to hear Barelli speak. She once spent the night stranded in a train station at the Civita Castellana by herself; her only company in the waiting room was a sailor, drunk and eventually comatose.[16] By 1930 Barelli led almost five hundred thousand young Italian women.[17]

In France Mademoiselle Marie du Rostu directed the youth section of the French Women's Patriotic League, the French version of Barelli's Italian organization. In 1924 Christine de Hemptinne started a Belgian counterpart. Two years later, in 1926, the same year Sofía initiated Mexico's JCFM, Christine was elected president of all the worldwide affiliated national young Catholic women's associations. Essentially, Christine was the president of the youth section of the IUCWL, while Steenberghe-Engerin remained the executive president of the IUCWL, administrating the women who were married or over thirty-five years old.[18]

All three women—de Hemptinne from Belgium, Barelli from Italy, du Rostu from France—would meet and come to know Sofía during her trip to Europe. Christine de Hemptinne was first on Sofía's list.

Sofía's nervous anticipation of her first meeting with Christine only increased as she approached the address she'd been given. The de Hemptinne home appeared to be some kind of "palace." Was this where she lived? Sofía, with small travel bag in hand, stood before a "palatial door."[19]

She knocked . . . no answer. Had she traveled all this way to come to the wrong place?

Sofía knocked again. Very slowly the enormous door opened. A woman appeared, speaking formal French to Sofía. No . . . the woman explained . . . she was not part of the de Hemptinne family. She was the doorwoman. She lived in a small house of her own, contiguous with the rooms Christine used as offices. The de Hemptinne family actually lived in a still larger complex of buildings at the next corner. It seemed to Sofía that Christine did, in fact, "live in a palace," she later wrote Miranda.[20]

The family de Hemptinne appeared the epitome of sophistication. They were gracious hosts—formal, yet quite charitable. The count, Alexandre de Hemptinne, was a "very proper man," Sofía described to Miranda, "and distinguished." Thin, almost completely bald, with a salt-and-pepper Van Dyke, the count wore small, wire-frame spectacles atop an enormous nose, a feature only slightly less striking than his twin pitch-black hedgerow of eyebrows. He was a physicist of some renown, a lauded professor at the Catholic University of Louvain. The countess, according to Sofía's description, was "very tall and of medium build, with a very distinguished air and very elegant."[21] A woman of more delicate features than her husband, the Countess de Hemptinne was, for Sofía, the quintessence of decorum. Christine's younger brother Marc also introduced himself. He'd recently received his doctorate in science and was starting a career in physics like his father.

Father, mother, son—they were everything Sofía expected of a wealthy, Catholic, ennobled family. She considered them people worthy of emulation. Except for Christine . . . Christine de Hemptinne was nowhere near the person Sofía expected to meet.

After the minor problem of finding the correct home, Sofía later told Miranda that a new and more troublesome problem presented itself... Christine. "In her bearing and appearance," Sofía explained to Miranda, Christine "contradicts the picture of her home" and her family. "I have no idea," she continued, "why they do not do something so that Christine dresses and presents herself better." Sofía described Christine as having the "hands of a cook"; she was disheveled and unkempt.[22]

It seems odd criticism, at least on first glance. Why the hands? Of all the potential aspects Sofía chose to mention, she highlighted Christine's dishpan hands and her manner of dress. Sofía's critique rested on comportment. Her sense of social class shines through. For Sofía, the educated, those with means, should know better—should *behave* better—than others; they had a duty to act in line with their station. "One's appearance," she later wrote Miranda, "should correspond with what one is." The issue was particularly important as Christine mentioned a potential visit to the United States she'd been planning, perhaps even a visit to Mexico, if Sofía felt it timely. Sofía outwardly supported Christine's proposed visits, but privately held misgivings. If Christine undertook her mission as she was "it would fail," Sofía reported bluntly to Miranda.[23]

Proper comportment, for Sofía, whether class or gender comportment, had an instructional quality. There was an ideal way of being—in presentation, in etiquette, in dress, even in travel. Living up to that ideal, Sofía believed, was a method of teaching, of uplifting one's friends, one's neighbors, of society's uneducated—of assisting the poor who, she argued, had neither the means nor the models of how to live in a Christian manner. Living up to the ideal in all areas of life, not only the spiritual, was a way of Christianizing society. And so Sofía's view of a Christian society was not classless by any means. But it was not, in her view, a static entity either, where one's station was unchanging. The poor and uneducated could rise through education. The training of the elite was *for* the uplift of all of society's classes. It was an inclusion of the less fortunate into the culture of the fortunate. According to Sofía, Christine, in presenting herself falsely, wasn't living up to the ideal. (Christine wasn't a cook, after all, she was the daughter of a count.) And if she wasn't living up to the ideal, she wasn't being a good teacher.

The teacher, for Sofía, should lead by attraction. Students should want what their teachers have. Would anyone want what Christine had to teach, Sofía wondered? She felt the strength of Christine's character, the spiritual good she had to offer, would never reach others if they dismissed Christine on first glance.

The count and countess weren't oblivious to their daughter's lackluster appearance. Perhaps they perceived Sofía's reaction to Christine and felt Sofía might do something for her. It's unclear who made the first move, whether Sofía believed it her duty or Christine's parents decided to say something. Either way, the count confided to Sofía: "I have not been able to convince my daughter to spend what I would want her to spend on her personal appearance."[24] Sofía took it as a personal challenge. She would try to convert Christine.

The first obstacle was Christine's perspective on fashion and beauty. Sofía later recalled that Christine "was part of an organization in which any female grooming was attributed to vanity and was therefore avoided."[25] Christine had recently presided over an international women's congress where the delegates made rigid declarations about fashion. The resolutions included a "renunciation of fashions, sports, and customs harmful to health." "Christian decency," the document continued, required that "evening gowns, sportswear, or costume dress" maintain "something of a sleeve." Bare shoulders were considered indecent. "The most important aim," the female delegates decided, "is to instruct young women in the very great responsibilities that provocative and immoral fashion brings with it." According to Christine's thinking, one should always be "able to recognize a Christian woman among the rest."[26] A Christian woman, Christine believed, was recognized by her *rejection* of style, beauty, and adornment. Christine's desire to set herself apart as a Catholic woman by her appearance resulted in her wholesale rejection of all fashion, even more modest varieties, as anti-Catholic.

Sofía neither recommended provocative dress nor the abandonment of modesty. Indeed, Sofía's manner of dress was conservative by the standards of Parisian haute couture. But her view on fashion differed from Christine's. She believed that attention to an appropriate fashion sensibility was essential. One could be *in* the world and not *of* the world and still wear feminine clothing. Dowdy skirts and frumpy frocks, Sofía felt confident, were not a given for the Catholic woman. Sofía set about trying to convince Christine of that notion. A bit more Catholic couture in Christine's wardrobe, Sofía believed, might actually assist Christine's work as a professional Catholic activist.

Sofía chose her approach with Christine carefully. Her purpose was not to offend the influential woman she'd just met. Over the next several days Sofía spent time with the de Hemptinnes. When Christine was occupied, the count personally escorted Sofía in his chauffeured automobile to the artistic and cultural sites of Ghent. A dinner was held in Sofía's honor. Oriental tapestries hung by the dozens on the walls of the de Hemptinne family home. Statues and pricey paintings adorned the palatial mansion. Like Sofía's father, Christine's father supported his daughter's social activism, albeit on a scale far grander than Francisco del Valle could manage. The count donated a three-story house to Christine for her headquarters of the international women's organization. "Praise God there are rich people that know how to be so generous," Sofía wrote Miranda. "May there come a time when such luck comes to us in Mexico."[27]

Despite their differences, Sofía and Christine became fast friends. First impressions aside, Sofía realized they had much in common. Both were single women leading large movements. In a moment of vulnerability Sofía confided in Christine about her troubles in Mexico—how she faced what seemed endless resistance to Catholic Action, as well as resistance to her own leadership. Christine encouraged Sofía; she too had been attacked by Catholics. Christine, Sofía later described, "went through the same problems that I have had to face." Christine confided to Sofía that she had been denounced before the local bishop and even before the Belgian cardinal. She went so far as to tell Sofía that "only because of her social position and the money she donates has she remained in the leadership" of the women's associations. That knowledge comforted Sofía, but only slightly. "It is comforting in part," Sofía told Miranda, "although not edifying to see that the same beans are cooked everywhere"—a quip Sofía took from *El Quijote*, by which she meant that the same trials were experienced everywhere.[28]

As their shared vulnerability grew, Sofía felt the time was right to broach the issue of Christine's manner of self-presentation. The count and countess had "tired of preaching to [Christine] about the necessity of being more conscientious with her appearance." Sofía stepped in as a new friend. Yet she didn't sugarcoat the issue. "I gave it to her tough," Sofía reported to Miranda. It was essential, Sofía told Christine, to use more of her money to buy clothes that might aid her presentation to the world. It would be "a means of making her apostolate more effective," Sofía stressed.[29]

It wasn't the first time Christine had heard these suggestions. Usually, however, they'd come from her parents, with all the parent-child baggage that implied—a desire for independence, a clash of wills, a distrust in an older generation's appraisal. Now it was coming from a peer; a woman who, although certainly not as rich and socially well-positioned as Christine, was still, nonetheless, a counterpart. Christine had just met Sofía, but she seemed to trust her. She could be vulnerable with Sofía and valued a straight opinion. Christine thought about the suggestion and reluctantly agreed to set aside more money to buy a wardrobe for travel and for conference presentations.[30]

The count's daughter believed she'd found the woman she was looking for, a woman to help extend the IUCWL to Latin America. This had been on Christine's agenda. Bonds with Catholic women from the United States' National Council of Catholic Women had been formed already.[31] European extension was proceeding on pace as well—Italy, France, Belgium, England, and also Poland had affiliated with the IUCWL.[32] Latin America, Christine knew, was ripe for Catholic Action and female organizing. Christine began to believe that Sofía del Valle, a Mexican woman who had lived through the recent persecution and who, despite innumerable difficulties, had still managed to build the JCFM, would make a perfect representative for Latin American women. Sofía could speak three languages, was educated, and had an opinion—all of these factors would be important in bridging the cultural worlds separating European elites and Latin America. It was virtually terra incognita for many European women. Christine set in motion plans to invite Sofía to the annual bureau meeting of the IUCWL. It was taking place in Warsaw in late May and early June. Christine would see if Sofía had what it took to bridge the Catholic women's movement across the seas.

A few more days in Ghent with the de Hemptinnes and Sofía was ready to travel to Bruges and then back to her sister. Bruges had one important function for Sofía. She attended a dinner with the Dominican Father Ceslas Rutten. Rutten's Belgian Social Secretariat had been the model for Alfredo Méndez Medina's Mexican version, established in 1920. Rutten was impressed with Sofía's ability to communicate the needs and problems of her country. He recommended that Sofía speak about Mexico to a broader audience; perhaps, Rutten mentioned, Sofía could find time to give small conferences in Bruges, Brussels, Ghent, and Liege in the spring? Maybe, Rutten prodded, Sofía might even raise some money for Mexico? "I had never thought about money," Sofía later wrote Miranda. She added: "these are things the Little Lord does." Sofía, excited about the prospect, was also reticent. She presented the idea to Miranda in one letter, asking him "to petition the superior [church] authorities" whether something like this was even possible for her to pursue.[33]

As with the nuns in London, here again, with Father Rutten, Sofía was confronted with encouragement to speak about Mexico. She was reluctant to run with the plan until her superior—male—authorities gave her permission.

Sofía had much to contemplate as she returned to Consuelo for Christmas at Val Notre Dame. She arrived in the late afternoon on December 24. But she made sure to write Miranda. As she finished reporting on the events of her travels, she made known her desire to be with him during Christmas. "And so," she ended her letter, "in the heart of Jesus we will be united and He more than anyone will bring to pass what I would have wished if I were there and not in exile."[34]

Sofía felt the pain of separation from Miranda. She felt in exile. Yet she believed that her spiritual connection with Miranda could bring them together, even though physically they were far apart.

After writing Miranda, she had dinner and then began a Christmas vigil. Sofía and the nuns sat in prayer before the consecrated Host in the chapel. She didn't get to bed until past two in the morning. Uncertainty about her role in a new international arena still dogged her as she turned in. How much was she supposed to accomplish on her own volition? And then, what should she leave to men and to priests—her "superiors"?

21

Terrible Beasts

She's alone. She opens her mouth, calls for help, but the cries are muffled. Wants to scream. There's no sound. Only terror.

Sofía woke up. Nightmares again.[1]

Sofía was still at the Assumptionist convent in Belgium. The terror of the dream receded as the knowledge of her surroundings took hold. She was warm, safe. Consuelo, her sister, was there asleep. It was Christmas Day. Fog hung dense and persistent about the thin trees outside Sofía's window on the grounds of the convent. She hoped afternoon sunbreaks might pierce the Christmastide gloom of the Meuse Valley.

Her spirits lifted as the day came on. She confided in Consuelo about the dream. The dreams had been growing more intense, Sofía told her younger sister, ever since leaving Mexico. Sofía believed the cause was the opposition back home—the resistance against Miranda and against her. Letters from Miranda began detailing how the Jesuits, Alfredo Méndez Medina among them, were behind some of the attacks against Catholic Action. Sofía was spitting mad about that piece of news, in particular. "If I were of sufficient authority there," Sofía fumed, "I would send Dn. A.M.M. and the others, the Bernardos, Romero, Iglesias, and Cuevas, and some others besides, to the mission field in the *Congo*." The "A.M.M." Sofía referred to was none other than Alfredo Méndez Medina; the others were the surnames of many of the most prominent Mexican Jesuits at the time. Sending these "friends"—a word she used ironically—to Africa "would be the only way to cut off the infection at the root and avoid grave troubles for the church itself," she vented.[2]

Exiling the Jesuits was a joke, but only partially so. She couldn't understand how men from the Society of Jesus, "whose only reason of being is to serve the church," she added, could be such an "embarrasement."³

Part of her anger was due to personal affront. She knew these men; Méndez Medina had been an early mentor of hers. Yet the other part of her anger was perspective. She didn't see the world as they did. She strongly believed in submission to authority, not in subverting it. She was incensed that these Jesuits thought they "knew more than the Holy Father himself," who, as pope, had constantly recommended Catholic Action for Mexico and for the entire Catholic world, for that matter.⁴

Sofía took solace in the words of the Gospel: "If they persecuted me they will likewise persecute you," she wrote Miranda, trying to encourage him, but also clearly trying to encourage herself. Sofía desired to be a rock for Miranda, a sentiment she echoed in several strongly worded letters.⁵ But Sofía was having difficulty forgiving men like Méndez Medina. Her constant repetition of "I forgive them" in her letters to Miranda seemed to imply forgiveness was an effort of her will more than a desire of her heart.⁶ Sofía urged Miranda not "to waste time searching for the root of the intrigues and machinations of these *friends*."⁷ She chalked up Jesuit hatred of Miranda and hatred of Pascual Díaz, hatred for Catholic Action itself, to envy. They were envious, Sofía believed, of the favor of the pope toward Miranda and Sofía's mission. Catholic Action was Pius XI's idea, she emphasized to Miranda. Miranda shouldn't forget that. "If for some reason I should regret not being [in Mexico]," Sofía reminded Miranda, "it is for not being able to help you remain calm and to be a *rock* amid the tempest."⁸

Anger, bitter feelings toward Mexican Jesuits, concern for Miranda—Sofía was suffering nightmares as a result. She confided in her sister Consuelo. Consuelo tried to lighten her older sister's mood. This vulture in your dream, Consuelo said with a sly smile, "sounds just like *Mamá* or one of her satellites."⁹ The two laughed thinking about Señora del Valle's strict temperament and their memories of childhood. The two sisters didn't have much time left together. Consuelo was going to El Salvador after the New Year. And the next destination for Sofía was France.

22

Winter in the City of Light

It was nearly dark and extremely cold when Sofía's train arrived in Paris, and the city stretched out illuminated. Paris had been one of the first major world cities to install public street lighting in the 1800s; gas fueled thousands of lamps. Electricity followed. Had Paris's nom-de-plume—City of Light—been granted by its power judged in megawatts or by Paris's central place as a beacon of the Enlightenment? The question of origins, by the 1930s, had become murky. And so whether the name came from the light of illumination or from that of intelligence, Paris glowed.

Finding affordable accommodations was first on Sofía's agenda.

North of the Seine in January 1931 the Parisian couturiers were showing their spring lines. Monochrome was out; colors were in. Long, slim silhouettes were also in: dresses that flared at the bottom, sometimes slightly, sometimes dramatically, always tapered more at the waist than the hemline. Print chiffons, starched chiffons, plain satins, and triple georgettes were the mode for dress wear. Divided skirts, often voluminous, made a splash—basically billowing trousers that followed the 1920s pajama fad. Pants for women were still controversial. The divided skirt was an early acceptable version of the female trouser. Gabrielle Chanel—"Coco" as she was called—resident of the Ritz on the Place Vendome north of the Seine, released one of the most popular divided skirts that season.[1]

Coco's glitzy neighborhood was too pricey for Sofía. South of the Seine was more in Sofía's price range. She wanted a room for just 25 francs a night. Sofía inquired at pensions and even at hotels. All were booked. No vacancy. "It might appear untrue," she wrote Miranda, "but Paris is flooded with students, of all categories, above all by ones who know some witchcraft, which has made it impossible to find an all-included room within my price range because everything is taken.... The economic crisis," Sofía continued, "is being felt by everyone, which keeps people at home and does not permit the luxury of travel."[2] In early 1931, this was how Sofía felt the growing global depression: first, in a lack of funds for Catholic Action back in Mexico; second, in the inability to find cheap housing in Paris. She visited the Protection of Young Women, an institute established for single women whose mission was to provide job assistance and housing for women in Sofía's position. Finally, she found a room at the Pension du Bretagne located at 2 rue Cassette, just a five minute walk from the famous Church of Saint-Sulpice.

Situated in Paris's sixth arrondissement, Saint-Sulpice was not only a church but also a neighborhood. The shops near the church became well-known for retailing sacred objects used in devotional practices. "Saint-Sulpician" came to signify a particular style of religious art, one that was made cheaply and mass-produced. Factories on the outskirts of Paris churned out terracotta Madonnas, wooden Sacred Hearts of Jesus, plaster saints, chintzy beaded rosaries, and sentimentalized holy cards in the tens of thousands. Retailers around Saint-Sulpice first began selling the assembly line devotionalia in the late-nineteenth century. It was modern production techniques meeting a market demand for religious items the working class could afford. Manufacturers using cheap materials could quickly respond to devotional religious fads. New saints, insisted the retailers, needed to hit the streets and shops immediately. Many critics viewed Saint-Sulpician art with raised eyebrows and disdain. Elite fashionistas viewed Coco Chanel's use of cotton instead of satin or silk similarly. It was an era of mass production, whether in the world of haute couture or Catholic devotionalism. Jacques Maritain, for instance, a Catholic philosopher and influential political theorist—a man of refined French sensibilities—loathed the Saint-Sulpician aesthetic or, better said, lack thereof. The Saint-Sulpician plague, he said, had grown worldwide, "harmful to the spread of religion." Saint-Sulpician art, he raged, promoted a "kind of bitter contempt" for the artisanal, truly inspired painting, sculpture, or poem.[3]

Whether in devotional art or high fashion, Paris in the 1930s was feeling the maddening rush of mass production and consumption.

Once Sofía settled in at 2 rue Cassette, letters from Miranda began to arrive. It was a relief. Finally, news from home. Yet the tidings from Miranda were far from consoling. Attacks from Méndez Medina and other Jesuits had continued. Catholic Action was still under assault. So too was Cultura Femenina.[4]

Attacks seemingly appeared from everywhere. It wasn't just Méndez Medina and the Jesuits that bothered Sofía. It was the "Catholic Ladies"—the Damas Católicas. Their organization had been around since 1913. Their leader and president, Elena Lascuráin de Silva, had been in her position for a decade. During the Cristero War the Damas had officially disassociated from the Catholic Defense League. When Catholics made the decision for armed violence, the Damas claimed to have no part. The reality was different. Lascuráin and her husband, Fernando Silva, housed cristeros recently released from the Islas Marías penal colony—cristeros who then went back into the fight after leaving the Lascuráin family. The national secretary of the Damas, Clara Arce, and her sister, Angelina, also were engaged in helping cristeros. So too was Juana Pitman de Labarthe, another Damas leader.[5] Sofía knew these women. She'd been introduced to Méndez Medina in 1922 through some of them. During the rebellion, Sofía and Miranda took a hard line against any woman in Cultura Femenina who hid their interactions with "the dissidents," as they called them. Sofía found herself at odds with many of the Damas leaders when the peace came in 1929.

Now that the rebellion had ended, what remained was lingering bad blood. Sofía was everywhere touted by Miranda, preferred by him for important tasks in Catholic Action. Sofía had had a seat at the table in deciding quite a bit of Mexico's Catholic future. Lascuráin, the Arce sisters, Pitman, and another woman, Refugio Goribar de Cortina, were in charge of the newly reorganized Damas Católicas, the Mexican Catholic Women's Union (UFCM). These women had watched as their beloved Damas Católicas organization was wrenched from them and transformed into the UFCM. Lascuráin spoke of the "sacrifice" in changing their "already historic name."[6] Perhaps Sofía seemed, to the Damas leaders, too eager to fall in line with Miranda's and Pascual Díaz's wishes—too eager and also too ready to receive attention and applause for her work. Sofía wrote Miranda of "the gossip initiated" in Mexico before her European travels. The gossip, whatever content it may've had, infuriated Sofía. She interpreted it as "a case of jealousy."[7] But that gossip, most likely about her and her actions, was something she wanted to escape, yet it was still affecting her emotional state.

Sofía read Miranda's letters with growing concern. In one letter, Sofía learned that Miranda felt pressured to demote Juana Arguinzóniz as managing director of Cultura Femenina in Sofía's absence. It's not clear the motivation behind this move. Nor was it clear who was pressuring Miranda. Perhaps leaders of Catholic Action felt a man would better fill Sofía's position. Rafael Dávila Vilchis was then the managing director of the Social Secretariat when Miranda was absent (and Miranda often was absent on fundraising trips). Dávila Vilchis was proposed as a candidate to take over for Juana Arguinzóniz. When Sofía left Mexico, she'd stepped down from the presidency of the JCFM. First the JCFM and now Cultura Femenina seemed to be slipping from Sofía's control. Matters were made worse when Sofía discovered that Miranda and Pascual Díaz would be leaving Mexico for several months—first traveling to the United States and then to Rome. Sofía pleaded with Miranda to keep Juana Arguinzóniz, a woman she trusted, in charge of Cultura Femenina, even "without title," she wrote. It wasn't as though Sofía disliked Rafael Dávila Vilchis. But she knew him well. She'd served with him in 1928 and 1929 while Miranda was in Europe. Sofía knew Rafael had no extensive vision for Cultura Femenina like her, like Miranda, or like Juana. Writing from Paris, Sofía was unsure of the future.[8] *Would she even be able to return to Mexico?*

She learned from Miranda that the opposition had become quite intense. "In anticipation," Sofía wrote, "that God allows me to return and resume [my work] at Cultura I would not want to have to displace Rafael from the leadership of Cultura and [thereby] not be able to work with [Juana] adequately." There seemed, to Sofía, a real possibility that her exile was permanent. "If I do not return," she agonized to Miranda, "then you would be in complete liberty to name whoever seems best to you."[9]

After reading several of Miranda's letters Sofía felt she had to act, at least in a small way, to ease her anxiety. She went to Mass that morning, then a second time in the afternoon, and a third in the evening. She instituted a clear schedule. It would also give her more time to pray—her rock-solid solution to all the problems in her life. "I pray incessantly," she wrote Miranda, "that Our Lord gives you light and frees your heart from the passion that darkens your way and that you and your superiors are given the ability not to be weak."[10] Sofía was exerting pressure, first through prayer and second by appealing to Miranda's character, his manhood even. She had written Miranda once that she felt like his complement. Even like the stem of a flower, which holds up the bud. Sofía was putting her role to use. She would make him stand up. Miranda, Sofía demanded, should not be weak during a time of trial. She, in other words, was not backing down. And neither should Miranda, a priest, a man placed in a position of power.

Order and control were allusive during that winter in Paris. Good news appeared in that Juana Arguinzóniz remained in charge of Cultura Femenina. But Sofía, as Miranda had discovered during his own travels, couldn't control events from Europe. Sofía's health declined once again. She went on a strict diet to combat a new bout of pain caused by liver inflammation. The weather challenged her spirits. "Here the temperature varies enormously and very quickly," she complained in one letter. "Some days it is extremely cold and snows and then other days less cold and almost does not appear to be winter in Paris." The infrequency and unpredictability of letters from Mexico affected Sofía's mood. "Today has been a tremendously sad Sunday," she told Miranda.[11] No letters had arrived, despite several sent to Juana, many more to Miranda, even to Leopoldo Ruiz y Flores and Pascual Díaz. "I have no desire to visit things here," she wrote in low spirits, "I still have yet to go to any museum!"[12] "After God," she confided in Miranda, "it is you who sustain me and will help me continue to move forward."[13]

Her schedule was one thing she could control. Mornings she woke at 7:30, went to Mass at 8:30 or, "when the cold is very intense," she went at 9:00. "I listen to two Masses and a little bit more and then I have breakfast around 10:00." Sofía made appointments or visited

Catholic institutions—observing their methods, making contacts—until 12:30. She returned to her pension and had lunch, then went back to her room: "I recite the rosary and rest until 2:00." More appointments in the afternoon followed, or if not, "I write or begin to read." At 5:00 she went to church again to "see if I might be able to catch some blessing from the Most Holy [sacrament of communion]."[14] Leaving the church Sofía passed Parisians of all sorts. Perhaps she even saw an aging Gertrude Stein returning home to 27 rue de Fleurus after a long walk with her poodle, called Basket, on the quays of the Seine.[15] Stein and her partner, Alice Toklas, lived not far from Sofía in Paris. The Catholic woman, Sofía del Valle, and the Lost Generation's godmother, Gertrude Stein, were just two more of Paris's tiny islands of life floating past one another in a sea of electric light.

At 7:00 p.m. Sofía was back at her accommodation—a light dinner, then to her room to finish her daily prayers, perhaps to read a bit more, or even to do some sewing. She described to Miranda that 9:30 was bedtime. "Usually I am able to fall asleep easily." After a few hours she woke and stayed awake "at times one to two hours, depending on my mood and the preoccupations that I have." She would make linden flower tea, which settled her stomach, hoping it would calm her nerves and help her return to sleep. "And this is how my days go," she wrote Miranda, "taking advantage of everything that I can regarding acquaintances to make myself useful."[16]

The sublimation of her anxiety in a rigid schedule only went so far. She was still unable to go a day, she confided to Miranda, "without thinking of anything but of you, of the ministries, of the difficulties, in searching for a reversal of these difficulties and in praying all the time for everyone and for everything and especially in offering it all for you, your health, and your difficulties."[17]

Keeping her appointment book full during the winter of 1931 allowed Sofía less time to worry about Mexico. It also made her feel she was making the most of her European exile. At the end of January she was invited to attend a study week put on by the Patriotic League of French Women. Mademoiselle Marie du Rostu led the section for young women and also sat on the bureau of the International Union of

Catholic Women's Leagues. She was the French counterpart to Christine de Hemptinne in Belgium. Present also at the study week would be Signorina Armida Barelli from Italy. After meeting de Hemptinne, du Rostu and Barelli were next on Sofía's list of important Catholic women to contact in Europe. Sofía instantly bonded with both women at the study week. "We became good friends," Sofía wrote of Barelli. "They sat us together in front with the representatives of Belgium and Canada: she calls me *chérie*." Barelli called Sofía "dearie."

Yet reminders of Sofía's difficulties in Mexico followed her to the study week. Angelina Arce, a member of the Damas Católicas, which had now been reorganized as the Mexican Catholic Women's Union (UFCM), unexpectedly showed up at the study week. "Now you see," Angelina told Sofía with a bit of pleasure, "I also have come to study." Sofía and Angelina went a few rounds, exchanging passive-aggressive verbal punches.[18] Angelina and her group, the UFCM, were among those that resented Miranda's oversight. Sofía dreaded the thought that Angelina might spread rumors about her back in Mexico. She tried her best to be cordial but to limit interaction with Angelina. "If not," Sofía feared, "even here gossip could be spun of what I said or left unsaid!" Despite Sofía's annoyance at Angelina Arce's appearance, the study week was beneficial. "I believe this week has been worth a large part of the trip, as I see a lot of substance in the work being developed.... Believe me," she wrote Miranda, "because of everything this trip has begun to mean for me, I am now the one to give thanks to those people who by their attacks contributed to my having to leave Mexico, as they have no idea the very great good they have done for me and for our ministries! ... For my part," she continued, "not only do I forgive them but I am grateful to those who have pushed me to these lands!" Yet forgiveness and gratefulness were one thing. She wasn't ready to allow her detractors credit for their behavior. "I am only sorry that they won't be credited with any merit for all the good that I am getting out of it."[19]

The study week proved to Sofía, once again, that she had a talent for speaking about Mexico. She received sympathy wherever she went. Almost all the questions from French women at the event concerned Cultura Femenina. The week had enlarged her vision about what might be possible in an international realm. "We need to foster and enlarge our international relations," she advised Miranda, "to be more effective and strong in the fight against evil, which also has received international support, and up until now has been more effective than us in [fighting] for good!"[20] She caught a glimpse of Catholic women uniting internationally, engaging in a mutual fight against anti-Catholic forces that had also created international networks. Maybe she would play a part in fostering that future, she seemed to be considering—not just for Mexican women, but a future for the Catholic Church across borders.

Paris had a way of highlighting contrasts. Paris high fashion decked the New Woman out in the latest tradition-rejecting modes. Paris was famous for its music halls and cabarets. They provided freedom to some, like Josephine Baker, an African American woman who became the toast of Parisian society. She danced and sang nearly nude at the Casino de Paris; her act was done wearing only a skimpy string of bananas.[21] Motion pictures, increasingly popular, captured the mores of the dance hall in vivid detail. Yet Paris was also pious. Every week it seemed Sofía attended a conference or sat in on a study session sponsored by groups such as the Patriotic League of French Women or the French Young Women's Catholic Association. Both groups had memberships of over one million in the 1930s.[22] The female branch of the Young Catholic Worker movement also had a tremendous following. Its young leader, a woman named Jeanne Aubert Picard, made it her mission to reach out to single women working in factories.

Everywhere Sofía looked, the New Woman contrasted sharply with Catholic True Womanhood. Paris's contrasts played out vividly in the press. Catholic headlines contained the latest document written by the pope on marriage, *Casti connubii*. It upheld the sanctity of marriage. Divorce was not compatible with the Catholic faith. The document opposed eugenics and sterilization, but also prohibited any artificial means of birth control. It fulminated against abortion. Marriage, according to the papal document, was for procreation. Only "natural reasons either of time or certain defects" should prevent partners from procreative sex.[23] Some interpreted the pope's statement as an allowance for natural family planning. Others said it merely referred to instances of infertility and menopause.

But the core issue in *Casti connubii* was the New Woman. The document roundly rejected her. The pope condemned the notion that "woman is to be freed at her own good pleasure from the burdensome duties properly belonging to a wife as companion and mother... freed from the cares of children and family, [that she] should, to the neglect of these, be able to follow her own bent and devote herself to business and even public affairs... even without the knowledge and against the wish of her husband may be at liberty to conduct her own affairs, giving her attention chiefly to these rather than to children, husband, and family."[24]

Paris, a city both pious and profane, carried headlines of the pope's words. Yet Paris newspapers also ran stories of gossip, scandal, and sexual misdeeds. In January 1931, for instance, Paris newspapers reported on a celebrity marriage and its bitter demise. The celebrity in question was Jeanne Aubert—an actress, not the same Jeanne Aubert Picard who led the Young Catholic Workers. When Aubert, the actress, was offered money by her rich American husband to remain in the marriage, Aubert told an interviewer: "It would choke me. I must be independent. I must have my own life."[25] The tale of the "saucy Parisienne," one article stated, "was particularly intriguing because it presented the modern question of whether a woman should devote her time to the home or to a career."[26] Sofía probably viewed tabloid stories such as these as unfortunate consequences of the disintegration of marriage and family life, which the pope had recently spoken about.

Sofía's view of a woman's duty was far closer to the pope's than to Jeanne Aubert's. Certainly she saw a role for women in public affairs, even business. But the issue of a woman's role in society, for Sofía, was always a choice for *both* family responsibility and public activism. That, at least, was her ideal. She was under no illusion that fulfilling family obligation and public activism would be easy. It would mean sacrifice. What Sofía rejected was the New Woman's assertion that a woman could, even should, choose personal fulfillment, career, or public ambition over and above family. She made a clipping of *Casti connubii*, the pope's publication on marriage, and sent it to Miranda. Sofía told him to pass it along to a mutual acquaintance. In this case, the individual was a man. Sofía felt, despite the document's strong words toward the New Woman, the pope was also speaking to men. They had obligations to fulfill as well. She hoped the pope's words "might at least cause some remorse" in the wayward husband, whom both she and Miranda knew.[27]

Perhaps Paris's contrasts seemed so stark to Sofía because she was new to the city. It wasn't as though Mexico City didn't have its contrasts too. It had its cabarets, it fashions, its *chica moderna*, or modern girl, on display. A new squadron of all-female police officers had formed in Mexico City in 1931.[28] The Mexican civil code declared: "Husband and wife have the same authority and voice in the house." In France, in contrast, the Napoleonic Civil Code stated that "a husband owes protection to his wife; a wife obedience to her husband."[29] Despite the legal formalism, Paris highlighted for Sofía the gulf between her own imposed order and the disordered city she encountered. The roles men and women played seemed confused to Sofía. "There are things here that very much test my patience!" she wrote Miranda. "Imagine that at the hotel, for room attendants, there are men, and in contrast, for the table service, a young woman. As if it would then be logical to have rooms inhabited by men attended by women!" Clear sexual and gender ideas guided Sofía's outlook. She might have been forward-thinking on valuing women's education, even perhaps allowing herself to break the mold—in travel, in leadership—where other women should not, but she still envisioned a society where men and women played their separate parts. "One goes on the trains," Sofía continued, "and finds there are female conductors! I have no idea why it does not occur to them to put everyone in their proper place!"[30]

One is tempted to see something else, besides merely pious disdain, behind Sofía's comments on women in traditionally male jobs. Perhaps Sofía felt so keenly the difference between the New Woman and Catholic True Womanhood because she herself felt anxious to maintain control in Paris, to maintain a sense of respectability in a situation uncommon for many Catholic women of her day. She was, in fact, a single woman living alone, with quite a lot of freedom. How conscious was Sofía that much in her life smacked of the New Woman? Her independence, her education, even aspects of her fashion sense—these realities perhaps made her all the more ready to differentiate herself from Paris's blatant forms of female liberation. "Anyway," she told Miranda, "every country has their issues and one has to adjust to them."[31]

Paris could do Paris. Sofía would do Sofía.

23

Doubt

Winter in Paris tried to hang on during March and April 1931. And so too did Sofía's doubts—even despite a brief visit to Lisieux, the Norman town 120 miles north of Paris where Thérèse Martin had lived and died and now remained immortalized as St. Thérèse of the Child Jesus. Sofía arrived in Lisieux as one weary pilgrim among many. She was awed by the love she encountered for St. Thérèse as she walked into the Carmelite chapel, La Chappelle de la Chase, as it was known. The small convent chapel where Thérèse had worshiped in life—behind a latticed choir grille as a cloistered nun—had become a "little piece of heaven," Sofía later described.[1] There, the nations had left their offerings. The nave's walls and niches were covered in thanksgiving prayers, called ex-votos. Military crosses and medals revealed the love French soldiers had for Thérèse during and after World War I, before she'd even been declared a saint. There were "crutches, marble slabs, diminutive airships, rings, crosses fashioned from trenches." One writer described it as "an arsenal of warlike trophies unequaled in the history of saints."[2]

Overwhelmed by the atmosphere of prayer and thanksgiving, Sofía knelt close to the main altar where the remains of the Little Saint lay in marbled repose. Sofía began to weep. "I do not know how to tell you what happened to me," she later told Miranda, "but I simply kneeled and began to cry without being able to think or say anything." Sofía's fear, her anxiety, her anger at how she'd been treated by Catholics back in Mexico, seemed finally to find escape as they transfigured in tears. They became an offering to God through St. Thérèse. "My Little Saint," she prayed, "here am I, you know everything I carry in my heart." "I was there an hour or so," she later wrote, "and when I stood up I felt renewed." She looked around at the walls of the chapel covered in gratitude to the saint. "Lisieux is a little piece of heaven," she marveled, "one can *feel* grace at the feet of the Little Saint and one would wish . . . to never cease bathing in this peace and confidence in the mercy and love of God that breathes through these surroundings."[3]

Order and control were comforts for Sofía. What she encountered in St. Thérèse were trust and abandonment. If Sofía's time in "exile," as she'd called it, had taught her anything it was that she couldn't control the work in Mexico; the world was more disordered than she would've hoped. Praying at St. Thérèse's tomb was an act of letting go.

"It pains me to tell you," she later wrote Miranda, "all I prayed and said to the Little Saint, for you and for all your great needs, for the ministries, for the bishops, for Mexico, and for our enemies! My parents and siblings naturally had their rightful place in my petitions and then I said only this to her: 'My Little Saint, here am I. You know all I carry in my heart, make my purposes your own and obtain for me from the Lord the graces for which we are in such need.'" Sofía promised to dedicate part of *Juventud*, their monthly magazine, to St. Thérèse, that Mexican young women "might know [St. Thérèse's] spirit of confidence and abandonment that is the path to spiritual childhood."[4]

Yet after Sofía returned to Paris, the comfort of Lisieux faded and the light she received darkened like winter clouds stretched over Parisian skies.

Sofía's doubts weren't about Miranda and the work of Catholic Action in Mexico. It wasn't mistrust in her characterizations of individuals in France and Mexico, not even doubt about her capacity to plan and dream, which could swell like some warm southern breeze. The biting cold snaps that came were doubts about herself. How independent was she? Did she need to submit *everything* for Miranda's approval? Would she be up to the task to speak as *the* representative of Mexican Catholic women? Perhaps family responsibilities should come before her own work? Sofía began to second-guess herself and, like some surprising and unwelcome spring snow, these doubts persisted.

In Paris that spring, confidence could surge in Sofía when it touched on others—it was doubt about her own role that plagued her. She no longer fretted about the opposition to Miranda and Catholic Action. "Do you not believe Our Lord is with you?" she wrote Miranda. "I have the firm conviction that this is a trial"—Sofía referred to the resistance to Catholic Action—"which should not be given any importance because Our Lord sees into the depths of the heart and knows how to give to each according to his merit and He will not let His interests be left to those who, by their own actions, show themselves unworthy.... Not for one minute," she continued, "do I doubt that the cause of justice will triumph." Sofía wrote boldly: "All these intrigues do not worry me." The only "point of doubt," for her, was the resolve of Archbishop Díaz. She prayed constantly that he would "fulfill his duty in everything." Regarding the intriguers, Sofía felt "the class and measure of their Christianity" was clear. In one letter Sofía mentioned hearing news about Alfredo Méndez Medina. "I would prefer not to have anything to do with him," she reported concerning her former mentor at the Social Secretariat, "and content myself here with asking Our Lord to forgive him and help him with light and charity."[5]

Sofía's opinions and advice to Miranda revealed a developing certainty in the future for Mexico. "Each day my confidence is strengthening," she noted, "and in it rests all my forces." "Santa Teresita," she felt sure, "is my great collaborator."[6] From the warmth of her growing confidence Sofía envisioned plans—setting up a financial committee in Paris to pay for students to study in France was one example. She saw herself as the first of many women to study where she had studied. She laid out logistics, budgets, and potential meetings in her letters to Miranda.

Specialization was on Sofía's mind and on her agenda. The need to specialize was an all-important factor she'd gleaned from her time in France. "Form specialists" is the phrase Sofía had heard from Marie du Rostu. And Sofía was absolutely convinced that professional specialization was the strategy they should implement in Mexico. Catechists, she felt, should be trained teachers. Charity workers should be trained social workers. Poverty, hygiene, and sanitation—these were problems that Catholic nurses should confront. Sofía reminded Miranda that their job as leaders was, "as you have said," she prodded, "to wake up the sleeping and warm the tepid."[7] Though far away, Sofía wanted to keep the fire tended in Mexico.

But the distance between France and Mexico began to set in. Weeks passed and Sofía barely heard from Miranda. She wrote Rafael Dávila Vilchis several times. No answer came from the subdirector of the Social Secretariat. Sofía wanted to make progress on collecting books for Cultura Femenina's library. Four letters Sofía sent went unanswered. The cold winds of doubt returned. "My position as it now stands is proving uncertain and baffling," she wrote Miranda. About Rafael Dávila Vilchis she was perplexed. "This is the moment when he has not replied"—a moment, she wrote, when information from him was crucial. "If he has a pent-up cat that he is taking care of," Sofía wrote sarcastically, "then on my return, if God allows it, let's free him of it!!"[8] Sofía's humor about the reason for Rafael's silence seemed to cover her old fear of the future. Would she return? Did they need her? Was she wanted?

With no news from Miranda, Sofía's letters began being peppered with provisions, very tentative plans, everything needing Miranda's approval. Lack of word from Mexico "paralyzes me and I cannot take another step until receiving some indication," she wrote Miranda. "If you believe it advisable," she wrote. Also: "All of this, in proposal, I submit for your consideration" and "I would ask you to give me your opinion." Sofía's uncertainty appeared to mount with each new conditional clause she felt compelled to type.[9]

And then the snow came full force and the idea of spring seemed an illusion. Sofía received a letter from her sister, Matilde, who lived in Spain. Their grandmother had died. Sofía was heartbroken, but the situation became all the more difficult as the letter contained a tough question: Could Sofía come to Spain, Matilde asked, and help put their grandmother's affairs in order?[10] Matilde had stayed behind in Villaviciosa, the del Valle family's ancestral home, when Sofía had continued on to Mexico, developing her career as a Catholic activist. Matilde had sacrificed her desires to family duty. Should Sofía honor her sister's sacrifice by making one of her own? Matilde's request for help threw into doubt the rest of Sofía's time in Europe. Should she leave immediately for Spain? Would she have to drop the work still left unfinished?

If the death of her grandmother wasn't enough to deal with, it coincided with a huge opportunity. It was the biggest opportunity Sofía had received during her time in Europe. Christine de Hemptinne invited Sofía to take part in the annual bureau meeting for the International Union of Catholic Women's Leagues. It was to take place in Warsaw. Eighteen council members from eleven different countries would be meeting to strategize and plan for the entire IUCWL worldwide. Sofía would be given a seat at the table. She had the chance to direct policy for an organization of millions of Catholic women. Christine, the president of the youth section, had already spoken to the executive president of IUCWL about Sofía. Madame Steenberghe-Engerin, the executive president, wanted Sofía to be there. Sofía, realizing that attending the meeting would mean putting off her visit to Spain, quickly responded to Christine's letter. Sofía asked Christine whether "it would be worth the effort" for her to attend the Warsaw meeting. The reply from Christine, left no doubt. "Cherie Amie," it began. "Dear Friend: I spoke to Madame Steenberghe about your presence in Warsaw. She, like me, very much desires it from all points of view, for the reasons you say, and for the unstinting work we can do together in order to put our international movement in even better position to meet the needs of the whole world. The effort, indeed, is so great, that we must put our heads together in an effective and intelligent manner."[11]

Christine went on to suggest that Sofía meet her in Brussels, that she give a talk about Mexico at a small, two-day gathering in the city, and that then they would proceed by train to Berlin and on to Warsaw. It was all set to take place in the last week of May and the first days of June.

Sofía was presented with a choice. Would she go immediately to Spain or wait? If she went immediately, she would miss the Warsaw conference.

More than ever, Sofía wanted to hear news from Miranda. But Miranda, Sofía discovered, had left Mexico. He was en route to Los Angeles to meet with an American branch of the JCFM. Its members were emigrants recently arrived during the Cristero War, as well as Mexican-American young women, whose parents and grandparents had made Los Angeles home. The JCFM, just five years old, was connected from California to scores of cities, towns, and parishes in Mexico and connected also to Paris, where Sofía sat impatient for a response from Miranda. Building an international movement, Sofía perhaps felt at the moment, could be extremely irritating at times.

After California Miranda traveled to New York and from there he met with Archbishop Díaz. The two had planned a pilgrimage to Rome with at least a dozen or so Mexican Catholics. Sofía, with no news from Miranda, hoped to rendezvous with them either in Rome, where an international congress was taking place, or in France, where the Mexican pilgrims planned to visit Lourdes.[12]

Without "signs of life" from Miranda—Sofía used the phrase in one letter—she had to make a decision. Should she help her sister and fulfill her family obligation? And if so, what would that mean for her mission? Warsaw was an unmissable opportunity, Sofía felt sure. It would provide a chance to solidify her new relationship with Christine de Hemptinne, the chance also to meet other bureau members of the Women's Leagues, to "stretch the cord as much as possible," Sofía wrote in one letter, between the international movement and the Mexican one. Sofía made it clear in her explanations to Miranda that Warsaw was important. "My impression," she emphasized, "is that my attendance at this international meeting would be advantageous as [Christine] recommends, as I believe it would both profit me as much as the work itself; it also seems that Mexico and our national prestige would be well served."[13]

No letters came from Miranda. She couldn't help but write again. Sofía reiterated her desire to go to Warsaw and its larger utility—always in the conditional, submitting her plan to attend for Miranda's approval. But as time passed and no word arrived, Sofía's entreaties grew more impassioned. The conditional tone she used might make one believe she had an intractable choice to make: either Warsaw and the future or Spain and family responsibility. Yet Sofía refused to see it as an either/or problem. For her, the problem was coming up with a plan where she could do both. Sofía had always tried to balance her public career and domestic duties. And she believed she could do so now, once again. Before she heard a reply from Miranda she'd already told Matilde, her sister, she couldn't leave Paris immediately. She made, at least, a provisional decision. Allusions to guilt, or at least a realization that it wasn't the best-case scenario, showed in her letters to Miranda. "[Matilde] understood very well," Sofía explained, "as in her letter she told me it would make her very happy for me to be at her side at the moment, but she understood that it would not be possible, as I have already told her that I could be with her in Villaviciosa in early June, as the meeting in Warsaw will end on the fifth or sixth and I would then undertake to be with her soon after."[14]

Sofía may have learned how to balance family and calling, yet she also recognized her sister hadn't been afforded that chance. It's not entirely clear what went into Matilde's decision to stay in Villaviciosa to care for grandma del Valle. Was it family expectation as the eldest female sibling? Or was it her own sense of calling, or duty, without prodding from Sofía's parents? Or perhaps expectations, duty, and calling all colluded in the decision. Whatever the reason, or the conglomeration of them, Matilde's decision had cost her a life like Sofía's. Both were unmarried. According to Miranda, both had similar outlooks on life: the desire to "do something." Both never seemed drawn to either marriage or a nun's life. Miranda wrote when he visited Matilde that her existence in Villaviciosa was small and felt, to him, stifling. The full range of Matilde's skills and aptitudes, Miranda wrote Sofía, had gone undeveloped. With their grandmother's death, Sofía acknowledged the sacrifices Matilde had experienced, which she hadn't had to make. And perhaps, if Sofía was being honest, she hadn't been willing to make those same sacrifices. "In [Matilde's] letter," Sofía told Miranda, "she shared that this is a very difficult time for her, because ... she has had to decide about her life." Sofía endeavored to encourage her sister. "I let her know the pleasure it would give us for her to return to the bosom of the family, enjoying a little of the home life that she has been deprived of for so many years." Sofía told her sister of the "collaboration" in the "field of the apostolate" that she could experience in Mexico.[15] They would work together, Sofía wrote. She even let slip in one letter that Miranda had mentioned Matilde's potential work in Mexico. A new life could begin for her, Sofía proposed.

Doubt   237

"Despite being very expected"—the death of grandmother del Valle—"it still made a deep impression on me," Sofía confided to Miranda. "More than anything in thinking about poor Matilde alone and me not being alongside her!" It was something that Matilde "also deplored," Sofía continued, "but she understands that I will not be able to undertake the trip [to Spain] without completing my work here!" Everyone seemed to understand. Matilde let Sofía off the hook for the time being. Sofía's parents also wrote as much: "News from home has calmed me, both in how they received [the death] and in what pertains to me, as they understand the prolongation [of my trip] will be advantageous and they have accepted the postponement of my return more easily."[16]

Sofía's phrase "more easily" is telling. Maybe Sofía had had to give some explanation of her decision. Once that explanation had been provided, Sofía emphasized to Miranda that everyone had come on board—that once her rationale had been received by her parents they accepted it "more easily." Sofía's letters don't explain further. We might speculate that Sofía's parents, at first, thought it imprudent to prolong her stay in France. The phrase "more easily" might suggest the first go around wasn't so smooth, that at first her parents were less than understanding. Regardless, Sofía managed to satisfy her parents and, at the very least, to placate Matilde. From the available evidence, Sofía doesn't appear wracked by guilt. She treated the decision to postpone Spain as the rational choice. Yet there was doubt. Perhaps that explains her desire to hear from Miranda. What Miranda could offer was a bit of external reinforcement: that her course was the right one; that she'd reasoned correctly. Doubt, for Sofía, and its origin in fear—emotional, often irrational—couldn't always be conquered by logic.

"In that moment," Sofía later recalled thinking, "the idea came to me that I should not attend a meeting such as this without the authorization of His Excellency Archbishop Díaz, as my trip had been one of study and observation."[17] And so, if Sofía was going to go to Warsaw, she could no longer wait for a response. She'd have to go out and get one.

24

Lourdes

It's entirely unclear what Miranda and Díaz were thinking when their train pulled into Lourdes. The train that brought them there had traveled north from Rome, then west up the leg of the Italian boot and, finally, over the French border. From there, the train headed farther west to Lourdes, in the foothills of the Pyrenees. By all accounts, it was late afternoon when Miranda and Díaz arrived. Food and rest quite likely were on their minds. Maybe even the brewing conflict between the pope and Mussolini summoned their train-jostled attention. But, upon disembarking from the train, setting foot on the station platform, one thought had surely *not* crossed their minds. Miranda and Díaz had no idea that the first woman they'd see, the woman that now stood before them in saucer-eyed surprise, would be Sofía del Valle.

Sofía could hardly believe they'd all arrived in Lourdes, from opposite directions, at approximately the same moment.[1]

What seemed still more improbable, to Sofía, was that neither she nor they had planned the near-simultaneous arrival. Miranda and Díaz didn't know Sofía was coming to Lourdes. Sofía had only heard a bit of news from a third party that the two Mexican clergymen would, at some point, travel to the southern French city. "Without a doubt," Sofía later recalled, "the Holy Spirit, through the patroness of the JCFM, Santa Teresita of the Child Jesus, assisted me in a special way on my route toward Warsaw."[2] Sofía's road to the Warsaw conference began with the providential encounter in Lourdes.

Miranda and Díaz grappled with Sofía's unexpected appearance. As they picked up their bags, they approached her.

"What are you doing here, daughter?" Díaz asked, perhaps with a bit of concern.[3]

It was a legitimate question. What was she doing there? But for Sofía, the question was more personal and complex than a simple answer could reveal. She'd now spent months alone in Paris. The Mexicans she encountered were not friendly. Doubts about her place in Mexico affected her dreams. Her company had been elite Belgian, and then French, ladies who inhabited a whole world that she had only just glimpsed. Women of influence, of culture, and of conviction dominated that world. These women, who valued Sofía, who told Sofía they felt such affinity for her, were organizing an international movement that seemed to fit with what Sofía was trying to do in Mexico. She wanted to be part of it. Sofía had endured the very blurry present and now had glimpsed what her role might be in that world. But then... also there was her need, real or imagined, for permission from her superiors, her conflicting sense of responsibility to family and to vocation. There were issues of gender and models of womanhood old and new that, while she wouldn't have analyzed it in those terms, still were felt and had bearing on her actions. Despite everything, Sofía somehow knew, a knowing that seemed unshakeable, that all the waiting and enduring was leading her to Warsaw; so much so, in fact, that she didn't take Díaz's and Miranda's silence as an answer to her future. She hopped on the first train she could to track them down.[4]

As that was all too much to explain, Sofía decided, a far easier answer would have to do for the moment. "What are you doing here, daughter?" Díaz had asked. The question hung waiting for an answer.

"Looking for Your Excellency," is all Sofía could reply.

"But, why?" Díaz couldn't help but feel alarmed.

It was clear to Sofía she'd have to explain.

"Because," she began, "I have received an invitation from the international president of the Young Catholic Women to attend an international meeting of great importance in Warsaw and I did not dare go without your authorization."[5]

As Díaz registered the words, and his concern subsided—no one was ill, no one had died, there was no tragedy—it's likely one of the archbishop's broad-faced smiles appeared.

"Yes, daughter, yes," Díaz reassured her, "attend everything you are invited to, whatever it may be, and speak in favor of Mexico, so internationally discredited due to the religious persecution."[6]

It wouldn't have been the first time Díaz met well-intentioned initiative with a bemused smile. Díaz had smiled, too, when the young Miranda gave his opinion of the importance of preparing the future at the beginning of the Cristero War. But how important was Díaz's consent? Apparently Díaz didn't feel Sofía needed his permission in a case such as this, at least not for Sofía to go to the lengths she had to obtain it. Sofía's struggle about Warsaw was of her own internal making. This, as with Miranda's absence during the Cristero War, revealed Sofía's reticence to trust herself.

After hearing Díaz's encouragement, Sofía made to leave immediately for Paris. Perhaps she felt a tinge of embarrassment? Or perhaps she simply had a mission to fulfill and was focused on returning as soon as possible to the French capital? She still needed to obtain the proper travel visas, after all, and a speedy return was crucial. Regardless, it's probable she recognized that her brief appearance and fast escape could appear strange to Miranda and the other Mexican pilgrims traveling with Archbishop Díaz. And so Díaz halted Sofía before she could leave as rapidly as she arrived.

"First we will eat, daughter, then you will go," Díaz swooped in with a fatherly mandate.[7]

After eating with Díaz and Miranda, Lourdes receded behind Sofía as she took the train back to Paris. Receding too were her doubts. Whatever else transpired with Díaz and Miranda in Lourdes—conversations that have left no trace in the record—of this we can be sure: Sofía's conscience had been put to rest. She felt an explicit commission, a vote of confidence, from her male superiors. There was now no choice but to go to Warsaw. Nevertheless, many miles and new roadblocks lay ahead. And perhaps the biggest hurdle of all—Sofía's doubt whether she was up to the task ahead—still needed to be surmounted.

25

The Road to Warsaw

The German Embassy in Paris didn't operate according to the Lord's schedule. When Sofía arrived in Paris it was a Saturday. The embassy was closed and its visa-granting officials were unavailable. Yet Sofía calculated that if the Lord had properly summed the timetables of the trains of Europe, how hard would it be to convince Germans to work a little overtime? Such was Sofía's confidence as she telephoned the home of the German ambassador to France, Leopold von Hoesch.

Sofía explained her predicament to the courteous ambassador. Von Hoesch, according to Sofía's account, weighed her story and then—surprisingly—informed her that all would be fine. Take a taxi to the embassy, von Hoesch directed Sofía; he would grant the visa she needed. With the necessary paperwork complete, Sofía caught a train to Brussels, anxious to meet Christine de Hemptinne. From Belgium, they were soon on their way to Berlin and, after, to Warsaw.[1]

How plausible is Sofía's story? First, there's the unexpected encounter with Archbishop Díaz and Miranda on the Lourdes railway platform. Then, the German ambassador to France shows Sofía surprising deference in granting her a travel visa on a weekend. Sofía's retelling of these details comes from an interview she gave some forty years after the events. Only one letter from Miranda, dated May 29, directly relates to Sofía's travel to Poland. In it, Miranda mentions Sofía should already be on her "route to Warsaw."[2] But the letter neither mentions Lourdes nor comments on von Hoesch's courtesy. Certainly other letters, now lost, might've contained supporting evidence: for example, notes of gratitude for the hand of Providence in her arrival at Lourdes or God's assistance in being granted the visa in the nick of time. Sofía often made sure to describe in detail what she considered divine help in her other letters to Miranda. In this instance, that doesn't appear to be the case. So the fact remains that Sofía's recounting of the process that got her to Warsaw comes only in an interview she gave when she was over eighty years old. Can we trust her memory?

Perhaps it doesn't matter. There are more important aspects of Sofía's memory than the exactitude of detail. Time indeed has a way of compressing or extending in the memory. A more interesting question is, What did the process mean for Sofía? For her, the trip was crucial. She looked back on it as a turning point in her career. It convinced her, by the very circumstances enabling her to go—divine assistance included—that God approved of her future work, not just in Mexico, but also in an international arena. The road to Warsaw was important for what it said to Sofía about herself. That is, she had the talent and aptitude for international work. She saw an alignment between her skills and her passion. The happy coincidences of the journey provided her evidence that she was not stepping out of the path marked out for her as a Catholic, as woman, and as a Mexican. Actually, for her, the divine aid she received suggested the opposite. She was stepping *into* the path, even if the way forward meant proceeding in a manner out of the ordinary for Catholic women of her day. It wasn't ordinary for a single, Catholic woman to travel alone in Europe. It wasn't ordinary for bishops and priests to entrust a laywoman with the job of speaking on behalf of the Catholic Church. And so, the details of divine aid in her account, in her memory, were just as important as the outcome of the journey. Divine assistance meant divine approval.

The reliability of Sofía's memory is important only insofar as it reveals something about the kind of miracles she expected. Regarding the trains of Europe and the calculation of their intersection, not much can be said. It is possible. Sofía's paper trail, her letters, end in April 1931. It leaves off when Sofía had written, time and again, for approval for her journey to Warsaw. What seems certain is that Sofía's memory of her mad dash to Lourdes is compressed. The train from Paris to Lourdes would've taken at least a day; the trip from Rome to Lourdes even longer. Perhaps in reality the journey to Lourdes and back, the meeting with Díaz and Miranda on the platform, was a longer process than she remembered. But it was etched in Sofía's mind as miraculous. It relieved her doubts about the appropriateness of the trip, and did so even while maintaining what, to her, was a proper relationship with church authorities.

Then there was the miraculous visa in Paris. Would a German ambassador grant such a request, and so quickly, on a Saturday? Maybe. Sofía certainly had tact. She knew how to present herself to those of rank as someone trustworthy and, indeed, worthy of the effort. And we know something of the German ambassador, Leopold von Hoesch. He was a career diplomat who served Germany under the kaiser, then under the Weimar Republic (1919–33), and, finally, under the Nazis, albeit reluctantly for the latter, until his untimely death in 1936. (He dropped dead from a heart attack while dressing in his London residence.) It was said the strain of serving Hitler while trying to maintain Anglo-German peace—he had been transferred from France to England in 1932—became too much for him in the end.[3] Others, in contrast, note the suddenness of his demise and the appointment of the bellicose Joachim von Ribbentrop in his place as proof of foul play.[4] In any case, von Hoesch represented the best of German liberal statesmanship in the era.[5] But would the stately diplomat have granted a last-minute visa to Sofía? Von Hoesch, despite his decorum, had a touch of sentimentality. The ambassador was known as a beloved dog owner. When his hapless Alsatian named Giro chewed on an exposed wire and promptly died of electrocution in 1934, von Hoesch had the pet honored with burial outside the German embassy in London. The inscription on Giro's grave reads: "*Ein Treuer Begleiter!*" A true companion.[6] Von Hoesch, the liberal German diplomat, the mannered patrician, the sentimentalist who showed proper respect even to his pets, does appear to be a man who could be bothered on a Saturday for a much-needed visa. However it happened, the fact remains that Sofía received permission to travel properly documented to Berlin, the last stop before crossing into Poland.

It wasn't a miraculous cure she experienced, or the apparition of Mary, or the appearance of angels. Trains and visas fit with the kind of favors showered from heaven by Thérèse of Lisieux. Sofía's spiritual hopes were of a modern variety, suited to the ordinary, the humdrum, of modern society. God could work, Sofía believed, in the most humble of lives and God could do it even in the most unassuming of situations—in train timetables and in correct passport stamps. These favors were all the more special for Sofía because she could see God's guidance in her pilgrimage through the complexities of the contemporary world. She didn't have to withdraw from the world to live a spiritual life. She journeyed into the world to find it.

A mixture of relief, excitement, and gratitude played within Sofía as the train carried her to Brussels. Christine de Hemptinne and her personal secretary met Sofía at the station. They were delighted. Sofía attended several meetings in Brussels and in Jette over the next several days. She spoke briefly about Mexico. Soon the bureau members of the IUCWL began to arrive. At least a half dozen traveled with Sofía and Christine on the train from Belgium to Berlin and then on to Warsaw.[7]

Among Sofía's companions on the train were some of the world's most influential Catholic women: Armida Barelli and the Countess Maddalena Patrizi from Italy, Marie du Rostu from France, Christine de Hemptinne from Belgium, and Mary G. Hawks from the United States.

Hawks, a native of New Jersey, was the president of the National Council of Catholic Women (NCCW). A slight, white-haired woman, she never married and traveled relentlessly in pursuit of unifying the disparate collection of pious societies, charity groups, and philanthropic organizations that made up America's far-flung attempt at Catholic Action. In 1932 there were at least eighteen hundred organizations affiliated with the NCCW. Mary Hawks tried to get a grip on as many of these organizations as she could. Hawks and the female program staff of the NCCW were indefatigable. As national president, Hawks "addressed meetings in fourteen cities in nine different states" from October 1931 to October 1932. Agnes Regan, executive secretary and a permanent fixture of the NCCW for over thirty years, visited thirteen cities in ten states during the same period; Margaret Lynch, assistant executive secretary, visited nine cities in five states; Dr. Ann Nicholson, a field agent, traveled to eleven cities in eight states.[8] None of these women were married and neither were they nuns. Miranda in one letter called Agnes Regan the "Sofía here in Washington."[9] The comparison was apt, if not exact. Regan was a bit older, already in her fifties in 1930. She had been a teacher, principal, and school board member in San Francisco. She moved to Washington and oversaw the administration of the NCCW.[10] She also ran the National Catholic School of Social Service, which had received two students from Mexico. Hawks and Regan, who worked closely with Rev. Burke, helped make the NCCW possible, despite the reticence of some American bishops. Many were suspicious of Catholic laywomen. To some, a woman's place was in the home, and only in the home. The public battle to protect Catholicism was a man's job, not a woman's, ran the argument. Leaders like Mary Hawks, Agnes Regan, Margaret Lynch, and Ann Nicholson believed otherwise. Hawks wrote Burke one letter lamenting the lack of confidence from American bishops. "Why must we spend so much time," she asked, exasperated, "convincing the bishops that the NCCW is 'useful and necessary?'"[11] Mary Hawks was the lone representative sent from the United States to the Warsaw meeting. Hawks and Sofía became good friends over the course of the journey.

One gets a keen sense of the importance the bureau of the Catholic Women's Leagues played in the lives of women like Mary Harks and Sofía del Valle. In one report, Hawks described the NCCW's participation at the Warsaw conference as "one of the most important developments of the year."[12] In Warsaw the national presidents, each laboring within their own national contexts, found in one another strength, inspiration, and direction.

It comes as no surprise, then, that Sofía and the other women on the train to Warsaw had much to discuss. Sofía remembered they needed a train compartment for ten people. It's tempting to imagine the women talking, laughing, sharing their stories, describing the particular challenges and headaches of their work. Sofía felt herself one of these women. Christine had wanted Sofía there, to introduce her, to vouch for her. "The journey was very pleasant," Sofía later recounted. They had a delay in Berlin; the women disembarked to attend Mass. "Returning to the train," she remembered, "we chatted without ceasing about all the activities, both theirs and my own, in an atmosphere of sincere friendship and camaraderie." As the women carried on, a man sat close to the window: the lone male in a compartment full of animated women. Sofía recalled feeling bad for the man. The women continued to chat together, while the man by the window stared with bemused disinterest at the countryside as the train rolled from Germany into Poland.[13]

26

Borders

> Most fantastic and, as it proved, most disastrous of all the follies of Versailles was the creation of the free city of Danzig and what was called the Polish Corridor.
>
> H. G. Wells, *The Shape of Things to Come*

Where Germany ended and Poland began was a sticky issue in 1931. Poland, as a national territory, with borders to call its own, was recreated in the aftermath of World War I. The Treaty of Versailles's redrawn map of central Europe outraged Germans to the extreme. A good chunk of the new Poland split Germany in two. This chunk of Poland, the so-called Polish Corridor, separated East Prussia from Germany proper. (It was an area roughly the size of Connecticut and Rhode Island.) The "narrow neck of land" did provide Poland access to the Baltic Sea, but it created a border nightmare for German travelers between Germany and East Prussia.[1] The journey between the two Germanys meant crossing Polish territory. Poland, for its part, was equally impassioned to maintain its new borders intact. A special "sealed" train service was available, which crossed the Polish Corridor. German travelers could traverse the Corridor without applying for a special visa. But there was a downside, in that often not even the windows of the train could be opened. Sabotage also happened, as in 1925, when parts of the track were unstaked from position and the train derailed, killing twenty-five.[2] That event was a rarity. More often, Polish border enforcement was simply zealously thorough.[3] Even travel that wasn't sealed, like the train Sofía rode from Berlin to Warsaw, was vigilantly surveilled. And the trip from Berlin to Warsaw definitely required a Polish visa. The issue of the Polish Corridor only grew more enormous after the Nazi ascent to power in 1933.[4]

In August 1939 Hitler demanded an east-west "German Corridor" to cut through the north-south Polish one. Poland rejected the claim. In September Germany invaded Poland and, with it, began another world war.

And so, in the spring of 1931, Sofía and the women with her bound for Warsaw traversed the Polish Corridor. It's unclear exactly when during the two hours it took the train to cross that narrow chunk of Poland, but, at some point, Sofía realized she'd completely forgotten to get a Polish travel visa.

Sofía's mad rush from Lourdes to Paris, the last minute German visa: it had all happened so quickly. Even if she would've remembered, there had been little time to contact the Polish embassy.

As the train slowed its pace into the first Polish border checkpoint, the women in Sofía's compartment began reaching for their travel documents. Sofía felt a sudden rush of heat to her face and a deepening dread in the pit of her stomach. The Polish authorities made way from car to car, stopping at each compartment. Finally, they arrived at hers. She reluctantly handed the official her passport.

"No visa for Poland," he declared. "You will have to return to Berlin, to the embassy of Poland in Berlin, for the visa."[5]

Sofía looked at Christine for help; perhaps Christine knew of some solution? A return to Berlin would put Sofía's whole trip in jeopardy. She would miss the conference in Warsaw.

Christine had no help to give. She returned Sofía's pleading look with one of annoyance and disbelief.

"How could you have let this happen?" Christine interrogated Sofía.

The women in the compartment were stunned. Sofía's dread only deepened. Her gaze met the impatient official once again.

"To Berlin! To Berlin!" is all he would say.

She could provide no explanations to either Christine or the other women. The man who'd been sitting by the window stood and followed the border agent out of the compartment. At least, perhaps Sofía thought, she'd be spared further embarrassment in front of a stranger. She had no other option but to begin taking her luggage down from the shelf above the seats. She would disembark and try and catch the next train back to Berlin.

"Anguished" was the word Sofía used to describe the experience.[6] She didn't know what to do. She prayed to the Holy Spirit; she asked Santa Teresita, under her breath, to intercede on her behalf. Sofía didn't record the expressions on the faces of her traveling companions, nor their words, if any, as she awkwardly gathered her things. Maybe her embarrassment was such that she didn't dare meet eyes with any of them.

Sofía turned to go, bag in hand, which felt somehow heavier than usual. At the compartment door the man who'd been sitting by the window, who had quickly left after the border agent, had returned. He stood blocking the exit. *Perfect*, she perhaps thought, *someone else to witness my less than graceful departure.*

She began to excuse herself to pass when suddenly the man grabbed Sofía's suitcase. He promptly hoisted it above the seats on the luggage shelf.

"I have been listening," he said as he fit the bag into place, "to your conversation during the trip and I realize that you all are going to a good thing."

Sofía looked at the man, confused.

"I am a Polish official." He spoke in accented French. "I spoke on your behalf to the authorities."

The man reached into his pocket. "Here is my card. When you arrive go to this address." He pointed to the card. "Pay 100 złoty; it is the fine for having forgotten the visa."

Looking down at the card and then at the Polish official, Sofía was speechless.

"I hope your stay in Poland is very fruitful," the man said smiling.[7]

Without another word, the Polish official turned on his heels and left the train compartment.

It's quite reasonable to picture the train car exploding in a torrent of thanksgiving. What is certain is that Sofía sensed, once again, the care of Providence. "I felt," she later recalled, "the desire to get down on my knees and thank [the official] for his intervention." As the dread in her stomach vanished, as the train once again trundled forward, Sofía directed her gratitude elsewhere: "I thought that those to whom I should give thanks were the Holy Spirit and Santa Teresita, those whom I had called upon from the depths of my heart and those who had interceded for this very unexpected solution."[8]

Passing the Polish Corridor, for Sofía del Valle, became just one more modern miracle. In retrospect, perhaps, it provided her further evidence that she had been right to go to Warsaw. Despite doubts about whether she should've gone immediately to see her sister in Spain, or doubts about whether she had the appropriate permission from her male superiors, Providence, she believed, had made the way for her. Sofía wasn't looking back.

27

Bridges

Warsaw was a city rich in culture and beauty in 1931; that is, before war came a decade later and reduced the city to rubble.

After Sofía's long journey, she was absolutely thrilled to get there. She and the other travelers made their way to their lodgings, accommodations built for young women, which had a chapel attached. They gathered and gave thanks to God. They began preparations for the bureau meetings and the general conference that were about to begin.

For Sofía it was an arrival. The road to Warsaw had been long. She'd had to make hard decisions. There had been loneliness in Paris. There had been her need for order and control, her desire for approval from Miranda, her uncertainty about whether to come to Poland, even her doubt about putting off family responsibilities until after the trip. The trains of Europe, for her, appeared attuned to the workings of a divine plan, and that divine plan had been proved by the favor of German and Polish officials. God's safe conduct, she believed, had allowed her to cross what was perhaps the most fiercely disputed territory in Europe at the time. "I can't sufficiently explain," Sofía later remembered, "all that my attendance at a meeting of such grand stature . . . meant for me."[1] Women from all over Europe attended. Ideas and experiences unknown to Sofía were discussed. It was a personal vindication for Sofía. The sacrifices had been worth it, she believed. What she learned there, Sofía recalled, would benefit "the realization of our projects and our work in Mexico."

After three days Sofía felt full of so many new experiences, new ideas, new friends. As the morning session ended on the last day, Christine waved for Sofía's attention. Christine looked as though she had something to discuss. She smiled briefly and approached.

"Are you ready? Christine asked with enthusiasm.[2]

"For what?" Sofía was confused. She had no clue what Christine meant.

"Haven't you seen the program?"

Sofía searched her memory. "I have been following each day." She had the feeling she'd missed something.

"You're on the program for this afternoon," Christine informed her. "Didn't my secretary tell you?"

"No," is all Sofía could muster, panic beginning to set in.

Sofía could see a look of disappointment on Christine's face. It was the same look she'd given Sofía on the train, where the Polish visa fiasco had unfolded.

"Well, I'm sorry." Christine was blunt. "But you have to speak."

Christine bounded away, abruptly ending the exchange. Sofía could feel, as she recalled, "the blood draining to my feet." Panic gripped her. She left the hall where the session had just ended. She hurried back to the conference accommodations and went straight to the small chapel. It was empty. The only presence was that of Christ consecrated, in the form of dissolvable bread, set inside the ornate tabernacle on the altar. She kneeled facing it and made the sign of the cross. She looked up at the small, white, round wafer. Sofía had come to speak with Jesus.

"Have I come here for this?" she asked aloud. "To make a fool of myself and leave Mexico in the dirt?"

Her gaze fell, her forehead rested on folded hands.

"I am going to leave." The thought came to her from somewhere inside. "I'll just say an urgent telegram called me back to Paris."

Time passed in silence. The desire to escape grew.

"Cowardly," she thought. She couldn't run away. That would be worse, she reflected.

A different thought passed through her mind, swirling up like the others from inside, but this thought blew in stronger, with more force than the possibility of flight.

"If the Lord," she began to remember, "has taken me through the difficulties I have faced on this journey, he will not leave me, in representing Mexico, a frightened idiot incapable of presenting a speech."

A verse from the Bible, like a gust of fresh wind, added to her resolve: "But when they deliver you up, take no thought how or what ye shall speak: for it shall be given you in that same hour what ye shall speak."

Sofía lifted her eyes back to the altar. She made a deal with Jesus.

"I will endure the fear and You speak for me."

With that, she got to her feet, left the chapel, and returned to her room. She changed clothes to look presentable. She drank a clear cup of chicken broth, steadied herself, and returned to the conference salon.[3]

Sofía nervously waited for her turn to speak. Mary Hawks, the delegate from the United States, sat beside her. The salon was full, adorned with flowers Sofía didn't recognize. Her name was listed second-to-last on the program: "Catholicism in Mexico" was all it said. After her, the delegate from the Vatican was to speak, a nuncio; he would close the assembly. Sofía later remembered that moment: "My frame of mind was such that I was unable to think even of an outline for my talk. I put myself in God's hands; I prayed and waited my turn."[4]

As the speaker ended, Sofía discreetly made a sign of the cross over her breast. "Lord, for you I endure the fear," she prayed silently, "give me your light and You speak for me."

Sofía whispered to Mary Hawks by her side to pray. She rose feeling weak in the knees. Walking to the podium she took a breath and began speaking in French, the official language of the conference. She talked for a solid thirty-five minutes. Yet, for the life of her, she couldn't recall a word of it. All Sofía knew was this: when she finished, the salon erupted in a standing ovation of applause.

The sound and force of it, Sofía remembered, carried her back to her seat. Mary Hawks stood smiling, clapping as well. Sofía, finally sitting, caught a glimpse of Christine's face, beaming approval.

In the coming decades, Christine would look back on Sofía's appearance as crucial for the IUCWL and for its successor (after 1952), the World Union of Catholic Women's Leagues (WUCWO). In one talk to a large women's conference in 1960, Christine credited Sofía with helping to create an "Atlantic Bridge." "You know how Sofía del Valle told us of you," Christine told her American audience, "and how the contacts began."⁵ The "contacts" Christine meant began with Sofía's speech in Warsaw.

But in 1931, as the applause subsided in the salon, the pope's delegate rose to the podium. Sofía, relieved, gave silent gratitude: "Thank you Lord, apparently you spoke very well for me," she prayed to herself, delighted.

The papal delegate shuffled some papers, looked briefly at Sofía, and finally said to the audience: "I had prepared my discourse for this session." He began slowly. "But the words of the woman from Mexico have profoundly impressed me and I would like to refer to some of them."

Taken aback, Sofía looked at Mary Hawks by her side and whispered for Mary to take notes. "Write down what he says that I said," Sofía told Mary quickly, "so I can know what my talk was actually about."⁶

The remainder of Sofía's stay in Europe felt, she recalled, like the relief that comes after passing an arduous exam. She had passed the test. It felt like freedom.

After her speech there were further congratulations, there were promises to pray for Mexico, there was even a telephone call from the Mexican ambassador to Poland extending to Sofía words of thanks for her splendid talk. The attitude of the ambassador was itself miraculous, Sofía remembered. She had just spent a half hour explaining Catholic resilience amid persecution and, here on the phone, an official of the Mexican government was busy congratulating her on it. She felt divine assistance once again. To Sofía, Warsaw felt like victory. She proved to the Catholic ladies—influential, cultured, and intelligent—that she belonged with them and that she had something important to say. And perhaps, most importantly, she proved to herself she could stand alone—without her father, without Miranda, without men.

Doubts still came from time to time. Even after Warsaw she remembered: "I probably was not going to be able to return to Mexico."⁷ Despite lingering worries, she was more sure of her mission, whatever form it would take, than ever before. She would work to bridge the gap between Mexico and the world.

From Warsaw Sofía traveled to Rome. There she was received by friends of Armida Barelli.[8] The Vatican in the summer of 1931 was in the throes of a battle with Mussolini over Catholic Action. While Pius XI secretly tried to settle the dispute with the Duce, Sofía obtained a brief private audience with the pope. She could barely contain her excitement as she described the meeting to Miranda: "I come to give you great news! Today I have had the great blessing of seeing the Holy Father in private audience and I could not tell you what happened to me when I found myself alone before him."[9]

Sofía's dress was long, black, and silk, "very elegant," she recalled. She'd borrowed it from a Protestant woman who was staying at the same boarding house as Sofía.[10]

As Pius XI approached the kneeling Sofía, he reached out his hand, she kissed it and also his ring.

"Are you from Mexico City?" He asked in French.

Sofía said, yes, she was.

Pius XI "looked very sad," she later remembered.

Sofía began by saying she had come on behalf of Mexican young women, "to prostrate myself before his feet," she later reported to Miranda. She told the sad pope that she was bringing him "the security of our filial adhesion and the assurance of doing everything in our power to bring about, through Catholic Action, the great desire of his heart, the reign of Christ on earth!"[11]

Pius XI appeared "very fatherly," Sofía recalled. He looked at Sofía through small, round spectacles with thick lenses. She remembered that he encouraged her efforts, difficult as they were, he said. The pope then prayed for a "great generosity of spirit," as Sofía described the Holy Father's words to Miranda. Pius blessed Sofía and blessed also the holy rosaries Sofía had brought with her, one of which Sofía had set aside for Miranda.[12]

The audience with Pius XI was brief. Sofía then met secretary of state Eugenio Pacelli, who replaced Gasparri as the Vatican's second-in-charge. "They have chased me out like a dog," Gasparri told one friend after being fired from his position. "I am the one who made the librarian a pope and a sovereign," he complained to another, "and he chased me out worse than a mangy dog! He will pay me for it! Believe me, he will pay me for it." Gasparri had no less severe words for Pacelli. When Pacelli came to Rome to begin his new position Gasparri greeted him with a rebuke: "You have come to take my place! You should not have accepted! They exploited me, and now they send me away! You will see what kind of man the pope is!" Pacelli was mortified. Gasparri, the astute, kindly parish pastor, the diplomat, was venting years of anger. Gasparri could be overheard, muttering to himself, in the halls of the Vatican: "They have chased me out like a dog!"[13] One might speculate that Gasparri's parrots learned some new phrases from their rattled master.

For Pacelli, Pius XI remained an unknown quantity as he began his new job. In an early run-in, Pacelli had given consent to an Italian bishop to bless a Fascist banner. When the pope learned of it, he gave Pacelli a stripping down. "I told you, Holy Father," Pacelli mustered up the courage to reply, "that I would be incapable of carrying out the functions of the secretary of state."[14] Pacelli was a genius with an eidetic memory. He'd been trained in Rome and was the son and grandson of papal loyalists. But he'd spent the last decade in Germany. Pacelli therefore returned to Rome as an outsider, overshadowed by Pius's "forceful personality" and undermined by his subordinates. One subordinate in particular was Giuseppe Pizzardo, an undersecretary in the secretary of state office. Pizzardo and Pacelli were friends. But Pizzardo was also head of Italian Catholic Action, which meant he took advantage of Pacelli's vacillations. Pizzardo constantly honey-tongued into the pope's ear a hard line on Fascist aggression. Everyone, it appeared, considered Pacelli a nonentity. The bespectacled Pacelli would prove more formidable than his detractors believed. He would not be fired as some onlookers whispered in the apostolic palace. He would act more cleverly, with more circumspection, with a keener eye, than many thought him capable. He placed his strategy on maintaining relations with Fascist Italy and even with Nazi Germany. He believed diplomacy was the key to institutional survival.[15] Pacelli would succeed Pius XI as pope, continuing the Pius line as Pius XII (1939–58). But all of that lay in the future. In 1931 Pacelli was still on a steep learning curve with little to no leg up to ease his ascent as the Vatican's leader in diplomacy and political affairs.

Sofía didn't know it, but even then, June 26, Pius had secretly spirited out of the Vatican copies of an upcoming letter of protest. The letter, published June 29, was called *Non abbiamo bisogno* (On Catholic Action in Italy). It lambasted Mussolini's attacks on Catholic Action in Italy. And although, in the end, Mussolini's grip on Catholic Action only tightened, the pope was dead set on making Catholic Action work around the globe. It's tempting to think that a faithful and ardent laywoman such as Sofía, so dedicated to the work of Catholic Action in Mexico, only confirmed the pope's resolve on the issue.

Over the coming year Mexico's religious conflict reignited. The peace worked out by Leopoldo Ruiz fell apart. Pius XI and Pacelli admonished Mexican church leaders to think only in Catholic Action, not in armed defense. The Vatican had no desire for another Cristero War. The Mexican Jesuits, the "friends" Sofía wrote Miranda about—those like Alfredo Méndez Medina who put up resistance to Catholic Action—received their own marching orders. Although he didn't send them to the Congo, as Sofía might've wanted, the Jesuit father general, Wlodzimierz Ledóchowski, penned a special rebuke to Mexican Jesuits. Under no uncertain terms, Ledóchowski emphasized, were Mexican Jesuits to resist any longer their duty to support Catholic Action.[16]

Sofía, for her part, left Rome and met her sister, Matilde, in Spain. Together they mourned their grandmother. Sofía was able to fulfill her family duties finally, even if her work had delayed her from attending to them. Matilde had decided her own future. She traveled with Sofía back to Mexico. Quinta Sofía was receiving back, in Matilde, a daughter who'd spent most of her adult life in Europe.

Sofía's worst fears never materialized. For all her anxiety about a return to Mexico, in reality she received a hero's welcome. Resistance to Catholic Action seemed to wane, at least as renewed conflict with the government provided an impetus for greater unity. And with Vatican support over the ensuing months, Sofía's and Miranda's place in the Catholic Action structure became more sure. Sofía was elected to a new term as president of the JCFM. Cultura Femenina received fresh vigor from its returning dean, who brought back a renewed vision. The future still needed to be prepared, Sofía believed. Education, training, and outreach became her focus once again. The JCFM's monthly magazine, *Juventud*, even featured Sofía's portrait on its front cover. Other than the Virgin of Guadalupe, Sofía was the first woman to appear on the cover of *Juventud*.[17]

Sofía del Valle was back.

Interlude

WALLS

Recently
Snob Bistro Londres, Mexico City, 2:08 p.m.

We sit down for lunch and I notice the walls of the restaurant are floor-to-ceiling windows. The light from the wall of windows gives the restaurant a shadowless glow. Afternoon sun, high-skied and squintingly bright outside, provides the interior dining room with yawn-inducing warmth.

I take out my Olympus WS-852, put it on the table, and hit the record button. The four old ladies are here, as well as Tere Huidobro and Héctor. They're laughing. Several conversations are happening at once.

I hear María Elena Álvarez de Vicencio, the former legislator, finish her sentence: "not respecting the vote," she says, speaking to Tere across the table. I'm trying to ladle my tortilla soup without missing what she's saying.

"The police detained us when we did propaganda," Álvarez de Vicencio continues. "They considered it social dissolution to speak against the government and the president."

Álvarez de Vicencio tells us about the early days of political activism for the Catholic-inspired PAN party. She tells me that it was very hard, in the fifties and sixties, to get people—especially politically minded Catholics—to vote at all. They mistrusted the outcome, she explains. Álvarez de Vicencio's father was a cristero. A family member of hers even had to change his name after the uprising in order to work and avoid reprisals.

As I finish the soup, I remember to ask the four ladies a question I've had for a while. I put my spoon down and wait a beat before speaking.

"As educated Catholic women, did you experience opposition in the church or from Mexican society?"

For a moment, the four women look confused. Maybe they didn't understand my Spanish?

Guadalupe Aguilar Fernández, the social worker, interprets my question as a statement about class. Did they, as educated, comparatively wealthy urban leaders experience push back from poorer Catholics from the provinces? That's what she thinks I'm asking. It's a good question, so I don't try to clarify. Aguilar Fernández explains that by the fifties and sixties the JCFM was very concerned about development, literacy, primary education—these were their goals, she emphasizes. She wants me to know she was aware of the gap between the educated, urban Catholic Action leadership and the majority of Mexico's rural population.

María Eugenia Díaz Gastine understands my question differently.

"Being Catholic," she says, this was the "stigma" she felt. "You're one of those *mochos*," she remembers hearing. In Mexico, *mocho* is the common insult leveled at a particularly pious and conservative Catholic. For her, being Catholic was where she felt prejudice, not necessarily for being an educated woman.

The ex-president's mother-in-law, Mercedes Gómez del Campo, points out that Sofía nurtured friendships with people of other religions and those with no religion at all. She mentions Sofía's relationship with feminist organizations, her participation in Mexico's 1975 World Conference of the International Women's Year, held in Mexico City—Gómez del Campo points to these as evidence that Sofía endeavored to transcend the Catholic *mocho* stereotype.

"She didn't judge others," Gómez del Campo says as an afterthought.

Álvarez de Vicencio chimes in. "Accepting others as they are and not as we are."

She tells me about the 1975 Women's Conference. It was promoted by the United Nations. It was the first international gathering of its kind. Everyone from Gloria Steinem and Betty Friedan to Mother Teresa attended.[1] It initiated a decade-long UN program dedicated to global women's rights.[2] It also led to March 8 being dedicated as International

Interlude: Walls 261

Women's Day. Sofía was a promoter of that initiative. Yet, Álvarez de Vicencio tells me, the PAN didn't support the 1975 conference. Sofía, in contrast, *did* support it. Over time, Álvarez de Vicencio's position, as well as that of the PAN, has shifted. For instance, as a Mexican senator, Álvarez de Vicencio supported the establishment of quotas for women in education, in the professions, and in government. "It's been a change in the PAN," she says. "It cost a lot of work."

For all of these four women, Sofía del Valle was significant in trying to bridge the gap between the conservative Catholic Church and Mexican society. A wall had been erected between Catholic culture and the mainstream of Mexican political life. The religious conflict initiated that separation. And its memory reinforces it. The women see Sofía as embracing the world before many other Catholics were willing to admit a world "out there" existed.

Sofía didn't believe in walls, they tell me.[3]

PART 5

Catholic Vagabond

28

Miss del Valle Goes to Washington

Sofía was forty-two when she crossed the U.S.-Mexican border on May 1, 1934. Two photographs from the era depict the image Sofía projected. The first is undated, but her age and appearance suggest the mid-1930s. From what we know of her in the 1930s, she was keenly aware of her mission to educate young women. She's reading a book; sitting next to her is a younger woman, also reading.

Even while making her tour of the United States, lecturing about the religious conflict, raising funds, extending her network of Catholic allies for Mexico, she was invested in Mexico. The work of building Cultura Femenina and the JCFM was constantly on her mind. Books played a large part in the vision she was seeking to realize. Sofía's vision was to link femininity and intelligence. A woman who studied was not less feminine, she argued, but more so because she developed her God-given intelligence.

"Show me your books! And I will show you who you are!" The JCFM's bulletin often printed the saying in its pages.[1]

Another picture captures Sofía at a more informal moment. She looks directly at the camera—hands clasped and dangling over drawn-up knees. She sits on steps outside an unknown location. Is it Quinta Sofía? Cultura Femenina?

Her head tilts slightly to the side and her smile is genuine, comfortable. Pearls, a ring on her finger—this is a self-assured Sofía, at home in her own skin. Sofía's mission to the United States would require all of the intelligence and the self-assurance she could muster.

In late April 1934 Sofía del Valle's train rolled north through Mexico's countryside—over mountain passes, through arid land, through towns and cities. Its terminus was the border: Laredo, Texas. Laredo was only a temporary stop; Sofía's final destination was Washington

21. Sofía del Valle (*left*), ca. 1934. Photograph, Archivo Histórico del Arzobispado de México, base Miguel Darío Miranda, caja 8a.

DC. The fight for Mexico's future had once again, and not for the last time, compelled her to travel abroad.

From the window of the Pullman sleeper car, Sofía saw the horizon as a permanent fixture in the distance. Only pieces of it became visible to her line of site, just beyond the bending track.

The hills, the trees, the cactus, and sagebrush—the trackside features came one by one from out of the blurry horizon and finally paralleled her window's view. Just as quickly they sped by, as though running to some point in the direction she'd just traveled.

Sofía had time with her thoughts as the train sped north. Her future mission in the United States weighed on her mind—a mission to collect money for Mexican Catholic Action and, more important, to win American friends for Catholic Mexico.

Sofía knew her plan. She would contact Archbishop Leopoldo Ruiz y Flores in San Antonio. He would provide introduction letters for her to U.S. bishops. Archbishop Diaz, in Mexico, had already written half a dozen American bishops on her behalf.[2] In Washington she'd meet with Rev. Burke and the National Catholic Welfare Conference. She'd do what she'd always done. Plan, pray, hope for the best. The plan was as fixed as the horizon. Only time would tell what it offered up. And

22. Sofía del Valle, ca. 1934. Photograph, Archivo Histórico del Arzobispado de México, base Miguel Darío Miranda, caja 8a.

so with nothing but anticipation for company, Sofía's thoughts turned to the past, to reflection, to the last couple of years in Mexico.

Flashes of people, places, and moments appeared and then receded like the view out her train window. She saw herself returning from that long European trip in 1931. Warsaw had taught her to trust herself, taught her also to make new initiatives. Sofía had established ties to an international Catholic world. She strengthened those links. There were visits of prominent women from the United States. Sofía acted as tour guide for American women in Mexico City. There was the December 1931 celebration of the four-hundredth anniversary of the apparition of the Virgin of Guadalupe. She proudly showed off the JCFM's gains at the celebration. The foreign visitors were impressed. By 1932 the JCFM had 9,363 members in nineteen dioceses.[3]

Juana Arguinzóniz was still a rock for Sofía in Cultura Femenina. But others too: Aurora de la Lama, Consuelo Cueto, the Ziegler sisters (Emma and Felícitas), the Olivera sisters (Eugenia, Teresa, and Margarita), as well as Isabel Gibbon and Guadalupe Gutiérrez Velasco.

Sofía couldn't help but smile when she thought of Guadalupe Gutiérrez Velasco. Lupe was short, barely over five feet tall. She wore owlish glasses and chain-smoked. She had the personality of a wise-cracking

Miss del Valle Goes to Washington 267

sea captain. Lupe was a journalist by training and a keen editor; she ran *Juventud*, the JCFM's monthly magazine. Her diminutive stature and round spectacles earned her the nickname *Ratón*, or "Mouse."[4]

In the spring of 1932 Sofía and Lupe embarked on a first national tour of Mexico. If links had been made internationally through Sofía's European tour, forging strong national ties would take no less time and travel. Sofía and Lupe cut a C-shaped swath through Mexico's Catholic heartland and through points north. The pair covered over one thousand miles. They rode trains from Guanajuato—Mexico's geographic center—north to Zacatecas, to Durango, and Torreón, to Saltillo, Monterrey, and, finally, to Laredo and the U.S.-Mexican border. Along the way they were met with "flowered farewells" at the train stations.[5] Enthusiastic JCFM groups hailed them as Catholic celebrities. In Saltillo a group of young women even caravanned Sofía and Lupe to Monterrey, just to take part in the meetings in that city. But the duo also encountered "little generosity" in some places, "very little preparation" in others.[6] *Juventud* magazine was virtually unknown in several spots.[7] The trip, Sofía knew, had been crucial for the movement's future. Sofía soon lost her voice from so many speaking engagements. In one rural parish, in Zacatecas, one young JCFM acolyte remembered Sofía speaking from the local church pulpit—the first woman she'd seen do so.[8] The woman later remembered Sofía loudly calling the young women gathered to social work. The visit became a catalyst for the local JCFM's work in the parish.

Sofía and Lupe's national tour put a face on Catholic Action for many young women. It also provided a mouthpiece. Lupe worked to increase the monthly subscriptions of *Juventud*. The publication provided a printed version of the Catholic culture Sofía was trying to create. It carried fashions, an advice column, doctrine, announcements, and feature writing. It also published photographs of the leadership of diocesan and parish JCFM groups. Each issue of *Juventud* carried the names and faces of young women throughout Mexico. Young women waited in anticipation to see their own pictures featured in the pages of *Juventud*—their hair cropped short, sometimes in hats, all dressed in ready-made fashions increasingly available outside Mexico City. In

1932 *Juventud* had only 1,316 subscribers; in 1934 it had 4,288. Much remained to be done, Sofía knew. Even as the JCFM membership rolls had tripled in 1934—to 31,107—only some 13 percent of its members subscribed to the monthly magazine.[9]

Another image came from the horizon ahead, a memory of mounting persecution. Sofía saw the face of Leopoldo Ruiz y Flores, whom she would meet with in San Antonio. He'd been forcibly exiled two years previously, in 1932—considered a traitor by the Mexican government. The peace he'd helped to forge had disappeared. The momentary freedom the JCFM and Cultura Femenina had experienced was gone. Even on that first national tour, Sofía and Lupe had exercised caution. They told civil authorities that their trip was a "school outing," hiding the Catholic activism that had been their real intention.[10] Behind the National Revolutionary Party, ex-president Calles still exerted control. After him, another president, Lázaro Cárdenas (1934–40) sought to make a cultural and psychological revolution. Education became the mechanism. A so-called socialist and sexual educational curriculum was mandated. Schoolteachers became "missionaries" of the state.[11] The clergy became the enemy.

Sofía had seen the propaganda. Revolutionary magazines printed cartoons. Rapacious priests sought to beguile and despoil the nation's children. The Mexican state was intent on instituting secular education in the nation's new public school system. Sofía's Catholic liberal arts school once again came under the threat of closure by police authorities.

To the acute problem of persecution came the gnawing fear of economic disaster. Money was still a problem. The Depression in the United States and Mexico—and worldwide—kept growing. Poverty in Mexico meant poverty for Catholic Action. It seemed incredible to Sofía that this, of all times, would be the opportune moment to fundraise in the United States for the JCFM and Cultura Femenina. But there weren't many options. Miranda and Archbishop Pascual Díaz commissioned Sofía to travel on this mission—raise awareness, they told her, raise money.[12] These were the twin goals of Sofía's trip.

But again, Sofía could only dwell so long on that unknown part of the trip head. Rising up into Sofía's mind came the face of Miranda.

23. "The clerical reaction stalks [its young prey] with the intent to betray the homeland once again. Teachers and students should defend the socialist school with their lives." Photograph, Archivo Histórico del Arzobispado de México, base Pascual Díaz Barreto, caja 7.

His face showed new lines of worry, of age; his chin now had the first signs of sagging jowls. But Miranda's face was still quick with a smile—and there was his ever-present cigar, which he always brought out to smoke in moments of leisure.[13] Miranda's presence in Sofía's life was extensive, although they shared fewer moments alone than during the first years of the JCFM and Cultura Femenina. He still visited Sofía's family every couple of weeks. Miranda relied on Sofía's father, Francisco, for friendship and advice. Miranda relied too on Sofía to run Cultura Femenina virtually by herself. Sofía, for her part, leaned on Miranda. She needed a sounding board, someone sympathetic to the demands of leadership. But gone were the days when Sofía felt she had to ask for permission for every move, for every new initiative. She needed him, but she could survive on her own.

"You are of the opinion that it is for everyone's good that you are not among us," Sofía had written Miranda when he was on yet another journey away from Mexico. "But we are not of the same opinion, especially when I feel ready to sack the whole thing, as . . . I have to decide on an enormity of things that I would rather you decide on, or at least [us] together, or if necessary me, but with previous consultation or counsel!"[14]

The train jostled and slowed and Sofía snapped out of her traveling reveries. The U.S. border approached. Sofía took a long breath, let it out slowly, and reminded herself of the plan. She had letters of introduction. She had contacts in the United States.

Sofía processed through immigration without incident. But the border agent grilled Sofía on her itinerary. Sofía said she was visiting her sister, a nun, in Philadelphia. She left it at that. The official eyed her intently, making sure she presented no threats. She wasn't a smuggler and she didn't appear to be a Mexican crossing the border to work. The official stamped her travel visa: Approved 1 May 1934.[15]

29

The Plan

> How strange to remember typewriters, with their jammed keys and snarled ribbons and the smudgy carbon paper for copies.
>
> Margaret Atwood, *Stone Mattress*

Sofía punched the keys of the typewriter with force.

Click, clack, clickety, clack.

She'd been in the United States for over a month.

The machine's type bars glided better now that it was fixed. It was a small satisfaction to see tiny lettered hammers lever up to the black platen, or roller; the tiny hammers moved slightly more easily than they had before. With a gratifying *thwack, thwack* she channeled the ball of anxiety and anger in her chest, down through her arms, and then through her fingers.[1]

Click, clack—thwack, thwack—clickety, clack.

She pushed hard on the key tops. Harder than usual. And with each tiny hammer strike, she gave the paper, and Miranda—the letter's intended recipient—a piece of her mind in Courier font.

It had been twenty days since Miranda's last letter.

Click, clack—thwack, thwack—clickety, clack.

Sofía was angry. She needed final approval from Miranda for the plan she'd worked out during her time in Washington.

Thunka. Sofía hit the space bar.

Thnk—

Nothing happened. The space bar stuck—again—on Sofía's borrowed typewriter. Her borrowed typewriter.

Ay, ¡Que pena! How annoying, perhaps Sofía muttered under her breath.

Sofía had planned to bring her own typewriter to the United States. It had proven too expensive to ship and too impractical to carry with her luggage. She was stuck with this typewriter, at least for the time being. Miss Lynch, from the NCWC, had lent it to her.

"A little old machine," Sofía typed Miranda. "It is serviceable, but not good."

The old front-strike typewriter had given out completely in the last few days of her stay in Washington, before she was finally able to leave the nation's capital and visit Philadelphia. Thankfully, she'd found someone to service it. And she was now with her sister; "Mother Hortensia," Sofía called her. Hortensia was a nun of the Assumption convent school, Ravenhill, located in Germantown, a Philadelphia suburb.[2]

The exterior serenity of the convent had done nothing for Sofía's interior turbulence. And it wouldn't. Not until Miranda wrote her. She wasn't asking for permission, so much as needing his backing for a plan she'd already formulated.

How different were her two rooms with en suite bathroom in the peaceful Assumptionist convent, her sister for company, the simplicity of the nuns' devotions and teaching vocation. How different her experience in Philadelphia felt from the mad rush of the American capital.

Miss del Valle—as the Americans had taken to calling her—had spent a month in Washington DC. May 1934 was filled with introductions, meetings, speaking engagements, excursions, tea and conversation—and then more introductions and meetings. *Where had it gotten her—all this running around?*

She'd gained contacts. Plenty of them. Many were well placed. Some were priests, others were laywomen. All had expressed sympathy for Mexico. But whether these contacts would pan out—would they really provide financial assistance to Sofía?—was another question altogether.

During the month of May Sofía wrote other letters to Miranda— ones typed with less force and with greater hopes. She received a kind welcome from Agnes Regan and Margaret Lynch. They were the executive secretary and assistant executive secretary of the National Council of Catholic Women—two of the most powerful behind-the-scenes women in the American Catholic Church. Lynch had visited Sofía in Mexico in December 1931. Regan and Lynch provided cheap lodgings for Sofía at the National Catholic School of Social Service. "Miss Lynch and Miss Regan," Sofía wrote Miranda, "couldn't be more lovely and decent toward me."³

Sofía's first lead for a potential donor came on an outing with Miss Lynch. It was the three-hundredth anniversary of the first Roman Catholic Mass held in the British North American colonies. They should attend the ceremony, Lynch proposed, and visit Saint Clement's Island, where the original Mass had taken place three hundred years ago. Lynch invited two other women besides Sofía. One of them owned a car and the four made a day of it. Sofía felt relieved to get out of the city. "I was feeling extremely depressed," she admitted to Miranda in one letter, "and my liver was bothering me." The drive in the country south of Washington revived Sofía. We drove on "some lovely roads," she later described, "and as nature is blossoming at the moment, the trees and forests are a marvel."⁴

The drive gave Sofía a chance to share with the women. She told them her efforts to set up a meeting with several American cardinals; her inability, up to that point, to do so; her doubts about the next steps to take. "Here the women are of the opinion," Sofía commented to Miranda, "that I should do nothing without the authorization of His Excellency [Archbishop Ruiz]."⁵ Sofía wasn't so sure. Didn't she already have his blessing? Sofía wanted to remain in line with church authority. But "this is what is detaining me," she wrote regarding new authorization from Archbishop Ruiz.

After a few hours in the car, the women arrived in southern Maryland. On the banks of the Potomac, the women attended Mass and had lunch. A gas-powered boat ferried them the fifteen minutes it took to reach Saint Clement's Island. Looking south they could see the shores of northern Virginia; to the west, in the distance, the mouth of Chesapeake Bay. A forty-foot cross marked the spot where three centuries before a group of English Catholics had come ashore in the New World. The birthplace of religious liberty in America is how Miss Lynch perceived the monument. "Miss Lynch asked that there in that place," Sofía later recounted, "we pray collectively for religious liberty in Mexico." The women bowed their heads and took each other by the hand. They prayed. "It very much pleased me to do so," Sofía wrote Miranda, "and you have no idea how fervently we made that supplication to Our Lord."[6]

The prayer ended. Sofía and the women lingered awhile as they waited for a boat off the island. Miss Lynch struck up a conversation with Sofía. The Catholic Daughters of America, Lynch had heard, were interested in Mexico. Lynch personally knew the organization's leader—its supreme regent—Miss Mary Duffy. The Catholic Daughters were the female counterpart to the Knights of Columbus. The Knights established their association in Mexico in 1905. Both the U.S.-based Knights and the Mexican Caballeros de Colón had been involved in the religious conflict. (The American Knights raised money and lobbied the U.S. Congress; they specified their money was not to buy arms for cristeros, much to the chagrin of the Mexican Caballeros.)

While they waited for the boat, Lynch told Sofía that it seemed as though Miss Duffy desired to extend the female Catholic Daughters of America to Mexico, like the male Knights of Columbus had done. The Catholic Daughters, Miss Lynch thought, were just "waiting for the current political agitation to pass in order to achieve something there" in Mexico. Perhaps Miss Duffy might be an important contact? Lynch offered.[7] Yes, Sofía began thinking.

The Catholic Daughters had more than 170,000 members in 1934. During the past decade they'd given over three million dollars in charitable and educational donations.[8]

"In such a providential way the conversation about Miss Duffy came about," Sofía reported to Miranda. "To me, naturally, on the one hand, their interest seems really good because it favors our plans," she continued. But Sofía had doubts. Money from the Catholic Daughters was one thing. If the group desired to set up their own organization it had the potential to diminish Mexican-led authority over Catholic Action. Sofía submitted the lead to Miranda. She wanted instructions. Yet her mind was already turning. We could "open the doors for them," Sofía wrote, imagining how the relationship might develop. "They could be in some form 'patrons' of Cultura," Sofía's liberal arts college.[9] Sofía decided she'd have to pay Miss Duffy a visit.

In the meantime, Sofía pursued as many opportunities as she could. Even if no immediate help in financial terms seemed probable, Sofía couldn't be sure if there might not be some unforeseen good to come of the contacts she made.

Sofía had plenty of meetings. There was Father Wilfrid Parsons, a Jesuit and the director of *America* magazine, an influential Catholic publication. Then there was John A. Ryan, the "New Deal" priest, as he was sometimes called. He advocated social reforms and was sympathetic to President Roosevelt's programs for economic recovery. There was also Edmund Walsh, another Jesuit, a diplomat by training and professor at Georgetown University. He was Pope Pius's point man on missions to the Soviet Union and to Mexico. And there were others besides.

But the question, for Sofía, was how to turn goodwill into rent for Cultura Femenina? Miss Anna Dill Gamble of York, Pennsylvania, was one of Sofía's contacts. Gamble invited Sofía to speak at the Harrisburg Diocesan Council of Catholic Women. Gamble had originally met Sofía in Mexico and became a true ally for Sofía's work. She campaigned tirelessly for peace. Gamble sat on several international organizations; she'd even been part of a delegation that spoke before the League of Nations on issues of women's rights and peace initiatives. Gamble also operated as a member of the NCWC's recently established Latin American Bureau. She was a good contact to have.[10]

Sofía accepted Gamble's invitation. She wasn't sure what would come of it. "I do not believe," she wrote Miranda, "that it will benefit my goals, although perhaps it might create an atmosphere of goodwill." And at the moment, Sofía would take goodwill. She stayed at Gamble's home in York. She attended a dinner and then gave her lecture. Sofía felt overwhelmed by the reception she received. The questions from the audience kept coming. In a short couple of hours Sofía managed to correct false impressions among Americans about Mexican Catholicism. It astounded Sofía—not only the good she felt she was doing, but the prejudices she encountered. Gamble's activism and the

Latin American Bureau, Sofía reported to Miranda, "in reality are very favorable for us because they help to diminish prejudices." Gamble proposed a series of lectures for Sofía. She'd come back in the fall and speak to the Women's Clubs in Pennsylvania; perhaps even elsewhere, as Gamble had contacts throughout the United States. Again, Sofía mentioned the goal of "diminishing prejudices and myths" among Americans about Mexicans.[11]

Even potential American allies revealed a layer of prejudice barely hidden below the surface of cordialities. At dinner in York, where Sofía delivered her lecture, a parish priest—a Father Brown—delved into conversation with Sofía. She was their invited Mexican guest. The priest, between bites of supper, mentioned he'd thought that perhaps Sofía knew of a Mexican priest of "high character" that he, Father Brown, could bring to the United States—"it might help him and assist him in getting ahead" in life, Father Brown offered. But, of course, he "wouldn't want an Indian," Father Brown told Sofía. He wiped his mouth on a cloth napkin. "But a young man from a fine family who may have had difficulties because of persecution and would want to work in these parts"—in the United States, Father Brown indicated.[12] Sofía said she'd think on it and left it at that.

Father Brown "told me many things that I will fill you in on," Sofía later wrote Miranda—his comments were "very American." Yet Sofía also felt vindicated, in part, by Father Brown. As the priest forked-and-knifed his dinner, he turned to the table and spoke to the women seated there. "He told them, the [American] women, that those among them who had customarily devalued Mexicans, but could see this Mexican young lady"—Father Brown motioned toward Sofía—"who had more culture than them, who dressed as well as or even better than they, who was very good looking and who was also spiritually superior to them for the kind of life and the type of work she was carrying on; that if they didn't understand the foolishness of their thinking, then they weren't Christian, etc. etc."[13]

Father Brown "told me many things . . . that were very American but true," Sofía wrote Miranda.

The Plan   277

It's difficult to untangle the threads of condescension—toward the American women, toward Sofía ("very good looking," according to Father Brown)—from the positive support the priest gave Sofía. For her part, Sofía didn't appear offended. She took Father Brown's compliment and reported it to Miranda as both "very American" but also "true." She perhaps felt the prejudice of Americans, especially of American women, toward Mexicans more keenly than Father Brown's sexism. And maybe the tone of male superiority aired by the priest was not her main concern at the time. Her mission was for Mexican Catholics. Perhaps she'd also learned there were other approaches, more subtle but effective, in gaining the respect of male priests.

The interaction with Father Brown tells us something about how whiteness worked in Sofía's life. In Mexico, Sofía had all the privilege associated with a European heritage—access, education, culture, influence. Her ability to speak English, the lightness of her skin, her fashion sense—all these factors enabled her to access those same privileges in the United States. But her whiteness in the United States was constantly under scrutiny. To many Americans, Mexicans were not white. As one historian notes, Mexicans in the United States inhabited a "nebulous [legal] category: people who did not meet a commonsense or scientific definition of whiteness but who nonetheless possessed its legal privileges."[14] As a Mexican resident in the United States, Sofía had to perform her whiteness.

At any rate, the speaking engagement in York gave Sofía an idea. Perhaps fundraising and the work of diminishing prejudices had to go hand-in-hand. The money wouldn't come until American Catholics got to know the *real* story of Mexican Catholics.

Sofía felt herself the right storyteller for the job. Storytelling took time however. Sofía felt pressure to get results now. In one letter, Miranda reminded Sofía that Archbishop Díaz would want funds in the near term. Sofía confided in Miranda. "All these preparations," she wrote, "seem to take so much time and I feel as though time is slipping by, but I do not see a way to accomplish anything faster."[15] Miranda, a man who had spent time in the United States himself—doing a very similar job to Sofía's—tried to ease Sofía's mind. "The form of action this time," Miranda wrote, "giving in order to receive, changes and differs greatly from earlier visits. Therefore I believe difficulties will not be lacking. However a way may be opened in some places at least."[16] Miranda encouraged Sofía to stay the course.

But that was twenty days ago. Sofía struck the keys of her "serviceable," borrowed typewriter. There had been positive momentum—yet still no money. She'd finally had several meetings with Rev. John J. Burke, the tall, affable priest who had done so much to bring peace to Mexico in 1929. Burke understood Sofía's predicament. At NCWC headquarters in Washington, Sofía had found real advice, real sympathy. With Burke, she felt "real hopes." "From all the others," Sofía typed Miranda, "I receive attention and interest, but in a platonic way, and naturally this is not enough for me." The Americans Sofía met were friendly enough, but not particularly passionate about her cause.[17]

Sofía worked out the plan, as it stood, with Burke. Wait until the fall—that had been Burke's advice. Sofía should return to the United States then. Catholic women's colleges would be in session again. She would give lectures to parish and diocesan women's clubs—to the colleges as well. Sofía, on Burke's advice, decided to affiliate Cultura Femenina with the International Federation of Catholic Alumnae. It had eighty thousand members.[18] Its president, Elizabeth Brennan, was on board with Sofía's plan. Brennan knew how to raise funds. She'd campaigned for thousands of dollars for the Mary's Monument at the National Basilica in Washington.[19] Sofía needed time to prepare lectures, to gather statistics, to make slides and visual aids. She would come with facts, which the Americans would want, Burke said.[20] The plan for the fall was a lecture tour. *But what about now?*

Sofía set her sights on Miss Duffy's Catholic Daughters of America. Burke was opposed to Miss Duffy's Mexico proposal. He wrote Duffy a letter saying as much—a letter he read to Sofía. Burke wanted Sofía to be aware of his opposition, especially in the current political climate in Mexico.[21]

Sofía saw an opening. Perhaps, she suggested to Burke, they could leverage the Catholic Daughters' desire to help into a financial contribution? Burke believed it possible. He warned Sofía that Miss Duffy and the Catholic Daughters had a very independent streak. Regan and Lynch of the National Council of Catholic Women had been pulling their hair out trying to get the Catholic Daughters on board the Catholic Action bandwagon. They'd had little success. The Catholic Daughters of America "felt themselves very important," was how Sofía relayed it to Miranda. But she had to try with Miss Duffy. "So my concern was to see this trip, so as not to result in something useless, provide some immediate benefit.... I keep thinking," Sofía wrote, "of the Catholic Daughters."[22]

Sofía took her anxiety and anger out on the old typewriter. There was only silence from Mexico. She needed letters from Miranda, from Díaz, from Ruiz—new letters that made a specific financial appeal to Miss Duffy. The U.S. apostolic delegate had been little help. She met with him, Msgr. Amleto Cicognani. The Italian diplomat was cordial, but not forthcoming. He sympathized with Sofía, but said it wouldn't be his place to write a letter to the Catholic Daughters asking for money.[23]

And so Miranda was her lifeline. She knew Miranda and Archbishop Díaz were busy with the Catholic Action Assembly happening in Mexico. But couldn't they take a moment away and support her on a mission they had commissioned?

"As I am very mad," Sofía typed—*thwack, thwack*—to Miranda, "I will not say anything else on the subject, except to ask that you send me some word, even if it is just a telegram, if you cannot send anything else, so that I will know how to proceed."[24]

Thunka. Sofía hit the spacebar. It worked. Small mercies.

She finished her letter to Miranda. She hoped his reply came in time for her meeting with Miss Duffy. Duffy was supreme regent of the Catholic Daughters of America, an organization with deep pockets in an age of economic depression.

30

The Deception of Miss Duffy

Sofía stood on the doorstep of the home of Miss Mary Duffy in South Orange, New Jersey.

She came dressed to impress. "I had on my little red tailored dress," Sofía later wrote in a letter to Miranda. "Little" didn't mean immodest. It still fell below Sofía's knees. "Little," for Sofía, meant her "trusty" or "favorite" red dress. It was the dress she used to project confidence to a sometimes skeptical American audience in a foreign land. Sofía topped off her outfit with a small-brimmed straw hat, slanted over one eye. She wore white gloves.[1] Sofía was ready to make her pitch to Miss Duffy.

Confidence had welled in Sofía—in herself, in her mission—over the last few weeks. Miranda finally answered Sofía's letters. The Catholic Action Assembly in Mexico had consumed his attention. He apologized and had good news. "I went to see [Archbishop Díaz]," Miranda reported to Sofía, "and we spoke about your work. He told me that he had read the plan with all due attention and that he had approved it in its entirety."[2]

Sofía had the backing of Miranda and Díaz. Ruiz y Flores also supported Sofía. The exiled Mexican apostolic delegate in San Antonio wrote a specific appeal to Duffy. He requested financial support. Sofía had that letter in her valise as she stood on Miss Duffy's doorstep in South Orange, New Jersey.[3]

Rev. Burke, NCWC point man, gave Sofía a vote of confidence as well. Burke admitted it would be easier just to name Sofía the official representative of Catholic Action to raise funds in the United States. Sofía inflated with pride. "If it were possible," Sofía related to Miranda, "[Burke] would wish the efforts of Catholics to obtain economic help for Mexico to be centered around me, and I would officially be the representative of the delegate [Ruiz y Flores] and the archbishop of

Mexico, as a pontifical director of Catholic Action, to seek and obtain this assistance." Sofía took the compliment. It felt like validation. Burke, an extremely important U.S. clergyman, had recognized Sofía's value. She let Burke's comment stand on its own. Sofía distanced herself from the recommendation—almost as though whispering an aside to Miranda, assuring him she wasn't campaigning for such a role. "This is much more than I could hope for," she made sure to add. "But I am telling you so you know how they think here."[4]

Still, even if there were too many complications in Sofía being named an official representative—she wasn't ordained; she was a single laywoman—Sofía recognized her unique advantages. "I believe," she wrote, "there exists a favorable environment for me among all these good people, by the grace of God, not because I deserve it, and it is an opportunity that should not be wasted." Sofía viewed her gender and her background as an asset: "I also believe that it seems to them"—the Americans—"that around me no 'suspicion' could be raised that this has any political character." Being a woman, Sofía felt, lessened the impression that she was politicking in the United States. Her seat on the international bureau of the IUCWL also helped. "With my international contacts I can offer more than others who have only a national perspective on the issues."[5]

Sofía straightened her dress one last time, pushed her shoulders back, and knocked on Miss Duffy's door.

The American woman answered the door. She was cordial. Miss Duffy led Sofía into her home. They sat and began with small talk. The conversation soon tended toward Sofía's purpose in the United States. Sofía reached for her valise. She handed Miss Duffy the "clear petition"—the letter from Ruiz asking the Catholic Daughters for financial assistance. As Duffy began to read, Sofía couldn't quite make out what effect the letter was having.

Whatever pleasantness existed in Mary Duffy's face vanished as soon as the American woman looked up from the letter to Sofía's waiting gaze.[6]

Sofía's heart began to thud in her chest.

She later described Miss Duffy's face as revealing "a sharp change in aspect." The American woman explained, through pinched lips, that "she could do nothing."

"Only in the Assembly" of the Catholic Daughters, Duffy continued, could the matter be discussed. Miss Duffy handed the letter back to Sofía. She noted Sofía's ill-timed request. The National Assembly of the Catholic Daughters wouldn't be for another year. Not until July 1935, she said with precision.

Sofía later summarized Duffy's response: "Totally and completely negative."[7]

Miss Duffy once again broached the subject of Mexican fundraising. "But why wouldn't the Catholic Women's Council help?" Miss Duffy asked.

Sofía sensed there was something behind the question.

Miss Duffy added: "Since they make so much noise." The statement lingered.

Answering Miss Duffy required care. Sofía had heard the rumors. Who was in charge of the American Catholic women's movement? Miss Duffy's Catholic Daughters and the National Council of Catholic Women—run by Miss Regan and Miss Lynch—had a difference of opinion on that question. The NCCW promoted Catholic Action. That meant all organizations had to submit to the NCCW's authority. Miss Duffy was jealous of her autonomy. She wanted to keep the Catholic Daughters independent.[8]

Sofía tread lightly.

"I explained to her," Sofía later wrote, "that [the NCCW] were going to help but that we had hoped to spread the help around so that it would not be overly burdensome on anyone." The conversation, and Miss Duffy's disposition, "softened" after that.[9] Whatever simmering contentions Duffy had with the NCCW seemed no longer liable to boil over into her chat with Sofía.

Miss Duffy set out to explain her side of the story regarding Mexico. The Mexican Caballeros de Colón, she argued, had written her directly. They made an appeal for the Catholic Daughters to establish itself in Mexico, just as the Knights of Columbus had done thirty years previously. Duffy had taken the issue up with the American apostolic delegate, Msgr. Cicognani. "Go into the water thoroughly," is how Duffy said the delegate had responded—apparently a positive affirmation for the American woman.[10] The problem, Duffy confided in Sofía, started once Rev. Burke and Ruiz became involved. Both had recommended that Duffy wait until a more favorable climate existed in Mexico.

Sofía listened. She felt Duffy had her facts wrong, but didn't correct the American woman. Later, Sofía wrote both Ruiz and Miranda of "Miss Duffy's deception." Sofía felt misled. Duffy had signaled a desire to help Mexico, but had placed Sofía in limbo—for a year or more. Some internal feud with the NCCW existed, Sofía understood. But she didn't like it. Sofía had been made to feel the pawn in a chess match between American Catholic women.

When the meeting ended, Miss Duffy asked what Sofía had on her agenda. She planned to see Bishop Walsh of New Jersey, Sofía said. Duffy explained that the next day was the only time Walsh received visitors. "I can't guarantee you any luck with him," Duffy added. The American woman offered lodging for Sofía at the House of Assistance run by the Catholic Daughters. Sofía hadn't planned on staying overnight. But she took Duffy up on the suggestion. She possessed a letter from Ruiz to Bishop Walsh. Perhaps he would provide a measure more of support? Duffy made a quick telephone call and told Sofía that a Miss Higgins would attend to her. As the two women walked to the door, Miss Duffy handed Sofía ten dollars—as a "personal contribution."[11]

Sofía smiled and said thank you. As she stepped over the doorstep, Sofía waved a "very friendly" farewell. It was a mask she wore. "You can imagine," Sofía wrote Miranda, "how much heartache I felt inside."[12]

Wind and rain and thunder played loudly outside Sofía's window all night as she tried to sleep.

"I had a terrible stormy night," she wrote Miranda.[13]

The disastrous meeting with Miss Duffy had left Sofía feeling particularly storm-drenched. The pleasant breeze of Providence had been replaced, quite literally, by an unrelenting squall.

After leaving Miss Duffy, Sofía took the train from South Orange to Newark. She hadn't planned on an overnight stay. But with the potential to meet Bishop Walsh, she bought clothes to sleep in and a change of underwear. She checked in at the Assistance House. Miss Higgins, the director, was friendly enough. She took Sofía to dinner a few blocks away at a tea room. Afterward, they listened to the radio back at the lodging. Sofía wanted to put the day behind her. She asked Miss Higgins if there was a Catholic church nearby. She wanted to attend Mass the next morning. With that, Sofía went to bed. The rain began and didn't stop.

"After such an awful night," Sofía later wrote Miranda, "I woke up to go to Mass."[14] Sofía slipped into the only clothes she had—the red tailored dress. She tried to compose herself. It was a new day.

Sofía descended the stairs and found Miss Higgins waiting. Higgins said she would accompany Sofía to Mass herself. They'd go together.

Outside the rain came down in sheets. Sofía had left her raincoat in her luggage—her luggage in storage at the train depot. All she had were the nightclothes and the red dress she was wearing. She'd even left her umbrella neatly packed in that stored luggage. Miss Higgins loaned her a "brand new" umbrella as well as "a pair of shoes a size-and-a half bigger than my feet," Sofía later described.

The two women slogged through the downpour to the church and back.[15] Water trickled uncomfortably down her arms, her back, her legs. Her hat—her straw hat—had traveled off its slanted perch and now hung indecorously, completely covering one eye.

Miss Higgins lent Sofía a pair of dry stockings. But dry stockings were not nearly the half of it. Sofía's red dress clung wet to her body. She had to peel it off and asked Miss Higgins for a pair of slippers and a dressing gown. She spent the next several hours trying to iron the red dress dry. As she did, the calf-length suit contracted above her knees. She couldn't meet Bishop Walsh that way. She worried it would cause a scandal. Sofía and several women spent the next hour trying to stretch the skirt—ironing it out—but to no avail. She'd have to go as she was. She reformed her hat and set off to meet Bishop Walsh. "I left with a feeling of *deliverance*," Sofía later wrote, "and I made my way to the bishop's office."[16]

Miss Duffy's warning that Bishop Walsh might not receive her proved unwarranted. Walsh was warm and accommodating. Sofía immediately apologized to Bishop Walsh about her dress. The prelate replied with humor, "These are trials that the Lord permits. Do not worry."[17] Sofía was put at ease. She gave her pitch to Bishop Walsh. He was impressed with Sofía. He asked whether Miss Duffy, a woman of influence in his diocese, had done anything for Sofía.

No, Sofía told him. She explained the situation to Bishop Walsh.

"I don't like it at all," the bishop replied. "They could do very much if they wanted because all they are good for is to raise money."[18]

Sofía later described the bishop as a man who "was not a saint of [Miss Duffy's] devotion."

"Well my dear," Walsh continued, "we must do something for you now and we will do all we can for the future." He gave Sofía a donation of twenty-five dollars. But he did more than that. Walsh had his secretary, Msgr. Delaney, coordinate club meetings for Sofía's return in the fall. Walsh even sent a sizeable donation to Ruiz y Flores in San Antonio.

"His kindness and interest," Sofía wrote Miranda, "compensated my *decepción* of the day before and all the other sacrifices."[19] The word Sofía used—*decepción*—finds an English equivalent in discouragement or disappointment. It doesn't mean to deceive. But yet, it was clear that Sofía experienced a betrayal of a sort. She believed—she expected—Mary Duffy to help and she had not. It left Sofía feeling bewildered, disappointed, and to an extent, deceived.

Sofía had won a donation for the present. With this, she proved the worth of her mission to Miranda, Ruiz, and Díaz. She understood it wasn't much. But she asked all three—Miranda, Ruiz, and Díaz—to trust the Lord and to trust her. "You do not know," she wrote, "how sorry I am that our, or better said, 'Our Plans' have not turned out as we had hoped; however, I believe that is it a *temporary disappointment* [and] that something much more *substantial* than anything we imagined [will be forthcoming]."[20] There was a promise of more to come in the fall. Before leaving the United States, Sofía made sure to make the possibility of donations a basic part of her speaking tour.

By the summer of 1934 Sofía was wanted back in Mexico. She briefly visited Chicago on her way through San Antonio to report to Ruiz y Flores. Sofía then went on to Mexico City, where she attended the congress of the JCFM, where she was elected treasurer of the national bureau. During her stay, she attended to Cultura Femenina and JCFM leadership. American Catholic tourists visited, a not-unusual event, as female Catholic activists came and went during the 1930s. To Sofía, the situation in Mexico worsened daily. Cultura Femenina needed a secure source of funding. Catholic schools, even private ones held in homes, were raided and closed. She felt antsy to tell the story of what was going on in Mexico. Sofía's anxieties increased about money. She confided in a letter to Ruiz that God was in control and that her mission was being placed in his hands.[21]

It was time to return to the United States.

31

Consider the Lobster

It was November 1934. Sofía had been back in the United States less than two months, and in the last two weeks everything seemed to fall apart.

The Mysterious Sofía had happened. She'd been caught up in a scandal not of her own making. But she was still suffering its consequences. Sofía's letters to Miranda—confidential letters written from Washington DC—had somehow been intercepted. By whom, she didn't know. But she could guess: the Mexican secret police. The letters were leaked to the press; to *El Nacional*, no less, the official newspaper of the Mexican government. The articles claimed Sofía was an "agent" of the Mexican bishops. If only her authority were actually that official. "Fortunately," Sofía later remembered, "my letters were signed Sofía."[1] They carried only her first name. "From that came the mysterious part," she recalled. "I was deeply concerned for the effect a thing like this could have on my family," Sofía described. "At the same time I worried about the false accusation." The editorial stated: "fanatical Mexican agents and the high prelates of the clergy continue with this work of treason to the nation." The paper accused Sofía of national betrayal. That came as a blow. "My only intent," Sofía wrote Miranda, "is to *inform* and awaken interest so that they help us financially; the rest is in God's hands."[2] *El Nacional*, Sofía despaired, had twisted her words: "When Sofía says 'so that they help us financially,'" the newspaper asserted, "that is, with resources for the rebellion."[3] The charge was baseless. Sofía wasn't in the United States to start a rebellion in Mexico. But it still hurt. It was a personal affront to Sofía's sense of patriotism—wasn't she working for Mexico?

But worse still, it hurt Sofía's public image. She had worked hard to protect that image. Now, the Americans she'd been trying to win over—Burke, Montavon, Regan, Lynch, even the Vatican's American delegate, Msgr. Cicognani—all had reason to doubt Sofía's claims about herself. All the American suspicion of Mexicans—some latent, some plain—that Sofía had felt would only be made worse by the Mysterious Sofía scandal.

"I have already seen Father Burke," Sofía had written Miranda on October 10 (in the letter leaked to the press) "and he was very attentive." She continued, in that same leaked letter, on a less positive note: "However it seems [American Catholics] are a little 'worried' at my arrival and, in my view, would like to help but do not know how and on the other hand they fear that my initiative comes from some other place."[4] Sofía didn't expand on that, but perhaps she felt the Americans doubted her mission, that they thought her mission was connected to something more radical. What is clear is that Sofía felt misunderstood.

Back in May, it had been Burke who'd helped Sofía craft the plan for a lecture tour. She couldn't figure out his reticence now that she'd actually arrived to begin that tour. Regan and Lynch, the leaders of the National Women's Council, were friendly, but didn't want to shoulder the logistics of the tour. Montavon, legal director of the NCWC, "continues in the same manner as always," Sofía had written in that October 10 letter, "without understanding our problems and believing himself, we might say, almost infallible." Sofía had been worried about how the NCWC staff viewed her work even before the Mysterious Sofía scandal erupted. "I believe they fear," she wrote Miranda, "I am operating outside of *my faculties*; that is, that I will initiate or suggest some practical means of help.... I believe," she continued, "that the delegate here"—she meant Cicognani—"fears any commitment."[5]

If Sofía felt like she was already positioned uncomfortably on a wobbling stool before the scandal, now she had the feeling of falling. The Americans viewed her with some species of suspicion or annoyance or reserve that she couldn't quite figure out. The Mysterious Sofía affair seemed like the last swift kick to her tottering stool.

The scandal was still making news in the American press. She was depressed, a bit lonely, and even a bit afraid. She feared losing the trust of Americans, but also the confidence of Archbishop Díaz and

Ruiz y Flores. Díaz had wanted results for her mission—real donations. Momentum was beginning, Sofía believed. She'd spoken at the national conventions of both the Women's Council and at the Catholic Alumnae during October. The lectures and appointments were just beginning. There was interest, sympathy—but no real money yet. She had barely been able to convince Díaz, with Miranda's help, that another stint in Mexico was worth the effort. She felt distance between herself and Diaz. When Sofía visited Ruiz in San Antonio in late September, Ruiz picked up on Sofía's concern—"a thorny nail" is how Ruiz described it, "the impression that Sr. Díaz had little confidence in her."[6] Fortunately, Sofía and Díaz had cleared the air—through Ruiz's and Miranda's mediation. But fear, that Sofía's authorities didn't have complete confidence in her, remained. Sofía tried to make up for that potential lack of trust by writing a flurry of letters to Ruiz. She wrote details, schedules; she wrote about contacts and the people she met with and hoped to meet. She trusted herself. But she wanted them—her male superiors—to trust her as well.

And there was good reason for fear—at least in terms of the lack of confidence from some individuals. Ruiz trusted Sofía. But he also had to defend himself against his own superiors. And these superiors didn't trust Ruiz or his strategy of using Sofía as a freelance intermediary. Many of Ruiz's letters had been published in *El Nacional*. Also, Ruiz published an angry apostolic letter, which the Mexican government took as an affront. The U.S. apostolic delegate, Msgr. Cicognani, was furious with Ruiz over the letters. And Cicognani gave the Vatican an earful about it. Ruiz's use of "laypeople"—a woman no less—was "dangerous," wrote Cicognani.[7] He stated in one letter to the Vatican that Sofía's mission would provoke profound distrust in the American public and with the U.S. government. Cicognani felt the leaked letters had damaged the process then in motion to again settle the religious conflict through diplomatic channels. Burke was then involved in those plans, which could explain his own reserve toward Sofía. The Mysterious Sofía scandal angered Cicognani. Sofía had little idea about Cicognani's negative reports to the Vatican. But Sofía could feel Cicognani's lack of trust through his icy interactions with her.

If Sofía felt fear from the lack of trust given by her superiors, fear also came from another direction. She'd been told Mexican agents in the United States were seeking her out. The source was the Jesuit editor of *America* magazine, Wilfrid Parsons. His contacts in the State Department had told him that the Mexican consulate in New York had information on Sofía.[8] Parsons counseled caution. She shouldn't go out at night alone, Parsons told Sofía; she shouldn't take a taxi by herself. After the Mysterious Sofía scandal—a scandal that centered on intercepted correspondence—precautions would have to be taken. Sofía didn't stop writing Miranda letters; she simply wrote under different names. She addressed Miranda as "Mr. Alex," while she became "Rose Queen," "Mary del Val," and "María Victoria" (the latter was actually a play on her own given name—María Sofía Victoria del Valle). Her letters were often penned or typed in English—sometimes only the first page would be in English, while subsequent pages reverted to Spanish. If authorities were on the lookout for "Sofía"—a belief that Sofía, Father Parsons, and just about every other Catholic clergyman Sofía came in contact with held as fact—then she would be "Rose Queen." Father Parsons instructed Sofía not to lecture in Spanish. Mexican officials might hear of the event, Parsons believed, through city and neighborhood informants.[9]

In one extreme precaution, Cardinal Dougherty of Philadelphia assigned a bodyguard to Sofía. "Miss del Valle," Dougherty told her, "you should know that during your stay in Philadelphia you will have a bodyguard whom you should totally ignore but he will follow you everywhere as I know that you are in some danger." When Sofía arrived at one lecture in Philadelphia, Cardinal Dougherty announced that all journalists present would have to leave the room before the lecture could begin. "All this," Sofía later remembered, "due to the publicity that had been given to the 'mysterious Sofía' affair."[10]

But was Sofía really in danger? Prominent American priests and bishops clearly believed as much. Sofía herself expressed anxiety about reprisals for her family in Mexico City. She evidently welcomed the bodyguard assigned to her and took the advice from Father Parsons to change her name in public, to use pseudonyms in correspondence, and never to travel alone or take taxis at night. But was she in real danger? How much did the Mexican Secret Service care about the Mysterious Sofía?

The Ministry of the Interior controlled the Mexican Secret Service. At the time it was named the Directorate of Political and Social Investigations (Dirección de Investigaciones Políticas y Sociales). The directorate had agents in the United States. They operated mainly along the U.S.-Mexico border. During the Cristero War of the late 1920s, agents surveilled Catholic dissidents. The directorate even employed the services of a female agent during the rebellion.[11] Less is known about Mexican Secret Service agents in the United States during the 1930s.[12] The directorate focused operations on political dissidents, such as General Antonio Villarreal, who was in U.S. exile after losing the presidential election of 1934 to Lázaro Cárdenas. Supporters of Villarreal planned an insurrection on U.S. soil. Mexican Secret Service operatives interrupted those plans and intercepted arms and munitions smuggled from Los Angeles and Laredo, Texas, in 1934 and 1935.[13] In January 1935, after one Villarreal supporter was arrested in the United States, the *Baltimore Sun* reported that among the documents seized in the dissident's quarters "were purported to contain letters from Catholic priests and other papers naming leaders of the alleged anti-Government movement."[14] This was two months after the Mysterious Sofía affair. It's quite likely that Sofía del Valle was indeed a person of interest to the Mexican Secret Service.[15]

Person of interest or not, the fears of U.S. clergymen voiced on Sofía's behalf appear overblown. Maybe Sofía would've lost her passport; worst case she might've been detained when crossing back into Mexico. The precautions set up by American churchmen—bodyguards, not taking taxis alone—point to a belief that Sofía's personal safety, perhaps even her sexual purity, was in jeopardy. These dark imaginings held by American clergymen—of devious Mexican agents intent on corruption—appeared on the silver screen not long after the Mysterious Sofía affair. Actor Peter Lorre portrayed a sex-crazed "Mexican" spy in Alfred Hitchcock's film *Secret Agent* (1936). Americans of all stripes, it seems, whether Catholic or otherwise, shared these dark fantasies of

Mexican spies. American clergymen intended to keep Miss del Valle out of their clutches.

In the scandal's immediate aftermath, Sofía decided to visit Canada. Ruiz had counseled as much when he broke the news to her in Washington DC. After meeting with Ruiz, Sofía returned to her room at the National Catholic School of Social Service. She wired Father Muckle of Toronto. A few hours later, a reply came: she was to travel to Albany, stay overnight, and then go on to Canada.[16]

As Sofía packed her bags she received a telephone call. Two Mexican priests studying at the Catholic University of America were checking in on her. They offered to take her to the train. Their kindness was a relief, Sofía remembered. The two priests helped Sofía with her bags at the station and she simply expected them to leave afterward. With a smile, they said no.

"We are going to take you to eat lobster on the bank of the Potomac River and then drop you off back here for the train taking you to Albany."[17]

Sofía suppressed a laugh as she received her plate of lobster at the restaurant. It was a bit of peace—some divine provision—after the frenzy of the Mysterious Sofía scandal. "How to thank God," she later remembered, "for his assistance in the difficult moments that I encountered."[18]

The lobster dinner reconfirmed what she knew about herself. She knew what she wanted. Money for Cultura Femenina. To move the needle—even slightly—on American Catholic prejudices toward Mexico. And if Sofía knew what she wanted, she knew she couldn't give up now.

32

Golden Hour of the Little Flower

> Cards on the table, Padre, cards on the table. Why are you cooling off on me? Why are you criticizing the things I'm doing?
>
> Franklin D. Roosevelt speaking to Charles E. Coughlin

If image and propaganda had been used against Sofía, perhaps she could use those very same tools for the good of her mission. Sofía needed a mouthpiece; someone to shout the message of Mexican Catholic persecution to Americans. The Mysterious Sofía scandal had hindered her ability to be that mouthpiece. She worried in a letter to Ruiz about the potential fallout from the affair in Mexico.[1] What she needed was someone to speak for her.

Sofía need only turn on her radio for a potential candidate. No one seemed to be shouting louder in 1934 than Father Charles E. Coughlin—the most famous Catholic priest in America.

Coughlin was a Detroit area priest. He'd risen to national fame by hosting a weekly broadcast called the Golden Hour of the Little Flower. Every Sunday, at 3:00 p.m. CST, Coughlin's sermons filled the airwaves of American homes in the Midwest and Northeast. His rich baritone, touched with a slight Irish brogue—"church" sounded like "charrch"—was heard on WOR Newark and across the country on WTMJ Milwaukie, on WHO-WOC Des Moines, and on WOL Washington.[2] He was heard in Philadelphia, St. Louis, and Chicago, and also in Omaha, Cincinnati, and Cleveland. By late 1934 some thirty stations broadcast Coughlin.[3] His weekly radio hour became an immovable fixture around which the rest of American life seemed to turn. In Massachusetts, for instance, one local high school was known to take an extended time out during football games played on Sunday afternoons. The players, coaches, referees, and spectators listened to Coughlin and, afterward, the game resumed. One historian describes how many Americans "long remembered the familiar experience of walking down streets lined with row houses, triple-deckers, or apartment buildings and hearing out of every window the voice of Father Coughlin blaring from the radio. You could walk for blocks, they recalled, and never miss a word."[4] The "Radio Priest," as he was called, received more mail than anyone else in America. One hundred secretaries handled the correspondence. Station WOR Newark ran a poll asking, "Who Was the Most Useful Citizen?" Coughlin won the contest. Station WCAU Philadelphia asked listeners whether they'd rather hear Coughlin or the New York Philharmonic—Coughlin won 187,000 votes to 12,000.[5]

But in 1934, Coughlin was a messenger no one seemed able to control. Coughlin's own bishop, Michael Gallagher of Detroit, admitted as much in a letter to a fellow bishop. "He cannot control himself in the excitement of oratory," Gallaher wrote of Coughlin, "much less can anybody else control him."[6]

What was Coughlin saying so loudly? His radio sermons treated a range of topics—at first mainly issues of particular concern to Catholics, such as religious and moral education. Increasingly, however, he moved on to current events and more provocative issues. With popularity came boldness. Coughlin tackled birth control, divorce, and Prohibition. He openly talked about American politics by the early 1930s. The Central Broadcasting System, afraid of government censorship, broke its contract with Coughlin in 1931.[7] The Radio Priest started his own network in response. He promoted monetary reform, he shamed President Hoover's handling of the Depression-era economy, he warned of the threat of Communism, he lambasted the crooked dealers of Wall Street—the J. P. Morgans, the DuPonts, the Rothschilds. He appealed to a broad constituency, framing his talks as ecumenical—for all Americans of goodwill, whether Catholic, Protestant, or Jew, the Radio Priest intoned. In time the Jews would be singled out as enemies, targets of Coughlin's antisemitic bigotry. But in the mid-1930s, Coughlin kept his personal antisemitism muted.[8] Instead, Coughlin pointed a righteous finger at the moneyed elite, at "satanic" conspiracies, at corrupt bankers—he even coined the term "banksters" to highlight Wall Street's alleged gangsterism. Coughlin was, in his own opinion, the voice of America's "little guy"—those farmers and working poor and factory laborers who'd been hit hardest by economic disaster.[9] He often claimed that Catholics, Protestants, and Jews were united on the issues he spoke about. At the height of his fame in the mid-1930s, perhaps forty million Americans listened to Father Coughlin, the Radio Priest.[10]

Coughlin had the kind of platform that could make Sofía's message heard. Yet using someone else as mouthpiece was risky. The personality and perspective of the messenger just might influence the message. In late 1934, Sofía decided it was worth the risk.

After Sofía escaped to Canada in November 1934, in the fallout from the Mysterious Sofía scandal, she felt less afraid. Canada had given her hope. She felt support from Father Muckle in Toronto. She gave lectures in French in Quebec and Ottawa and lectures in English while visiting Toronto and Hamilton. Sofía spoke to the Canadian Catholic Women's League and met the Canadian apostolic delegate. She received a donation of $150, which she proudly reported to Ruiz.[11] The trip had improved her outlook. She no longer felt a nagging sense that her mission was doomed to failure. Her next destination was Detroit.

Sofía knew who Father Coughlin was and she knew that Father Coughlin was a man she had to speak with. She wrote Ruiz from Canada that her plan was to go and see Bishop Gallagher and Coughlin about "saying something on the radio."[12] It's unclear what Sofía meant. Did she think she would speak on the radio? Or was her plan to convince Coughlin to devote all, or part, of one of his sermons to the Mexican persecution? Either way, Sofía believed Coughlin could assist her. It was the Canadian Father Muckle who introduced Sofía to Detroit's bishop, Michael Gallagher. And Gallagher, the Radio Priest's ecclesiastical superior, as well as the Radio Priest's staunch protector, told Sofía that Coughlin wanted to meet her.[13]

Father Coughlin broadcast from the Shrine of the Little Flower in Royal Oak, Michigan. It was one of many newly dedicated American homages to the recently canonized Thérèse of Lisieux. Bishop Gallagher had himself been in France during the canonization of St. Thérèse. The bishop looked to a dynamic young priest—one he'd been keeping his eye on, the Canadian-born Charles Coughlin—to pioneer a new parish in Royal Oak where St. Thérèse's shrine was to be built.[14]

The project was an immediate failure. Coughlin faced bankruptcy and later claimed bigotry and resistance from the local Ku Klux Klan. The story, unsubstantiated by historians, went that the KKK burned a fiery cross in front of the church only weeks after the new parish opened. Whether the burning cross ever happened is unclear. But for Coughlin, it was the story he told—how he patted out the flames with his own garments; how he stood stone-faced when confronted with anti-Catholic bigotry; how he cried to the heavens for strength.[15]

Heaven seemed to answer—but God worked through natural means in Coughlin's case. The priest's friendship with a local radio broadcaster and his cozy relations with local management at General Motors turned the tide of the parish's fortunes. Coughlin started broadcasting in 1926. Virtually free airtime and a large advertiser in General Motors proved a perfect match. Coughlin established the Radio League of the Little Flower. For just one dollar listeners could join the league; even the deceased could be enrolled by their living loved ones. Coughlin assured that the dearly departed would be "remembered in the daily Mass offered at Calvary Hill, Jerusalem." Money flowed into the Shrine of the Little Flower. "Dollars flooded in and were carried in gunny sacks to the bank," according to one historian's description.[16]

Money was on Coughlin's mind in the early 1930s. He insisted that America's Depression could only be righted through inflationary reform. Raise the price of silver, Coughlin recommended. Inflationists like Coughlin believed that as silver prices rose, so too would the capital behind it—farmers and the destitute would then have access to capital and money with which to pay off debts. *Time* magazine featured Coughlin on the cover of its January 1934 issue. Photographed with the priest was Senator Elmer Thomas of Oklahoma. Coughlin became a sort of spiritual and political advisor to Thomas in the senator's crusade to raise silver prices.

The 1934 *Time* magazine cover shows Coughlin seated, leaning close to the senator, Coughlin's gaze fixed on the camera—a pose suggesting whispers passing between the legislator and the priest. Coughlin wears a plain gray suit, his neck wrapped in a thick, white clerical collar. Coughlin's strong, stubborn jaw clenches impenetrably, lips pursing in a tight, thin line. Round spectacles do little to hide the priest's arched eyebrows. Coughlin postures either a supremely satisfied confidence in his God or a smugness of believing he knows better than his fellow man.[17] Perhaps both.

By 1934, when Sofía met Coughlin, the priest had erected a 150-foot tower depicting Christ on the cross. Coughlin said it was the "cross they could not burn," though it stood no less illuminated than the one on fire in Coughlin's imagination—scores of electric lights floodlit the limestone structure.[18] Coughlin had a private study built at the top of the large tower, which loomed over the church. He penned his radio sermons there, a Great Dane by his side. By the time Sofía visited Royal Oak, a gift shop sold signed portraits of Coughlin, silver rosaries, and even a silver-plated automobile gearshift lever. One contemporary noted the shop's profits were "the highest in the holy trinket retail field." It went on like that until one zealous church lady hid a chain in her purse; once inside, she used it to smash the shop to pieces, like some sort of modern exorcism of moneychangers from the house of God.[19]

But in 1934 that scene still lay in the future. At the time of Sofía's visit, business was booming. Sofía was hopeful that Coughlin's radio listeners would shower on her and on her mission a small measure of the "rain of roses" she saw accumulating at the Shrine of the Little Flower.

Sofía met Coughlin at the home of Bishop Gallagher. "He was very kind," Sofía recalled of Coughlin, "and showed a deep interest in the plight of Mexican Catholics." They spoke at length about Sofía's experiences in Mexico. They discussed Father Pro and other martyrs. Coughlin had, in fact, installed a small votive shrine in his church dedicated to Father Pro.[20] It quickly became apparent to Sofía that Coughlin had no intention of allowing Sofía to talk on the radio. Coughlin alone spoke on the radio. He was using Sofía for research. Coughlin asked Sofía for printed materials; perhaps propaganda distributed secretly in Mexico, he suggested, which he could study. Coughlin planned to dedicate his Christmas broadcast—set for Sunday, December 23—to discuss the Mexican situation.

Bishop Gallagher returned to the room where Sofía and Coughlin had been meeting. As they were saying their goodbyes, Gallagher invited Coughlin to lunch with Sofía. Sofía was scheduled to give a lecture at a nearby convent. Would Coughlin like to watch? Gallagher asked. Coughlin agreed and the two men accompanied Sofía to her talk.[21]

Sofía felt encouraged by the meeting, even excited by the prospect of Coughlin's Christmas sermon being heard by millions of Americans. But she expressed doubts to Ruiz whether Coughlin's program would have the "appropriate tenor."[22] Perhaps it would be too political? Sofía wondered. It appears Sofía was aware that Coughlin's charisma could be a double-edged sword—sharp enough to cut through American indifference, but also potentially dangerous to the message Sofía wanted broadcast. She desired American economic assistance and solidarity. She didn't want to be a prop for Coughlin's American political vision.

Unfortunately, that was just what Coughlin sought to promote. He wielded the radio sermon of December 23 to attack President Franklin Roosevelt's New Deal, the series of laws and institutions created to save the American economy from Depression. The persecution of Mexican Catholics became a convenient straw man to hack apart before taking a swipe at FDR. "The government of the United States," Coughlin accused, "from Wilson down to our President Roosevelt has aided and abetted the rape of Mexico." If Mexico was suffering, Coughlin told his listeners, it was the fault of American policies. "From Wilson to Roosevelt Mexico has fallen the full depth into the slimy cesspool of barbarism."[23]

The Radio Priest charged ahead, denouncing Mexico's socialist and sexual education program. On this Sofía and other Catholics could agree. Sofía, Miranda, and Catholic Action rejected the new Mexican public education program as godless. But Coughlin went for sensation. The claims he made were fantasies. "Blush not!" he said to his radio audience, "for in your mind's eye you will see little children stripped naked—little children of both sexes, not only taught to examine themselves but taught, by performance in the class room, how to commit copulation with each other." Coughlin suggested that "natural and unnatural sins against the flesh" were perpetrated in the Mexican public schools—by this he meant both heterosexual and homosexual violation. He demanded that Americans do something about "the sodomy that cries to heaven for vengeance" because of the Mexican socialist and sexual education initiatives.[24]

At the end of the broadcast, Coughlin revealed his political aim. "Purposely I have saved the first principle of our sixteen points for this day, which is dedicated to the Christ Child." He was referring to the sixteen points of his new political organization—the National Union for Social Justice. Even as he met with Sofía in November, Coughlin was founding the new political party. He used the interview with Sofía, and the eventual broadcast, to bolster his political objective—the dismemberment of FDR's New Deal. Coughlin wanted to scare Americans by using Mexico as an example. "Moscow is here!" he said, "the league of the godless is encroaching while we sit idly by with a wicked complacency." He pointed to his organization, the National Union, as a way out of impending doom—"Freedom of religion, freedom in education because the child does not belong to the state!"[25]

Coughlin made headlines in the press for his broadcast on the Mexican persecution—for that, Sofía was glad. But most newspapers commented on Coughlin's vitriol toward Roosevelt and the current American ambassador to Mexico, Josephus Daniels.[26] The issue of Mexican persecution was lost amid Coughlin's harangues of FDR. Worse still, Coughlin reinforced American racist ideas of Mexicans: their supposed backwardness, barbarism, and passivity. That was not the message Sofía wanted broadcast. She sought publicity for the Mexican situation and she needed money for Catholic Action. Yet she didn't want to achieve those goals by furthering Americans' racist ideas about Mexicans.

The meeting with Coughlin, and the priest's eventual broadcast, was the first of several experiences Sofía had with American speakers and writers—Catholics who saw themselves as allies of Sofía and the church in Mexico, but all of whom had their own particular American domestic political agendas. Coughlin was one, but there were others. After leaving Detroit, Sofía gave an interview for Michael Williams, editor of the Catholic publication *Commonweal*. The eventual article in *Commonweal* about the Mexican situation did not mention Sofía. It used the issue of Mexican persecution to lambast the silence of Protestants and Jews on the subject. Religious freedom, wrote the *Commonweal* editors, "is not only an issue in Mexico: it was an issue in Russia yesterday, and state totalitarianism conquered; it is today an issue in Germany; tomorrow it may be an issue in the United States as well." Mexico was a tale of what could happen in the United States if Americans—Catholics, Protestants, and Jews—did nothing to stop it. *Commonweal*, while purporting to uphold religious liberty, made sure to take a jab at Protestants and Jews while reporting on Mexican Catholic persecution.[27]

By 1935 American clergymen began publishing books on the Mexican situation.[28] Sofía found these men to be temperamental allies. Bishop Francis Clement Kelley produced *Blood-Drenched Altars* (1935), while Jesuit Wilfrid Parsons published *Mexican Martyrdom* (1936). Sofía assisted both authors with research, information, and background stories for their books. Although she thought she was helping promote the cause of Mexican Catholic Action, both books offered little in the way of a true picture of Mexico's situation. They were sensational accounts, partisan screeds promoting American intervention in Mexico. Sofía wrote to Ruiz of her disappointment. "Although I have done it willingly in order to help Mexico, Your Eminence knows how the people of this country are. They propose writing a book in just a few weeks, and the superficiality and the inaccuracies of this frighten me." Sofía learned firsthand the danger of letting others be her mouthpiece. "But you have to take things as they are," Sofía wrote Ruiz.[29]

What did American Catholics see when they looked at Mexico? Like incantations spoken over a simmering cauldron of racist ideas, American words about Mexico formed the wispy specters of a beastly and ignorant people south of the border. The incantations sounded like Father Coughlin. "Never in the heart of Africa," he said, "could be found the savagery of Mexico's present government."[30] Coughlin told millions in his radio sermon of December 23, 1934—the radio sermon he had promised Sofía he would give—that "Mexico . . . is pleading on her knees and asking us in the name of the Infant Christ whom we revere at this moment to have pity on her and cease associating ourselves with her crucifixion."[31] Coughlin's view was not far from other American Catholics. Only the degree of vehemence, of frothing-at-the-mouth invective, set Coughlin's view apart from the mainstream American Catholic view. The core was the same: Mexico, a land of barbarism, was led by atheists, communists, and Indians; Mexico's only saving grace was its Catholic European culture, which was being beaten to a bloody pulp. For instance, one popular lecturer at Notre Dame University, who spoke in defense of Mexican Catholics, made sure to remind his audience: "It is essential to remember that Mexico is not really a white man's country. . . . Mexicans, for the last one hundred years have been held in ignorance by a government whose power depends largely on this ignorance." Only the Catholic Church, he said, was "largely responsible for the steady growth of a lasting culture in Mexico."[32]

In an attempt to hurt Mexico's government with their words, American Catholics reinforced racial and cultural stereotypes of Mexicans. Racist words soon took on flesh in cartoons published by Catholic newspapers. The *Brooklyn Tablet*, a consistent defender of the Mexican Catholic Church, ran a cartoon captioned, "Freedom in Mexico." The cartoon appeared in November 1934, as the education crisis in Mexico ramped up, as American Catholics demanded the recall of U.S. ambassador Daniels, and as Sofía was still reeling from the Mysterious Sofía scandal. The cartoon depicts Mexico's government as a corrupt politician—fat, sloppy, and smiling baffoonishly. Alongside this character are other figures in cahoots with the first: one is labeled "Gov't Grafter"; the other, "Social Racket." The three men—caricatured with dark, supposedly Indian or mestizo facial features—look on as a fourth figure menacingly stands over a Hispanic, supposedly white, individual who represents religious freedom; a broken sign with "Freedom of Speech" and "Freedom of Education" lies tattered beside the knocked-

24. "Freedom in Mexico" through the eyes of American Catholics. *Brooklyn Tablet,* November 8, 1934, p. 8.

down Hispanic man on the ground. The figure looming above him holds the butt-end of a pistol ready to strike. The corrupt officials look on—one says to his companion: "He must take it out on someone."

The cartoon suggests that the persecution of Mexican Catholics was a diversion from the Mexican people's real enemies—the corrupt government and moneyed interests of the social elite. The cause of religion and the cause of freedom in Mexico were both embodied in a white individual who had been knocked to the ground. In the distance, on the other side of the Rio Grande, in the United States, the Statue of Liberty shines a beacon of freedom. America is the fount of liberty, the cartoon argues. And Mexico, a land of atheists, communists, and revolutionaries—all coded as Indians or mestizos—was a land of barbarism. Mexico's only saving grace was its Catholic culture, depicted as white.

Sofía encountered these images, and the racist ideas behind them, during her tour of the United States. Using others as a mouthpiece was a fraught proposition, she came to realize. She couldn't trust the job to someone else. She'd have to be the one to speak directly to Americans. Despite her fears, especially after the Mysterious Sofía scandal, she assumed responsibility for correcting the image Americans had of Mexican Catholics.

33

On the Road

Controlling the image of Mexican Catholicism utterly exhausted Sofía. From 1935 to 1937 Sofía visited scores of cities between Washington DC and Seattle and between St. Paul and Chicago. She traveled mainly in the East however, working back and forth along the Catholic networks of power and money located between New York, Philadelphia, Boston, Baltimore, New Jersey, and Washington. Fatigue set in, not only due to a grueling schedule, but because she became the face of the church in Mexico to the people she met. Sofía offered herself in place of the racist cartoons, the sensational books, and the condescension of Father Coughlin. She felt the weight of every word she spoke, each interaction, every answer she gave, because Sofía knew that the impression she left with her audiences would be the image Americans took with them of Mexico.

Sofía felt she had to be remarkable, extraordinary. Listeners inspected everything about her. They tested her intelligence. After listening to Sofía, one professor at the Catholic University of America felt satisfied that "every member of the audience had become 'sapientior'"—that is, wiser.[1] (The professor's use of the Latin word apparently showcased his qualifications to judge on matters of intelligence.) American audiences assessed Sofía's English. One American mother superior from New York wrote: "The matter of her lectures is, of course, above all interesting and timely, but the manner of them and the English is also extraordinarily good. Miss Del Valle has a vocabulary which is far richer and more varied than many people who are born English-speaking. There is but the faintest trace of a foreign accent, only enough to give charm to the pronunciation."[2] When Sofía spoke in Cleveland, one of the city's Catholic newspapers introduced her to its readers as "the leading Catholic woman of her country," that Sofía was "young, attractive and energetic," that she was "not guilty of the faintest accent." The newspaper went on to describe Sofía as pious, but also fashionable. "Though deeply religious, Senorita Del Valle definitely is not out of touch with the world as her sleek New York clothes prove."[3]

Sofía carried Mexico with her to small impromptu tea parties, to Catholic girls' schools, to conferences and congresses organized by elite lay societies. Miss Duffy's Catholic Daughters of America sized her up. So too did the women of the International Federation of Catholic Alumnae. The men of the Knights of Columbus, influential in American politics, gauged whether to trust Sofía. Protestants and Jews heard Sofía speak at specially arranged interfaith meetings. Parish congregations and communities of male and female religious, priests, and priests-in-training at several seminaries—all looked for a way to generalize about Mexico in the presentation of a singular Mexican woman. A promotional brochure about Sofía's mission—circulated internally among American Catholics—reported that Sofía gave over five hundred lectures in her first two years traveling in the United States.[4]

During the first half of 1935, in addition to lectures within her East Coast nexus (Philadelphia, New York, Baltimore, Washington DC), she made a trip to the Midwest—to Chicago, St. Paul, Milwaukie, Great Falls (Montana), and St. Louis, as well as to the West, in Seattle at the National Conference for the Catholic Alumnae, and was invited to speak in British Columbia, Canada, and Portland, Oregon.

Controlling the image, carrying that image on her face, conveying it with her words, showcasing it with her outfits, embodying the Mexican Church, was a daunting task.

Sofía was tired.

In Philadelphia Sofía often found rest with the Mothers of the Assumption, where her sister Hortensia—known by everyone as Mother François—was mother superior. The convent would be a refuge for her throughout her time in the United States. Sofía's schedule was grueling. In one twenty-four-hour period, she traveled from New York to Baltimore to give a lecture at 2:00 p.m., then on to Newark, New Jersey, that same day to give a talk at 8:30 p.m. that evening. By 10:30

p.m. she was back on the train for a return trip to Baltimore, arriving at 2:10 a.m. in order to give a lecture there at 10:00 a.m. and another later that afternoon. Sofía spent the next day in bed with a headache but still managed to draft a list of questions she had been asked during her talks, which she would later work through with the help of Miranda in order to construct the best possible answers for future lectures.[5]

Sofía's schedule drained her spiritually as well as physically. The monotony of her schedule bothered her; she had no time to reflect, to maintain her interior spiritual vitality: "I have been so occupied with my lectures and with all the interviews that so many people have wanted with me . . . that there are times that I do not notice the days passing. I live almost automatically and I do not have time to reflect on all that is happening and the consequences of so many hardships, but I can only put myself in God's hands."[6] Sofía found comfort and control in daily Mass and Communion. She was forced to trust in Providence, which provided a narrative of her role in God's global plan. God brought to her, Sofía believed, those individuals who could help her carry out her mission. The mission to the United States would only be a success with the help of sympathetic, well-connected Catholics *and* with spiritual aid. She wrote to Ruiz y Flores: "Once again, I ask [Your Excellency] to keep me in your prayers . . . especially that Our Lord concedes through the special intercession of St. Teresita [Thérèse of Lisieux] that this effort might be as successful as we have hoped, as I feel a great responsibility on me with all the efforts and sacrifices that [Your Excellency] and Father Miranda have made to facilitate these trips, and I would like to see your sacrifices amply compensated with the fruit of my meager efforts abundantly blessed by God."[7] In every conversation she believed that perhaps Providence had arranged the meeting; the circumstances were not mere happenstance. She set about to work for the good of the Catholic faith and the interests of Mexico and trusted that an unseen hand was guiding her movements, her words, and her lectures. She understood her limitations: a single woman in a country that was not her own, with limited resources—both financial and social—and fighting the preconceptions and prejudices of Americans toward women and Mexicans. But she felt herself to be an instrument of Providence nonetheless—a tool—and Providence was using her to carry out an important work.

Sofía perceived Providence to be working in bringing to her the right people who could assist in her mission. In Boston she befriended Elizabeth Ward Loughran, a graduate of Trinity College and a woman with numerous connections within the city's Catholic community. (Loughran later became the private secretary of Cardinal Cushing of Boston.)[8] Elizabeth Loughran had short hair she wore in curls, a round face, and round glasses, which magnified kind, intelligent eyes. When Loughran heard Sofía speak about Mexico she immediately offered to connect her to individuals of influence: the rector of the city's seminary, Jesuits at Boston College, and several prominent priests in the vicinity. Loughran received a master's degree from Boston University and, eventually, a doctorate from Emmanuel College. She worked for four years in the field of Latin American history under Professor C. H. Haring of Harvard. She published an article for the *Catholic Historical Review*.[9] When Loughran wasn't pursuing research, she organized the Trinity Speakers Bureau—a coterie of intellectual Catholic women who gave lectures in the Boston area on an array of topics. Elizabeth and Sofía were instant friends. They understood one another. Neither was married—both committed their lives to serve the social and educational mission of the church. Sofía wrote that when "I arrived in Boston to prepare the terrain there I met, or better said Providence took care of putting me before a young woman who would serve as my 'Guardian Angel' there." Throughout Sofía's time in the United States, Loughran would remain a trusted friend, constant encourager, and key contact who helped introduce her to Boston's Catholic elite.[10]

It's likely that Sofía met Dorothy Day in 1935 or 1936, although no documents from the archive can confirm they crossed paths. Only a few years before, Dorothy Day helped establish *Catholic Worker*, both a newspaper and a movement. Day's long-time co-leader in this project was Peter Maurin, a man twenty years older, a French Catholic activist trained in the latest social Catholic teachings in Europe. Together, Dorothy and Peter opened soup kitchens, shelters, and centers for workers in the midst of the Great Depression. The movement began in

New York, but then spread across the country. By 1936 *Catholic Worker* had 150,000 subscribers. They took the Catholic "third way"—a path between capitalism and socialism—to a radical extreme: marching with striking workers, rejecting militarism, embracing pacifism.[11]

Members of Catholic Worker protested at the Mexican consulate after the Mysterious Sofía scandal. Religious liberty in Mexico became an important issue for the movement. Dorothy Day worked with the Baltimore Bureau for the Defense of Religious Liberty in Mexico.[12] Sofía often worked at the Baltimore Bureau, too; she translated Spanish-language documents into English. It became an important point of return and departure during Sofía's lecture tour. Dorothy was an American who, in her early life, saw more viable solutions to the social question in the political Left—in socialism—than in religion. Dorothy moved to Greenwich Village, lived a Bohemian life, took a lover, had an abortion, got pregnant again, and had a child out of wedlock.[13] Having a child reawakened her spiritual search. She decided to have her daughter baptized in the Catholic Church; Dorothy herself converted in 1927. For six months between December 1929 and June 1930 Dorothy lived in Mexico City.[14] There's no evidence Dorothy met Sofía then. Sofía was a cradle Catholic, a Mexican who ran in social circles Dorothy Day despised. Day had committed to radical poverty; she probably considered Sofía too bourgeois for her taste. Dorothy was a woman of the world trying to find a home in the church; Sofía, a churchwoman trying to find her place in the world opening before her. Dorothy wanted radical change; Sofía, incremental education.

Yet seemingly divergent paths have a way of crossing. Both shared a calling to celibate life. They were laywomen wholly devoted to a Christian restoration of society. For Dorothy it was the solidarity of picket line and soup kitchen; for Sofía, the service of the schoolhouse and the intellectual education of the new Catholic woman. Both had a social calling. "I had prayed that some way would open up for me to do *something*," Dorothy later wrote in her memoir, "to line myself up on their side, to work for them, so that I would no longer feel that I had been false to them in embracing my new-found faith."[15] Sofía too longed to do *something*—a longing that led to her vocation of service.

Both women attached themselves to men by choice, first out of seeming necessity, then less so over time. The authority male priests had over their lives gradually diminished. They were professional lay workers, increasingly with one foot in church work, the other in civil society.

When Sofía wasn't working at the Baltimore Bureau, she traveled. Life on the road for Sofía taught her to trust Providence. Control and order were hard to come by—Sofía had to put faith in the control and order offered by Providence. Sofía felt herself to be a modern Esther, called to such a time as this; her mission, like that of her biblical model, would be to help save a people from destruction through her humble acceptance of God's mission.

Carrying the image of Mexico meant upholding an ideal model of female activism. Sofía remained conscious of appearances. How she presented herself mattered. Her dress and her relations with ecclesiastical authorities, especially men, were intentionally orchestrated. On a trip from Mexico to Washington DC, Sofía stayed a few nights at the Convent of the Incarnate Word in San Antonio, where Ruiz y Flores lived and ran the apostolic delegation. On the morning of her departure, she went to Mass and received Communion, as was her daily custom. When Mass went long she had to hurry to leave in order to catch her train. Onboard, she wrote Ruiz about several business matters, which she hadn't remembered to tell him in their face-to-face meetings. However, she made sure to extend her apologies for her quick departure, not wanting the sisters of the convent of the Incarnate Word to think she had simply left *a la francesa*, or without regard to propriety and decorum.[16]

Bearing the image of Mexico required Sofía to keep all the pieces of her identity in place—a gender ideal as well as a class ideal. She needed to be fashionable but also modest, concerned for the working class but also respectable. Sofía's ideal of female activism had a clear element of social class. She'd begun her career as an activist by forming professional associations of workingwomen. Once in the United States, her preoccupation with workingwomen continued. During her already daunting schedule, Sofía gave classes in New York City to Latin American immigrants on the principles and practice of Catholic

Action.[17] This group was made up of women living in New York who came from around the Spanish-speaking world: the Caribbean, especially Puerto Rico, as well as Central and South America. Sofía modeled the group on the JCFM, giving it the name of the Iberoamerican Young Women's Association. It was parish-based, and an American priest was assigned its first ecclesiastical assistant.[18]

Sofía's class status often translated into class paternalism: she believed that she had the responsibility to educate, train, and "lift" workingwomen of a lower-class status through moral instruction. Catholic class distinctions were not hers alone but came imbedded in Catholic Action. A committed elite, often urban and of a higher social status, were the ones appointed to spread Catholic social doctrine. The apostolate, or mission, of the hierarchy, was first imparted to an elite laity in every sense of the word: educated, most often urban, of financial means, and "whiter," who shared in a cosmopolitan culture and who idealized French, Spanish, Belgian, Italian, and German Catholic piety and practice. As an elite Catholic woman, Sofía felt called to educate young workingwomen, imparting to them the apostolic mission she had received from the male hierarchy. The Catholic feminine ideal contained a distinct class dimension.

Throughout her time in the United States, recognition made Sofía feel uncomfortable and revealed the importance of modesty within the Catholic female ideal. In Springfield, Massachusetts, she received a medal from a local Catholic college, given "to the woman that has accomplished some outstanding work." The award was given out at a graduation ceremony, held for the girls of the college. Before diplomas were handed out, three speeches were given by young women on Mexico: "The Church and Spanish Mexico," "The Church and Republican Mexico," and "The Church in Mexico Today." Then the local bishop spoke at length on Sofía and her work. Sofía wrote, "I do not understand how these gentlemen have taken notice of me." Yet, she put herself in the hands of God and accepted the honor in name of Mexican Catholic women, although she wrote, "I wanted to disappear under my chair."[19] The young women of the college offered her a precious bouquet of flowers, and afterward they had a reception in her honor. While maintaining modesty was important to Sofía, her mission in defense of Mexico also became a mission to embody an ideal Catholic femininity.

Bishops took special note of Sofía's model womanhood. In Boston in July 1936 she spoke in one of the "morning salons" that were celebrated in the parks of the great summer residences of some of the wealthy Catholics in the city. The cardinal archbishop of Boston heard about the event and sent her a note, wishing her success. Then through a female friend of the cardinal, Sofía was contacted for a private audience. The visit took place over tea, and the cardinal lavished Sofía with praise, telling her how happy and satisfied he was that Sofía was speaking in his diocese and that she represented "a model of womanhood that he wanted to be spread in his archdiocese."[20] Sofía remembered she'd luckily decided to wear gloves that day, as she had painted her nails and knew the cardinal was "a severe man when it came to the look and appearance of women." "I always made sure to adjust myself to the environment in which I worked," she recalled, "and so I painted my nails, albeit in pale colors, so that no one would think that Mexican women were not up to date in fashion."[21] It was a balancing act. Painted nails were a must for some Americans—unpainted nails necessary for others. Sofía's little white gloves came in handy.

Keeping all the pieces together—holding her gender, her class, her religion, her nationality in alignment—became difficult. When confronting American racist ideas Sofía pushed the boundaries of respectability. Yet even in this, Sofía mounted her counterattacks with a nod toward prudence. She expressed her opinions but with tact, even when they conflicted with the ideas of bishops, priests, and laymen. In an early meeting with Rev. Burke, the influential priest frankly stated that Sofía's mission to raise public opinion among American Catholics would certainly benefit the Mexican church, especially if the enthusiasm she encouraged resulted in financial assistance for Mexican Catholic Action. However, Burke continued, he believed that the Mexican government could not care less about American Catholic public opinion; on this point Sofía sharply disagreed and made sure to express her contrary point of view.

Sofía constantly contended with the prejudices of American Catholics toward their Mexican brothers and sisters. In Boston, John E. Swift, a judge and the future leader of the Knights of Columbus, invited Sofía to a tea, where she made her presentation about the Mexican religious conflict. A question and answer period followed, and to Sofía's annoyance, Swift pointedly asked, "Miss del Valle, do you think that the Mexican people would ever take into consideration their annexation to the USA?" Sofía replied without missing a beat: "They would never give a minute's thought to that idea. They know very well the way you have treated your Indians."[22] In a letter to Ruiz y Flores about the incident, Sofía recounted that Swift had nothing to say after that. Yet, she wrote, the question had put her in a difficult position, her answer had to be given "with a lot of diplomacy [and] without offending even while saying something that would be truthful and definite."[23] She felt the answer perhaps a bit forthright, but within the boundaries of tactful conversation. Sofía felt she'd been inspired by the Holy Spirit in her reply. The interchange was disheartening nonetheless. She wrote Ruiz: "But just imagine [Your Excellency] these ideas among those who might want to help us. You can see that they do not understand our problems except through the eyes of 'satisfied Americans.'"[24] Sofía found herself in a gendered world, with boundaries around what was acceptable behavior for women. But she had to speak articulately, pointedly, and even a bit sharply in overcoming inherent condescension toward women. And in her role as a representative of Mexican Catholics, she had to use these same skills to battle American racial and national biases.

Sofía's gendered performance also came under critique from American women. Again, in Boston, she was invited to speak to a meeting of the Junior League, a philanthropic organization composed of the wealthy elite of the city. Sofía took care, as usual, to make sure her physical presentation was just as pristine as her speech. Her hair, dress, shoes, purse—everything was fashionable and neatly ordered. During her lecture, she noticed that many in the crowd were more interested in how she looked than in what she said: "I knew that God would help me and that my mother, the Virgin of Guadalupe, would give me victory in the challenge. After the conference, we were offered a tea and I had the pleasure of being congratulated by various participants both for my English and for my attire. Some of the women told me: 'We never thought that a Mexican could present so well.'"[25] In another incident she was asked whether the clothes she wore were made in Mexico or if when she was in her country she wore feathers. She replied that the clothes were indeed made in Mexico and the only feathers she wore were in her hats.[26]

National and racial stereotypes came in a gendered package, requiring Sofía to overcome prejudices against Mexico, and with it notions of Mexico's perceived racial "otherness," through a performance of ideal Catholic femininity: being well dressed, fashionable, and articulate and having self-effacing humor. For example, after one lecture, a member of the audience asked if she was a nun. Sofía replied in reference to her well-dressed outfit, "Do I look like a nun?"[27] The audience laughed uproariously, and any tension in the question-and-answer session dissipated.

Sofía's continuing work on behalf of Cultura Femenina and Catholic Action in Mexico did not go unnoticed among Europe's elite Catholic women. Her friendship with Christine de Hemptinne, who remained president of the youth branch of the IUCWL, provided an important contact with the leadership of the European Catholic women's movement. Sofía had affiliated Cultura Femenina and the JCFM with the Union Internationale in 1930. She had attended the 1931 congress with de Hemptinne and was again invited to speak at the 1937 meeting in Belgium. The leader of the IUCWL, Madame Steenberghe-Engerin, presented her as the representative of Latin America at the congress. "It appears that *Diosito* has wanted to use me as a mouthpiece for Latin America," Sofía wrote Ruiz, "as I had many opportunities to intervene in the discussions that helped bring a clearer understanding of our mentality and our problems."[28] She attended the sessions for young women, as well as the ones dedicated to Catholic Ladies. There, she was given an opportunity to give her point of view from a Latin American perspective. In all, approximately twenty-two countries were represented.

After the conference, Madame Steenberghe-Engerin tasked Sofía with a mission to Rome. En route she gave several lectures in Paris and then traveled to the Eternal City. There she met with Giuseppe Pizzardo, Pius XI's point man for the Roman model of Catholic Action.[29] About the meeting she wrote Ruiz y Flores that Pizzardo

> surprised me with his attention and cordiality and I had a conversation with him for close to three hours. In it, we touched on various points, especially on Mexico, naturally, and I believe that I was able to shed some light with respect to our situation and especially regarding the constructive work of Catholic Action. He told me things that I will tell [Your Excellency] when we meet, he asked me for my impressions of things [in the United States], and we left on the best of terms. [He] asked me to write to him every so often, providing him information regarding various issues that I hope to indicate to [Your Excellency].[30]

The next day she had tea with the sisters of a Mrs. Macauley, widow of Nicholas Brady, an American Catholic who had been involved in negotiations to give money to the cristero cause during 1927. Sofía spoke at a gathering of aristocratic Catholic women about Mexico. After further meetings with Francesco Borgongini-Duca, another Vatican official, she wrote that she was able to "bathe myself in the atmosphere of Rome and renew myself internally in the catacombs and in the magnificent basilicas, especially in St. Peter's."[31]

Sofía discovered what so many others have found—a lot of work for little payoff. Although less successful than hoped, Sofía raised a not-inconsequential sum. The exact figures are hard to calculate, as the documentary evidence is incomplete. Before April 1935, the date when a bank account was opened in New York City, the donations sent back to Mexico were spotty at best. Sofía did not always provide a detailed accounting of the money sent during this earlier period; also, much of the money collected went toward her travel expenses, as well as to her own family. It had been decided that the sum of one hundred dollars a month would be sent to her family because her contributions remained an important part of her parents' income during this period. From April to June 1935 Sofía's lectures raised $1,393.37, and $420 from these funds went to the Social Secretariat, the JCFM, and Cultura Femenina. Between January 1936 and June 1937 she raised another $6,728.52, of which $3,186.70 was sent to Mexico, divided between her family (a little more than half, $1,605.80) while the rest was provided to Cultura Femenina and Mexican Catholic Action ($1,580.90). Of the other remaining money, $2,687.65 was used for expenses. Thus, from April 1935 to June 1937, she raised a rough sum of $2,000 for Catholic organizations. It does seem that she was able to collect more than this amount, as many of her letters report receiving additional donations. However, it is not possible to say with any accuracy exactly how much, because these additional funds were allocated among expenses, money to her family, and funds sent directly to Mexican Catholic ministries.[32]

Sofía's mission officially ended in 1938. Yet she wasn't done with the United States. For over twenty years, beginning in 1934, Sofía traveled nearly annually to the United States to give lectures on Mexico. The networks she established in the mid-thirties remained intact throughout those two decades. When money for Cultura Femenina was scarce, she went north. Sofía recalled in her unfinished memoir that Cultura Femenina's accountant would approach her with bad financial news. "Sofía," the accountant would say, "the funds are getting low; we might have only enough to cover rent for this month."[33] Sofía remembered that that was her cue "to consider traveling to the U.S." Small donations from her network in the United States—an East Coast circuit between Philadelphia, Newark, New York, Washington, and Boston—covered operating expenses. By the early 1940s Sofía charged a going rate of sixty dollars per lecture: fifty dollars went to Cultura Femenina and ten to traveling expenses.[34] Cultura Femenina remained small. At the beginning of Sofía's U.S. tour there were only fourteen students in 1935, and Eugenia Olivera wrote from Mexico that money was almost nonexistent.[35] A high of eighty students in the late twenties and early thirties eventually declined to half that number by the forties and fifties. Sofía never sought multitudes. She wanted leaders. And these she trained in abundance: women who would lead Catholic Action, who would become journalists, social workers, and future politicians.

As the 1930s came to a close, the order and structure of Sofía's life altered. The men Sofía knew and trusted and worked with began to disappear. Archbishop Pascual Díaz died in 1936. Rev. John Burke, the American priest who supported Sofía in the NCWC, also died that same year. Archbishop Leopoldo Ruiz y Flores, the exiled apostolic delegate much maligned by ex-cristeros, lost his job as Rome's envoy in 1937. The Vatican fired Ruiz. Officials in Rome—Giuseppe Pizzardo and Eugenio Pacelli—lost trust in Ruiz's ability to function effectively. He was prone to publishing rash statements, they believed; he'd become estranged from the Mexican bishops during his exile in San Antonio.[36] The Vatican looked elsewhere for new leadership of the Mexican hierarchy. They chose Luis María Martínez to be the next archbishop of Mexico City. In a highly unusual move for the Vatican, Rome named Martínez the apostolic delegate as well. The decision enabled Martínez to get around the Mexican government's refusal to allow a nuncio in Mexico. Martínez would be both the head of the Mexican bishops *and* the intermediary to the Vatican. Ruiz y Flores returned to Mexico as a simple archbishop, without a mission for Mexico's future. He had been one of Sofía's spiritual advisors. Ruiz died in 1941, defending until the end his role in bringing about peace to Mexico and putting a stop to the Cristero War. Sofía now had fewer authorities to lean on.

In 1937 everything changed for the two men closest to Sofía— Miguel Miranda and Francisco del Valle, Sofía's father. Miranda was made bishop of the Mexican diocese of Tulancingo, located in Hidalgo almost sixty miles from Mexico City. A picture taken in the mid-thirties shows the importance of Miranda to the del Valles. Miranda stands in the center, towering over Sofía and her family. Sofía's sister Ana María and her husband, Angel Huidobro, are there. Sofía's mother wears a contented smile. Sofía's father looks happy. The men have a glass in hand, perhaps in toast to Miranda's presence. Sofía stands on the end, with Sofía's mother standing between her and Miranda. And like her mother, Sofía too looks down in the moment before the picture was to be taken.

25. *Standing, left to right*: Sofía, Mama del Valle, Miranda, Angel R. de Huidobro, Francisco del Valle, Ana María R. de Huidobro de del Valle; (*seated*) unidentified. Personal collection of María Teresa Ruiz de Huidobro Márquez.

It's tempting to imagine a scene like this photograph taking place at Quinta Sofía after Miranda's appointment as bishop in 1937. Miranda not only had a close relationship with Sofía, but also with Sofía's parents. The del Valles supported Miranda, first during the death of Miranda's father, and then his mother, in the late 1920s. Miranda frequented family dinners at Quinta Sofía. While Miranda traveled, he inquired after the health of Sofía's parents; he wrote letters to her parents and received letters from them. Miranda chose Francisco, Sofía's father, to be his *padrino*, or godfather, when Miranda was ordained bishop.[37] The ceremony took place at the Basilica of Guadalupe. The *padrino* sat in a seat of honor, to one side of the altar of consecration. Francisco witnessed as Miranda received miter, staff, and pectoral cross. Sofía, from the congregation, saw Miranda receive the bishop's ring. "Receive the ring," the consecrating bishop told Miranda, "the symbol of fidelity, in order that, adorned with unspotted faith, you may keep, inviolably, the Spouse of God, namely, His Holy Church." The response from Sofía's lips, as from all those in the sanctuary, was "Amen."[38] Miranda's vows were to the Bride of Christ, the church.

Francisco Jr., the del Valle's son who died in 1921, would've been the same age as Miranda—forty-three. It's not unlikely Sofía's parents felt Miranda to be a surrogate son, taking joy in Miranda's honor of becoming a bishop, proud that their daughter, Sofía, had linked herself to such an accomplished and energetic clergyman. Perhaps Miranda was both the priest-son they never had and the closest thing to a son-in-law for their daughter Sofía. The two roles—priest and son-in-law—are contradictory, but Miranda's special relationship with Sofía and Sofía's parents suggests as much. When Miranda received his appointment as bishop, it seems no flight of the imagination to think that they celebrated at Quinta Sofía, that toasts were lifted in Miranda's honor, that smiles were worn openly and unguarded.

Amid the celebration for Miranda's future, Sofía felt fear for the next steps. In practice, Sofía had directed Cultura Femenina for almost a decade. But with Miranda's departure, Sofía harbored some anxiety for the new responsibility placed on her shoulders. She alone would be in charge. She would be dean and director—Cultura Femenina would succeed or fail on her direction alone. "Padre Miranda," Sofía remembered, "to our great desolation was named bishop of Tulancingo . . . from that time the institute came under my direction." Sofía rejoiced with Miranda, but privately felt the weight of responsibility in her new role. "Great was my anguish in feeling responsible," she recalled, "for the life and continuation of the youth." Sofía played down her skill and ability; she pointed to God's help and the assistance of other women. "I placed myself in God's hands," she said, "and with the collaboration of some brilliant ex-students we continued the work."[39] Her long-time friend and assistant, Juana Arguinzóniz, and Isabel Gibbon, a future JCFM president, were two collaborators. Sofía leaned on these women in the coming years.

As Miranda transitioned to Tulancingo, Sofía took charge of outfitting and decorating Miranda's new residence in the city. Sofía remembered doing so as a sign of affection from the JCFM, the organization Miranda had helped found. Sofía proposed using the furniture and home décor from the residence of the apostolic delegation in Mexico City. It wasn't being used since the new archbishop, Luis María Martínez, was named the apostolic delegate. He didn't need two residences. "Yes, *hija*," Martínez told Sofía when she asked permission, "it is a very good idea."[40]

If Sofía publicly outfitted Miranda's new home as a gesture of goodwill from the JCFM, she privately took exclusive control over the process. Sofía personally did Miranda's interior decorating. "The red doilies that were sent," she wrote Miranda, "are for your bedroom on either side of the bed, and the blue ones that you have are for the guest bedrooms." She told Miranda where to place the rugs, to remember that it can be slippery getting out of the bathtub without a proper bath mat, to use the two large bath towels she sent him during the winter months, as the houses were not heated in Tulancingo. Sofía sent flowerpots of roses and carnations and said she would send more, or others, if Miranda preferred different plants. If Sofía had to let Miranda go she would continue to be his complement. She made sure Miranda had what he needed in his new position.[41] One gets the sense she decorated Miranda's home the way she would've done it if she were moving in. Perhaps she absorbed herself in ordering Miranda's home as a way to expend her own anxiety over his permanent absence. They'd spent long months apart while he traveled, or while she was abroad. But their point of return had always been the "nest," their code for Cultura Femenina. Miranda's new appointment was different. Sofía was under no illusions: Miranda's assignment in Tulancingo had changed the proximity of their relationship.

Had it changed the nature of their relationship? He'd received the ring of commitment to the church. He was a bishop now, no longer a simple priest. Maybe Sofía's home decorating was an attempt to reconstruct their "nest" elsewhere and so to resist the potential for Miranda's consecration as bishop to alter the intimacy of their friendship. "I will be coming there very soon," Sofía wrote after Miranda was settled, "for a nice, long chat. Write me a few lines so I know how everything is going."[42] Miranda may have left Mexico City, but Sofía determined to continue with Miranda as she had before. She had a commitment to him—an intimacy with him—that went beyond their partnership in Cultura

Femenina and the JCFM. "You already know," Sofía wrote him, "that you are and always will be ours, or better said, we will always feel yours."[43]

The year 1937 was significant for another reason. The celebration of Miranda's consecration as bishop was probably the last time Sofía was together with both Miranda and her father. Francisco del Valle died at Quinta Sofía just weeks after Miranda's consecration. No letters speak about his death, and Sofía doesn't mention it in her unfinished memoir. Among the papers of Alfredo Méndez Medina is a prayer card, issued on the first anniversary of Francisco's death. The card reminded the faithful to pray for the soul of the departed. Sofía's silence on the subject is strange. She loved her father and respected him greatly. "My father was an extremely charitable man," Sofía remembered many years later, "extremely interested in helping people, and so we saw that when they went to father, he always spoke to us of the necessity of taking care of our brothers, of others." It was Francisco who first taught Sofía the value of education. Francisco facilitated Sofía's first endeavors to train factory women in Mexico City. She credited her parents for her life's successes. "If the work I have done has some merit," Sofía later reflected, "80 percent of it is due to the very great simplicity of the Christian education my parents gave me, always confirmed by their example." Sofía remembered, for instance, watching her father give an employee another chance after the worker came to the job drunk. "My father was good and tolerant like that, as the man needed the job."[44] One del Valle family member recalled Francisco sitting in his favorite chair in Quinta Sofía, smoking a good cigar, sipping a glass of cognac, and wearing a contented smile.[45] "Life in *América* is rough," Francisco would say with a wink as he nursed his drink, watching the rings of cigar smoke waver and waft away.

Sofía's silence on her father's death reveals not indifference but, rather, how devastating the blow was for the family—and for Sofía personally.[46]

While traveling, she struggled with guilt that, in her work for the church she was abandoning her family. In one letter Sofía wrote Ruiz that she worried about the "sickness of my parents."[47] In another letter she thanked Ruiz for his "comforting exhortations to my parents." After one visit home, she commented how it had been a needed "encouragement to my parents."[48] Sofía noted in her unfinished memoir that her initial travels organizing Catholic Action had meant leaving her mother alone. The del Valle's longtime nanny stepped in to keep the elder Sofía company. "I had peace of mind knowing she was in good hands." Sofía emphasized the "very generous and unselfish collaboration that my parents gave me, especially in the last years of their lives."[49] Sofía constantly tried to balance the call to work and the responsibility to family. It was her ideal and, to her, it required sacrifice to keep her work in the world from outweighing her duty to family. Perhaps Sofía's silence over her father's death reveals a bit of how hard the balance was.

As Sofía approached fifty, perhaps she felt, not for the first time, a sense of frightening independence. She was left without Miranda as leader of Cultura Femenina and the JCFM. Her father was dead. Only Sofía's mother and sister Matilde remained at home. But so much of her life over the past decade had been spent in frightening independence. She'd learned to live in it and had succeeded because of it. "I have led since my arrival in this land," Sofía wrote about her time in the United States, "the life of a pilgrim."[50] She'd become a frequent client of American railways. "A good part of my life," she continued, "I spend on the road. The seed that is being sown is little by little beginning to bear the desired fruits that we have hoped: prejudices diminishing, slander refuted, clear exposition of the present situation, the affection won of these our brothers for their brothers on the other side of the border, interest to do something to help us, prayer and penitence for us, and economic help for our needs."[51] Sofía continued to have a home at Quinta Sofía. She'd also established a feeling of home in the world. Any fear she may have had about the future was eased in the company of so many friends, scattered abroad. "It is good to have friends everywhere," she wrote to one American woman, "don't you think?"[52]

While Sofía finished her work in the United States in the spring of 1938, the English novelist Graham Greene, a somewhat recent and reluctant convert to Roman Catholicism, visited Mexico. Much of Miranda's and Sofía's work in the United States was about broadcasting the Mexican situation to as wide an audience as possible. Graham Greene desired to do just that—but on his own terms. Miranda facilitated Greene's trek through the Mexican states of Nuevo León, San Luis Potosí, Veracruz, Tabasco, Chiapas, Oaxaca, and Puebla.[53] Greene also made two stops in Mexico City.

The novelist, in his own words, absolutely hated Mexico. He was sick with dysentery, and perhaps his dour view of Mexico was made worse by his yet-to-be diagnosed mood disorder. "The dysentery was as bad as ever," Greene wrote in his 1939 travel memoir, *The Lawless Roads* (published in the United States as *Another Mexico*). "I watched anxiously for the blood which would mean hospital and no escape for weeks from this country which I hated."[54] And there was probably something to the probability that his travels triggered a bipolar swing—for instance, Greene himself, after later reading his travel diary, was unable to adequately account for just why he had been so negative during the trip.[55] Regardless, his journey, made with one English eyebrow cocked in dry irony, gave him enough fodder for his nonfiction travelogue as well as his most famed novel, *The Power and the Glory* (1940). The novel, loosely based on the religious persecution in the state of Tabasco, follows the ill-fated appointment of an anonymous "whiskey priest" with his eventual execution at the hands of government soldiers. Greene's protagonist is a bad priest. He drinks and fathers a child by one of his parishioners. Yet the priest doesn't flee the state as so many others do; he stays for reasons unknown even to him. Some unseen hand holds him within the persecution in order that he may fulfill his duty as a priest. Despite controversy over the novel—it wasn't exactly the sort of publicity Miranda and Sofía wanted—Greene's sensitive portrayal of the persevering faith of ordinary people within the frame of their frail humanity eventually found favor with Catholics—even the pope.[56]

Miranda appears in Greene's *The Lawless Roads*. He's called the bishop of Tulancingo—"dark, stout, and young, he reminded me a little of an Italian diplomat," Greene writes. Miranda and Greene go for a drive around Chapultepec Park in one section of the book. The two discuss the religious persecution; they talk about Father Pro and about a young member of the JCFM who was killed by radicals during a riot at a Mexico City church.[57]

"The Church needed blood," Miranda tells Greene as they drive. "It always needs blood."[58]

Greene did not name Sofía, who was in the United States at the time. Cultura Femenina, however, receives mention. "And the work goes on," Greene writes. "A training college for girls started at the time of the worst persecution to instruct leaders among the laity numbered six in 1926; now fifty-six thousand have been trained in theology and dogma." Greene's statistics lump Cultura Femenina with Catholic Action but, still, the unflappable Englishman is impressed by the perseverance of these young women. This seemingly ordinary Catholic women's association had, implausibly, "been lent the dignity of death," he notes.[59] The cadre of young women, led by Miranda and the unnamed Sofía, those of tea parties and prayers and "little meetings after Benediction"—groups that aroused suspicion in England, Greene adds—had been the ones to carry on the faith in Mexico. "This was headquarters," Greene describes one clergy gathering, "where they made blueprints—interminably—for a peaceful and holy world."[60] Miranda and Sofía were always preparing the future—Graham Greene recognized as much.

Near the end of Greene's dark description of Mexico the narrative pivots toward European fascism. On the eve of World War II—and in the midst of it by the time his two books were published—Greene uses Mexico to provide a dystopian forecast for Europe. The kind of "Total" state Greene sees in Mexico—squashing freedom of conscience with every altar toppled, every church closed—he bitterly predicts that Europe's future portends something similar. The only glimmer Greene seemed to spot in the descending darkness was the light of ordinary Catholics like those he encountered in Mexico, who, with their tea parties and their prayers, with their ribbons and medals, kept carrying on regardless of resistance.

But even perceptive seers can get their prophecies wrong. While Europe indeed descended into darkness and war, things improved in Mexico. It was as if Greene's dark clouds traveled back across the

Atlantic with him and Mexico's shadow passed. The policies of revolutionary anticlericalism—socialist education, especially—produced diminishing returns, as one historian of the period has argued. At every level, from the local school, to state politics, to the National Palace, Catholics resisted the state's education policy. New secular rituals couldn't dislodge local saints and national devotions such as the Virgin of Guadalupe. For many Mexicans, the Virgin of Tepeyac perfectly embodied La Madre Patria—The Motherland. The nationalist overtones of Guadalupe's protection had been too long ensconced in the national character; the revolution couldn't tear her out. President Cárdenas foresaw that much and struck a conciliatory stance with the new archbishop of Mexico, Luís María Martínez. As early as 1935–36, agents of President Cárdenas were in high-level secret talks with Mexican church officials. Sofía didn't recognize the meandering shift of the anticlerical cloud cover. Virtually no one did. Yet by 1938, even as Graham Greene imagined his hunted whisky priest, Archbishop Martínez gave Cárdenas backing for the Mexican government's oil nationalization. It was a move that infuriated the United States but ingratiated Cárdenas toward his erstwhile church enemies. The two men—Martínez and Cárdenas—were both from the same Mexican state, Michoacán. They understood one another and they understood politics. The antichurch laws stayed on the books and would remain so until the 1990s. But governing meant pragmatism and compromise. Martínez and Cárdenas were experts at both.

Sunbreaks appeared in the skies above Mexico's church-state relations. In late 1938 Sofía and the JCFM led a pilgrimage of two thousand Catholic women through Mexico City.[61] The very public event went unimpeded by Mexican authorities. Conflict over religion in public life remained, especially on the state level, where local politics still saw scuffles, even violence, between Catholics and revolutionary strongmen.[62] At the national level, however, the skies were all but clear. "In exchange for state tolerance of Catholic education," one historian writes, "and for as long as it was unmolested in the exercise of the cult, the church would support—no longer critique or rival—revolutionary social projects in a spirit of common patriotism."[63] Revolutionary anticlericalism was replaced by revolutionary nationalism—and the Catholic Church began to bask in the glow. The church could get behind nationalism. It offered a shared vision for the future, especially as the church began openly promoting Catholicism as a basis for national identity. And as long as the church stayed within boundaries, the government allowed Catholic ritual and ceremony to support civic unity. Archbishop Martínez understood the national quid pro quo. When Martínez felt one Catholic journalist had criticized the government too harshly, the archbishop squashed the dissent. "Don't forget," Martínez admonished, "*I'm* the one who milks the cow."[64]

For Sofía, the realization of the passing cloud of persecution was slow. American women, friends of Sofía, could plainly see that Sofía had done much to assist the Mexican church. Margaret Lynch, NCCW secretary—a woman who'd felt that Sofía was something of a headache in 1934—had changed her opinion. Lynch wrote of Sofía: "She has made every sacrifice for the cause of religion all her life and is continuing to do so. In fact, I consider her little short of a martyr."[65] But had Sofía's mission made any lasting impression? Was anything getting better? Sofía wasn't sure. In a 1940 letter, Lynch tried to encourage Sofía, going so far as to connect Sofía's work to the general trend of improving conditions in Mexico. "Your work in Mexico and the prayers said for Mexico seem to be having some effect," Lynch wrote. "Surely God will ultimately bring Mexico into the light and reestablish the hope and church activities as in former years. Our press here seems encouraged that the new regime is at least less anti-Catholic."[66]

President Manuel Ávila Camacho (1940–46) led the new regime Lynch mentioned in her letter. Cárdenas left office and with him, the most radical revolutionary policies softened. A conservative military officer, Ávila Camacho stated to the surprise and delight of Catholics, "I am a believer" during his inauguration in 1940. None of Sofía's letters refer to the president's statement, but surely Sofía, like so many other Mexican Catholics, took it as a sign of something better.

And it was better—the years of persecution and catacombs lay behind. And now the Mexican state needed the church. The state needed an ally who could marshal support for its programs of economic development, for its entry into World War II on the side of the United States and, eventually, after the war, the state found in the church a willing ally against Communism. When the United States declared war on Japan and Germany in December 1941, Mexico followed suit in 1942. Archbishop Martínez exhorted Catholics to support the war effort. Mexican women, Sofía included, were asked by their country, and by their archbishop, to join the cause.[67] Sofía del Valle, the woman who had not even ten years prior been labeled a traitor by the Mexican government, became a patriot.

34

La patria Calls

> If the whole world is set on fighting, what happens when we are at peace? What happens when there is no one left to work?
>
> Sofía del Valle

"Mexico is in a state of war," Sofía wrote in the July 1942 issue of *Juventud*, "and, in this perilous hour, duty calls all Mexicans to respond promptly to the Mother's call."[1] Mexico and the world were at war when Sofía wrote those words. Sofía's connections to the International Union of Catholic Women's Leagues were almost totally severed during the conflict. She received scant and spotty news of Christine de Hemptinne's travails in Europe, and Sofía feared for her European friends.[2] At home in Mexico, Sofía witnessed her society mobilizing. Mexico sent into harm's way just a single squadron of fighter pilots, nicknamed the Fighting Tigers. But regardless of numbers, Mexico was at war. The Catholic Church in Mexico—Sofía included—dedicated their time and energy to drum up support for the war effort. Perhaps Sofía felt the irony: Just a few years earlier the government was the Catholic Church's persecutor. Now, Sofía was calling Catholics to support the Mexican government.

After the war, while visiting Rome for an IUCWL congress, Sofía had a brief conversation with Pope Pius XII. A young Vatican official, Giovanni Montini (the future Pope Paul VI), a friend of Sofía's, ushered her up to the front of the crowd of women assembling before the pope.

"Mexico is going better, is that not so?" The pope beamed at Sofía.

"Yes, Holy Father," Sofía replied. "Even to the extent that yesterday's persecutors today desire their sons to be priests!"

Pius XII, the man who had once been Eugenio Pacelli—the man who took Gasparri's job and who saw his diplomacy of appeasement wither and die before Nazi atrocities—smiled at Sofía. "Mexico is a comfort to my heart," the pope said.[3]

Finally, Sofía felt, her patriotism and her activism were both in alignment with the Mexican government under President Ávila Camacho.[4] Now, more than ever, Sofía told the readers of *Juventud*, Mexico needed women of intelligence prepared to protect Mexico for future generations. "The present generation is the depositor," she wrote in *Juventud*, "and [our generation] is obligated to guard and to multiply the magnificent patrimony we have inherited, to transmit it intact and enriched to the generations to come." Whether as mothers, wives, or women devoted to service, Sofía called the JCFM to attention. "Member of Juventud," she wrote, "translate this love [of country] into deeds developed with due preparation to serve *la patria* (the homeland) with firm commitment and with the fervor of your enthusiastic youth, fulfilling all those responsibilities for which the present hour calls."[5]

Sofía was no warmonger. She'd always presented herself as a pacifist. During the Cristero War she'd committed the JCFM and Cultura Femenina to nonviolent activism. After World War II she committed her time to United Nations initiatives and was a member of several peace organizations such as Pax Romana. Was her call to support the Mexican war effort consistent with her commitment to peace? Sofía appeared to believe it was. She couldn't change policy—she could, however, aid those most affected, those most vulnerable to the consequences of war. Peace could only come, she believed, if someone was there to work for wars' victims. "How many times, in the course of these years . . . have we prayed . . . for the coming of concord, for peace between men? But peace has not come," Sofía wrote to the young women of the JCFM. Now that Mexico had found itself in the midst of a war it did not ask for, the duty of the JCFM was to come to the call of *la patria*—that was Sofía's message. Young women, committed to sacrifice, to bettering themselves, to using all of their gifts—their intelligence, their femininity, even their call to be mothers—was what the nation needed, Sofía argued. True patriotism, Sofía wrote, was not an appeal to revolution, but a call "to education, morality, useful reforms, that is authentic patriotism."[6] Sofía's bluff, that she had been training a generation of young women who could be of service to their nation, was being called. She wasn't going to let the moment pass without laying down a hand flush with aces.

In the war years *Juventud* magazine touted the image of an intelligent woman. The editors in charge of the JCFM's magazine in the 1940s were Lupe Velasco, Aurora de la Lama, Isabel Gibbon, and Eugenia Olivera. Both in content and in appearance, the magazine reflected the link between femininity and the intellect. *Juventud* gave its readers a picture of what kind of woman the nation needed in wartime. Prepared women, smart women, professional women—women useful to their families, to *la patria*, and to the world.

The covers of *Juventud* used striking visuals to link femininity and intelligence. Eugenia Olivera, a woman of fair complexion and blonde hair, contracted with Tufic Yazbek to take the cover photos for the magazine. Yazbek, born in 1915 and of Lebanese descent, co-owned one of the most important portrait studios in Mexico City in the 1930s and 1940s. He took still photos of movie stars like Dolores del Río, Mexico's first Hollywood starlet.[7] By the 1950s Yazbek and his brother Alfredo moved into advertising and commercial photography. Their client list included Avon, Smirnoff, Tecate, Manchester Shirts, Disneyland, Coca-Cola, and Nestlé.[8]

The difference between the *Juventud* covers before Yazbek and after Yazbek was hard to miss. Before Yazbek began taking pictures, *Juventud* covers displayed art with ideological content but without an aesthetic tug. The covers were monochrome drawings, religious art, and icons. There were photos of Mary, photos of *santitos* (little saints), churches framed in black-and-white, even one creative drawing of four dark-haired Mexican women—one running a machine, one standing, another teaching a child, the fourth holding stalks of grain—all positioned over an outline map of Mexico.[9] The message was there—the JCFM had a mission for Mexico. These were serious young women, according to the magazine; women committed to a Catholic vision of nation-building, economic assistance, and education. And even though their membership roster contained thousands more names of women from cities than from the countryside, *Juventud* acknowledged that the rural campesina had a place in their vision for Mexico. The ideological thrust of the magazine was of a movement of young women who were smart, professional, and trained—useful to a modernizing society. Yet it wasn't at all glamorous; not until Eugenia Olivera, with Sofía's oversight, hired Tufic Yazbek, "photographer of the stars."[10]

Yazbek's covers of *Juventud* displayed actual members of the JCFM— but always beautiful members and mainly women with very light skin, dressed in modern fashions. It wasn't until the 1950s that *Juventud* placed a mestiza of mixed ethnicity on the cover.[11] One cover from the 1940s pictures a pious old woman with her face in wrinkled hands holding a rosary; another depicts two women in profile wearing rebozos reminiscent of Yazbek's still photos of Dolores del Río from the film *María Candelaria* (1944). Yet as with the pictures of Dolores del Río, the *Juventud* covers by Yazbek portray white glamour girls dressed in traditional garb. The point of these covers is their subjects' piety— coded traditional—not a valorization of indigenous beauty. Within the pages of *Juventud* in the 1940s, rural campesinas were photographed, but they would have to wait nearly a decade to be pictured on the cover.

Yazbek's covers likely struck readers as modest counterparts to the fashion magazines of the era. *Juventud* pictured an ideal—first in spirit and, after Yazbek, in body as well. The women in the *Juventud* covers exude confidence; they smile, they wear makeup, their hair, clothes, and accessories all in place. Inside *Juventud* a thumbnail reproduction of the cover came with a caption, describing the meaning of the image. Yazbek's first cover was published in April 1941. It's a close-up portrait of a young woman, her gaze slightly lifted and to the left, smiling. Flowers frame her hair. The caption reads: "A member of the JCFM knows how to smile because she is young and appreciates life; because she is pure and carries peace in her soul; because she knows how to lift her eyes to the heavens; because she carries desires and drives and hopes. Member of Juventud! Smile always with gratitude, with purity, with elevation, with sincerity, with love." It's unclear who wrote the caption, but it echoes sentiments expressed by Sofía. She often spoke about

26. "A member of the JCFM knows how to smile." *Juventud*, April 1941.

the importance of gratitude. Sofía too smiled with uplifted chin; she urged the development of a joy that was both authentic and chaste.[12]

A few months later *Juventud* celebrated the fifteenth anniversary of both the JCFM and Cultura Femenina. The cover image is of Cultura Femenina students. The photo caption melds the idea of "joy" and "satisfaction" with "desires to know" and "readiness to give." "These expressive faces," the inset reads, "know how to become serious and fix their eyes, now mischievous, on their textbooks, on their wise professors." It goes on to note the "arduous work" that study could be, but that study produced the satisfaction that came with winning the prize—intelligence and achievement.[13]

The August 1941 cover explicitly links femininity and intelligence. Two fashionably dressed young women read a book together—one appears to be pointing out a line in the text to the other. Aurora de la Lama, Sofía's protégée and a woman who briefly traveled to the United States with Sofía in 1937, wrote the cover article. She describes in detail the qualities of "feminine intelligence." She points out the differences between men and women, in keeping with Catholic gender ideals. She also notes physiological differences. It's true, she writes, that men and women are differently created. But to her, this is a benefit, one that has unique advantages for women in education. They learn faster than men, she contends. The female intelligence, de la Lama writes, is imbued with "subtlety"; the female brain, she argues, is made of less dense material, which allows a woman's brain to put up less of a fight to new ideas, "accelerating in this way their transmission and their organic responses; thence proceeds an astounding rapidity in intellectual endeavors." The different biology of a woman's nervous system, according to de la Lama, is a "gift." A woman's biology, she continued, assists in creating "an unprecedented number of associations, making ideas richer and more complex." Under examination, she writes, female intelligence "is not essentially an infertile terrain, as some might claim."[14] As a gift from God the intelligence should be cultivated, de la Lama emphasizes.

De la Lama's article buys into many essentialist stereotypes of women—they are more intuitive and more sensitive than men; their biology more simple. The article also acquiesces on the issue of a wom-

27. "Feminine intelligence and study." *Juventud*, August 1941.

an's vocation. "The majority," she concedes, are called to marriage or religious life. In cultivating their intelligence, women would be a "companion and helper to their husband in accordance with the Holy Bible"—complements to their husbands in his business, in his career, in his projects. Yet in opposition to the misogyny that often accompanied female stereotypes, de la Lama argues women's differences actually made women equally capable of intelligence. Women learned differently than men, she argues, but had equal aptitude. Women, de la Lama insists, didn't have to become like men to be intelligent. "The women on our cover," she writes, "are not less feminine for having their hands on a book; they are feminine precisely because they know how to take advantage of the light and teaching that study offers them."[15]

During World War II Sofía made it clear to JCFM members that patriotism required preparation. *La patria*, she argued, needed professional women, but also mothers who could adequately train the next generation. Sofía, too, was asked to be a mother—of a sort. Polish refugees from German advances wound up in Mexico. Catholic Relief Services arranged their resettlement in Santa Rosa, Guanajuato. President Ávila Camacho gave the refugees official asylum. One of Sofía's friends from the United States, Eileen Egan, an activist who had worked with Dorothy Day's *Catholic Worker*, helped with logistics and support of the refugee camp.[16] One day Egan knocked on Sofía's door in Mexico City and asked Sofía to house two young boys, the sons of a noble Polish family who had recently arrived in Mexico. Their father had died during their flight from Poland and their mother had stayed in Guanajuato with two other young siblings. Sofía opened Quinta Sofía to the boys; she helped the boys and the rest of the family eventually settle in the United States. For years after the war, Sofía stayed in contact with the family. She spoke often of the boys and followed their careers closely.[17]

The pages of *Juventud* reveal a tension. Was the mission to train professional, educated laywomen, many lifelong celibates, or to train mothers? In fact, even as active women like Sofía and her close circle were highlighted, the magazine also extoled motherhood and religious life. *Juventud* covers pictured proud women standing in front of a waving Mexican flag; it also published covers of a woman holding an infant, and another cover of a woman doing housework.[18] In each issue a page listed announcements of weddings, often accompanied by photos. JCFM members entering religious life also were listed in the announcements. The tension lay in the JCFM's leadership. Many of them, like Sofía, were unmarried—and contentedly so. Articles in *Juventud* introduced readers to lay celibacy—"The Third Way: The Celibate in the World," Aurora de la Lama titled one article. As with the issue of feminine intelligence, de la Lama once again appealed to science in her argument. "Statistics show," she writes, "that a third of women do not wed." How prevalent lay celibacy was among the JCFM is not clear. Perhaps Sofía and her circle were the exception that proved the rule—most Catholic young women aspired to marriage or, if they felt a calling, to religious life. Sofía and her protégées like Aurora de la Lama tried to carve out a third option: the professional celibate laywoman.[19]

Sofía and many of her early protégées aged out of the JCFM by the 1950s. The route of lay celibacy appears to have closed after they left, virtually disappearing in the pages of *Juventud*.[20] In 1953 Mexican women were finally able to vote in national elections. Catholic women, in the main, supported it. But by that time many professionally and politically minded women had bolted from the JCFM and church ranks. Professional women no longer needed the church for opportunities to participate in civic life.[21] JCFM membership reached its peak after World War II—110,000 members in 1960.[22] After the war the ground in which Catholic activists like Sofía had planted deep roots shifted under their feet. The landscape was forever changed.

The year 1945 brought a farewell to arms but a costly peace—bought in lives and destruction. War was over. Sofía's path to Europe and the wider world was once again open. Sofía knew she had to be one of those ready to serve the peace. Rebuild—that was the vision circulating across the Atlantic. Sofía cheered the birth of the United Nations in 1946. UNESCO—the United Nations Educational, Social, and Cultural Organization—sparked her imagination.[23] Here, she believed, was a truly international society that could draw on the expertise and commitment of nongovernmental associations to rebuild. Sofía vol-

28. Sofía del Valle, 1950. Personal collection of Adriana Garza Ramos.

unteered almost immediately to be Mexican Catholic Action's delegate for foreign relations. For the next twenty years she worked in this capacity—attending UNESCO gatherings as a delegate for the IUCWL and its successor, founded in 1952, the World Union of Catholic Women's Organizations. She traveled throughout Mexico providing UN educational resources and participating in government-funded literacy programs. She networked between government and Catholic activists committed to economic development.

By 1957 Cultura Femenina closed its doors. There's no evidence Sofía fought Miranda's decision to shutter the college. Sofía, it seems, believed the school had served its purpose. A Catholic university was founded in Mexico City, the Universidad Iberoamericana, under Jesuit auspices.[24] Cultura Femenina graduates continued to meet periodically, bound by a common vision and with a common older sister in Sofía del Valle.

It was clear Sofía's networks spread far and wide. Maria von Trapp and her musical children sang in Mexico City in 1950. "After Panama," Trapp wrote, "we flew to Mexico City, where we were invited by an old friend of ours, Sofía del Valle, to a Mexican dinner." It's unclear how Sofía met the famous singing family. Perhaps Sofía's sister, Hortensia, made the introduction as the von Trapps had connections to the Assumptionist nuns in Philadelphia.[25] "We listened," Maria continued, "to [Sofía] tell of the persecution of the Church in the 1930s when she, with priests hidden in her house and Holy Mass being offered in her cellar, had been in constant danger of death. Sometimes the Blessed Sacrament had been entrusted to her care, and she had risked her life to bring it to condemned prisoners." Was this the story Sofía told? Or, had Maria Augusta von Trapp embellished the story Sofía related? Either way, Sofía, as an ideal, a model to be emulated, a woman of sacrifice and commitment, was already well established.[26]

Catholics in Mexico, in the United States, and in Europe recognized Sofía. She worked with Maryknoll Father John Considine on awakening American Catholics to serve as missioners in Latin America.[27] "It is all right to come to Mexico as tourists," she told one women's gathering in Kansas City, "but come as Catholic women, too." Sofía urged her listeners, Americans and Mexicans both, to "unite our strength and activities for peace in the world."[28] She received medals from women in the Midwest, peace prizes from American organizations—and Sofía was awarded Vatican honors.[29] In Mexico City's La Profesa Church Sofía knelt with several other women as they received their honorary titles as Damas de la Santa Sepulcro. Sofía's vision expanded to making contacts with women

29. Sofía (*center left*) holding hands with two women from an African delegation of the WUCWO, 1961. Archivo Histórico de la Unión Femenina Católica Mexicana.

from Africa and Asia. A picture taken at a 1961 WUCWO conference shows Sofía clasping hands with Catholic women from around the globe.

But by the 1960s Sofía felt her energy fading. She served as treasurer on the short-lived Mexican Committee for John F. Kennedy's Alliance for Progress.[30] She wrote to Miranda while the sessions of the Second Vatican Council met. Her letters were of a personal nature. She had little to say about the details of Vatican II. She wrote Miranda lamenting not being able to greet him before his departure for Rome; she offered prayers for him and the important work of the council; she even mentioned being the godmother in a ceremony for Luz Longoria Gama, one of only four official women auditors to the Second Vatican Council.[31]

Historians speak of a new "emerging laywoman" appearing in the 1960s: women who interpreted Vatican II's pronouncements—metabolizing or rejecting them as the case may be—but finding newfound freedom to engage in the work of the church and the world.[32] Perhaps Sofía knew she didn't need a council for all that.

La patria Calls 339

Sofía's actual reach into the workings of the Mexican church diminished, even as her profile and notoriety as a well-known Catholic activist increased. She commented only briefly, and vaguely, on Mexico's 1968 Tlatelolco massacre, when government troops gunned down student activists before the opening of the Olympic Games in the city. She referred to the present—in her 1972 interview—as a time of confusion.[33] The methods she had advocated all her life—training first, action second—had been seemingly reversed by many Catholic activists. Action was now privileged over preparation, Sofía found. She worried about that. Some priests advocated revolution; others called for liberation. Sofía mourned what, to her, felt like the loss of a coherent way of working in the world. Extreme passions, Sofía believed, not study, motivated action in the world she encountered when she turned eighty years old.

"Currently I find our present moment one of great disorientation among the Catholics of Mexico," Sofía said in that 1972 interview.

Yet for all her misgivings, she acknowledged that often "some of us [Catholics] have not had a broad Christian social sensitivity," which she could see as a root cause of many of the problems upsetting Mexico and the world. The church, Sofía admitted, had failed to provide solutions. Christians had to claim part of the blame for "this species of world revolution," she said.

Sofía slowed down by the early 1970s. She wanted to spend more time with her family. UN general secretary Kurt Waldheim (1972–81) initially rejected her letter of resignation, disappointed that Sofía wanted to step down. She had experience and an institutional knowledge he wanted to maintain while beginning his leadership of the UN. Sofía reminded Waldheim she'd worked for the UN for over twenty years—she was already eighty.[34]

In 1971 Sofía, nearing retirement, wrote Miranda that the letter she'd just written him had some mistakes, which she apologized for, "but . . . both me and the typewriter are fit for the museum . . . in this age of electric typewriters and computers!"[35]

Perhaps Sofía paused a moment, staring at her old, well-used typewriter. She had made her decision—a difficult one, painful, even; but, she knew, necessary. The time had come to stand aside.

Postlude

DAY'S END

Recently
Somewhere in the suburbs, Mexico City, 4:25 p.m.

There's a garden outside Tía Babi's small home. Green and verdant, it constantly catches my eye as I'm speaking with Tere and Héctor, and as I'm getting to know our host, Tía Babi. Her given name is Adriana Garza Ramos, but everyone in the family universally knows her as Tía Babi. She's the daughter-in-law of Ana María del Valle, Sofía's sister.

The *viejitas*, the four women who knew Sofía, graciously gave us—Tere, Héctor, and me—a lift from Snob Bistro to Tía Babi's home. There has to be more to discover.

We sit in what feels like a shop of antiques: upholstered davenports, intricately latticed wood-back chairs, vases, glass bowls. There are old pictures framed handsomely.

No nonsense—that's how Tía Babi strikes me. She's a straight talker; blunt even. She's got a dry wit and a husk to her voice. She's rail thin and smartly dressed in a pantsuit. It's as if I've journeyed up the mountain on pilgrimage only to find the sage who's been waiting for me is Joan Rivers. I really like Tía Babi.

Afternoon light streaks in slants and shards through the living room. Outside, the garden's branches move light and shade around as a breeze swirls in and out and then it's still.

Where do I begin?

I realize my questions are too specific. They feel irrelevant. Tía Babi sees my hesitation. She begins, not unkindly, saving me from making the first move. I decide to listen.

"I met Tía Popi when I was nineteen years old."

It was 1953. She tells me about her relationship to the del Valles. Her first contact with the family was not with her future husband, Paco, but with Paco's sister. Eventually, Tía Babi says, Paco convinced her to marry him. They had two children—both grown now with children of their own.

I'm listening, trying to keep the family history straight. Ana María was Sofía's younger sister. Ana María had six children. One of those sons—Paco—was Tía Babi's husband. Another one of those sons—José Luis—was Tere's father. Ana María and her husband, Angel, lived in Spain during the Civil War. She only returned to Mexico in 1948, after Angel's death. Ana María and five of her children—one stayed behind in Spain—moved into Quinta Sofía.

I shake out of the mental genealogy and see that Tere's taking the photo albums out of her brightly colored cloth bag.

"Oh, how beautiful!" Tía Babi coos as she begins to look at Tere's pictures. She tells Tere to go upstairs. Bring down more photographs, she says, and don't forget the framed one by her bed.

The photo albums have now multiplied in the living room. I ask to take digital snapshots and begin rapidly click-clicking my way through the black-and-white pictures.

Tía Babi's albums tell me the story of Sofía's last decade. Sofía retired in 1972. She died in 1982. She spent those years with family. Ana María's kids and grandkids fill the photos from those years. Sofía is pictured with laughing toddlers and adolescents growing into teenagers. I also realize that Quinta Sofía, the family home, was being lost in those years. Chunks of it, a once large plot, were slowly sold off. Yet the family continued to meet. Tere and her cousin—another Ana María, the professor at Johns Hopkins—told me about these family get-togethers. Birthdays. Holidays. All these photos are in the garden.

Sofía's public role receded in those last ten years. She remained an advisor for Catholic Action and the JCFM. Sofía also sat on the leadership committee for Aurora Arrayales's feminist organization.

"I only go when they ask for counsel," Sofía told Alicia Olivera in 1973, "and since they very rarely ask for advice, very rarely do I go."

In 1975 Sofía supported the UN Conference on Women held in Mexico City. She promoted the annual International Women's Day that came out of the event. But her exact role in the assembly—whether she attended or simply acted in an advisory capacity—is unclear from the sources. There are questions about the UN Conference I haven't been able to answer. For instance, Mother Teresa visited Mexico for the first time during the 1975 Women's Conference. Eileen Egan, Sofía's friend, even traveled with Teresa. Did Sofía meet Mother Teresa at the conference? Perhaps their paths crossed.

My thoughts turn to a letter written by Sofía. It's the last letter I was able to find in the archive written by her. She addressed it to Pope John Paul II in 1979. The pope visited Mexico that year—the first visit of a reigning pope to Mexico, and only the second time a reigning pope had visited Latin America.

"We cannot," Sofía began, "nor could we ever, in all our lives thank you enough for your visit to Mexico. It has awakened in our people, a little bit ignorant, yes, but at root completely Christian, such a happy and promising reaction for future Catholicism in Mexico."[1]

Sofía, near the end of her life, had hope for the future. Perhaps she felt, in part, that her work and Miranda's work had been part of what kept Mexico "at root completely Christian." Or was it an old woman's wishful thinking? Catholic Action was in decline. The organization was nowhere near the height of its strength as it was in the 1930s to the 1950s. Characteristically, Sofía looked on "future Catholicism" with an attitude of hope. That was faith, for Sofía—the resolve to attach the now to the not yet.

Sofía's letter to John Paul is a story. She narrates how Polish Catholics gave her strength when she visited Warsaw in 1931, about how, a decade later, she returned the favor to Polish refugees in Mexico. Sofía continued to see her story, like that of the Catholic Church, as one that was universal—one that crossed borders and connected people.

But was the letter ever sent? Did John Paul ever read it?

Sofía's letter, I remember, says only one line about its context: "Draft of a letter from Srta. Sofía del Valle to SS John Paul on his visit to Mexico."

There's no proof the letter was ever sent. And even if it was, I have no way to corroborate whether John Paul II ever read it. The Vatican archive isn't accessible for 1970s documents. Yet other evidence recommends the letter. Miranda, for example, was a cardinal in 1979. Sofía herself had longstanding connections in the Vatican. Sofía might reasonably have met John Paul during his visit to Mexico. Perhaps Sofía leveraged her insider status to get the letter into the pope's hand?

I have the sense that the letter is an instance of history's ruins—the material remains of a past preserved but no longer understood in its context, its lived quality, its meaning. Is the letter evidence of triumph or tragedy? Is it Sofía's last statement of who she was and what she did for the church? Or is it the whisper of a life fading into silence? There's no one to tell me the letter's story. The job of a historian is to salvage what we can from history's ruins. There's no guarantee I'm right, but I'd like to think Sofía sent the letter, that John Paul read it, that Sofía was remembered in the Vatican—that Sofía's letter is a metaphor for Latin American Catholicism's bold new voice at the end of the twentieth century...

Tía Babi, Tere, and Héctor are looking at a framed photograph of the del Valle family. Tía Babi begins telling a story about the photo.

The del Valle family had it taken in Switzerland, probably sometime around 1910. Each of the eight children is engaged in some task—Clara's playing her piano; a few of the children look over Clara's shoulder; Sofía seems to be laughing at some joke told by Hortensia; Sofía's father, Francisco Sr., is intent on his kid's activities; Sofía's mother glances up from her newspaper chidingly.

"I like it," comments Tere, "because it gives you an idea of what kind of family they were ... very caring, very united."

Tía Babi disagrees. "No, each one with their own role." She sees them as a family of different personalities, different interests—as independents.

I wonder whether Tía Babi's description explains something about Sofía's family—why Sofía was really the only one wholly committed to public church work. The del Valle family was a Catholic family, but also a modern one. Self-determination and individuality defined the family's contours as much as authority and responsibility.

Tía Babi describes Sofía's domineering personality in contrast with Ana María's compliance. Enrique, the youngest brother, was a polished gentleman—he received his education in England, Tía Babi tells us—while Francisco Sr. always projected informality and humor.

Afternoon is fading into evening and there's still more I want to know from Tía Babi. I need to understand Sofía's relationship with Miranda—especially at the end of their lives. They met in 1925 and corresponded for over fifty years. They worked side-by-side. They shared an intimate friendship. *What became of their relationship in old age, in the twilight of life?*

Other family members have told me their memories of Sofía and Miranda—of Miranda attending family events, patting the children on the head, Sofía and Miranda sitting by each other in the garden of Quinta Sofía, presiding over the festivities like doting grandparents.

I've pieced together a partial story from archival evidence. In 1979 Sofía and Miranda received a joint honor at the fiftieth anniversary of Catholic Action. It was Sofía's last appearance at a Catholic Action event. I think about them receiving an award together: Sofía, dignified, her chin up, a flower pinned to her lapel; Miranda, slouched a bit, his nose and ears grown into grandfatherly proportions, eyes sparkling behind thick horned-rim glasses.

Is this the future they had imagined? Did all their work, all their sacrifices, feel worth it?

Sofía's health deteriorated after 1979. The friend who helped Sofía with her memoir—the mother of María Eugenia Díaz Gastine, one of the *viejitas* I interviewed—wrote a brief page about Sofía in those last years.

"She always had the Rosary close to hand," the friend wrote. All who visited Sofía received encouragement. Sofía told them she'd pray for them and their needs. "In her last days," Sofía's friend continued, "God tested her, to finish the work of purifying her and enriching the crown of her merits."[2]

Sofía's old age was yet another test.

By 1980 friends of Sofía wrote Miranda that Sofía needed full-time live-in help. Arthritis had put Sofía in a wheelchair. The friends proposed a fund be established for Sofía's care. No retirement plan awaited Sofía. She'd received little inheritance from her parents. The friends wanted to keep the plan a secret. Sofía, they knew, was proud, jealous of her independence. "With maximum discretion," they wrote Miranda, "so that Sofía doesn't become aware and feel bad for our intervention."[3] Miranda happily obliged. But by the spring of 1981 it became clear that Sofía needed more care than her family or friends could provide.

Díaz Gastine's mother wrote: Sofía's "age—she was about to turn ninety—her illnesses, in addition to arthritis, the aches and pains of advanced age, and the worst of it: her loss of sight, which had almost completely slipped away; all of this required special care, constant tending, and her present circumstances were not conducive for her situation. So, because of the impossibility of finding a suitable apartment and a person dedicated to care for her continually as her condition required, all of which became too costly, the decision was made to select a rest home."[4]

Sofía went to a home in Cuernavaca. Díaz Gastine's mother recorded that Sofía emphasized it was her own choice: "After thinking about it before God," Sofía wrote to her friends, "I have decided to go to Cuernavaca."[5] It had a chapel and a chaplain who provided the Catholic sacraments.

Even if the choice to go to Cuernavaca wasn't much of a choice—there weren't any other reasonable options for Sofía's care—it seems characteristic of Sofía to own the decision. She wanted to feel she'd chosen it. Order and control continued to be comforts. She spent a year in Cuernavaca before her death in 1982.

I ask Tía Babi for more. I want to hear Tía Babi's views on Sofía's relationship to Miranda. "I have lots of letters," I begin, "between Miranda and Sofía in the twenties and thirties . . . they had an intimacy between them . . . a great friendship."

"Who knows," I continue haltingly, "if perhaps things were different . . . perhaps there would've been something more romantic?"

"I don't think so," Tía Babi says with confidence.

I immediately regret my question. Of course Tía Babi doesn't think Sofía and Miranda could've had a romance! I think to myself.

"Señor Miranda had a horrible face!" Tía Babi says almost to herself.

"What?" I almost choke. I'm taken off guard.

In a whisper, Tía Babi says she doesn't want this taped. She pauses; seems to consider it. She proceeds anyway—on the record.

"He was ugly as can be!" Tía Babi says in English.

I'm surprised at Tía Babi's statement. "You mean Miranda?" I ask.

She nods. Tía Babi's telling me that a romance between Sofía and Miranda never happened—not because of commitment, celibate vows, obedience to a calling; she's telling me a romance never happened because Miranda "was ugly as can be."

"And she was beautiful," Tía Babi adds. She tells me about Sofía's perfume and Sofía's sophistication—her femininity. Tía Babi strikes a pose for us: her hands slightly bend at the wrist; she produces a coy slant of her eyes and a coquettish smile. Tía Babi says that's how Sofía was.

"I'm telling the truth," Tía Babi says and returns to her normal position.

"Señor Miranda was an intelligent man. Such high intelligence." Tía Babi strings out the word "intelligence" for emphasis. "With a great sense of humor," she adds, "attractive in some sense."

I realize I'm never going to get a better answer about Sofía and Miranda. Were there romantic sentiments between Sofía and Miranda? Even if never articulated, did they have private thoughts of what might've been if life were different?

If love can also mean emotional intimacy, if it can mean mutual support and commitment, if it can mean genuine admiration and sacred partnership—if love can mean these things, Sofía and Miranda had them in abundance.

And maybe, I think, I've already received an answer. Sofía once wrote that she considered herself Miranda's "complement." In his way Miranda reciprocated. He called Sofía his "most faithful and inseparable crown." They loved one another within the boundaries of their time and their choices.

Eventually Tía Babi says: "If there was anything more [between them], I don't know."

Shadows stretch across Tía Babi's living room. The mood shifts. I'm not sure what Tía Babi wants to tell me. Sadness contracts her usually animated face.

"When Tía Popi was completely..." Babi falters, looking for the right word.

"Ill?" Tere suggests.

Tía Babi accepts the word. "She was no longer seeing anyone except for my husband and me. We had taken her to a place in Cuernavaca."

I nod, acknowledging that I'd learned as much from my research.

"On two occasions," Tía Babi continues, "Señor Miranda went to see her. But Paco wouldn't let him see her."

I try to put together what Tía Babi's telling me. Paco was Sofía's nephew and Tía Babi's husband. At the end, Sofía had deteriorated to the point where Paco wouldn't let anyone visit Sofía—not even Miranda.

"No one is going to see my aunt," Tía Babi affects the voice of her husband, "except me and my wife."

"Was this a quick decline?" I ask.

"Well, yes," Tía Babi says. She wants me to understand just how bad it got. She tells me that Sofía had dementia. I'm aware that she's explaining this so I might understand the decision, made by Paco, not to let anyone see Sofía at the end.

"No one... no one." Tía Babi takes the voice of her husband again; firm, resolute. "You're not going to see her, not after the woman she was."

I can't come up with anything except a slow nod of my head.

"And he never let anyone see her."

Later, I will try to make sense of Sofía's illness, her decline. Dementia, I will learn, steals the past in reverse. Memory centers in the brain deteriorate. Short-term memory goes first because the hippocampus—the place where new memories form—is attacked first. Older memories, the ones made over and over throughout life, stored in the cerebral cortex, remain untouched for a time. I will discover that dementia, of which Alzheimer's disease is the most virulent type, can be imagined as a shelf of diaries. The diaries represent one's memories. The disease initiates a cascade of falling "diaries" beginning with the most recent and ending with the earliest. Dementia is an unlearning.[6]

I will wrestle with Sofía's terrible unlearning. Dementia stole Sofía's education, her years of self-formation. Dementia dissolved the glue of Sofía's personality—forged over decades of persistence, of independence, of travel, of standing alone...

Later, I will ask myself whether the historian is equipped to interpret such loss.

I sit uncomfortably on the couch. Tía Babi and Tere are silent a moment.

"We went to see her every week," Tía Babi says. "Paco and I; my children were too young." She pauses. "It was very painful."

Tía Babi explains how they received a call at six in the morning on July 21, 1982. Sofía died peacefully in her sleep. Tía Babi and Paco hurried to Cuernavaca. Paco dealt with arrangements. It was Tía Babi who sat with Sofía's body.

"When she died, I'm not going to say I didn't feel anything, but really, it wasn't her anymore. Even physically. Her mind. Her energy."

I'm quiet as I listen.

It's as if she's saying all this to convince herself that she and her husband made the right decision in allowing no one to see Sofía. Tía Babi explains that individuals close to Sofía questioned the decision. She adds that Miranda blessed Sofía outside her door at the rest home on both of his visits.

I ask her how Miranda took the decision.

"As a gentleman," Tía Babi says. There's a weight to the moment. "He never saw her again." She pauses. "This is sad."

"Yes," is all I can say, feebly.

"Do you understand? Tía Babi asks me the question.

"Yes, I understand."

There's more force to my voice than I intend. I don't know whether she's asking me if I understand her Spanish, or whether I can empathize with the decision made by her and her husband.

"No," Tía Babi repeats, "but do you understand the fact that [Paco] didn't let anyone see her?"

I take another needed breath.

"Yes. I understand." I look down at my feet for a second, then back at Tía Babi. "I think it's a decision that no one can judge from the outside . . . it's something very intimate."

Tía Babi nods her head but says nothing right away. She simply agrees with a closed lip *mmm-hmmm, mmm-hmmm*.

Tere breaks the silence. She wants to know whether a priest performed last rites—did Sofía make her last confession?

"Confess?" Tía Babi raises her voice. "Teresa by God!" She turns on Tere incredulous. "What did she need to confess?"

The discussion is done for Tía Babi.

She turns to me with confidence. Something of her earlier mischief returns to her face. "I'm sure she is in heaven, but I am very progressive." She says it with a slight smile and a glance at Tere.

"I don't think you knew any of this, did you?" Tía Babi asks.

"No," I say.

"I don't think anyone knew," Tía Babi explains to Tere and me.

The light in the room is almost gone, but no one moves to turn on a lamp.

Tere is describing her memories of Sofía's funeral—Tía Babi as well. They remember flags and banners and hundreds of members of Catholic Action and the JCFM attending. Tere tells Tía Babi the story of the crypt at the Metropolitan Cathedral, how Sofía's ashes came to be deposited there.

"Now all three are resting together," Tere says. "My father, Carlitos, and Tía Popi."

"I don't know," Tía Babi says. "In my family, when you lose someone you keep them here"—she points to her chest—"and you keep them shut up tightly so they will never leave . . . but you never visit cemeteries or tombs . . . only hearts full of joy."

Tía Babi waits a moment, then continues.

"I never go to the cemetery. Never. Never. Never. Not even to see Paco." "But it was my father's tradition," Tía Babi adds. "I think he didn't like death."

In her own way, Tía Babi seems to feel the same.

"What always impressed me," Tía Babi says of Sofía, "was not her sanctity, but her humanity."

And that's all. Tía Babi ends there. She turns to Tere and they begin talking about other photos.

As they talk, I remember a Catholic magazine published an article honoring Sofía a month after she died. I found Miranda's last published words about Sofía in that memorial edition: "I have never found a more generous and committed woman to the service of the church." It strikes me that the article's description of Sofía echoes Tía Babi's memory. "We believe that Sofía del Valle, with her life, anticipated what the Second Vatican Council said about what it means to be a Christian laywoman: a woman of the church in the heart of world, a woman of the world in the heart of the church."

Shuffling from her hands to mine, Tía Babi sets pictures of her daughter and son on my lap.

Her daughter: Oh, Tía Babi concedes, her daughter doesn't look much like Sofía—though, she comments, her daughter does look like a del Valle.

Her son: "This is the child Tía Popi left Señor Miranda for . . . he's fifty years old now; he doesn't look like that anymore."

I almost miss Tía Babi's comment. *Sofía left Miranda for this child?* Tía Babi doesn't seem to be divulging a secret as much as honoring Sofía's choices: the commitment to celibacy and the commitment to love. Perhaps her words are an acknowledgement of what might've been and what was. The meaning I make of Tía Babi's comment is this: Sofía didn't have a husband and didn't have a son—yet she loved a man and she loved a young nephew all the same.

I think about what Tere told me of her relationship to Sofía—the gift of the pearl necklace, the first stockings—stepping into Tere's life as a mother figure when Tere's mother was out of the picture.

Sofía had the love she wanted.

Tere and Tía Babi, Héctor as well—he's been mostly quiet during the conversation—begin to talk among themselves. They share pictures. Memories. Laughs of recognition at their younger selves and their relatives.

We have so many biographies of popes and presidents. We have so many biographies of saints and revolutionaries. Currently, there are almost as many Catholic women in Mexico as total Catholics—men and women combined—in Italy. Forty percent of the world's Catholics live in Latin America. It is women, especially women in Latin America, Africa, and Asia—who provide the portrait of the world's "average" Catholic. Sofía's story deserves to be told because, increasingly, the Catholic world is made up of "Sofías": lay women, sacramentally active, members and leaders alike of community associations; single and married women, who keep the faith alive in their parishes, in their cities, and in their nations. But who remembers them?

It's almost completely dark outside now. There's almost nothing to see in the garden. I say my goodbyes as Tía Babi and her family carry on together. I realize there were no secrets to uncover after all—not really—no Mysterious Sofía; only questions that had been left unasked; only time spent with an old woman in a late afternoon was necessary to hear these stories. Sometimes what we take as lost history is simply a lack of intention and a commitment to listen.

How do you tell the story of a life?

Listen.

Héctor tells me the visit has been proof of divine things. I don't know how to answer and just nod. I turn to Tere and she only says we'll be in touch.

If I were family, I think to myself, maybe it'd be enough to keep the memory of my visit, my day, locked inside—like Tía Babi—never to visit cemeteries and tombs.

All I know is I've got to visit Sofía's ashes.

Matins

A FEW DAYS AFTER

Recently
Uber, Nissan Sentra, Mexico City, 9:24 a.m.

It's been almost a week since my day with some of Sofía's surviving family members. The Uber I'm riding in, with warm sun and cool air hitting me in the face, will only cost 7 USD to get me to the downtown cathedral where Sofía's ashes remain. I admit to myself that I feel old. I feel rich. I feel like an old, rich gringo tourist.

The Uber driver, Rodrigo, looks at me in the rearview mirror.

"Here to visit the Centro Histórico for the first time?" he asks me in Spanish.

I don't have the energy or confidence to tell him this is not my first time. I play along. It feels good to hear someone tell me about his city. Rodrigo clearly loves it. Always the tourist—that's how I feel, no matter that you have a piece of paper claiming you're an expert in Mexican history.

We're nearing downtown. I tell Rodrigo to let me off up the street from the Metropolitan Cathedral and the Zócalo, a massive plaza that flattens out at the church's southern doorstep. We've now passed Mexican 7-Elevens called OXXOS, passed bookstores and Starbucks, passed places called Erotika Sexyshop, passed also the beautiful and aptly named Palacio de Bellas Artes. And then there are spits of not-yet-cooked Tacos al Pastor hanging out of sidewalk eateries—these red, raw, throbbing cones of meat. In a matter of hours there'll come from them a taste sweet and spicy and lightly charred and like everything good about food, all in a tiny corn wrapper. We pass all this stuff, this mélange of chaotic city, and then the pavement turns to faded cobblestone and it feels hopeful, like despite all the ways the present disregards the past, somehow something remains.

Despite the homogenization of Mexico City, a process happening in so many other gargantuan urban centers, the city tries, in small ways, to maintain its distinct presence. Honestly, though, it's just sometimes really hard to perceive.

Welcome to globalization, I think.

I'm walking now on Avenida Cinco de Mayo, meandering in a sea of humanity straight toward the cathedral that looms in the distance. The clash between the present and the past feels jarring. *Where is the past I've devoted so much time to investigating?*

Change happens. A banal statement, surely. But the experience of change usually happens in incremental, basically imperceptible ways. I've spent so much time trying to picture these streets as they looked almost one hundred years ago. And now that I'm here, at the end of my pilgrimage, it feels strange not to encounter them as I've imagined. My mind is playing this time-lapse, fast-forward tape where all of the change happens in five minutes.

"The past is a foreign country; they do things differently there."

This is an often-quoted line, almost a cliché, but I've always liked it. At the moment, however, it feels false. Unlike foreign countries, which often still exist over time, the past has vanished; they don't do anything there at all, these people from the past. We historians try to have them live again, if only for a few hundred pages.

This will become increasingly clear to me, as later that day after my visit to Sofía's ashes, I will sit at a Starbucks built right next to a different church meaningful to her story: La Profesa, a church just blocks away from the Metropolitan Cathedral. La Profesa was where Sofía first heard a call to service, where she announced, after the Cristero War, the coming out of the youth movement to Mexican society, where Sofía received, on bended knee, the Vatican's highest honor for a woman. Now there's a Starbucks next door to La Profesa.

Or, it's like later that day when I will search—again, after my visit to Sofía's ashes—for 9 Motolinía Street where the first Cultura Femenina classes took place; Motolinía Street where Miranda and Sofía built their movement together. And then I found it: 9 Motolinía Street is now your one-stop shop for eye exams, eyewear, and various ophthalmological accessories. There's an army of hawkers outside advertising their services, very aggressively, with little flyers. The building still looks early twentieth century: faded rose-colored walls and stone-framed façade, squat with a second floor built on by Sofía del Valle's father. Its central staircase, once grand, has now been split in two: on one side of the wall they do eye care; eyewear on the other. I ask a guy sweeping the floors, who works there, about the building. I even show him a picture taken of the place from the early 1920s: Alfredo Méndez Medina is seated front and center before the grand staircase; Sofía stands behind him, young and wearing a bell-shaped cloche hat. Sweeping Guy seems interested. He refers me to Security Guard, who tells me there is no way I can take a photo. I ask, as politely as I can, if I can speak to The Owners.

A few minutes click by.

I can see Security Guy talking to two impatient people wearing sunglasses. The Owners. I try my luck and introduce myself. They begrudgingly shake my hand. My entreaties about history, documenting change over time, are brushed aside.

Who owns the past? I ask myself. It all seems too much to process, so later I will write about it at that Starbucks in the ruins of La Profesa's shadow . . .

Back in the present, I've just emerged from the Uber, walking on cobblestone toward the Metropolitan Cathedral, still trying to visit Sofía's ashes. I make my way through the wrought iron gate in front of one of the oldest cathedrals in the Americas. They've built viewing windows in the stone pavement; thick Plexiglas looks down onto pre-Hispanic ruins on which the cathedral was built in the 1500s. I barely stop to ponder the irony—lamentations of a lost past, which itself was built on a still longer lost past—because I want to see if I can gain access to the crypt below the cathedral where Sofía is buried.[1]

The Metropolitan Cathedral is cavernous inside and dark. It was built to make you look up, which I do instantly. Diagonal columns of light transect with solid, straight Doric pillars. Lining the walls are small chapels with altars, sixteen of them. But the main event is the baroque high altar. Massively tall, the Altar of the Kings soars in ornate gold. A gaggle of tourists, wearing shorts, flip flops, and tank tops, are clearly identifiable from the plainly dressed Mexican parishioners, seated and getting ready for the Mass. I'm not here for this, so I hurry my way to a small stone staircase on the west side of the cathedral: the stairs to the crypt. As I descend a sign confronts me: Only Family Members Allowed. I continue on. Tere Huidobro, Sofía's grandniece, has given me permission to visit. I hope her word is enough.

At the bottom of the stairs a kind of macabre hybrid of reception desk and votive chapel awaits. The woman behind the desk eyes me sourly. I fold my hands, trying to seem respectful. I explain. I give the number to Sofía del Valle's niche: #4809. Surprisingly, I have access. I have to surrender my passport and register in a three-ring binder. There's a uniformed security guard. Another woman is busy lighting candles on the votive-chapel half of the atrium.

There are hundreds of mausoleum-styled niches containing the cremated remains of the dead. Some have names etched in the marble, others only numbers, still others are clearly the loved ones of the wealthy. The lighting above the expensive niches is motion sensitive; the quality of marble, multicolored and solid looking, contrasts with the half-inch-thin marble facades of the other resting places.

Finally, at the very end of a long, low hallway I see it: #4809:

Fundadora de la Juventud Catolica
Femenina Mexicana

Sofía del Valle
1891–1982

Jose Luis Ruiz de Huidobro del Valle
1930–2010

Carlos Alfonso Ruiz de Huidobro del Valle
1940–2016

The names of Tere Huidobro's father and uncle are etched below Sofía's name. They were two of Sofía's nephews. Both are encased with her. The circular emblem of the JCFM is also carved on the marble niche. Apostolate—Eucharist—Heroism; the motto of the JCFM encircles an ancient Christian symbol, the Chi Rho, written in the Greek letters XP. I've seen this same symbol etched on the tomb of early Christians and martyrs in Rome. There's a hum of the electrical system that inhabits a dark passage beyond Sofía's resting place. Organ music and indistinct singing filter through the floor above, where Mass has begun.

The urge is overpowering to find where Miranda has been laid to rest. I can't help but wander through the labyrinth of the mausoleum. By chance I turn right, as I always seem to do, and happen upon a wooden doorway, slightly propped open. The room clearly seems important. I can see shimmering light reflected off precious stones and skilled masonry. It contains the Crypt of the Archbishops. Directly above this crypt's ceiling is the Altar of the Kings.

Here lie almost all of Mexico's highest-ranking bishops. I find the name of Mexico's first, Bishop Juan de Zumárraga, a man disbelieving of the young convert's story of the appearance of the Dark Virgin. Entombed also, behind the small altar in niches #38, #39, and #40, are Pascual Díaz and Luis María Martínez and finally... Miguel Darío Miranda; men who in death are kept separate from the woman they built the church of Christ with—in the case of Miranda, seventy-seven steps away from the humble, less ornate niche of Sofía del Valle. She was a woman Miranda once called his Most Faithful and Inseperable Crown. Those seventy-seven steps speak volumes about the choices Sofía and Miranda made, and the world they inhabited. Kept apart in death, so much of their lives were lived together.

I make my way back from the Crypt of the Archbishops to Sofía del Valle's niche resting place. I walk, counting off those seventy-seven steps. At the end of my pilgrimage to find the Mysterious Sofía I have no idea what to do. I reach a hand up to touch the marble façade where her name's inscribed. If I apply any more force it feels like the flimsy stone will give way. My heart starts a moment. That's not the way I want this to end.

I pray briefly, something private, which will remain with me, between Sofía and me, something I keep with me as I climb the stairs back into the church above and retrieve my passport.

I've done matins now. I've had my morning prayers, and so I step quickly by tourists and the seated churchgoers and head straight out into the blinding light of Mexico City's central plaza from the darkness of the cathedral.

Postscript

Excerpt from the Unfinished Memoir of Sofía del Valle
(reproduced textually)

The Hon. Bishop [name missing in orig.] of Kansas City who was very interested in Mexico and the suffering of Catholics during the persecution, made several visits to Mexico in the time of General Calles and spoke with many of those held prisoner in the police inspection [yard] in order to have direct information regarding the situation in the country. In one of my conferences in Kansas City which he attended, he said to me: "Sofía, you have to write a book about all your work. I even have a publisher in New York and also a title for the book: Mysterious Sofía." I thanked him for his suggestion but unfortunately I never had time to write the book.

Notes

Prologue

1. You'll notice, too, that I call the two main characters, that is, Sofía del Valle and Miguel Darío Miranda, "Sofía" and "Miranda." There are two "Miguels" in the book—the martyred Jesuit Miguel Agustín Pro being the other—and I decided to call Miguel Miranda "Miranda" in order not to confuse the reader. There was no intention to reinforce gender bias in using Sofía's first name and Miranda's surname. In much of their long correspondence to one another, over fifty years, Sofía always signed her letters "Sofía," while Miranda's signatures varied between "Miranda," "Miguel Darío," "Miguel," and "MDM." I went with "Miranda" for the sake of simplicity and clarity. Here are some sources that informed my thinking on male biographers writing the lives of women: Heilbrun, *Writing a Woman's Life*; Cahill, *Writing Women's Lives*; Brekus, *Sarah Osborn's World*; Sensbach, *Rebecca's Revival*; Bonnie Smith, *Confessions of a Concierge*; White, *Remembering Ahanagran*.
2. Both Catholics and secular social welfare advocates in Mexico displayed a changing vision of the poor and the strategy to "redeem" them; see Sanders, *Gender and Welfare*, 30.
3. This is changing. Recent work on the Cristero War has shown how the conflict became an important part of Mexican-American identity, and that the Cristero years are well-remembered among certain communities. However, outside Mexican-American and Catholic circles, the conflict is largely unknown (at least in my opinion). See Young, *Mexican Exodus*.
4. This is a topic being taken up by an increasing number of scholars; see Andes and Young, *Local Church, Global Church*; and Bonner, Denny, and Connolly, *Empowering the People of God*.
5. Jenkins, *Next Christendom*.

1. Days of the Dead

1. The clerical conspiracy was published in *El Nacional*, October 27 and 28, 1934. Details of religious celebration and pilgrimage can be found in the

New York Times, October 28, 30, 31 and November 1 and 2, 1934. The Mexican government's defanaticizing policies are detailed in Bantjes, "Idolatry and Iconoclasm," 87–120.
2. Ruiz y Flores, *Recuerdo de recuerdos*, 102–3.
3. The best, most concise English-language treatment of the Cristero War is still Meyer, *Cristero Rebellion*.
4. The supposed apparition of the Virgin Mary to Juan Diego is a contentious subject. Scholars and devotees both debate whether it happened, when it happened, and when the devotion actually began in Mexico. "Then it happened," for me, is simply an acknowledgement that the Virgin of Guadalupe became an important bridge, over time, between an imported European Catholicism and indigenous rituals and traditions. See, for example, Taylor, *Theater of a Thousand Wonders*; Poole, *Our Lady of Guadalupe*; Chávez, *Our Lady of Guadalupe*; and Matovina, *Theologies of Guadalupe*.
5. Brading, *Mexican Phoenix*.
6. Wright-Rios, *Revolutions in Mexican Catholicism*, 105.
7. Much has been written on revolutionary anticlericalism and the spectrum it encompassed—from rabid antireligion to Christian anticlerical reformism; see Blancarte, "Personal Enemies of God."
8. Quotes taken from the *New York Times*, "Clashes in Mexico Today Are Feared," October 28, 1934, 23.
9. *New York Times*, "Clashes in Mexico."
10. Young, "Calles Government," 63–91.
11. A recent edited edition of a portion of Sofía del Valle's memoir provides information on her early life, supplementary information regarding her fundraising tour, and other anecdotal material; see Olimón Nolasco, *Sofía del Valle*, 86.
12. *New York Times*, "Clashes in Mexico."
13. *New York Times*, "Clashes in Mexico."

2. The Sophie Letters

1. *New York Times*, "Ruiz Denies Catholic Plot; Mexican President Strikes at Church, October 31, 1934, 1.
2. Elizabeth Kite to Agnes Regan, November 1, 1934, ACHRCUA, RNCCW, box 117, folder 1.

3. Miss del Valle

1. Agnes Regan to Elizabeth Kite, November 5, 1934, and Elizabeth Lynch to Agnes Regan, memorandum, October 13, 1934, ACHRCUA, RNCCW, box 117, folder 1.

4. The Mastermind

1. Ruiz's attitudes toward armed rebellion are laid out in Butler, "Keeping the Faith," 9–32; for the activism of the cristero diaspora, see Young, *Mexican Exodus*.
2. *New York Times*, "Sedition in Mexico Laid to 2 Prelates," November 12, 1934, 11.
3. There is evidence that Ruiz began to tire of the Vatican's soft, diplomatic approach after his exile to the United States. However, mastermind of an American armed intervention in Mexico, he was not. See Solis, "La difícil situación."
4. *New York Times*, "Ruiz Denies."
5. The educational reform came into force on December 1, 1934. For the classic treatment, see Vaughn, *Cultural Politics*.
6. Del Valle to Ruiz y Flores, May 19, 1934, 4rv in "Sofía del Valle," ASV, AM, fasc. 28.
7. See, for example, the conflicting interpretations offered by Alan Knight and John Mason Hart: Knight, *Mexican Revolution*; Hart, *Revolutionary Mexico*.
8. *New York Times*, October 31, 1934.
9. And it wasn't just Catholic women who participated in informal networks of political persuasion. See, for example, Threlkeld, *Pan American Women*.
10. *New York Times*, "Ruiz Denies."
11. Olimón Nolasco, *Sofía del Valle*, 84–88.

Interlude: Tere Huidobro

1. Tere Huidobro's full name is María Teresa Ruiz de Huidobro Márquez. Her cousin, also Sofía's grandniece, is Ana María Rule, a professor at Johns Hopkins University. Sofía's niece, a daughter of Ana María, is named María Teresa Ruiz de Huidobro del Valle. She was a member of the Assumptionist Order and lives in Baltimore, Maryland. She now goes by Terry Huidobro. In the book, unless noted otherwise, Tere Huidobro refers to Sofía's grandniece in Mexico, with whom I spent a day of interviews, and not Terry Huidobro, who lives in Baltimore.

5. Little Flowers

1. Alicia Olivera Sedano de Bonfil, the investigator with whom Sofía del Valle spoke in 1972 and 1973, was a rising historian. Her first book, which began as a simple undergraduate thesis in history, was one of the earliest

attempts to tell an academic account of the cristeros. Her own supervisor at the UNAM, Mexico's National University, advised against it. "*No se meta en ese tema, Alicia, no le ha caído suficiente polvo.*" Not enough dust had fallen on the subject; she shouldn't touch it. But she did touch it and began to challenge the conventional narrative of the Cristero Rebellion, which up until then had been seen as a painful, though irrelevant, period in the nation's history.

Olivera pioneered a method of oral history in Mexico, one she fought for despite resistance from the old guard, perhaps a mix of historical negligence as well as misogyny—it was 1953 when she finished her undergraduate degree in history, the same year women achieved the right to full suffrage in Mexico. The history of *los de abajo*, the underdogs, the story forged from the grassroots, was developing a picture of the revolutionary era, not based in written documentation, but the nuanced memories of the participants. Olivera, often accompanied by her young son on these interviews, traveled collecting stories from *viejitos* of the revolutionary generation, those still living who had seen history firsthand. See Olivera Sedano, *Aspectos del conflict* and also Oikión Solano, "In Memoriam," 234–42. For Olivera's interview with Sofía del Valle, see Olivera/del Valle, 1972–73.

2. Olimón Nolasco, *Sofía del Valle*, 17–25.
3. Hernández, "From Conquest to Colonization," 291–322.
4. DeLay, *War of a Thousand Deserts*.
5. Bunker, *Creating Mexican Consumer*, 8.
6. Hernández, "From Conquest to Colonization," 305–6.
7. Hernández, "From Conquest to Colonization," 304–6.
8. The sponsorship of Spanish relatives, who then immigrated to Mexico, was a process dating back to the colonial era; see Brading, *First America*, 294.
9. ADG, "Vida de Sofía del Valle."
10. The literature on Thérèse of Lisieux is enormous. See, for example, Nevin, *Last Years*. On the links between Catholic piety and devotion to Thérèse see, for example, McCartain, "Sacred Heart," 53–67; Losel, "Prayer," 273–306; Burton, *Holy Tears, Holy Blood*, esp. chapter 2; Pope, "Heroine without Heroics," 46–60.
11. Losel, "Prayer," 277–78.
12. McCartain, "Sacred Heart," 64.
13. McCartain, "Sacred Heart," 64.
14. Pope, "Heroine without Heroics," 59.
15. McCartain, "Sacred Heart," 56.
16. Pope, "Heroine without Heroics," 59.

17. Pope, "Heroine without Heroics," 52.
18. Losel, "Prayer," 281–84.
19. Losel, "Prayer," 274.
20. Arrom, *Women of Mexico City*; Arrom, "Mexican Laywomen," 50–77; Chowning, "Catholic Church," 197–237; and Chowning, *Rebellious Nuns*.
21. Rupp, *Worlds of Women*; Mitchell and Schell, *Women's Revolution*; Stephanie Smith, *Gender and the Mexican Revolution*; Olcott, *Revolutionary Women*; and Olcott, Vaughn, and Cano, *Sex in Revolution*.
22. Losel, "Prayer," 280–86.
23. Yeager, "In the Absence," 207–42.
24. Blum, *Domestic Economies*, 108.
25. Gutiérrez Casillas, *Jesuitas*, 49.
26. Olimón Nolasco, *Sofía del Valle*, 25.
27. Olimón Nolasco, *Sofía del Valle*, 25–26.
28. Olivera/del Valle, 1972–73.
29. Olivera/del Valle, 1972–73.
30. Sofía to Miranda, December 24, 1930, AHAM, MDM, caja 162, exp. 9.

6. Sofía's Belle Époque

1. In fact, Lascuráin donated the land on which *La Sagrada Familia* was built; see Gutiérrez Casillas, *Jesuitas*, 49.
2. Hanson, "Day of Ideals."
3. Sofía del Valle's memories of her relationship with Jewish young women might have been filtered through a post-Vatican II understanding. However, the interwar years were an important period of intellectual change in interfaith relations. See Moore, "Philosemitism," 262–97.
4. Olimón Nolasco, *Sofía del Valle*, 40.
5. Kreisel Shubert, *Out of Style*, 225–27.
6. Kreisel Shubert, *Out of Style*, 48–60.
7. Olimón Nolasco, *Sofía del Valle*, 34–35.
8. Olivera/del Valle, 1972–73.
9. Kahan, *Celibacies*, 19, 60.
10. Abbott, *History of Celibacy*, 389–91.
11. Cummings, *New Women*, 174–75; Hartmann-Ting, "National Catholic," 101–19.
12. "Sofía del Valle," ASV, AM, fasc. 28.
13. Olimón Nolasco, *Sofía del Valle*, 40–47.
14. Gonzales, *Mexican Revolution*, 60–95.
15. The classic work on Zapata is Womack, *Zapata*.
16. Olivera/del Valle, 1972–73.

17. Olimón Nolasco, *Sofía del Valle*, 48–50.
18. Olimón Nolasco, *Sofía del Valle*, 56.

7. Vocation

1. The dialogue is from Olivera/del Valle, 1972–73. I was able to listen to the recording of the interview with Sofía del Valle at the Instituto Nacional de Antropología e Historia (INAH). The archivist informed me that it was recorded on the same machine that we were listening to it on.
2. Olivera/del Valle, 1972–73.
3. Johns, *City of Mexico*, 26.
4. Johns, *City of Mexico*, 23.
5. Porter, *From Angel to Office Worker*.
6. Hershfield, *Imagining*, 24–34.
7. Johns, *City of Mexico*, 37.
8. Davis, *Urban Leviathan*, 27.
9. The "use of women as sexual objects to sell products," writes Nichole Sanders, was a common practice; see Sanders, "Gender and Consumption," 1–30.
10. Hershfield, *Imagining*, 34; Johns, *City of Mexico*, 37.
11. Olivera/del Valle, 1972–73.
12. Olivera/del Valle, 1972–73.
13. Andes, "Catholic Alternative," 535–39.
14. Andes, "Catholic Alternative," 539–42. Italics in original.
15. Andes, "Catholic Alternative," 541–43.
16. Olivera/del Valle, 1972–73. The dialogue is quoted from the transcript of the interview with Olivera; the author has imaginatively recreated the exchange between Sofía and Méndez Medina.

8. Respectable Telephone Operator

1. ADG, "Vida de Sofía del Valle."
2. Davis, *Urban Leviathan*, 58.
3. Porter, "De obreras," 279–315.
4. ADG, "Vida de Sofía del Valle."
5. Hershfield, *Imagining*, 24, 108, 111.
6. ADG, "Vida de Sofía del Valle."
7. Olimón Nolasco, *Sofía del Valle*, 55–56.
8. Olimón Nolasco, *Sofía del Valle*, 56.
9. Andes, "Catholic Alternative," 542.
10. Olimón Nolasco, *Sofía del Valle*, 54.

11. Andes, "Catholic Alternative," 542–43.
12. There is debate about the relative strength, as against Jalisco, of the Mexico City Catholic labor movement. For a counterpoint, which argues that the Mexico City-Guadalajara tensions actually bolstered the movement as a whole, see Aguirre Cristiani, ¿Una historia compartida?
13. Curley, *Citizens and Believers*, 177–182.
14. Davis, *Urban Leviathan*, 45–46.
15. "Growth and Present Development," 3–4.
16. "Development of Telephone Plant," 16.
17. "Some Facts," 28–38.
18. Porter, "De obreras," 285.
19. Mercer, *Telephone*, 50.
20. Mercer, *Telephone*, 50–52.
21. Blum, *Domestic Economies*, 77; Hershfield, *Imagining*, 111.
22. Porter, "De obreras," 297–98.
23. Blum, *Domestic Economies*, 122.
24. Blum, *Domestic Economies*, 73–77.
25. Porter, "De obreras," 288.
26. Porter, "De obreras," 290.
27. Porter, "De obreras," 279–80.
28. Porter, "De obreras," 298.
29. Porter, "De obreras," 311–12.
30. Olivera/del Valle, 1972–73.
31. Olivera/del Valle, 1972–73.
32. Schell, *Church and State Education*, 140–41.
33. Curley, *Citizens and Believers*, 170.
34. Porter, "De obreras," 295.
35. Olivera/del Valle, 1972–73.
36. ADG, "Vida de Sofía del Valle."
37. Andes, "Catholic Alternative," 545–48.

9. Preparing the Future

1. During the summer of 1925, Miguel Miranda carried on an active correspondence with Alfredo Méndez Medina. Miranda kept Méndez Medina informed of the transition process at the Mexican Social Secretariat. They maintained an amiable relationship, even if Méndez Medina felt Miranda's strategy of focusing on education and training—as opposed to union organization—was misguided. In particular, Méndez Medina supported Miranda's efforts to create a female Catholic organization that would reach

out to lower-class women, in contrast to the class conscious Catholic Ladies Association. See Correspondencia III, 1925, AHSSM.
2. Olimón Nolasco, *Sofía del Valle*, 58.
3. Many religious orders dedicated themselves to the training of young girls before the 1910 Revolution, but Cultura Femenina was unique in its focus on the liberal arts education of Catholic women. See Torres Septién, *La educación privada*.
4. Instituto de Cultura Femenina, Horarios, Calificacciones, 1928–32, AACM, JCFM, sección 5.5.
5. Boylan, "Feminine," 176–77.
6. Hershfield, *Imagining*, 3–6.
7. For a groundbreaking study on photography in revolutionary Mexico, its uses, and the way photographers expressed social and political commitments through the medium, see Mraz, *Photographing the Mexican Revolution*.
8. Knight, "Mentality," 22–29.
9. Olimón Nolasco, *Sofía del Valle*, 60.
10. Olimón Nolasco, *Sofía del Valle*, 60.
11. Miguel Darío Miranda was no obscure figure in the history of the Mexican Catholic Church, as will be seen in the pages of this book. The scene has been reconstructed from Miranda's memoirs, as narrated in "pleasant table conversation" to Msgr. Francisco María Aguilera González, while Miranda "savored a Havana cigar." See Aguilera González, *Cardenal Miguel Darío Miranda*, ix, 117–18.
12. The quote comes from a letter written by a consultor (elected advisor) in the Mexican Jesuit province to the leadership in Rome. The consultor lamented the "nationalist" strain in the Mexican province and named Pascual Díaz and Méndez Medina among those whom should be watched out for. Díaz, as bishop of Tabasco, was seen as a natural leader of the Mexican Jesuits. However, in the course of the Cristero Rebellion, Méndez Medina and Díaz would be at odds over the strategy of armed defense. Méndez Medina was one of the most hawkish of Jesuits; Díaz, on the other hand, was one of the most pragmatic conciliators. The Mexican Jesuits would be a significant obstacle to Díaz's plan to pacify cristero militancy after 1929; see Alejandro Villaseñor SJ to R. P. José Barrachina, July 15, 1923, ARSI, PM, Epistolae, 1006-X (Consultori), 53.
13. Martínez Assad, *El laboratorio*, 33–34, 303; on the schismatic church, see Butler, "Sotanas," 535–58 and Butler, "God's *Campesinos*?," 165–84.

14. The basic physical description of Pascual Díaz is based on Quirk, *Mexican Revolution*, 146–47. Quirk, in turn, based his appreciation of Díaz's character on the reports made by the French minister to Mexico at the time, Ernest Lagarde. Both Quirk and Lagarde were hardly charitable, at times even quite racist, in their evaluation of the man: "[Díaz's] Indian eyes, like carved pieces of obsidian, seemed to glow with the primordial energy of the volcanic fire behind them" (Quirk); "intriguing and intolerant" (Lagarde).
15. Aguilera González, *Cardenal Miguel Darío Miranda*, 117–18.
16. Fallaw, *Religion and State Formation*, 22.
17. An unintended consequence of the interdict was the empowerment of the laity, many of whom did just about everything priests did, save for the consecration of the Eucharist. See, for example, Butler, "Su Hija Inés," 1249–94.
18. Published on June 14, 1926, in the *Diario Oficial*, the reform of the penal code comprised thirty-three articles, including suppression of the Catholic press, political speech by members of the clergy, and expressions of worship outside of legally registered church buildings. It effectively nationalized church buildings, requiring an inventory of the furniture and religious articles each contained. An interim neighborhood group was to take control of the churches until the inventory was complete. In essence, the clergy feared the regulations were essentially making them into religious functionaries of the state. Mr. Ovey to Sir Austen Charmberlain, July 6, 1926, 65–67, BNA, FO, Mexico, FOA4054/48/26.
19. The Vatican desired the bishops to make a unified decision; see Andes, *Vatican*, 81–84.
20. Bailey, *¡Viva Cristo Rey!*, 91n65.
21. Bailey, *¡Viva Cristo Rey!*, 97–98.
22. Andes, *Vatican*, 90.
23. Aguilera González, *Cardenal Miguel Darío Miranda*, 117–18.
24. Aguilera González, *Cardenal Miguel Darío Miranda*, 117–18.
25. Aguilera González, *Cardenal Miguel Darío Miranda*, 117–18.
26. Aguilera González, *Cardenal Miguel Darío Miranda*, 117–18.
27. Aguilera González, *Cardenal Miguel Darío Miranda*, 117–18.

Interlude: Family Albums

1. Hershfield, *Imagining*, 130–31.

10. The Catacombs

1. Many Mexican Catholics made special reference to this, likening their experience of underground worship services as their own "catacombs."

2. Weis, "Pious Delinquents," 185–210.
3. Aguilera González, *Cardenal Miguel Darío Miranda*, 123.
4. Aguilera González, *Cardenal Miguel Darío Miranda*, 123–24.
5. In 1979 Sofía described the incident to historian Barbara Miller. See Miller, "Role," 57–58.
6. Acevedo y de la Llata, *Yo, la Madre Conchita*, 19–20.
7. Miller, "Role," 57–58.
8. Acevedo y de la Llata, *Yo, la Madre Conchita*, 12.
9. Acevedo y de la Llata, *Yo, la Madre Conchita*, 14–15.
10. Acevedo y de la Llata, *Yo, la Madre Conchita*, 15.
11. Curley, "Transnational Subaltern Voices," 105.
12. Acevedo de la Llata, *Yo, la Madre Conchita*, 17.
13. Acevedo de la Llata, *Yo, la Madre Conchita*, 19–23.
14. Miller, "Role," 57–58.
15. Miller, "Role," 57–58.
16. Olivera/del Valle, 1972–73.
17. Miller, "Role," 132.
18. Olivera/del Valle, 1972–73.

11. The Voyage

1. Miranda to José Mora y del Río, January 23, 1928, AHAM, MDM, caja 273, exp. 23; "Sette anni di lavoro, del Segretariato Sociale Messicano," June 19, 1928, ASV, AES, pos. 523–24, fasc. 238.
2. Roberto Hutchinson to [Pascual Díaz], August 13, 1928, AHSSM, Correspondencia III 1925.
3. Miranda to Martín Tritschler y Córdova, arzobispo de Yucatán, Washington, May 8, 1928, AHAM, MDM, caja 271, exp. 43.
4. Acevedo y de la Llata, *Obregón*, 121–22.
5. Heilman, "Demon Inside," 23–60; Weis, "Revolution on Trial," 319–53.
6. The dialogue in this section is taken from Acevedo de la Llata, *Yo, la Madre Conchita*, 27–30.
7. "Breve Noticia de la muerte del P. Miguel Pro, SJ," ARSI, PM, Negotia Specialia, Varia, 1408, De persecutione religiosa in Mexico et praesertim de martyrio B. Michele Pro SJ.
8. López-Menéndez, *Miguel Pro*; Dulles, *Yesterday in Mexico*, 312–16; Ramírez Torres, SJ, *Miguel Agustín Pro*; Carreño, *El P. Miguel*; Butler, "Trouble Afoot?, 157–59.

9. "Breve Noticia de la muerte del P. Miguel Pro, SJ," ARSI, PM, Negotia Specialia, Varia, 1408, De persecutione religiosa in Mexico et praesertim de martyrio B. Michele Pro SJ.
10. "Breve Noticia de la muerte del P. Miguel Pro, SJ," ARSI, PM, Negotia Specialia, Varia, 1408, De persecutione religiosa in Mexico et praesertim de martyrio B. Michele Pro SJ.
11. López-Menéndez, *Miguel Pro*, xxvi.
12. Acevedo y de la Llata, *Yo, la Madre Conchita*, 30–34.
13. Antonio Galán SJ to R. P. José Barrachina, Rector del Colegio de Belen, Havana, Cuba, December 29, 1927, ARSI, PM, Negotia Specialia, Varia, 1408, De persecutione religiosa in Mexico et praesertim de martyrio B. Michele Pro SJ.
14. Butler, "Mexican Nicodemus," 271–306.
15. Acevedo y de la Llata, *Obregón*, 97–98.
16. Weis, "Pious Delinquents," 199–206.
17. Olivera/del Valle, 1972–73.
18. Aguilera González, *Cardenal Miguel Darío Miranda*, 127.
19. Olimón Nolasco, *Sofía del Valle*, 61–62.
20. *New York Times*, "Calles Police Seize 225 in Raid to Close Catholic Seminary," January 27, 1928, 1.
21. Aguilera González, *Cardenal Miguel Darío Miranda*, 128.
22. Miranda to Sofía, New Orleans, March 29, 1928, AHAM, MDM, caja 162, exp. 9.
23. It should be noted, for example, that if Sofía and Miranda had wanted a "carnal liaison," the period of the Cristero War would've been perfect cover, as ecclesiastical control over religious mores became relaxed. Special thanks to Matthew Butler for this point.
24. Olimón Nolasco, *Sofía del Valle*, 62–63.
25. Aguilera González, *Cardenal Miguel Darío Miranda*, 129.
26. Aguilera González, *Cardenal Miguel Darío Miranda*, 129.
27. Miranda to Sofía del Valle, on board the ss *Monterrey*, March 12, 1928, AHAM, MDM, caja 162, exp. 9.
28. Miranda to Sofía del Valle, Havana, March 16, 1928, AHAM, MDM, caja 162, exp. 9.
29. Miranda to Sofía del Valle, Havana, March 16 and 24, 1928, AHAM, MDM, caja 162, exp. 9.
30. Miranda to Sofía del Valle, New York, May 17, 1928, AHAM, MDM, caja 162, exp. 9.

12. The Test

1. Miranda to Sofía del Valle, New Orleans, March 29 and April 3, 1928, AHAM, MDM, caja 162, exp. 9.

2. ADG, "Vida de Sofía del Valle."
3. Miranda to Sofía del Valle, New Orleans, March 29, 1928, AHAM, MDM, caja 162, exp. 9.
4. Miranda to Sofía del Valle, New Orleans, March 29, 1928, AHAM, MDM, caja 162, exp. 9.
5. Miranda to Sofía del Valle, New Orleans, April 3 and 5, 1928, AHAM, MDM, caja 162, exp. 9.
6. Miranda to Sofía del Valle, on board train, April 10, 1928, AHAM, MDM, caja 162, exp. 9.
7. Miranda to Sofía del Valle, New Orleans, April 5, 1928, AHAM, MDM, caja 162, exp. 9.
8. Miranda to Sofía del Valle, New Orleans, April 5, 1928, AHAM, MDM, caja 162, exp. 9.
9. Cortés Rivera et al., "La vida."
10. Olimón Nolasco, *Sofía del Valle*, 63.
11. Cultura Femenina, 1928, AACM, JCFM, sección 5.5.
12. Miranda to Sofía, May 18, 1928, AHAM, MDM, caja 168, exp. 36.
13. María Victoria [Sofía] to Miranda, April 15, 1928, AHAM, MDM, caja 162, exp. 9.
14. María Victoria [Sofía] to Miranda, May 18, 1928, AHAM, MDM, caja 162, exp. 9.
15. María Victoria [Sofía] to Miranda, April 15, 1928, AHAM, MDM, caja 162, exp. 9.
16. Andes, *Vatican*, 98.
17. Curley to Miranda, Baltimore, May 14, 1928, AHAM, PDB, caja 48, exp. 10.
18. Miranda to Sofía, Washington DC, May 1, 1928, AHAM, MDM, caja 162, exp. 9.
19. Francisco del Valle to Miranda, Mexico City, Quinta Sofía, April 6, 1928, AHAM, MDM, caja 162, exp. 9.
20. McQueenan, *Closing Time*, 101.
21. Spoto, *High Society*, 20.
22. Larson, *Rosemary*, 148–49.
23. Miranda to Sofía, Philadelphia, April 19, 1928, AHAM, MDM, caja 162, exp. 9.
24. Miranda to Sofía, Washington DC, May 7, 1928, AHAM, MDM, caja 162, exp. 9.
25. María Victoria [Sofía] to Miranda, May 14, 1928, AHAM, MDM, caja 162, exp. 9.
26. Boylan, "Mexican Catholic," 105–6.
27. Miller, "Role," 87, 130–31.
28. María Victoria [Sofía] to Miranda, Mexico City, May 2, 1928, AHAM, MDM, caja 162, exp. 66.
29. María Victoria [Sofía] to Miranda, Mexico City, May 2 and 8, 1928, AHAM, MDM, caja 162, exp. 66.
30. María Victoria [Sofía] to Miranda, Mexico City, May 2 and 8, 1928, AHAM, MDM, caja 162, exp. 66.

31. María Victoria [Sofía] to Miranda, Mexico City, May 2 and 8, 1928, AHAM, MDM, caja 162, exp. 66.
32. María Victoria [Sofía] to Miranda, Mexico City, May 8, 1928, AHAM, MDM, caja 162, exp. 66.
33. Miller, "Role," 87, 130–31.
34. María Victoria [Sofía] to Miranda, Mexico City, May 12, 1928, AHAM, MDM, caja 162, exp. 66.
35. María Victoria [Sofía] to Miranda, Mexico City, May 12, 1928, AHAM, MDM, caja 162, exp. 66.
36. María Victoria [Sofía] to Miranda, Mexico City, May 8, 1928, AHAM, MDM, caja 162, exp. 66.
37. María Victoria [Sofía] to Miranda, May 14 and 18, 1928, AHAM, MDM, caja 162, exp. 9.
38. Kane, "'She Offered Herself Up,'" 80–119.
39. María Victoria [Sofía] to Miranda, May 14, 1928, AHAM, MDM, caja 162, exp. 9.
40. Sofía del Valle saw herself as especially devoted to Thérèse of Lisieux, the "Little Flower," but here reveals, perhaps, she was also influenced by Sacred Heart Theology—the idea of being a living sacrifice—as well as the Theology of the Cross, put forward by María Concepción Cabrera de Armida, whose symbol was a "Sacred Heart" nailed to a cross. And, perhaps, devotion to the Little Flower was not far off from these other currents, as Thérèse herself used her sickness and suffering as a special sacrifice for other "souls." See, for example, Burton, *Holy Blood, Holy Tears*, 47–50.
41. María Victoria [Sofía] to Miranda, May 14 and 18, 1928, AHAM, MDM, caja 162, exp. 9.
42. Coakley, *Women, Men*.
43. Schulenberg, *Forgetful of Their Sex*, 307–64.
44. For two recent books on Cabrera de Armida and her lasting influence on Catholic mysticism in Mexico, as well as her relationship with Father Rougier, see Sicilia, *Concepción Cabrera*; Sicilia, *Félix de Jesús Rougier*.
45. María Victoria [Sofía] to Miranda, May 14, 1928, AHAM, MDM, caja 162, exp. 9.
46. Stourton, "Secret Letters"; Merton, *Courage for Truth*.
47. M. Victoria [Sofía] to Miranda, April 20, 1929, AHAM, MDM, caja 162, exp. 9.
48. Miranda to María Victoria [Sofía], Washington DC, April 14, 1928, AHAM, MDM, caja 162, exp. 9.

13. Gasparri's Parrots

1. Miranda to Sofía, Paris, May 27, 1928, AHAM, MDM, caja 162, exp. 9.

2. Miranda to Sofía, on board train to Rome, May 30, 1928, AHAM, MDM, caja 162, exp. 9.
3. Edwards, *Roman Virtues*.
4. Information regarding Gasparri's special affection for his parrots—even their "green" plumage—and their ability to spout Latin phrases, comes from the following sources: "Statesman Retires," 34; Kertzer, *Pope*, 146–47; Morgan, *Listening Post*, 136–38.
5. Kertzer, *Pope*, 146–47.
6. Kertzer, *Pope*, 146–47.
7. Luca, "Memoria di Pietro Gasparri," 380–84; Roberti, *Il cardinale Pietro Gasparri*, 5–43.
8. Andes, *Vatican*, 14–15.
9. Kertzer, *Pope*, 111.
10. Kertzer, *Pope*, 147.
11. Stati Sessioni, 1926, ASV, AES, sessione 1292, stampa 1155.
12. Stati Sessioni, 1926, ASV, AES, sessione 1292, stampa 1155.
13. Morgan, *Listening Post*, 137.
14. Sir O. Russell to Foreign Office, January 10, 1928, BNA, Mexico, FO371/A181/31/26 and January 30, 1928, FO371/A689/51/26.
15. Mr. Ovey to Foreign Office, April 30, 1928, BNA, Mexico, FO371/A2864/31/26.
16. Miguel Darío Miranda, Nota dichiarativa, della realzione: Sette anni di Lavoro del Segretariado Sociale Messicano, Rome, June 18, 1928, 22r-24r, ASV, AES, pos. 523–24, fasc. 238.
17. Miguel Darío Miranda, Nota dichiarativa, della realzione: Sette anni di Lavoro del Segretariado Sociale Messicano, Rome, June 18, 1928, 22r-24r in ASV, AES, pos. 523–524, fasc. 238.
18. "Sette anni di lavoro, del Segretariato Sociale Messicano," June 19, 1928, ASV, AES, pos. 523–24, fasc. 238.
19. Card. Gasparri to Fumasoni-Biondi in Washington, cable, June 20, 1928, f. 11r, ASV, AES, pos. 523–24, fasc. 238.

14. A Long, Hot Roman Summer

1. Miranda to Sofía, Rome, June 19, 1928, AHAM, MDM, caja 162, exp. 9.
2. Miranda to Sofía, Rome, July 2, 1928, AHAM, MDM, caja 162, exp. 9.
3. Miranda to Sofía, Rome, August 5, 1928, AHAM, MDM, caja 162, exp. 9.
4. Miranda to Sofía, cable, Rome, August 25, 1928, AHAM, MDM, caja 162, exp. 9.
5. Miranda to Sofía, Rome, August 25, 1928, AHAM, MDM, caja 162, exp. 9.

6. On Toral, and his cohort of Catholic activists in Mexico City, see Weis, *God Restrains the Devil*.
7. Espinosa, "Student Politics," 533–62.
8. Dulles, *Yesterday in Mexico*, 362–70.
9. Dulles, *Yesterday in Mexico*, 374–75.
10. Heilman, "Demon Inside," 27.
11. Miranda to Sofía, Paris, October 14, 1928, AHAM, MDM, caja 162, exp. 9.
12. Miranda to Sofía, Rome, September 12, 1928, AHAM, MDM, caja 162, exp. 9.
13. Miranda to Sofía, Fribourg, October 8, 1928, AHAM, MDM, caja 162, exp. 9.
14. Francisco del Valle to Miranda, Quinta Sofía, October 1, 1928, AHAM, MDM, caja 162, exp. 9.
15. Enrique was married to Elena Pratt y Duarte, March 23, 1929. Because of the restrictions on religious sacraments, a judge married the couple at Quinta Sofía. One suspects a clandestine religious ceremony carried out by a priest also occurred, probably before the civil ceremony. Ancestry.com website, "Federal District, Mexico, Civil Registration Marriages, 1861–1950."
16. Miranda to Sofía, Paris, September 30, 1928, AHAM, MDM, caja 162, exp. 9.
17. Miranda to Sofía, Paris, October 14, 1928, AHAM, MDM, caja 162, exp. 9.
18. Miranda to Sofía, on the train from Oviedo to Madrid, October 24, 1928, AHAM, MDM, caja 162, exp. 9.
19. Miranda to Sofía, on the train from Oviedo to Madrid, October 24, 1928, AHAM, MDM, caja 162, exp. 9.
20. Heilman, "Demon Inside," 33.
21. Heilman, "Demon Inside," 33; Weis, "Revolution on Trial," 338.
22. Robert Weis argues, convincingly, that the trial also sought to publicize a prorevolutionary concept of Catholicism; Weis, "Revolution on Trial," 319–53.
23. This is the main argument made by Heilman, "Demon Inside," 24
24. Dulles, *Yesterday in Mexico*, 399.
25. Dulles, *Yesterday in Mexico*, 401.
26. Heilman, "Demon Inside," 42.
27. *El jurado de Toral*, 1:36.
28. Heilman, "Demon Inside," 42.
29. *El jurado de Toral*, 1:237–38.
30. Dulles, *Yesterday in Mexico*, 401–2.
31. Dulles, *Yesterday in Mexico*, 402–3.
32. Miranda to Sofía, Paris, November 22, 1928, AHAM, MDM, caja 162, exp. 9.
33. Miranda to Díaz, Paris, November 26, 1928, AHAM, PDB, caja 46, exp. 33.

15. The Return

1. "Shipping and Mails," *New York Times*, December 17, 1928, 52.
2. Drowne and Huber, *The 1920s*, 260; Fostick, *New York's Liners*, 36; Ancestry.com website, "New York, Passenger Lists, 1820–1957."
3. "14 Customs Guards Ousted in Rum Plot," *New York Times*, June 3, 1928, 1.
4. "Travelers Hold a Fete," *New York Times*, February 19, 1928, 120.
5. Miranda to Sofía, New York, December 21, 1928, AHAM, MDM, caja 162, exp. 9.
6. Miranda to Sofía, New York, December 21, 1928, AHAM, MDM, caja 162, exp. 9.
7. Carreño to Sofía, New York, July 7, 1928 [May 19, 1928], AHAM, MDM, caja 162, exp. 9.
8. Miranda to Sofía, New York, December 21 and 26, 1928, AHAM, MDM, caja 162, exp. 9.
9. Miranda to Sofía, cable, Rome, August 25, 1928, AHAM, MDM, caja 162, exp. 9.
10. Miranda to Sofía, New York, December 21, 1928, AHAM, MDM, caja 162, exp. 9.
11. Miranda to Sofía, New York, December 26 and 27, 1928, AHAM, MDM, caja 162, exp. 9.
12. Miranda to Sofía, New York, April 2, 1929, AHAM, MDM, caja 162, exp. 9.
13. Miranda to Sofía, New York, December 21, 26, 27, 1928, AHAM, MDM, caja 162, exp. 9.
14. Miranda to Sofía, Paris, September 30, 1928, AHAM, MDM, caja 162, exp. 9.
15. Miranda to Sofía, New York, December 21, 26, 27, 1928; and January 22 and 24, 1929, AHAM, MDM, caja 162, exp. 9.
16. Carreño to Miranda, New York, January 7, 1929, AHAM, PDB, caja 46, exp. 33.
17. John J. Burke to Philip R. McDevitt, June 26, 1928 and November 27, 1928, UNDA, CMCD, 17/07.
18. Carreño to Miranda, New York, January 7, 1929, AHAM, PDB, caja 46, exp. 33.
19. Pascual Díaz to Dwight Morrow, New York, July 24, 1928, AHAM, PDB, caja 45, exp. 11.
20. John J. Burke to Philip R. McDevitt, January 28, 1929, UNDA, CMCD, 17/07.
21. Díaz to Miranda, New York, January 10, 1929, AHAM, PDB, caja 48, exp. 10.
22. Díaz to Roberto Hutchinson, New York, January 28, 1929, AHAM, PDB, caja 48, exp. 10; Miranda to Díaz, Baltimore, January 27, 1929, AHAM, PDB, caja 48, exp. 10.
23. Miranda to Sofía, New York, April 23, 1929, AHAM, MDM, caja 162, exp. 9.
24. Fumasoni-Biondi to Miranda, January 13, 1929, AHAM, PDB, caja 48, exp. 10.
25. Fumasoni-Biondi to Miranda, January 13, 1929, AHAM, PDB, caja 48, exp. 10.
26. Miranda to Sofía, Washington DC, January 22, 1929, AHAM, MDM, caja 162, exp. 9.
27. Miranda to Sofía, Washington DC, January 24, 1929, AHAM, MDM, caja 162, exp. 9.

28. Miranda to Sofía, New York, April 27, 1929, AHAM, MDM, caja 162, exp. 9.
29. Miranda to Sofía, New York, April 27, 1929, AHAM, MDM, caja 162, exp. 9.
30. María Victoria [Sofía] to Miranda, undated April 1929 letter, AHAM, MDM, caja 162, exp. 9.
31. Sofía to Miranda, Mexico City, December 5, 1928, AHAM, MDM, caja 162, exp. 66.
32. Sofía to Miranda, Mexico City, April 20, 1929, AHAM, MDM, caja 162, exp. 9.
33. Miranda to Sofía, Washington DC, April 12, 1929, AHAM, MDM, caja 162, exp. 9.
34. Miranda to Sofía, New York, May 9, 1929, AHAM, MDM, caja 162, exp. 9.

16. The Peace

1. Ruiz y Flores, *Recuerdo de recuerdos*, 98–99.
2. John J. Burke to Philip R. McDevitt, May 25, 1929 and June 21, 1929, UNDA, CMCD, 17/07.
3. Valvo, *Pio XI*, 424.
4. Valvo, *Pio XI*, 424–25.
5. Ruiz y Flores, *Recuerdo de recuerdos*, 97.
6. "Mexico Rejoices in Church Peace; Throngs at Shrines," *New York Times*, June 23, 1929, 1.
7. "Algo de historia de la Acción Católica Mexicana y especialmente de la Juventud Católica Femenina Mexicana," undated, AACM, JCFM, 5.23, Historia 25 años 1926–1953.
8. "100,000 Mexicans Kneel at Shrine in Thanks for Peace," *New York Times*, June 24, 1929, 1.
9. "100,000 Mexicans."
10. Chernow, *House of Morgan*, 292.
11. "First Masses Said in Mexico in 3 Years," *New York Times*, June 28, 1929, 4.
12. E. Portes Gil to "A quienes corresponda," July 10, 1929, AGN, Ramo Presidentes, Emilio Portes Gil, 2/713/427.
13. Historia sin fecha, "Sofía del Valle," AACM, JCFM, 5.23.
14. Mr. Montavon to Father Burke, memorandum, December 12, 1930, ACHRCUA, GS, box 148, folder 11.
15. Mr. Montavon to Father Burke, memorandum, October 10, 1930, ACHRCUA, GS, box 148, folder 13; and Juana Arguinzóniz to Father John J. Burke, Mexico City, March 16, 1931, ACHRCUA, GS, box 148, folder 12.

Interlude: Las viejitas

1. María Elena Álvarez de Vicencio has been the subject of a recent biography: González Delgado, *Ambición de Igualdad*.

17. Out of the Shadows

1. "Algo de historia de la Acción Católica Mexicana y especialmente de la Juventud Católica Femenina Mexicana," undated, AACM, JCFM, 5.23, Historia 25 años 1926–1953.
2. "J.C.F.M. en la arquidiócesis," 11–14.
3. Aspe Armella, *La formación*, 19.
4. "Algo de historia de la Acción Católica Mexicana y especialmente de la Juventud Católica Femenina Mexicana," undated, AACM, JCFM, 5.23, Historia 25 años 1926–1953.
5. Boylan, "Mexican Catholic," 163–64.
6. Bailey, *¡Viva Cristo Rey!*, 285.
7. See Meyer, *Cristero Rebellion*, 202.
8. Meyer, *La Cristiada*, 1:323–29; 3:109.
9. Young, *Mexican Exodus*, 7.
10. Meyer, *Cristero Rebellion*, 178.
11. Pollard, "Pius XI's Promotion, 758–84.
12. The Roman model of Catholic Action became the pattern for the movement in Italy, Spain, and Latin America, while French and Belgian Catholic Action developed more specialized movements of workers based on "milieu." See "Note caratteristiche dell'Azione Cattolica" 15-IX-1961, Mons. Luigi Civardi, ASV, Concilio Vaticano II (Conc. Vat. II), busta 1176, comm. praeparatoria, XXIX–XXXVII, subcommissio I.
13. Lettera Autografa di S.S. Papa Pio XI "Vos Argentinae Episcopos," February 4, 1931, circa l'Azione Cattolica, ASV, Arch. Nunz. Argentina, busta 119.
14. Informe de los trabajos realizados por la Liga de Damas Católicas, December 1931, ASV, Arch. Nunz. Argentina, busta 119.
15. "Nuestra fiesta patronal," 5–8; "Algo de historia de la Acción Católica Mexicana y especialmente de la Juventud Católica Femenina Mexicana," undated, AACM, JCFM, 5.23, Historia 25 años 1926–1953.
16. "Nuestra fiesta patronal," 5–8.
17. "Nuestra fiesta patronal," 5.
18. "Palabras de nuestra presidenta," 11.

18. The New Woman

1. "Cultura Femenina, 1929–1933," María de la Luz Lazo de Conover, Mexico City, Enero de 1977, AHAM, MDM, caja 273, exp. 23.
2. Fiell and Dirix, *1930s Fashion*, 8–17.

3. "Cultura Femenina, 1929–1933," María de la Luz Lazo de Conover, Mexico City, Enero de 1977, AHAM, MDM, caja 273, exp. 23.
4. "Sociales," 10.
5. The phrase and the argument about Catholic women embodying both the "old" and the "new" in their activism is drawn from Cummings, *New Women*, 18–58.
6. "Cultura Femenina, 1929–1933," María de la Luz Lazo de Conover, Mexico City, Enero de 1977, AHAM, MDM, caja 273, exp. 23.
7. Informes de los Profesores, Cultura Femenina, Prefectura de Estudios, April 29, 1931, AACM, JCFM, sección 5.5.
8. Inst. de Cultura Femenina, 1928–1932, Calificaciones, AACM, JCFM, sección 5.5.
9. Inst. de Cultura Femenina, 1928–1932, Calificaciones, AACM, JCFM, sección 5.5.
10. Inst. de Cultura Femenina, 1928–1932, Calificaciones, AACM, JCFM, sección 5.5.
11. "Cultura Femenina, México, D.F.," ACHRCUA, GS, box 148, folder 12.
12. "Cultura Femenina, México, D.F.," AHAM, MDM, caja 175, exp. 24.
13. "Cultura Femenina, México, D.F.," AHAM, MDM, caja 175, exp. 24.
14. Cummings, *New Women*, 6, 19, 51.
15. Macías, *Against All Odds*, 3–17.
16. Lepore, *Secret History*, 21; Olcott, *Revolutionary Women*, 48, 205–6.
17. Boylan, "Mexican Catholic," 157–64; Schell, "Of the Sublime," 99–124.

19. Resistance

1. Alfredo Méndez Medina, SJ to Camilo Crivelli, SJ, April 28, 1930, Mexico City, ARSI, PM, Epistolae Mexico, 1010-V, 8.
2. Alfredo Méndez Medina, SJ to Camilo Crivelli, SJ, April 28, 1930, Mexico City, ARSI, PM, Epistolae Mexico, 1010-V, 8.
3. Leobardo Fernández, SJ to Fernando Gutiérrez del Olmo, José Demaux Lagrange, and Camilo Crivelli, April 10, 1931, ARSI, PM, Epistolae Mexico, 1010-XI, 4.
4. Alfredo Méndez Medina, SJ to anonymous, June 21, 1930, ARSI, OM, Epistolae Mexico, 1010-V, 10.
5. Miranda, after taking the helm of the Social Secretariat, wrote Méndez Medina constantly throughout the summer and fall of 1925; see AHSSM, Correspondencia III, 1925: Miranda to Méndez Medina, Mexico City, June 4, 1925; Méndez Medina to Miranda, León, Guanajuato, June 22, 1925; Miranda to Méndez Medina, Mexico City, June 26, 1925; Méndez Medina to Miranda, León, Guanajuato, June 26, 1925; Miranda to Méndez Medina, Mexico City, August 14, 1925; Méndez Medina to Miranda, León,

Guanajuato, August 16, 1925; Méndez Medina to Miranda, León, Guanajuato, September 25, 1925.
6. Alfredo Méndez Medina, SJ to anonymous, June 21, 1930, ARSI, PM, Epistolae Mexico, 1010-V, 10.
7. Leobardo Fernández, SJ to Fernando Gutiérrez del Olmo, José Demaux Lagrange, and Camilo Crivelli, April 10, 1931, ARSI, PM, Epistolae Mexico, 1010-XI, 4.
8. Sofía to Miranda, Paris, February 27, 1931, AHAM, MDM, caja 162, exp. 9.

20. *Les femmes internationales*

1. Ancestry.com website, "Border Crossings: From Mexico to U.S., 1895–1964."
2. Sofía to Miranda, London, December 9, 1930, AHAM, MDM, caja 162, exp. 9.
3. Sofía to Miranda, London, December 9, 1930, AHAM, MDM, caja 162, exp. 9.
4. Nemery, Hoet, and Nemmar, "Meuse Valley Fog," 704–8.
5. Vandevivere, Périer-d'Ieteren, and Boucher, *Renaissance Art in Belgium*, 72.
6. Robinson-Tomsett, *Women, Travel and Identity*, 87.
7. Robinson-Tomsett, *Women, Travel and Identity*, 89–90.
8. Pollard, "Pius XI's Promotion," 767–68.
9. Osselaer, *Pious Sex*, 172–84.
10. Arrom, *Volunteering for a Cause*, 75–80.
11. Rupp, *Worlds of Women*, 37–38.
12. Cummings, *New Women*, 192–94.
13. Holland, *Modern Catholic*, 258.
14. Rupp, *Worlds of Women*, 153.
15. Scaraffia, "Christianity Has Liberated Her," 275.
16. Scaraffia, "Christianity Has Liberated Her," 275–76.
17. Dawes, *Catholic Women's Movements*, 191–92; Ciriello, "Armida Barelli," 58.
18. Fayet-Scribe, *Associations féminines*, 120.
19. Sofía to [Miranda], Val Notre Dame, December 24, 1930, AHAM, MDM, caja 162, exp. 9.
20. Sofía to [Miranda], Val Notre Dame, December 24, 1930, AHAM, MDM, caja 162, exp. 9.
21. Sofía to [Miranda], Val Notre Dame, December 24, 1930, AHAM, MDM, caja 162, exp. 9.
22. Sofía to [Miranda], Val Notre Dame, December 24, 1930, AHAM, MDM, caja 162, exp. 9; ADG, "Vida de Sofía del Valle."
23. Sofía to [Miranda], Val Notre Dame, December 24, 1930, AHAM, MDM, caja 162, exp. 9.

24. Sofía to [Miranda], Val Notre Dame, December 24, 1930, AHAM, MDM, caja 162, exp. 9.
25. Olimón Nolasco, *Sofía del Valle*, 73.
26. "Extracto del informe del primer congreso internacional de la Liga Católica Femenil," *Juventud*, July 1930, 7.
27. Sofía to [Miranda], Val Notre Dame, December 24, 1930, AHAM, MDM, caja 162, exp. 9.
28. Sofía wrote Miranda in Spanish: "Consolador en parte aunque no muy edificante es ver que en todas partes cuesen habas." Sofía to [Miranda], Val Notre Dame, December 24, 1930, AHAM, MDM, caja 162, exp. 9.
29. Sofía to [Miranda], Val Notre Dame, December 24, 1930, AHAM, MDM, caja 162, exp. 9.
30. ADG "Vida de Sofía del Valle."
31. For example, NCCW president Mary Hawks was already a member of the bureau of the IUCWL; see Petit, "Organized Catholic," 83–100.
32. Diesbach, *WUCWO Story*.
33. Sofía to [Miranda], Val Notre Dame, December 24, 1930, AHAM, MDM, caja 162, exp. 9.
34. Sofía to [Miranda], Val Notre Dame, December 24, 1930, AHAM, MDM, caja 162, exp. 9.

21. Terrible Beasts

1. Sofía described her dreams to Miranda and mentioned one in particular during Christmas, when she was with her sister. Sofía to Miranda, Paris, February 15, 1931, AHAM, MDM, caja 162, exp. 66.
2. Sofía to Miranda, Paris, January 4, 1931, AHAM, MDM, caja 162, exp. 9.
3. Sofía to Miranda, Paris, January 4, 1931, AHAM, MDM, caja 162, exp. 9.
4. Sofía to Miranda, Paris, January 4, 1931, AHAM, MDM, caja 162, exp. 9.
5. Sofía to Miranda, Paris, January 4, 1931, AHAM, MDM, caja 162, exp. 9; and January 19, 1931, caja 162, exp. 66.
6. Sofía to Miranda, Paris, February 2 and 15, 1931, AHAM, MDM, caja 162, exp. 66.
7. Sofía to Miranda, Paris, January 4, 1931, AHAM, MDM, caja 162, exp. 9.
8. Sofía to Miranda, Paris, January 4, 1931, AHAM, MDM, caja 162, exp. 9.
9. Sofía to [Miranda], Val Notre Dame, December 24, 1930, AHAM, MDM, caja 162, exp. 9.

22. Winter in the City of Light

1. "By Radio from Paris," *New York Times*, January 26, 1931, X14; "Mme. Chanel to Aid Films," *New York Times*, January 20, 1931, 7; "Fashion Seen," 62–64.

2. Sofía to Miranda, Paris, January 11, 1931, AHAM, MDM, caja 162, exp. 9.
3. Schloesser, *Jazz Age Catholicism*, 196.
4. Sofía to Miranda, Paris, January 19, 1931, AHAM, MDM, caja 162, exp. 66.
5. Navarrete, *Por Dios*, 133–34.
6. Boylan, "Mexican Catholic," 115, 135.
7. Sofía to Miranda, Paris, January 25, 1931, AHAM, MDM, caja 162, exp. 66.
8. Sofía to Miranda, Paris, January 4, 1931, AHAM, MDM, caja 162, exp. 9.
9. Sofía to Miranda, Paris, January 4, 1931, AHAM, MDM, caja 162, exp. 9.
10. Sofía to Miranda, Paris, January 4, 1931, AHAM, MDM, caja 162, exp. 9.
11. Sofía to Miranda, Paris, January 25, 1931, AHAM, MDM, caja 162, exp. 66.
12. Sofía to Miranda, Paris, January 19, 1931, AHAM, MDM, caja 162, exp. 66.
13. Sofía to Miranda, Paris, January 11, 1931, AHAM, MDM, caja 162, exp. 9.
14. Sofía to Miranda, Paris, January 19, 1931, AHAM, MDM, caja 162, exp. 66.
15. Flanner, Thurber, and Ross, "Tender Buttons."
16. Sofía to Miranda, Paris, January 19, 1931, AHAM, MDM, caja 162, exp. 66.
17. Sofía to Miranda, Paris, January 19, 1931, AHAM, MDM, caja 162, exp. 66.
18. The run-in between Sofía and Angelina Arce, and the dialogue, comes from a letter Sofía wrote to Miranda. Sofía to Miranda, Paris, January 20, 1931, AHAM, MDM, caja 162, exp. 66.
19. Sofía to Miranda, Paris, February 2, 1931, AHAM, MDM, caja 162, exp. 66.
20. Sofía to Miranda, Paris, February 2, 1931, AHAM, MDM, caja 162, exp. 66.
21. Jules-Rosette, *Josephine Baker*, 50.
22. Foley, *Women in France*, 196.
23. "Casti Connubii," December 31, 1930, Papal Encyclicals Online, http://www.papalencyclicals.net/pius11/p11casti.htm.
24. "Casti Connubii," December 31, 1930, Papal Encyclicals Online, http://www.papalencyclicals.net/pius11/p11casti.htm.
25. "A Saucy Parisienne 'Tells All' About Her Chicago Millionaire," *Hamilton Evening Journal*, March 8, 1930, 18.
26. *Ogden Standard-Examiner*, January 5, 1930, 30.
27. Sofía to Miranda, Paris, January 11, 1931, AHAM, MDM, caja 162, exp. 9.
28. "Women Cops on Parade," *Hamilton Evening Journal*, March 8, 1930, 18.
29. Therbon, *Between Sex and Power*, 24, 90.
30. Sofía to Miranda, Paris, January 19, 1931, AHAM, MDM, caja 162, exp. 66.
31. Sofía to Miranda, Paris, January 19, 1931, AHAM, MDM, caja 162, exp. 66.

23. Doubt

1. Sofía to Miranda, Paris, February 10, 1931, AHAM, MDM, caja 162, exp. 9.
2. Comtesse de Courson, "Lisieux," 142.

3. Sofía to Miranda, Paris, February 10, 1931, AHAM, MDM, caja 162, exp. 9.
4. Sofía to Miranda, Paris, February 10, 1931, AHAM, MDM, caja 162, exp. 9.
5. Sofía to Miranda, Paris, February 15, 1931, caja 162, exp. 9; February 20, 27, and 29, 1931, AHAM, MDM, caja 162, exp. 66.
6. Sofía to Miranda, Paris, March 3 and 8, 1931, AHAM, MDM, caja 162, exp. 9.
7. Sofía to Miranda, Paris, March 3, 1931, AHAM, MDM, caja 162, exp. 9.
8. Sofía to Miranda, Paris, March 8, 1931, AHAM, MDM, caja 162, exp. 9.
9. Sofía to Miranda, Paris, March 18 and 24, 1931, AHAM, MDM, caja 162, exp. 9.
10. Sofía to Miranda, Paris, March 18, 1931, AHAM, MDM, caja 162, exp. 9.
11. Copy of a letter from Chr. de Hemptinne to Sofía, included in the letter from March 24, 1931, AHAM, MDM, caja 162, exp. 9.
12. For the classic history of the pilgrimage site, see Harris, *Lourdes*.
13. Sofía to Miranda, Paris, March 18, 1931, AHAM, MDM, caja 162, exp. 9.
14. Sofía to Miranda, Paris, March 18, 1931, AHAM, MDM, caja 162, exp. 9.
15. Sofía to Miranda, Paris, March 18, 1931, AHAM, MDM, caja 162, exp. 9.
16. Sofía to Miranda, Paris, March 18 and 24, 1931, AHAM, MDM, caja 162, exp. 9.
17. Olimón Nolasco, *Sofía del Valle*, 74.

24. Lourdes

1. ADG, "Vida de Sofía del Valle."
2. Olimón Nolasco, *Sofía del Valle*, 74.
3. Olimón Nolasco, *Sofía del Valle*, 75.
4. Olimón Nolasco, *Sofía del Valle*, 74.
5. Olimón Nolasco, *Sofía del Valle*, 75.
6. Olimón Nolasco, *Sofía del Valle*, 75.
7. Olimón Nolasco, *Sofía del Valle*, 75.

25. The Road to Warsaw

1. ADG, "Vida de Sofía del Valle."
2. Miranda to Sofía, Rome, May 29, 1931, AHAM, MDM, caja 168, exp. 36.
3. "Van Hoesch Dies; German Diplomat," *New York Times*, April 11, 1936, 7.
4. Johnson, *Our Man in Berlin*, 169; Roderick Jones, *A Life in Reuters*, 395–97.
5. Craig and Gilbert, *Diplomats*, 151.
6. Velten, *Beastly London*, 187.
7. ADG, "Vida de Sofía del Valle."
8. Regan, "Year's Work," 19–22.
9. Miranda to Sofía, Washington DC, April 17, 1928, AHAM, MDM, caja 162, exp. 9.
10. Petit, "Organized Catholic," 89–90.
11. Petit, "Organized Catholic," 100.

12. "Year's Progress," 17.
13. ADG, "Vida de Sofía del Valle."

26. Borders

1. Schmidt, *Folly of War*, 162.
2. "Corridor," 12.
3. "Poland Rounds Up Reds," *New York Times*, February 17, 1931, 12.
4. Shepard Arthur Stone, "In Europe's New Tenseness the 'Corridor' Looms Large," *New York Times*, March 19, 1933, XX3.
5. The dialogue is taken from ADG, "Vida de Sofía del Valle."
6. ADG, "Vida de Sofía del Valle."
7. ADG, "Vida de Sofía del Valle."
8. ADG, "Vida de Sofía del Valle."

27. Bridges

1. ADG, "Vida de Sofía del Valle."
2. Again, this memory comes from the unfinished memoir: ADG, "Vida de Sofía del Valle."
3. ADG, "Vida de Sofía del Valle."
4. ADG, "Vida de Sofía del Valle."
5. XVe Internationale Statutaire Vergadering evenals Internationaal Congres F.M.F.J.C., Rome April 19–23, 1960. "Hints for a Talk on WFCJWG," Hemptinne Papers, 14.12.18.
6. ADG, "Vida de Sofía del Valle."
7. ADG, "Vida de Sofía del Valle."
8. Sofía to Miranda, Rome, June 24, 1931, AHAM, MDM, exp. 162, exp. 9.
9. Sofía to Miranda, Rome, June 26, 1931, AHAM, MDM, exp. 162, exp. 9.
10. Sofía to Miranda, Rome, June 26, 1931, AHAM, MDM, exp. 162, exp. 9.
11. Sofía to Miranda, Rome, June 26, 1931, AHAM, MDM, exp. 162, exp. 9.
12. Sofía to Miranda, Rome, June 26, 1931, AHAM, MDM, exp. 162, exp. 9.
13. Kertzer, *Pope*, 154–55.
14. Kertzer, *Pope*, 155.
15. Ventresca, *Soldier of Christ*, 69, 86.
16. Andes, *Vatican*, 162–64.
17. *Juventud*, November 15, 1931, cover.

Interlude: Walls

1. Arvonne S. Fraser, "An Historic Step Forward," *Florida Today*, July 22, 1975, 3D.

2. For a recent, and important, look at the UN Conference in Mexico, see Olcott, *International Women's Year*.
3. "We haven't even asked you about Trump," María Eugenia Díaz Gastine said as we were finishing lunch. Flummoxed a bit, and pretending to finish my dessert, I tread lightly. I listened as the women told me how, to them, Trump's policies felt like a reversion to so many things. I didn't ask them to expand on that. But it made me think of the 1930s, when Sofía del Valle spent so much time in the United States. When jobs were scarce during the Depression, Mexican labor became problematic for many Americans. At least one million Mexicans faced coerced repatriation in the 1930s. In some ways, I remember thinking during that lunch, globalization just makes borders and walls seem that much more necessary. Fear has a way of causing people to erect barriers. I remember thinking of that quote by Mexican novelist Carlos Fuentes: "This isn't a border. It's a scar." The whole discussion about President Trump seemed too fresh, too disorienting, to include in the main text. But I considered it. How do historians talk about such contemporary subjects? Why don't we? Historians, it seems to me, are especially well-suited to talk about U.S.-Mexico relations in the era of Trump. Do we only get to say something in an Op-Ed? For a book on the repatriation of Mexicans and Mexican-Americans—some 40 percent of those coerced to leave the United States were American citizens—see Balderrama and Rodríguez, *Decade of Betrayal*.

28. Miss del Valle in Washington

1. "Libros," 14.
2. Pascual Díaz wrote to Cardinal Dennis Dougherty (Philadelphia), Archbishop Michael Curley (Baltimore), Archbishop John Glennen (St. Louis), Cardinal Patrick Hayes (New York), Cardinal William Mundelein (Chicago), and Bishop Joseph Walsh (Newark), April 14, 15, 16, 1934, AHAM, MDM, caja 178, exp. 71.
3. "N.C.C.W. Staff Afield," 31; "Algo de historia de la Acción Católica Mexicana y especialmente de la Juventud Católica Femenina Mexicana," undated, AACM, JCFM, 5.23, Historia 25 años 1926–1953.
4. Interview with Teresa R. de Huidobro del Valle, July 14, 2016 (Skype).
5. Sofía to Miranda, Durango, May 13, 1932, AHAM, MDM, caja 162, exp. 9.
6. Sofía to Doctor [Miranda], Monterrey, May 2, 1934, and Miranda to Sofía, May 4, 1932, AHAM, MDM, caja 162, exp. 9.
7. Sofía and Guadalupe Velasco to Miranda, April 20, 1932, AHAM, MDM, caja 162, exp. 9.

8. Interview with María Elena Álvarez de Vicencio, Guadalupe Aguilar Fernández, Mercedes Gómez del Campo de Zavala, and María Eugenia Díaz Gastine de Pfennich, March 20, 2017 (Mexico City).
9. "Algo de historia de la Acción Católica Mexicana y especialmente de la Juventud Católica Femenina Mexicana," undated, AACM, JCFM, 5.23, Historia 25 años 1926–1953; "Círculo de formación," 10.
10. Sofía to Miranda, Durango, May 13, 1932, AHAM, MDM, caja 162, exp. 9.
11. Vaughan, *Cultural Politics*, 12, 31, 34, 54.
12. ADG, "Vida de Sofía del Valle."
13. Aguilera González, *Cardenal Miguel Darío Miranda*, ix.
14. Sofía to Doctor [Miranda], January 25, 1933, AHAM, MDM, caja 175, exp. 15.
15. Ancestry.com website, "Border Crossings: From Mexico to U.S., 1895–1964."

29. The Plan

1. The letter's typographical errors are related to the spacing of words. Often two words are written without a space between, which was uncommon in most of Sofía's typed letters. Sofía mentions having the letter-hammers fixed. Sofía to Miranda, Philadelphia, June 3, 1934, AHAM, MDM, caja 162, exp. 9.
2. Sofía to Miranda, Philadelphia, June 3, 1934, AHAM, MDM, caja 162, exp. 9.
3. Sofía to Miranda, Washington DC, May 9, 1934, AHAM, MDM, caja 162, exp. 9.
4. Sofía to Miranda, Washington DC, May 9, 1934, AHAM, MDM, caja 162, exp. 9.
5. Sofía to Miranda, Washington DC, May 9, 1934, AHAM, MDM, caja 162, exp. 9.
6. Sofía to Miranda, Washington DC, May 9, 1934, AHAM, MDM, caja 162, exp. 9.
7. Sofía to Miranda, Washington DC, May 9, 1934, AHAM, MDM, caja 162, exp. 9.
8. Castagna, *Bridge across the Ocean*, 121; "The History of the Catholic Daughters of America," Catholic Daughters of America website, http://www.catholicdaughters.org/history.shtml.
9. Sofía to Miranda, Washington DC, May 9, 1934, AHAM, MDM, caja 162, exp. 9.
10. Sofía to Miranda, Washington DC, May 11, 1934, AHAM, MDM, caja 162, exp. 9.
11. Sofía to Miranda, Washington DC, May 11, 1934, AHAM, MDM, caja 162, exp. 9.
12. Sofía to Miranda, Washington DC, May 11, 1934, AHAM, MDM, caja 162, exp. 9.
13. Sofía to Miranda, Washington DC, May 11, 1934, AHAM, MDM, caja 162, exp. 9.
14. Jacoby, *Strange Career*, 132.
15. Sofía to Miranda, Washington DC, May 9, 1934, AHAM, MDM, caja 162, exp. 9.
16. Miranda to Sofía, Mexico City, May 16, 1934, AHAM, MDM, caja 162, exp. 9.
17. Sofía to Miranda, Washington DC, May 11, 1934, AHAM, MDM, caja 162, exp. 9.
18. Lacy, "Catholics and Catholicism," 1: 128.
19. Tweed, *America's Church*, 74–75, 77, 79.

20. Sofía to Miranda, Washington DC, May 19, 1934, AHAM, MDM, caja 162, exp. 9.
21. Sofía to Miranda, Washington DC, May 11, 1934, AHAM, MDM, caja 162, exp. 9.
22. Sofía to Miranda, Washington DC, May 19, 1934, AHAM, MDM, caja 162, exp. 9.
23. Sofía to Miranda, Washington DC, May 19, 1934, AHAM, MDM, caja 162, exp. 9.
24. Sofía to Miranda, Philadelphia, June 3, 1934, AHAM, MDM, caja 162, exp. 9.

30. The Deception of Miss Duffy

1. Sofía to Miranda, New York, June 20, 1934, AHAM, MDM, caja 162, exp. 9; ADG, "Vida de Sofía del Valle."
2. Miranda to Sofía, Mexico City, June 6, 1934, AHAM, MDM, caja 162, exp. 9.
3. Sofía to Miranda, New York, June 20, 1934, AHAM, MDM, caja 162, exp. 9.
4. Sofía to Miranda, Washington DC, May 19, 1934, AHAM, MDM, caja 162, exp. 9.
5. Sofía to Miranda, Washington DC, May 19, 1934, AHAM, MDM, caja 162, exp. 9.
6. The characterization of Miss Duffy comes from a photo in *N.C.W.C. Bulletin* 11, no. 4 (September 1929): 16.
7. The dialogue and description of this scene comes from Sofía to Miranda, New York, June 20, 1934, AHAM, MDM, caja 162, exp. 9.
8. Sofía to Miranda, Washington DC, May 9, 1934 and May 11, 1934, AHAM, MDM, caja 162, exp. 9.
9. Sofía to Miranda, New York, June 20, 1934, AHAM, MDM, caja 162, exp. 9.
10. Sofía to Miranda, New York, June 20, 1934, AHAM, MDM, caja 162, exp. 9.
11. Sofía to Miranda, New York, June 20, 1934, AHAM, MDM, caja 162, exp. 9.
12. Sofía to Miranda, New York, June 20, 1934, AHAM, MDM, caja 162, exp. 9.
13. Sofía to Miranda, New York, June 20, 1934, AHAM, MDM, caja 162, exp. 9.
14. Sofía to Miranda, New York, June 20, 1934, AHAM, MDM, caja 162, exp. 9.
15. Sofía to Miranda, New York, June 20, 1934, AHAM, MDM, caja 162, exp. 9.
16. Sofía to Miranda, New York, June 20, 1934, AHAM, MDM, caja 162, exp. 9; ADG, "Vida de Sofía del Valle."
17. Olimón Nolasco, *Sofía del Valle*, 69.
18. Sofía's encounter with the bishop comes from Sofía to Miranda, New York, June 20, 1934, AHAM, MDM, caja 162, exp. 9.
19. Sofía del Valle to Leopoldo Ruiz y Flores, Philadelphia, July 4, 1934, 5rv, ASV, AM, fasc. 28.
20. Sofía to Doctor [Miranda], July 11, 1934, AHAM, MDM, caja 162, exp. 9.
21. Sofía del Valle to Leopoldo Ruiz y Flores, Mexico City, July 27, 1934, 7r, ASV, AM, fasc. 28.

31. Consider the Lobster

1. ADG, "Vida de Sofía del Valle."

2. Intercepted letter found in Sofía to "Doctor" [Miranda], October 3, 1934, sent from The Mayflower Hotel, Washington DC, 60–62, FPEC, serie 010806, exp. 51, inventario 631, 2/3.
3. *El Nacional*, October 28, 1934, 4.
4. Sofía to "Doctor" [Miranda] October 3, 1934, sent from The Mayflower Hotel, Washington DC, 60–62, FPEC, serie 010806, exp. 51, inventario 631, 2/3.
5. Sofía to "Doctor" [Miranda] October 3, 1934, sent from The Mayflower Hotel, Washington DC, 60–62, in FPEC, serie 010806, exp. 51, inventario 631, 2/3.
6. Miranda to Sofía, October 5, 1934, AHAM, MDM, caja 162, exp. 9.
7. Solis, "El Vaticano," 129–30.
8. Sofía to Ruiz y Flores, April 3, 1935, 35v, ASV, AM, fasc. 28.
9. ADG, "Vida de Sofía del Valle."
10. ADG, "Vida de Sofía del Valle."
11. Young, "Calles Government," 63–91.
12. For a recent contribution to understanding the directorate in the 1930s, see Martínez Gobea, "De vigilantes."
13. *Corsicana Daily Sun*, January 5, 1935, 5.
14. "U.S. Gun Runners Hunted by Mexico," *Baltimore Sun*, January 6, 1935, 11.
15. I was unable to locate a mention of Sofía del Valle in the files of the IPS at Mexico's Archivo General de la Nación. However, Catholic Action and many of its members were under surveillance, as was one of the Jesuit priests, José Romero, named in one of the letters published in *El Nacional* at the same time as the "Mysterious Sofía." See "Pbro. Jose Antonio Romero," AGN, DGIPS, caja 307, exp. 2.
16. ADG, "Vida de Sofía del Valle."
17. ADG, "Vida de Sofía del Valle."
18. ADG, "Vida de Sofía del Valle."

32. *Golden Hour*

1. Sofía del Valle to Leopoldo Ruiz y Flores, Toronto, November 8, 1934, 13r, ASV, AM, fasc. 28.
2. Warren, *Radio Priest*, 25.
3. Brinkley, *Voices of Protest*, 101.
4. Brinkley, *Voices of Protest*, 83.
5. Sterling, "Coughlin, Father Charles," 658.
6. Boyea, "Reverend Charles," 211.
7. Sterling, "Coughlin, Father Charles," 658.
8. Modras, "Coughlin and Anti-Semitism," 231–47.

9. Soderbergh, "Rise," 10–20.
10. Brinkley, *Voices of Protest*, 92.
11. Sofía del Valle to Leopoldo Ruiz y Flores, Toronto, November 8, 1934, 13r, ASV, AM, fasc. 28.
12. Sofía del Valle to Leopoldo Ruiz y Flores, Toronto, November 8, 1934, 13r, ASV, AM, fasc. 28.
13. The close relationship between Coughlin and Gallagher is detailed in Tentler, *Seasons of Grace*, 323–39.
14. Tentler, *Seasons of Grace*, 411–13.
15. Brinkley, *Voices of Protest*, 82.
16. Warren, *Radio Priest*, 2.
17. *Time*, January 15, 1934 (cover).
18. Sterling, "Coughlin, Father Charles," 658; Barnouw, *Golden Web*, 42.
19. Warren, *Radio Priest*, 47.
20. ADG, "Vida de Sofía del Valle."
21. ADG, "Vida de Sofía del Valle."
22. Sofía del Valle to Leopoldo Ruiz y Flores, November 13, 1934, 14rv, ASV, AM, fasc. 28.
23. The text of Father Coughlin's December 23, 1934, radio sermon is in Coughlin, "Following the Christ Child!" 91.
24. Coughlin, "Following the Christ Child!," 93.
25. Coughlin, "Following the Christ Child!," 94–95.
26. Similar United Press stories made the rounds throughout the United States: "Coughlin Flays Mexican Stand," *Pittsburgh Press*, December 24, 1934, 1; and "Priest Slams U.S., Mexico Relationship," *News-Palladium*, December 24, 1934, 12. The *New York Times* also published a story focusing on Coughlin's attacks of Roosevelt, "Coughlin Condemns Our Policy in Mexico," *New York Times*, December 24, 1934, 9.
27. "The Supreme Issue of Mexico," *Commonweal*, November 23, 1934, 103–4.
28. Sofía del Valle wasn't the only individual to tour the United States speaking about Mexico. In fact, American clergymen, especially Francis Kelley, had done so since the 1910s. See, for example, Kelley, *Book of Red and Yellow*; and the British journalist, Francis McCullagh, *Red Mexico*.
29. Sofía to Ruiz y Flores, Chicago, March 7, 1936, 65r, ASV, AM, fasc. 28.
30. Coughlin, "Following the Christ Child!," 91.
31. Coughlin, "Following the Christ Child!," 91.
32. "Doctor James J. Walsh Speaks to Students in Wash. Hall," *Notre Dame Scholastic*, April 5, 1935, 4.

33. On the Road

1. Letter to Very Rev. John O'Hara, University of Notre Dame, October 12, 1934, ACHRCUA, RNCCW, box 117, folder 1.
2. "What Is Cultura Femenina?" 1938, ACHRCUA, USCCB General Secretary, box 148, folder 14.
3. *Cleveland Press*, Tuesday, April 15, 1941, ACHRCUA, RNCCW, box 117, folder 1.
4. "What Is Cultura Femenina, #1," introduction letter to promotional brochure, AHAM, MDM, caja 168, exp. 37.
5. Sofía del Valle to Leopoldo Ruiz y Flores, New York, November 29, 1934, 15rv, ASV, AM, fasc. 28.
6. Sofía del Valle to Leopoldo Ruiz y Flores, New York, November 29, 1934, 15v, ASV, AM, fasc. 28.
7. Sofía del Valle to Leopoldo Ruiz y Flores, on board the Sunshine Special, September 30, 1934, 10r, ASV, AM, fasc. 28.
8. Three-page testament written by Elizabeth Ward Loughran, personal collection of Lisa Loughran.
9. Loughran, "Role of Catholic Culture," 1–50.
10. O'Connor, *Boston Catholics*, 193–236.
11. Forest, *All Is Grace*, 248.
12. Day, *All the Way*, 85, 91–92, 294, 521.
13. Hennessy, *Dorothy Day*, 27–32.
14. Katherine Anne Porter visited Day in Mexico and briefly stayed with Dorothy and her daughter Tamar; see Walsh, *Katherine Anne Porter*, 107, 136, 144–45; Elie, *Life You Save*, 64–65. Dorothy Day published several articles for the Jesuit magazine *America* and for *Commonweal* while she lived in Mexico; Jordan, *Dorothy Day*, 7–20.
15. My emphasis. Day, *Loaves and Fishes*, 13.
16. Sofía del Valle to Leopoldo Ruiz y Flores, on board the Sunshine Special, September 30, 1934, 10r, ASV, AM, fasc. 28.
17. Sofía del Valle to Leopoldo Ruiz y Flores, New York, December 10, 1936, 77rv, ASV, AM, fasc. 28.
18. Olimón Nolasco, *Sofía del Valle*, 97, 100, 112.
19. Sofía del Valle to Leopoldo Ruiz y Flores, Baltimore, June 25, 1935, 47r, ASV, AM, fasc. 28.
20. Sofía del Valle to Leopoldo Ruiz y Flores, Philadelphia, August 25, 1936, 71r, ASV, AM, fasc. 28.
21. ADG, "Vida de Sofía del Valle."

22. Sofía del Valle to Leopoldo Ruiz y Flores, Chicago, March 7, 1936, 65r, ASV, AM, fasc. 28.
23. Sofía del Valle to Leopoldo Ruiz y Flores, Chicago, March 7, 1936, 65r, ASV, AM, fasc. 28.
24. Sofía del Valle to Leopoldo Ruiz y Flores, Chicago, March 7, 1936, 65r, ASV, AM, fasc. 28.
25. Olimón Nolasco, *Sofía del Valle*, 101.
26. Olimón Nolasco, *Sofía del Valle*, 103.
27. ADG, "Vida de Sofía del Valle."
28. Sofía del Valle to Leopoldo Ruiz y Flores, Rome, April 14, [1937], 104r, ASV, AM, fasc. 28.
29. Ventresca, *Soldier of Christ*, 66–67; Pollard, "Pius XI's Promotion," 759.
30. Sofía del Valle to Leopoldo Ruiz y Flores, New York, May 12, 1937, 81r, ASV, AM, fasc. 28.
31. Sofía del Valle to Leopoldo Ruiz y Flores, New York, May 12, 1937, 81r, ASV, AM, fasc. 28.
32. Sofía del Valle to Leopoldo Ruiz y Flores, New York, June 19, 1937, 84r-86r, ASV, AM, fasc. 28.
33. ADG, "Vida de Sofía del Valle."
34. "What Is Cultura Femenina?" 1938, ACHRCUA, USCCB General Secretary, box 148, folder 14.
35. "Cultura Femenina, 1935," Eugenia Olivera and Amparo Elguero de Rosales, AHAM, base PDB, caja 37, exp. 3.
36. Andes, *Vatican*, 169–70.
37. ADG, "Vida de Sofía del Valle."
38. McMahon, *Order Followed*, 29.
39. ADG, "Vida de Sofía del Valle."
40. ADG, "Vida de Sofía del Valle."
41. Sofía to Miranda, October 19, 1938, AHAM, MDM, caja 162, exp. 9.
42. Sofía to Miranda, November 24, 1938, AHAM, MDM, caja 162, exp. 9.
43. Sofía to Miranda, February 5, 1938, AHAM, MDM, caja 162, exp. 9.
44. ADG, "Vida de Sofía del Valle"; Olivera/del Valle, 1972–73.
45. Interview with Adriana Garza Ramos, Mexico City, March 20, 2017.
46. ADG, "Vida de Sofía del Valle."
47. Sofía to Ruiz, Baltimore, June 25, 1935, 48r, ASV, AM, fasc. 28.
48. Sofía to Ruiz, New York, January 13, 1937, 79r, ASV, AM, fasc. 28.
49. ADG, "Vida de Sofía del Valle."
50. Sofía to Díaz, New York, January 24, 1935, AHAM, PDB, caja 36, exp. 26.

51. Sofía to Díaz, New York, January 24, 1935, AHAM, PDB, caja 36, exp. 26.
52. Sofía to Margaret Lynch, Philadelphia, June 10, 1934, ACHRCUA, RNCCW, box 117, folder 1.
53. Aguilera González, *Cardenal Miguel Darío Miranda*, 162–63.
54. Greene, *Another Mexico*, 240.
55. Personal email correspondence with Richard Greene, December 8, 2017.
56. Godman, "Graham Greene's Vatican Dossier."
57. Greene, *Another Mexico*, 260.
58. Greene, *Another Mexico*, 261.
59. Greene, *Another Mexico*, 81.
60. Greene, *Another Mexico*, 264.
61. Montavon to Ready, memorandum, September 29, 1938, ACHRCUA, USCCB General Secretary, box 148, folder 14.
62. Fallaw, *Religion and State Formation*, 221.
63. Butler, "Catholicism in Mexico."
64. Butler, "Catholicism in Mexico."
65. Margaret Lynch to Elizabeth Connell, February 28, 1935, ACHRCUA, RNCCW, box 117, folder 1.
66. Margaret T. Lynch to Sofía del Valle, December 31, 1940, ACHRCUA, RNCCW, box 117, folder 1.
67. Halbert Jones, *War Has Brought Peace*, 37, 88.

34. La patria Calls

1. del Valle, "¡¡La patria en peligro!!," 12.
2. Margaret T. Lynch to Sofía del Valle, Washington DC, September 4, 1941, ACHRCUA, RNCCW, box 117, folder 1.
3. Olivera, "Charla con Sofía," 18–19, 34.
4. ADG, "Vida de Sofía del Valle."
5. del Valle, "¿Qué debemos?," 6, 23.
6. del Valle, "¡¡La patria en peligro!!," 12–13.
7. Hall, *Dolores del Río*, 223–24.
8. Fouad Elkoury, "Collector's Diary: Mexico," Bidoun, https://bidoun.org/articles/collector-s-diary-mexico.
9. *Juventud*, September 1, 1940.
10. The editors claimed that they'd "constantly been asked the name of our collaborator" who had been taking "the splendid photographs for our covers." In an inset, the editors revealed it to be Yazbek; *Juventud*, October 1941, 17
11. It's unclear when Yazbek stopped taking photos for *Juventud*, but the change in artistic direction is clear during 1949–1950. Portraits of women

were replaced with religious art. However, by 1951 *Juventud* frequently represented indigenous culture, and drawings of indigenous women, on its covers. On the September 1954 cover a portrait photograph of a mestiza young woman was published.

12. *Juventud*, April 1941, 7. (Many of the *Juventud* issues contain only the month and year of publication, without indicating volume and number.)
13. "Nuestra portada," 12.
14. de la Lama, "La inteligencia," 4, 7, 23.
15. de la Lama, "La inteligencia," 4, 7, 23.
16. Egan, *For Whom*, 11–50.
17. ADG, "Vida de Sofía del Valle."
18. *Juventud*, May 1941 (women holding infant); *Juventud*, February 1, 1942 (housework); *Juventud*, September 1942 (women in front of Mexican flag).
19. de la Lama, "La tercera ruta," 5, 7.
20. Torres Septien and Magaña, "Belleza reflejada," 55–87.
21. Cummings makes a similar argument for Catholic women in the United States; see Cummings, *New Women*, 195.
22. Interview with María Elena Álvarez de Vicencio, Guadalupe Aguilar Fernández, Mercedes Gómez del Campo de Zavala, and María Eugenia Díaz Gastine de Pfennich, March 20, 2017 (Mexico City).
23. Olivera/del Valle 1972–73; Rossi, "Status of Women," 300–324.
24. An all-female university, called the Colegio Motolinía, was incorporated into the National University (UNAM) as early as 1931. It appears Cultura Femenina increasingly lost its relevance as new avenues for women's education opened up; see Espinosa, *Jesuit Student Groups*, 78.
25. Interview with Teresa R. de Huidobro del Valle, July 14, 2016 (Skype).
26. Trapp, *Family on Wheels*, 112.
27. Hurteau, *Worldwide Heart*, 178–80; Sofía and John Considine appear in a photograph from 1946, taken at a luncheon for the Inter-American Commission of the NCCW (*Chillicothe Constitution-Tribune*, September 26, 1946, 13).
28. *Galveston Daily News*, Friday, August 12, 1960, 5.
29. Sofía received the "Women of America United for Peace" award during the Eisenhower administration (Olimón Nolasco, *Sofía del Valle*, 138); "Pinning a Heart of America Medal on Miss Sofía del Valle of Mexico City," reads one article ("Medals from Here to Mexico," *Kansas City Times*, February 15, 1963, 11).
30. Sofía wrote to Miranda from Washington, describing an Alliance for Progress conference led by JFK. At the event, she met the wife of Mexican

president Adolfo López Mateos (1958–64); see Sofía to Miranda, Washington DC, June 9, 1963, AHAM, MDM, caja 162, exp. 9.
31. Sofía to Miranda, November 19, 1963, and September 24, 1964, AHAM, MDM, caja 162, exp. 9.
32. Henold, "Woman—Go Forth!" 151–73.
33. Olivera/del Valle, 1972–73.
34. Miller, "Role," 137.
35. Sofía to Miranda, Mexico City, June 2, 1971, AHAM, MDM, caja 168, exp. 36.

Postlude

1. Sofía to Santisimo Padre, AHAM, MDM, caja 257, exp. 57.
2. ADG, "Vida de Sofía del Valle."
3. Glenda Blee et al. to Miranda, August 9, 1980, AHAM, MDM, caja 168, exp. 16.
4. ADG, "Vida de Sofía del Valle."
5. ADG, "Vida de Sofía del Valle."
6. Buijssen, *Simplicity of Dementia*, 36–38.

Matins

1. The Metropolitan Cathedral in Mexico City is the oldest and largest cathedral in all of Latin America. It was begun in the 1570s, but wasn't completed until the nineteenth century.

Bibliography

Archives and Manuscript Materials

AACM. Archivo de la Acción Católica Mexicana, Universidad Iberoamericana, Mexico City.

ACHRCUA. American Catholic History Research Center and University Archives, the Catholic University of America, Washington DC.
  GS. Records of the General Secretary.
  RNCCW. Records of the National Council of Catholic Women.

ADG. "Vida de Sofía del Valle." Personal Archive of María Eugenia Díaz Gastine de Pfennich, Mexico City. "Vida de Sofía del Valle," unfinished memoir.

AGN-DGIPS. Archivo General de la Nación, Dirección General de Investigaciones Políticas y Sociales, Mexico City.

AHAM. Archivo Histórico del Arzobispado de México, Mexico City.
  MDM. Base Miguel Darío Miranda.
  PDB. Base Pascual Díaz Barreto.

AHSSM. Archivo Histórico del Secretariado Social Mexicano, Mexico City.

ARSI-PM. Archivum Romanum Societatis Iesu, Provincia Mexicana, Rome.

ASV. Archivio Segreto Vaticano, Vatican City.
  AES. Affari Ecclesiastici Straordinari.
  AM. Delegazione Apostolica, Stati Uniti, Appendice Messico.

BNA-FO. British National Archive, Foreign Office Records, London.

FPEC. Fideicomiso Archivos Plutarco Elías Calles y Fernando Torreblanca, Fondo Plutarco Elías Calles, Mexico City.

Hemptinne Papers. Plaatsingslijst van het Archief Christine de Hemptinne, Papieren, Ch. de Hemptinne, Louvain.

Olivera/del Valle, 1972–73. Biblioteca "Manuel Orozco y Berra," Mexico City, Dirección de Estudios Históricos, INAH, Programa de Historia Oral, PHO-C/4/1, Entrevista con la Srta. Sofia del Valle, realizada por Alicia Olivera de Bonfil, los días 3 de Noviembre de 1972 y 14 de febrero de 1973, en la Ciudad de México.

UNDA-CMCD. University of Notre Dame Archives, Philip Richard McDevitt Papers, South Bend IN.

Published Works

Abbott, Elizabeth. *A History of Celibacy.* New York: Scribner, 2000.

Acevedo y de la Llata, Concepción. *Obregón: Memorias inéditas de la Madre Conchita.* Edited by Armando de María y Campos. Mexico City: Libro-Mex, 1957.

———. *Yo, la Madre Conchita.* Mexico City: Editorial Contenido, 1997.

Aguilera González, Francisco María. *Cardenal Miguel Darío Miranda: El hombre, el cristiano, el obispo.* Mexico City: IMDOSOC and CEP, 2005.

Aguirre Cristiani, María Gabriela. *¿Una historia compartida?: Revolución Mexicana y catolicismo social, 1913–1924.* Mexico City: IMDOSOC, 2008.

Andes, Stephen J. C. "A Catholic Alternative to Revolution: The Survival of Social Catholicism in Postrevolutionary Mexico." *The Americas* 68, no. 4 (April 2012): 529–62.

———. *The Vatican and Catholic Activism in Mexico and Chile: The Politics of Transnational Catholicism, 1920–1940.* Oxford: Oxford University Press, 2014.

Andes, Stephen J. C., and Julia G. Young, eds. *Local Church, Global Church: Catholic Activism in Latin America from Rerum novarum to Vatican II.* Washington DC: Catholic University of America Press, 2016.

Arrom, Silvia Marina. "Mexican Laywomen Spearhead a Catholic Revival: The Ladies of Charity, 1863–1910." In *Religious Culture in Modern Mexico,* edited by Martin Austin Nesvig, 50–78. Lanham MD: Rowman & Littlefield, 2007.

———. *Volunteering for a Cause: Gender, Faith, and Charity in Mexico from the Reform to the Revolution.* Albuquerque: University of New Mexico Press, 2016.

———. *The Women of Mexico City, 1790–1857.* Palo Alto CA: Stanford University Press, 1985.

Aspe Armella, María Luisa. *La formación social y política de los católicos mexicanos: La Acción Católica Mexicana y la Unión Nacional de Estudiantes Católicos, 1929–1958.* Mexico City: Universidad Iberoamericana, 2008.

Bailey, David C. *¡Viva Cristo Rey! The Cristero Rebellion and the Church-State Conflict in Mexico.* Austin: University of Texas Press, 1974.

Balderrama, Francisco E., and Raymond Rodríguez. *Decade of Betrayal: Mexican Repatriation in the 1930s.* Albuquerque: University of New Mexico Press, 2006.

Bantjes, Adrian A. "Idolatry and Iconoclasm in Revolutionary Mexico: The De-Christianization Campaigns, 1929–1940." *Mexican Studies/Estudios Mexicanos* 13, no. 1 (Winter 1997): 87–120.

Barnouw, Erik. *The Golden Web: A History of Broadcasting in the United States, 1933 to 1953.* Oxford: Oxford University Press, 1968.

Blancarte, Roberto. "Personal Enemies of God: Anticlericals and Anticlericalism in Revolutionary Mexico, 1915–1940." *The Americas* 65, no. 4 (April 2009): 589–99.

Blum, Ann S. *Domestic Economies: Family, Work, and Welfare in Mexico City, 1884–1943.* Lincoln: University of Nebraska Press, 2009.

Bonner, Jeremy, Christopher D. Denny, and Mary Beth Fraser Connolly, eds. *Empowering the People of God: Catholic Action before and after Vatican II.* New York: Fordham University Press, 2014.

Boyea, Earl. "The Reverend Charles Coughlin and the Church: The Gallagher Years, 1930–1937." *Catholic Historical Review* 81, no. 2 (April 1995): 211–25.

Boylan, Kristina. "The Feminine 'Apostolate in Society' Versus the Secular State: The Unión Femenina Católica Mexicana, 1929–1940." In *Right-Wing Women: From Conservatives to Extremists around the World*, edited by Paola Bacchetta and Margaret Power, 169–82. New York: Routledge, 2002.

——— . "Mexican Catholic Women's Activism, 1929–1940." PhD diss., University of Oxford, 2000.

Brading, David A. *The First America: The Spanish Monarchy, Creole Patriots and the Liberal State, 1492–1867.* Cambridge: Cambridge University Press, 1993.

——— . *Mexican Phoenix: Our Lady of Guadalupe; Image and Tradition across Five Centuries.* Cambridge: Cambridge University Press, 2003.

Brekus, Catherine A. *Sarah Osborn's World: The Rise of Evangelical Christianity in Early America.* New Haven CT: Yale University Press, 2015.

Brinkley, Alan. *Voices of Protest: Huey Long, Father Coughlin, and the Great Depression.* New York: Vintage, 1983.

Buijssen, Huub. *The Simplicity of Dementia: A Guide for Family and Carers.* London: Jessica Kingsley, 2005.

Bunker, Steven B. *Creating Mexican Consumer Culture in the Age of Porfirio Díaz.* Albuquerque: University of New Mexico Press, 2012.

Burton, Richard D. E. *Holy Tears, Holy Blood: Women, Catholicism, and the Culture of Suffering in France, 1840–1970.* Ithaca NY: Cornell University Press, 2004.

Butler, Matthew. "Catholicism in Mexico, 1910 to the Present." *Oxford Research Encyclopedia of Latin American History*, http://oxfordre.com/latinamericanhistory/view/10.1093/acrefore/9780199366439.001.0001/acrefore-9780199366439-e-23.

——— . "God's *Campesinos*? Mexico's Revolutionary Church in the Countryside." *Bulletin of Latin American Research* 28, no. 2 (April 2009): 165–84.

———. "Keeping the Faith in Revolutionary Mexico: Clerical and Lay Resistance to Religious Persecution, East Michoacan, 1926–1929." *The Americas* 59, no. 1 (July 2002): 9–32.

———. "Mexican Nicodemus: The Apostleship of Refugio Padilla, *Cristero*, on the Islas Marías." *Mexican Studies/Estudios Mexicanos* 25, no. 2 (Summer 2009): 271–306.

———. "Sotanas Rojinegras: Catholic Anticlericalism and Mexico's Revolutionary Schism." *The Americas* 65, no. 4 (April 2009): 535–58.

———. "'Su Hija Inés': Católicas laicas, el obispo Luis María Martínez, y el concepto religioso Michoacano, 1927–1929." *Historia Mexicana* 67, no. 3 (January–March 2018): 1249–94.

———. "Trouble Afoot? Pilgrimage in *Cristero* Mexico City." In *Faith and Impiety in Revolutionary Mexico*, edited by Matthew Butler, 149–66. New York: Palgrave Macmillan, 2007.

Cahill, Susan, ed. *Writing Women's Lives: An Anthology of Autobiographical Narratives by Twentieth-Century American Women Writers*. New York: Perennial, 1994.

Carreño, Alberto María. *El P. Miguel Agustín Pro, S. J.* Mexico City: Editorial Helios, 1938.

Castagna, Luca. *A Bridge across the Ocean: The United States and the Holy See between the Two World Wars*. Washington DC: Catholic University of America Press, 2014.

Chávez, Eduardo. *Our Lady of Guadalupe and Saint Juan Diego: The Historical Evidence*. Lanham MD: Rowman & Littlefield, 2006.

Chernow, Ron. *The House of Morgan: An American Banking Dynasty and the Rise of Modern Finance*. New York: Grove Press, 1990.

Chowning, Margaret. "The Catholic Church and the Ladies of the Vela Perpetua: Gender and Devotional Change in Nineteenth-Century Mexico." *Past and Present* 221, no. 1 (November 2013): 197–237.

———. *Rebellious Nuns: The Troubled History of a Mexican Convent, 1754–1863*. New York: Oxford University Press, 2006.

"Círculo de formación familiar." *Juventud*, September 1932.

Ciriello, Caterina. "Armida Barelli cucitrice di opere." In *Armida Barelli: Una donna tra due secoli*, edited by Benedetto Coccia, 45–114. Rome: Editrice Apes, 2016.

Coakley, John W. *Women, Men, and Spiritual Power: Female Saints and Their Male Collaborators*. New York: Columbia University Press, 2006.

"Corridor." *Time*, May 11, 1925.

Cortés Rivera, Hugo Eder, Diana Leticia Jiménez Gonzalez, Dalia Mariana Vazquez León, Adriana Alejandra Valdespino Gonzalez, and Rosalba Karina Villanueva Venegas. "La vida en la embajada de la Unión de Repúblicas Soviéticas Socialistas en México." Unpublished manuscript, Universidad del Valle de México, 2016.

Coughlin, Charles E. "Following the Christ Child." In *A Series of Lectures on Social Justice*, by Charles E. Coughlin, 84–96. Detroit: Radio League of the Little Flower, 1935.

Courson, Comtesse de. "Lisieux at the Present Day." *American Catholic Quarterly Review* 48 (January–October 1923): 142.

Craig, Gordon Alexander, and Felix Gilbert, eds. *The Diplomats: 1919–1939, Volume 1*. New York: Atheneum, 1965.

Cummings, Kathleen Sprows. *New Women of the Old Faith: Gender and American Catholicism in the Progressive Era*. Chapel Hill: University of North Carolina Press, 2009.

Curley, Robert. *Citizens and Believers: Religion and Politics in Revolutionary Jalisco, 1900–1930*. Albuquerque: University of New Mexico Press, 2018.

———. "Transnational Subaltern Voices: Sexual Violence, Anticlericalism, and the Mexican Revolution." In *Local Church, Global Church: Catholic Activism in Latin America from Rerum novarum to Vatican II*, edited by Stephen J. C. Andes and Julia G. Young, 91–116. Washington DC: Catholic University of America Press, 2016.

Davis, Diane. *Urban Leviathan: Mexico City in the Twentieth Century*. Philadelphia: Temple University Press, 1994.

Dawes, H. *Catholic Women's Movements in Liberal and Fascist Italy*. New York: Palgrave Macmillan, 2014.

Day, Dorothy. *All the Way to Heaven: The Selected Letters of Dorothy Day*. Edited by Robert Ellsberg. New York: Image Books, 2012.

———. *Loaves and Fishes: The Inspiring Story of the Catholic Worker Movement*. Maryknoll NY: Orbis Books, 2003.

de la Lama, Aurora. "La inteligencia femenina y el studio." *Juventud*, August 1941.

———. "La tercera ruta: El celibato en el mundo." *Juventud*, July 1, 1942.

DeLay, Brian. *War of a Thousand Deserts: Indian Raids and the US-Mexican War*. New Haven CT: Yale University Press, 2009.

del Valle, Sofía. "¡¡La patria en peligro!!" *Juventud*, July 1, 1942.

———. "¿Qué debemos a la patria?" *Juventud*, August 1, 1942.

"Development of the L. M. Ericsson Telephone Plant in Mexico." *L. M. Ericsson Review* 1, nos. 1–2 (January–February 1924): 16.

Diesbach, Geneviève de. *WUCWO Story*. Paris: WUCWO-UMOFC Secretariat, 2001.

Drowne, Kathleen, and Patrick Huber. *The 1920s*. Westport CT: Greenwood Press, 2004.

Dulles, John W. F. *Yesterday in Mexico: A Chronicle of the Revolution, 1919–1936*. Austin: University of Texas Press, 1961.

Edwards, Lisa M. *Roman Virtues: The Education of Latin American Clergy in Rome, 1858–1962*. New York: Peter Lang, 2011.

Egan, Eileen. *For Whom There Is No Room: Scenes from the Refugee World*. New York: Paulist Press, 1995.

Elie, Paul. *The Life You Save May Be Your Own: An American Pilgrimage*. New York: Farrar, Straus and Giroux, 2003.

El jurado de Toral y la Madre Conchita: Lo que se dijó y no se dijó en el sensacional juicio. Versión taquigráfica textual. 2 vols. Mexico City: Aloucin y del Llano, 1929.

Espinosa, David. *Jesuit Student Groups, the Universidad Iberoamericana, and Political Resistance in Mexico, 1913–1979*. Albuquerque: University of New Mexico Press, 2014.

——— . "Student Politics, National Politics: Mexico's National Student Union." *The Americas* 62, no. 4 (April 2006): 533–62.

"Extracto del informe del primer congreso internacional de la Liga Católica Femenil." *Juventud*, July 1930, 7.

Fallaw, Ben. *Religion and State Formation in Postrevolutionary Mexico*. Durham NC: Duke University Press, 2013.

"Fashion Seen at the Ritz in Paris/Garnet-Red with Pink." *Vogue*, January 15, 1931.

Fayet-Scribe, Sylvie. *Associations féminines et catholicisme: XIXe-XXe siècle*. Paris: Editions Ouvrières, 1990.

Fiell, Charlotte, and Emmanuelle Dirix. *1930s Fashion: The Definitive Sourcebook*. London: Carlton, 2012.

Flanner, Janet, James Thurber, and Harold Ross. "Tender Buttons." *New Yorker*, October 13, 1934.

Foley, Susan K. *Women in France since 1789*. New York: Palgrave, 2004.

Forest, Jim. *All Is Grace: A Biography of Dorothy Day*. Maryknoll NY: Orbis Books, 2011.

Fostick, John A. *New York's Liners*. Charleston SC: Arcadia, 2015.

Godman, Peter. "Graham Greene's Vatican Dossier," *Atlantic*, July/August 2001, https://www.theatlantic.com/magazine/archive/2001/07/graham-greenes-vatican-dossier/302264/.

González Delgado, Silvia. *Ambición de Igualdad: Biografía de María Elena Álvarez de Vicencio*. Mexico City: Partido Acción Nacional, 2016.

Gonzales, Michael J. *The Mexican Revolution, 1910–1940.* Albuquerque: University of New Mexico Press, 2002.

Greene, Graham. *Another Mexico.* New York: Viking, 1939.

"Growth and Present Development of the L. M. Ericsson Organization." *L. M. Ericsson Review* 1, nos. 1–2 (January–February 1924): 3–4.

Gutiérrez Casillas, José. *Jesuitas en México durante el siglo XX.* Mexico City: Editorial Porrúa, 1981.

Hall, Linda B. *Dolores del Río: Beauty in Light and Shade.* Palo Alto CA: Stanford University Press, 2015.

Hanson, Randall S. "The Day of Ideals: Catholic Social Action in the Age of the Mexican Revolution, 1867–1929." PhD diss., Indiana University, 1994.

Harris, Ruth. *Lourdes: Body and Spirit in the Secular Age.* London: Penguin, 2008.

Hart, John Mason. *Revolutionary Mexico: The Coming and Process of the Mexican Revolution.* Berkeley: University of California Press, 1997.

Hartmann-Ting, L. E. "The National Catholic School of Social Service: Redefining Catholic Womanhood through the Professionalization of Social Work during the Interwar Years. *U.S. Catholic Historian* 26, no. 1 (Winter 2008): 101–19.

Heilbrun, Carolyn G. *Writing a Woman's Life.* New York: W. W. Norton, 2008.

Heilman, Jaymie. "The Demon Inside: Madre Conchita, Gender, and the Assassination of Obregón." *Mexican Studies/Estudios Mexicanos* 18, no. 1 (Winter 2002): 23–60.

Hennessy, Kate. *Dorothy Day: The World Will Be Saved by Beauty; An Intimate Portrait of My Grandmother.* New York: Scribner, 2017.

Henold, Mary J. "'Woman—Go Forth!': Catholic Women's Organizations and Their Clergy Advisors in the Era of the 'Emerging Laywoman.'" *U.S. Catholic Historian* 32, no. 4 (October 2015): 151–73.

Hernández, José Angel. "From Conquest to Colonization: *Indios* and Colonization Policies after Mexican Independence." *Mexican Studies/Estudios Mexicanos* 26, no. 2 (Summer 2010): 291–322.

Hershfield, Joanne. *Imagining la Chica Moderna: Women, Nation, and Visual Culture in Mexico, 1917–1936.* Durham NC: Duke University Press, 2008.

Holland, Joe. *Modern Catholic Social Teaching: The Popes Confront the Industrial Age, 1740–1958.* Mahwah NJ: Paulist Press, 2003.

Hurteau, Robert. *A Worldwide Heart: The Life of Maryknoll Father John J. Considine.* Maryknoll NY: Orbis Books, 2013.

Jacoby, Karl. *The Strange Career of William Ellis: The Texas Slave Who Became a Mexican Millionaire.* New York: W. W. Norton, 2016.

"J.C.F.M. en la arquidiócesis de México." *Juventud,* April 1930.

Jenkins, Philip. *The Next Christendom: The Coming of Global Christianity*. New York: Oxford University Press, 2011.

Johns, Michael. *The City of Mexico in the Age of Díaz*. Austin: University of Texas Press, 1997.

Johnson, Gaynor, ed. *Our Man in Berlin: The Diary of Sir Eric Phipps, 1933–1937*. New York: Palgrave Macmillan, 2008.

Jones, Halbert. *The War Has Brought Peace to Mexico: World War II and the Consolidation of the Post-Revolutionary State*. Albuquerque: University of New Mexico Press, 2014.

Jones, Roderick. *A Life in Reuters*. London: Hodder & Stoughton, 1951.

Jordan, Patrick, ed. *Dorothy Day: Writings from Commonweal*. New York: Commonweal, 2002.

Jules-Rosette, Bennetta. *Josephine Baker in Art and Life: The Icon and the Image*. Urbana: University of Illinois Press, 2007.

Kahan, Benjamin. *Celibacies: American Modernism and Sexual Life*. Durham NC: Duke University Press, 2013.

Kane, Paula M. "'She Offered Herself Up': The Victim Soul and Victim Spirituality in Catholicism." *Church History* 71, no. 80 (March 2002): 80–119.

Kelley, Francis Clement. *The Book of Red and Yellow: Being a Story of Blood and a Yellow Streak*. Chicago: Catholic Church Extension Society, 1915.

Kertzer, David I. *The Pope and Mussolini: The Secret History of Pius XI and the Rise of Fascism in Europe*. New York: Random House, 2015.

Knight, Alan, "The Mentality and Modus Operandi of Revolutionary Anticlericalism." In *Faith and Impiety in Revolutionary Mexico*, edited by Matthew Butler, 21–56. New York: Palgrave Macmillan, 2007.

———. *The Mexican Revolution, Volume 2: Counterrevolution and Reconstruction*. Lincoln: University of Nebraska Press, 1990.

Kreisel Shubert, Betty. *Out of Style: A Modern Perspective on How, Why, and When Vintage Fashions Evolved*. Mission Viejo CA: Flashback, 2013.

Lacy, Tim. "Catholics and Catholicism." In *Encyclopedia of the Jazz Age: From the End of World War I to the Great Crash*, edited by James Ciment, 1:128. New York: M. E. Sharpe, 2008.

Larson, Kate Clifford. *Rosemary: The Hidden Kennedy Daughter*. New York: Mariner Books, 2016.

Lepore, Jill. *The Secret History of Wonder Woman*. New York: Vintage, 2015.

"Libros." *Juventud*, September 1932.

López-Menéndez, Marisol. *Miguel Pro: Martyrdom, Politics, and Society in Twentieth-Century Mexico*. Lanham MD: Lexington Books, 2016.

Losel, Steffan. "Prayer, Pain, and Priestly Privilege: Claude Langlois's New Perspective on Thérèse of Lisieux." *Journal of Religion* 88, no. 3 (July 2008): 273–306.

Loughran, Elizabeth Ward. "The Role of Catholic Culture in Uruguay." *Catholic Historical Review* 26, no. 1 (April 1940): 1–50.

Luca, Giuseppe de. "Memoria di Pietro Gasparri." *Nuova Antologia* 376 (1934): 380–84.

Macías, Anna. *Against All Odds: The Feminist Movement in Mexico to 1940*. Westport CT: Greenwood Press, 1982.

Martínez Assad, Carlos. *El laboratorio de la revolución: El Tabasco garridista*. Mexico: Siglo Veintiuno, 2004.

Martínez Gobea, Mireya. "De vigilantes y militantes: La presencia política femenina en los movimientos Sinarquistas y Almazanista en la ciudad de México y Zacatecas entre 1938 y 1943." MA thesis, Escuela Nacional de Antropología e Historia, 2018.

Matovina, Timothy. *Theologies of Guadalupe: From the Era of Conquest to Pope Francis*. Oxford: Oxford University Press, 2018.

McCartain, James P. "The Sacred Heart of Jesus, Thérèse of Lisieux, and the Transformation of U.S. Catholic Piety, 1865–1940." *U.S. Catholic Historian* 25, no. 2 (Spring 2007): 53–67.

McCullagh, Francis. *Red Mexico: A Reign of Terror in America*. New York: Carrier, 1928.

McMahon, Joseph Henry, ed. and trans. *The Order Followed in the Consecration of a Bishop, According to the Roman Pontifical*. New York: Cathedral Library Association, 1922.

McQueenan, Joe. *Closing Time: A Memoir*. New York: Viking, 2009.

Mercer, David. *The Telephone: The Life Story of a Technology*. Santa Barbara CA: Greenwood Press, 2006.

Merton, Thomas. *The Courage for Truth: The Letters of Thomas Merton to Writers*. Edited by Christine M. Bochen. New York: Farrar, Straus & Giroux, 1993.

Meyer, Jean A. *The Cristero Rebellion: The Mexican People between Church and State, 1926–1929*. Translated by Richard Southern. Cambridge: Cambridge University Press, 1976.

———. *La Cristiada*. 3 vols. Mexico City: Siglo XXI, 1973–74.

Miller, Barbara Ann. "The Role of Women in the Mexican Cristero Rebellion: A New Chapter." PhD diss., University of Notre Dame, 1981.

Mitchell, Stephanie, and Patience A. Schell, eds. *The Women's Revolution in Mexico, 1910–1953*. Lanham MD: Rowman & Littlefield, 2007.

Modras, Ronald. "Coughlin and Anti-Semitism: Fifty Years Later." *Journal of Church and State* 31, no. 2 (Spring 1989): 231–47.

Moore, Breanna. "Philosemitism under a Darkening Sky: Judaism in the French Catholic Revival (1900–1945)." *Catholic Historical Review* 99, no. 2 (April 2013): 262–97.

Morgan, Thomas B. *The Listening Post: Eighteen Years on Vatican Hill*. New York: Putnam, 1944.

Mraz, John. *Photographing the Mexican Revolution: Commitments, Testimonies, Icons*. William and Bettye Nowlin Series in Art, History, and Culture of the Western Hemisphere. Austin: University of Texas Press, 2012.

Navarrete, Heriberto. *Por Dios y por la patria*. Mexico City: Editorial Tradición, 1980.

"N.C.C.W. Staff Afield." *Catholic Action: A National Monthly* 14, no. 1 (January 1932): 31.

Nemery, Benoit, Peter H. M. Hoet, and Abderrahim Nemmar. "The Meuse Valley Fog of 1930: An Air Pollution Disaster." *Lancet* 357, no. 9257 (March 2001): 704–8.

Nevin, Thomas R. *The Last Years of Saint Thérèse: Doubt and Darkness, 1895–1897*. Oxford: Oxford University Press, 2013.

"Nuestra fiesta patronal." *Juventud*, June 1930.

"Nuestra portada." *Juventud*, July 1941.

O'Connor, Thomas H. *Boston Catholics: A History of the Church and Its People*. Boston: Northeastern University Press, 1998.

Oikión Solano, Veronica. "In Memoriam: Alicia Esperanza Olivera Sedano de Bonfil (1933–2012)." *Tzinzun Revista de Estudios Históricos* 57 (January–June 2013): 234–42.

Olcott, Jocelyn. *International Women's Year: The Greatest Consciousness-Raising Event in History*. Oxford: Oxford University Press, 2017.

———. *Revolutionary Women in Postrevolutionary Mexico*. Durham NC: Duke University Press, 2005.

Olcott, Jocelyn, Mary Kay Vaughn, and Gabriela Cano, eds. *Sex in Revolution: Gender, Politics, and Power in Modern Mexico*. Durham NC: Duke University Press, 2006.

Olimón Nolasco, Manuel. *Sofía del Valle: Una mexicana universal*. Mexico City: Instituto Nacional de las Mujeres, 2009.

Olivera, Eugenia. "Charla con Sofía." *Juventud*, December 1947.

Olivera Sedano, Alicia. *Aspectos del conflict religioso de 1926 a 1929: Antecedentes y consecuencias*. Mexico City: Instituto Nacional de Antropología e Historia, 1966.

Osselaer, Tine van. *The Pious Sex: Catholic Constructions of Masculinity and Femininity in Belgium, c. 1800–1940*. Leuven: Leuven University Press, 2013.

"Palabras de nuestra presidenta general en homenaje a S.S. el Papa Pío XI." *Juventud*, July 1930.

Petit, Jeanne. "'Organized Catholic Womanhood': Suffrage, Citizenship and the National Council of Catholic Women." *U.S. Catholic Historian* 26, no. 1 (Winter 2008): 83–100.

Pollard, John F. "Pius XI's Promotion of the Italian Model of Catholic Action in the World-Wide Church." *Journal of Ecclesiastical History* 63, no. 4 (October 2012): 758–84.

Poole, Stafford. *Our Lady of Guadalupe: The Origins and Sources of a Mexican National Symbol, 1531–1797*. Tucson: University of Arizona Press, 1995.

Pope, Barbara Corrado. "A Heroine without Heroics: The Little Flower of Jesus and Her Times." *Church History* 57, no. 1 (March 1988): 46–60.

Porter, Susie S. "De obreras, señoritas y empleadas: Culturas de trabajo en la ciudad de México en la Compañía Ericsson." In *Género en la encrucijada de la historia social y cultural*, edited by Susie S. Porter and María Teresa Fernández Aceves, 279–315. Mexico City: El Colegio de Michoacán/CIESAS, 2015.

———. *From Angel to Office Worker: Middle-Class Identity and Female Consciousness in Mexico, 1890–1950*. Lincoln: University of Nebraska Press, 2018.

Quirk, Robert. *The Mexican Revolution and the Catholic Church, 1910–1929*. Bloomington: Indiana University Press, 1973.

Ramírez Torres, Rafael, SJ *Miguel Agustín Pro: Memorias biográficas*. Mexico City: Editorial Tradición, 1976.

Regan, Agnes G. "Year's Work of the N.C.C.W. Reviewed." *Catholic Action: A National Monthly* 89, no. 10 (October 1932): 19–22.

Roberti, Francesco. *Il cardinale Pietro Gasparri: L'uomo, il sacerdote, il diplomatico, il giurista*. Miscellanea in memoriam Petri Card. Gasparri. Rome: Pontificia Universitas Lateranensis, 1960.

Robinson-Tomsett, Emma. *Women, Travel and Identity: Journeys by Rail and Sea (1870–1940)*. Manchester, UK: Manchester University Press, 2013.

Rossi, Joseph S., SJ. "'The Status of Women': Two American Catholic Women at the UN, 1947–1972." *Catholic Historical Review* 93, no. 2 (April 2007): 300–324.

Ruiz y Flores, Leopoldo. *Recuerdo de recuerdos*. Mexico City: Buena Prensa, 1942.

Rupp, Leila J. *Worlds of Women: The Making of an International Women's Movement*. Princeton NJ: Princeton University Press, 1997.

Sanders, Nichole. "Gender and Consumption in Porfirian Mexico: Images of Women in Advertising, *El Imparcial*, 1897–1910." *Frontiers: A Journal of Women Studies* 38, no. 1 (2017): 1–30.

———. *Gender and Welfare in Mexico: The Consolidation of a Postrevolutionary State*. University Park: Penn State University Press, 2012.

Scaraffia, Lucetta. "'Christianity Has Liberated Her and Placed Her alongside Man in the Family': From 1850 to 1988 (Mulieris Dignitatem)." In *Women and Faith: Catholic Religious Life in Italy from Late Antiquity to the Present*, edited by Lucetta Scaraffia and Gabriella Zarri and translated by Keith Botsford, 249–80. Cambridge MA: Harvard University Press, 1999.

Schell, Patience A. *Church and State Education in Revolutionary Mexico City*. Tucson: University of Arizona Press, 2003.

———. "Of the Sublime Mission of Mothers of Family: The Union of Mexican Catholic Ladies in Revolutionary Mexico." In *The Women's Revolution in Mexico, 1910–1953*, edited by Stephanie Mitchell and Patience A. Schell, 99–124. Lanham MD: Rowman and Littlefield, 2006.

Schloesser, Stephen. *Jazz Age Catholicism: Mystic Modernism in Postwar Paris, 1919–1933*. Toronto: University of Toronto Press, 2005.

Schmidt, Donald E. *The Folly of War: American Foreign Policy, 1898–2005*. New York: Algora, 2005.

Schulenberg, Jane Tibbets. *Forgetful of Their Sex: Female Sanctity and Society, ca. 500–1100*. Chicago: University of Chicago Press, 2001.

Sensbach, Jon F. *Rebecca's Revival: Creating Black Christianity in the Atlantic World*. Cambridge MA: Harvard University Press, 2006.

Sicilia, Javier. *Concepción Cabrera de Armida: La amante de Cristo*. Mexico City: Fondo de Cultura Económica, 2001.

———. *Félix de Jesús Rougier: La seducción de la Virgen*. Mexico City: Fondo de Cultura Económica, 2008.

Smith, Bonnie G. *Confessions of a Concierge: Madame Lucie's History of Twentieth-Century France*. New Haven CT: Yale University Press, 1985.

Smith, Stephanie J. *Gender and the Mexican Revolution: Yucatán Women and the Realities of Patriarchy*. Chapel Hill: University of North Carolina Press, 2009.

"Sociales." *Juventud*, February 20, 1932.

Soderbergh, Peter A. "The Rise of Father Coughlin, 1891–1930." *Social Science* 42, no. 1 (January 1967): 10–20.

Solis, Yves. "El Vaticano y los Estados Unidos en la solución del conflicto religioso en México: La génesis del *modus vivendi* real; México 1929–1938." PhD diss., Universidad Autónoma del Estado de Morelos, 2016.

———. "La difícil situación de la Iglesia Católica durante los primeros años del Cardenismo." Unpublished manuscript, 2015.

"Some Facts Concerning the Activities of L. M. Ericsson's Mexican Subsidiary." *L. M. Ericsson Review* 3, nos. 3–4 (March–April 1926): 28–38.

Spoto, Donald. *High Society: The Life of Grace Kelly.* New York: Random House, 2009.
"Statesman Retires." *Time,* January 6, 1930.
Sterling, Christopher H., ed. *Encyclopedia of Radio.* New York: Routledge, 2004.
Stourton, Ed. "The Secret Letters of Pope John Paul II." *BBC News Magazine,* February 15, 2016. http://www.bbc.com/news/magazine-35552997.
Taylor, William B. *Theater of a Thousand Wonders: A History of Miraculous Images and Shrines in New Spain.* Cambridge: Cambridge University Press, 2016.
Tentler, Leslie Woodcock. *Seasons of Grace: A History of the Catholic Archdiocese of Detroit.* Detroit: Wayne State University Press, 1990.
Therbon, Göran. *Between Sex and Power: Family in the World, 1900–2000.* New York: Routledge, 2004.
Threlkeld, Megan. *Pan American Women: U.S. Internationalists and Revolutionary Mexico.* Philadelphia: University of Pennsylvania Press, 2014.
Torres Septién, Valentina. *La educación privada en México (1903–1976).* Mexico City: El Colegio de México/Universidad Iberoamericana, 1997.
Torres Septién, Valentina, and Leonor Magaña. "Belleza reflejada: El ideal de la belleza femenina en el discurso de la Iglesia, 1930–1970." *Historia y grafía* 19 (2002): 55–87.
Trapp, Maria Augusta (with Ruth T. Murdoch). *A Family on Wheels: Further Adventures of the Trapp Family Singers.* Philadelphia: Lippincott, 1959.
Tweed, Thomas A. *America's Church: The National Shrine and Catholic Presence in the Nation's Capital.* Oxford: Oxford University Press, 2011.
Valvo, Paolo. *Pio XI e la Cristiada: Fede, Guerra e diplomazia in Messico (1926–1929).* Brescia: Morcelliana, 2016.
Vandevivere, Ignace, Catheline Périer-d'Ieteren, and Hughes Boucher. *Renaissance Art in Belgium: Architecture, Monumental Art.* Brussels: M. Vokaer, 1973.
Vaughn, Mary Kay. *Cultural Politics in Revolution: Teachers, Peasants, and Schools in Mexico, 1930–1940.* Tucson: University of Arizona Press, 1997.
Velten, Hannah. *Beastly London: A History of Animals in the City.* London: Reaktion Books, 2013.
Ventresca, Robert A. *Soldier of Christ: The Life of Pope Pius XII.* Cambridge: Belknap Press, 2013.
Walsh, Thomas F. *Katherine Anne Porter and Mexico: The Illusion of Eden.* Austin: University of Texas Press, 1992.
Warren, Donald. *Radio Priest: Charles Coughlin, the Father of Hate Radio.* New York: Free Press, 1996.
Weis, Robert. *For Christ and Country: Militant Catholic Youth in Post-Revolutionary Mexico.* Cambridge: Cambridge University Press, forthcoming.

———. "Pious Delinquents: Anticlericalism and Crime in Postrevolutionary Mexico." *The Americas* 73, no. 2 (April 2016): 185–210.

———. "The Revolution on Trial: Assassination, Christianity, and the Rule of Law in 1920s Mexico." *Hispanic American Historical Review* 96, no. 2 (May 2016): 319–53.

White, Richard. *Remembering Ahanagran: Storytelling in a Family's Past*. New York: Hill & Wang, 1998.

Womack, John, Jr. *Zapata and the Mexican Revolution*. New York: Vintage Books, 1968.

Wright-Rios, Edward. *Revolutions in Mexican Catholicism: Reform and Revelation in Oaxaca, 1887–1934*. Durham NC: Duke University Press, 2009.

Yeager, Gertrude M. "In the Absence of Priests: Young Women as Apostles to the Poor, Chile 1922–1932." *The Americas* 64, no. 2 (October 2007): 207–42.

"Year's Progress of N.C.C.W. Reported." *N.C.W.C. Review* 13, no. 10 (October 1931): 17.

Young, Julia G. "The Calles Government and Catholic Dissidents: Mexico's Transnational Projects of Repression, 1926–1929." *The Americas* 70, no. 1 (July 2013): 63–91.

———. *Mexican Exodus: Emigrants, Exiles, and Refugees of the Cristero War*. Oxford: Oxford University Press, 2015.

Index

Page numbers in italic indicate illustrations

Abelard, Peter, 127
Acción Femenina (magazine), 171
ACJM (Young Men's Catholic Association), 100, 141, 201
Advanced Institute of Feminine Culture, 68, 69, 70
Aguilar, Gregorio ("Father Goyo"), 122–23
Aguilar Fernández, Guadalupe, 171, 173, 175–76, 260–62
Alliance for Progress, xxi, 339
All Souls' Day, 94
Álvarez de Vicencio, María Elena, 171, 173, 174–75, 260–62
American National Council of Catholic Women (NCCW), 8
anticlericalism, 5
anticlerical laws, 135
Apaches, 20
Aquino, Maria Corazon, 119
Arce, Angelina, 226
Arce, Clara, 71, *71*, 222
Argentina, 20, 21
Arguinzóniz, Juana, 117, 153–54, 186, 191, 194, 223–24, 267, 319
Arrayales, Aurora, 175
assassinations, 102, 140–42, 155, 157, 158, 165
assimilation, 20
Association of Catholic Ladies, 50
Association of Ladies of Charity of Saint Vincent de Paul, 208–9
Atwood, Margaret, 272
Aubert, Jeanne, 228
Ávila Camacho, Manuel, 326, 329, 335

Babi, Tía, 341–42, 344–45, 346–51
Baker, Josephine, 227
Baltimore Bureau for the Defense of Religious Liberty, 309
Barelli, Armida, 210, 226, 245
Barousse, Consuelo, 194
Beals, Carleton, 115
Belgium, 206
Bell Telephone, 59
Benedict XV (pope), 210
Biondi, Fumasoni, 158
bishops: Catholic Defense League and, 78; church strike by, 73; decisions by, 76, 78, 157, 188; division of, 77; exile of, 95, 156–57; fundraising from, 115, 159–60; protection for, 138. *See also* Catholicism
Blood-Drenched Altars (Kelley), 301
Borgongini-Duca, Francesco, 315
Brady, Nicholas, 315
Brazil, 20, 21
Brown, Father, 277–78
Burke, John J., 6–7, 136, 147, 246, 279, 281, 289, 317

Bustos, Luis, 55–56

Calles, Plutarco Elías: anticlericalism of, 76; as executor, 104; José de León Toral and, 147, 149–50; leadership of, 57, 66, 77; National Revolutionary Party and, 269; resignation of, 146
Calles Law, 77–78, 367n18
Canada, 293, 296, 306
Capistrán Garza, René, 55
Cárdenas, Lázaro, 269, 325
Carrancistas, 95
Carranza, Venustiano, 41, 95
Carreño, Alberto María, 152–53
Casti connubii (article), 227–29
catacombs, 91–96, 367n1
Catholic Action: decline of, 343; fundraising for, 266, 281–82, 316; growth of, 186; international model of, 188–89, 210, 376n12; leadership of, 185; organization of, 134, 137, 168–69, 208–9, 219; resistance to, 200–203, 218, 219, 222, 233, 258
Catholic Association of Mexican Youth, 61–62
Catholic Daughters of America, 275, 279–80, 283–84
Catholic Defense League, 92, 100, 141, 147
Catholicism: activism in, xxii; All Souls' Day, 94; anticlerical laws, 135; Calles Law and, 77–78; catacombs and, 91–96; charity of, 233, xx; civil disobedience, 147; clerical conspiracy within, 3; Cristero War and, xx, 91; education and, 12, 299–300, 325; family planning viewpoint of, 227–28; fashion within, 70, 70, 71, 71; fundraising for, 145, 160, 281–82, 316; gender roles within, 161–62; international organization of, 215; labor movement within, 365n12; leadership in, 6, 317; marriage viewpoint of, 161, 227–28; martyrdom in, 67, 102–4, 189, 205; peace within, 79, 164–69, 187; persecution and, 91, 92, 95, 103–4, 105–6; prejudice within, 261, 276–78; propaganda efforts of, 92; relationships within, 127, 128; restrictions of, 75–76; saints, making of, 24, 103–5; schismatical movement of, 75–76; sexuality within, 72; social problems and, 47, 304; specialization within, 233; spiritual direction within, 126–28; Thérèse Martin and, 22–26, 231–32, 297–98, 371n40; union movement and, 57; victim soul, 125–26; violence to, 95, 100–101; women's role within, xxii–xxiii, 13, 26–27; World War I and, 133–34; World War II and, 327. *See also* Cultura Femenina
Catholic Labor Confederation, 137
Catholic Relief Services, 335
Catholic Worker (newspaper), 308–9
Catholic Workers Confederation, 99
celibacy, 38–39, 85–86, 177, 336
Central Broadcasting System, 295
CGT (General Labor Confederation), 57, 61–63, 65
Chanel, Gabrielle "Coco," 220, 221
charity, xx, 233
Chelsea piers, New York City, 152
Christ, identification with, 126

Cicognani, Amleto, 284, 289, 290
civil disobedience, 147
Clare of Assisi, 127
Colegio Motolinía, 391n24
Comanches, 20
Commercial University of Fribourg, 145
Commonweal (Catholic publication), 301
comportment, proper, 212
Concepción, María. *See* Conchita, Madre
Conchita, Madre: accusations of, 105; background of, 94–96; characteristics of, 104; José de León Toral and, 141, 142; Miguel Agustín Pro and, 101, 104–5, 126; raid of, 100; trial of, 146–50, 148; work of, 92–93, 96–97
conservatives, fight by, 20
Considine, John, 338
Cortés, Hernán, 4
Coughlin, Charles E., xxi, 294–301, 302
crime, 83
Cristero Rebellion, 5, 6–7, 79
cristeros, as resisters, 126, 200
Cristero War, xx, 4, 91, 359n3
CROM (Regional Confederation of Mexican Workers), 57, 66
Cruz, Roberto, 77, 95, 103, 104, 106
Cuauhtlatoatzin, Juan, 4–5
Cuba, 109–10
Cueto, Consuelo, 267
Cultura Femenina: advertising of, 196–97; attacks against, 222; challenges of, 72–73, 121, 124; closing of, 338; conditions in, 191, 193–95, 197–98; Feminine Brigades of St. Joan of Arc and, 121–24; finances of, 107–8, 158; founding of, 70; fundraising for, 145, 316; Graham Greene and, 324; growth of, 186; International Federation of Catholic Alumnae and, 279; leadership of, 99, 116–17, 122–24, 129, 153, 185, 223–24, 267, 319; mission of, 366n3; operation of, 114–17, 137; photo of, *194*, *196*, *197*; professors of, 116; purpose of, 80, 117; *Regulation for the Students of Cultura Femenina*, 194–95; resistance to, 202–3; vision of, 113, 226–27, 258–59; visitors to, 115, 195–96
Curley, Michael J., 118, 160

Damas Católicas, 209, 222
Daniels, Josephus, 300
Dávila Vilchis, Rafael, 223
Day, Dorothy, xxi, 308–10
Day of the Dead, 3, 6
Díaz, Pascual: accusation of, 11; background of, 74–75; as bishop, 4, 77; challenges of, 138, 156–57; characteristics of, 76, 367n14; death of, 317; exile of, 76, 78–79; influence of, 366n12; leadership of, 118; Miguel Darío Miranda and, 118; as peacemaker, 165, 166, 168; Plutarco Elías Calles and, 78; quote of, 6, 80; resistance to, 201; support from, 281, 290; travels of, 239–40; work of, 156
Díaz, Porfirio, 21, 40, 172
Díaz Gastine de Pfennich, Maria Eugenia, 172, 174, 178–79
drug violence, 83
Duffy, Mary, 275, 279–80, 281–84, 286

economic liberalism, 47
economy, 99–100, 269

Index   409

education: Catholicism and, 12, 299–300, 325; Mexico and, 299–300, 325; Sofía del Valle and, xix–xx, 33–34, 310–11; women and, 54, 64, 69
Egan, Eileen, 335
Elguero, Rafaela, 194
El Nacional (newspaper), 3–4, 6–7, 12, 288
Elorriaga, Angel, 39
Episcopal Committee, 80
Ericsson international, 57–58, 59, 60, 61–63, 65
Estrada, Genaro, 115
Eucharist, power of, 189–90
Europe: fashion in, 35–36, 221–22, 229; pollution in, 206; Sofía del Valle's travels in, 33–34, 204–8, 216, 220, 239–41, 245, 246–47, 249–51

family romance, as Catholic genre, 26, 28
fashion, 35–36, 46, 70, 71, 71, 220, 221–22, 229
female activism, xxii–xxiii
Feminine Brigades of St. Joan of Arc, 121–24
Fighting Tigers, 328
Flyckt, Bertil, 63
France: Catholic Action in, 210; fashion in, 220; laws within, 229; Sofía del Valle's travels in, 220–29; Thérèse Martin and, 22, 24, 231
Francis (pope), xxiii
Francis of Assisi, 127, 149
French Intervention, 19
French Young Women's Catholic Association, 227
Friedan, Betty, 261

Fuentes, Carlos, 383n3
fundraising: bishops and, 115, 159–60; Catholic Action and, 266, 281–82, 316; Catholicism and, 160, 281–82, 316; Cultura Femenina and, 316; Mexican Young Women's Catholic Association (JCFM) and, 316; Miguel Darío Miranda and, 159–60, 169; Social Secretariat and, 316; Sofía del Valle and, 269, 274, 275–76, 281–82, 312, 315–16

Gallagher, Michael, 295, 296, 298–99
Gamble, Anna Dill, 276–77
García Gutiérrez, Jesús, 70
Garrido Canabal, Tomás, 75–76
Gasparri, Pietro, 111, 118, 132–36, 138, 165–66, 256–57
Gemelli, Agostino, 143
General Labor Confederation (CGT), 57, 61–63, 65
General Motors, 297
Germany, 248–49
Gibbon, Isabel, 117, 186, 267, 319, 330
Gibson Girl, 35
global depression, 221
globalization, 354, 383n3
Goeury, Henri, 19
Goeury de del Valle, Sofía, 23, 29, 31, 32, *318*
Gollaz Gallardo, María Ernestina, 121
Gómez, Celia, 121
Gómez, Luis, 70
Gómez del Campo de Zavala, Mercedes, 172, 173, 176–77, 260–62
Goribar de Cortina, Refugio, 222
Greene, Graham, 76, 322–24
Gregorian University, 132
Grupo Carso, 82

Havana, Cuba, 109–10
Hawks, Mary G., 245, 246, 254–55
Heloise, 127
Hemptinne, Alexandre de, 211, 214
Hemptinne, Christine de, 207, 208, 210, 211–15, 235, 245, 253, 314
hepatitis, 114
Higgins, Miss, 285
Hitchcock, Alfred, 292
Hitler, Adolf, 249
Homer, 131
Huerta, Victoriano, 41, 49, 95
Huidobro, Ana María R. de, *318*
Huidobro, Angel R. de, *318*
Huidobro, Héctor, 83–84
Huidobro, Tere, 15–16, 83–86, 260–62, 342, 361n1
Huidobro, Terry, 361n1

Iberoamerican Young Women's Association, 311
immigration: to Mexico, 19–20, 21, 187, 335, 362n8; Sofía del Valle and, 19–20, 39–40, 42, 44, 335; to United States, 21, 187
Indios Bárbaros, 20
industrialization, in Mexico, 44
Industrial Revolution, xx
International Alliance of Women, 209
International Council of Women, 209
International Federation of Catholic Alumnae, 279
International Union of Catholic Women's Leagues (IUCWL), xxi, 209–10, 215, 235, 254, 328
Italy, 133, 210, 256–58, 352

Jalisco, Mexico, 56–57

JCFM (Mexican Young Women's Catholic Association): celebration within, 189; demographics of, 186–87; establishment of, 26, 69; fundraising for, 316; goals of, 261; leadership changes within, 223; location of, 186; membership within, 267, 336; mission of, 190, 193, 330–31; resistance to, 202–3; Sofía del Valle and, 258–59, 287
Jesuits, as resisters, 200
John of the Cross, 127
John Paul II (pope), 128, 343–44
Jones, Mary Hawkins, 194
Josefina College, 106
Juan Diego, 4–5
Juárez, Benito, 20, 21
Juventud (magazine): cover of, 232, 259, 329–33, *332, 334,* 335–36, 390–91n11; establishment of, 190; popularity of, 268–69

Kelley, Francis Clement, 301, 387n18
Kelly, Grace, 119
Kennedy, Rosemary, 119
Kite, Elizabeth, 8
Knights of Columbus, 61, 160, 275, 283

La Bombilla, 141–42
labor: Catholic-based, 53, 55–57, 60–61, 66, 137, 202; Ericsson international and, 57–58, 59, 60, 61–63, 65; Europe and, 47; Mexico and, 40, 41; United States and, 21; women and, 45, 60–61
La Familia Michoacana, 83
Lama, Aurora de la, 117, 186, 191, 267, 330, 333, 335, 336
La Profesa, 354

Lascuráin, Pedro, 33, 158
Lascuráin de Silva, Elena, 64, 71, 71, 222
Lateran Accords, 134
Latin America, Catholicism and, xxiii, 26–27, 131, 188, 215, 338, 352
The Lawless Roads (Greene), 323
League for the Defense of Religious Liberty, 78–79
Ledóchowski, Wlodzimierz, 258
Leo XIII (pope), xxii, 24
Lisieux Carmelites, 25
the Little Flower. *See* Martin, Thérèse
Lorre, Peter, 292
Loughran, Elizabeth Ward, 308
Luz Lazo, María de la, 193
Lynch, Margaret, 8, 9, 10, 245, 273–75, 280, 326

Maderistas, 41
Madero, Francisco I., 12, 33, 40–41, 49
Makar, Alexandr, 115
Manríquez y Zárate, Jesús, 160
Maritain, Jacques, 221
Marmol, Alfonso del, 112
marriage, Catholic view of, 161, 227–28
Martin, Thérèse, 22–26, 231–32, 297–98, 371n40
Martin, Zelie, 23
Martínez, Luis María, 317, 320, 325, 326, 327
martyrdom, 67, 102–4, 189, 205
maternity rights, 63
Maurin, Peter, 308
Maximilian, Emperor of Mexico, 19, 20–21
Medina, Alfredo Méndez: attacks from, 218, 219, 222; firing of, 66; focus of, 64; influence of, 46–47, 366n12; leadership of, 55, 57, 99; manifesto of, 47; as mentor, 107; Miguel Agustín Pro and, 103; Miguel Darío Miranda and, 365–66n1; orders to, 258; personality of, 68; photo of, 48, 56; resistance of, 200–202, 233; Sofía del Valle and, 46–47, 50; speech of, 50; tertianship of, 47; work of, 49–50
Mercer, David, 58
Merton, Thomas, 128
Metropolitan Cathedral, 355–57, 392n1
Meuse Valley, Belgium, 206
Mexican-American War, 20
Mexican Catholic Women's Union (UFCM), 170–79, 187, 222, 226
Mexican Martyrdom (Parsons), 301
Mexican Revolution, 44
Mexican Young Women's Catholic Association (JCFM): celebration within, 189; demographics of, 186–87; establishment of, 26, 69; fundraising for, 316; goals of, 261; leadership changes within, 223; location of, 186; membership within, 267, 336; mission of, 190, 193, 330–31; resistance to, 202–3; Sofía del Valle and, 258–59, 287
Mexico: Alvaro Obregón and, 140–42; anticlerical laws within, 135; casualties of, 187; catacombs in, 91–96; church and state within, 5, 325–26; church strike within, 73; civil war in, 41; communication systems within, 57–59; conditions in, 302, 303, 304; Constitution of, 41, 60–61, 62; consumer culture within, 46; criminal policy of, 147;

Cristero War and, 359n3; Days of the Dead in, 3; demographics of, 60; economy in, 99–100, 269; education in, 299–300, 325; faith of, 5; fashion in, 46; Fighting Tigers in, 328; government of, 20–21, 56–57, 325; immigration in, 19–20, 21, 187, 335, 362n8; industrialization in, 44, 53; insurrection in, 78; Jalisco, 56–57; labor in, 45; Mexico City, 44–46, 57, 229, 355–57; national revolution declassified files, xviii; overthrow conspiracy in, 3–4; peace in, xx, 164–69; photo of, *303*; population growth within, 44–45; poverty in, 359n2; Querétaro, 95–96; religious conflict in, xx, 258, 269, 270, 325; religious laws of, 77; revolution aftermath in, xx, 40–41; "Rosary Belt" of, 5; Sanborns in, 81–82; Secret Service of, 292; social revolution and, 5–6; Soviet Union embassy in, 115; strike in, 62; Tabasco, 75–76; Tanhuato, 6; tenement houses within, 45; theodicy of, 104; transportation in, 52; United States and, 301–2, 383n3; violence in, 83, 95, 100–101; war within, 95; women's employment in, 53; World War II and, 327

Mexico City, 44–46, 57, 81–82, 229, 355–57

Mexico City Labor Arbitration Board, 62, 63

Miranda, Miguel Darío: Alfredo Méndez Medina and, 365–66n1; arrest of, 92, 105–6; awards for, 345; as bishop, 317, 318; as cardinal, 344; characteristics of, 74, 347; Cultural Femenina and, 113; death of, 357; education of, 132; family of, 110; fundraising efforts by, 143, 145, 159–60, 169; Graham Greene and, 323–24; insurrection and, 79–80; leadership of, 122–23, 185; letter to, 14; mission of, 80; Pascual Díaz and, 118; personality of, 68; personal struggles of, 107, 119. 120, 143, 151, 154–55; photo of, *75, 318*; presentation to pope by, 136–38; as priest, 129–30; resistance to, 203; return of, 152–63; sickness of, 109–10; as Social Secretariat director, 67; Sofía del Valle and, 54, 68, 108, 109, 110, 111, 120–21, 125, 127, 128–30, 139–40, 154–55, 160–61, 162–63, 219, 269–71, 318–19, 320–21, 345–47; spiritual direction and, 127–30; support from, 281; travels of, 108, 109–11, 112–13, 117–20, 131, 132, 139, 143, 204, 223, 235–36, 239–40; del Valle family and, 111; work of, 74

Montavon, William F., 6–7, 169, 289
Montini, Giovanni, 328
Moore, Marianne, 33
Mora y del Río, José, 76–77, 110
Morgan, Thomas, 135
Morrow, Dwight, 136, 157, 168, 169
Mother Teresa, xxi, 261
Muckle, Joseph, 10, 296
Mussolini, Benito, 134, 258

Napoleonic Civil Code, 229
Napoleon III, 20
National Catholic Party, 95
National Catholic Welfare Conference (NCWC), 7

National Revolutionary Party, 269
National Union for Social Justice, 300
National University (UNAM), 391n24
National Workers Confederation, 56, 57
NCCW (American National Council of Catholic Women), 8
NCWC (National Catholic Welfare Conference), 7
Needleworkers Union, 54
New Orleans LA, 112–13
New Woman, 227–28
New York City, 152
Nicholson, Ann, 245
Nieto, Juan Correa, 149
Normal School for Catechism, 116
nuns, 38–39, 71, 77–78, 91–96, 106

Obregón, Alvaro, 57, 96, 140–42, 146, 150
The Odyssey (Homer), 131
Olivera, Alicia, 31, 43, 66, 361–62n1
Olivera, Eugenia, 186, 267, 330
Olivera, Margarita, 267
Olivera, Teresa, 267
One Happy Old Priest (Sullivan), 200
organized crime, 83
Orozco, Pascual, 40
Ortega, Dolores, 122, 123–24

Pacelli, Eugenio, 256–58, 317, 329
Padilla, Ezequiel, 150
pain, effectiveness of, 125–26
PAN party, political activism by, 260, 262
Paris, France, 220–21, 227
Parsons, Wilfrid, 276, 291, 301
Patriotic League of French Women, 227
Patrizi, Maddalena, 245
Pentecost, 189
Pérez, Patriarch, 148

persecution, 91, 92, 95, 103–4, 105–6
Pershing, John "Black Jack," 12
Picard, Jeanne Aubert, 227
Pilgrim People of God, xxii
Pio Latino, 131–32
Pitman de Labarthe, Juana, 222
Pius XI (pope): Catholic Action and, 219, 258; election of, 134; leadership of, 135, 138; Miguel Darío Miranda and, 136–38; possessions of, 171; Sofía del Valle and, 256
Pius XII (pope), 328–29
Pizzardo, Giuseppe, 257, 315, 317
Poland, 248–49, 343
Polish Corridor, 248
Portes Gil, Emilio, 146, 165, 166
The Power and the Glory (Greene), 76, 323
prejudice, 261, 276–78
priests, 72, 73, 116, 126–28, 132, 156–57. *See also* Catholicism
Pro, Humberto, 102–3, 141
Pro, Miguel Agustín, 101, 102–3, 126, 200
Pro, Roberto, 104
Professional Employees Union for Women, 54
professors, Cultura Femenina, 116
propaganda, Catholic, 92, 160
Protection of Young Women, 221

Querétaro, Mexico, 95–96
Quinta Sofía, 52, 74

Radio Priest, 294–301, 302
Randall, Margaret, 128
Ratti, Achille "Papa": Catholic Action and, 219, 258; election of, 134; leadership of, 135, 138; Miguel Darío Miranda and, 136–38; pos-

sessions of, 171; Sofía del Valle and, 256
Ravenhill, 119, 120, 273
Regan, Agnes, 8, 9, 10, 245, 246, 273–74, 280
Regional Confederation of Mexican Workers (CROM), 57, 66
Regulation for the Students of Cultura Femenina, 194–95
Rerum Novarum (Pope Leo XIII), xxii
Río, Dolores del, 330, 331
Rome, 118, 132, 256–58
Roosevelt, Franklin D., 7, 294, 299
"Rosary Belt" of Mexico, 5
Rostu, Marie du, 210, 225–26, 245
Rougier, Jesús, 101
Rubio, Pascual Ortiz, 115
Ruiz de Huidobro del Valle, José Luis, 16
Ruiz y Flores, Leopoldo: as apostolic delegate, 165; background of, 4; as bishop, 4; challenges of, 13, 138, 156–57; characteristics of, 11; clerical conspiracy role of, 11–12; death of, 317; firing of, 317; leadership of, 118, 134–35; negotiation terms of, 187; as peacemaker, 164–69; Plutarco Elías Calles and, 78; resistance to, 201; scandal of, 290; Sofía del Valle and, 14; statement of, 8; support from, 290
Russell, Odo, 135–36
Rutten, Ceslas, 216
Rutten, Georges, 49
Ryan, John A., 276

Saavedra, Dionisio, 70
saints, making of, 24, 103–5
Saint-Sulpice, 221

Sanborn, Frank, 81–82
Sanborns, establishment of, 81–82
Sanger, Margaret, 198
Santa Teresita, 22–26, 231–32, 297–98, 371n40
schismatical movement, 75–76
Secret Agent (movie), 292
Seminario Colegiar, 106
Servants of the Sacred Heart, 96
The Shape of Things to Come (Wells), 248
Silva, Fernando, 222
Slim, Carlos, 82
Smith de Goeury, Sofía, 30
socialism, 49
Social Secretariat: accusations of, 106; crisis within, 66–67; finances of, 99–100, 107; fundraising for, 316; leadership of, 49, 99; photo of, 56; rules for, 158–59; services of, 54; vision of, 55
Sodi, Demetrio, 149
Soviet Union, 115
specialization, use of, 233
spiritual direction, 126–28
Steenberghe-Engerin, Florentine, 209, 235, 314–15
Stein, Gertrude, 225
Steinem, Gloria, 261
Stone Mattress (Atwood), 272
The Story of a Soul (Martin), 25–26
Suárez, José Pino, 41
suffering, effectiveness of, 125–26
Sullivan, Thomas K., 200
Swift, John E., 313

Tabasco, Mexico, 75–76
Tagle, Ernest G., 9
Tanhuato, Mexico, 6
Teachers Professional Union, 54

Index 415

telephone companies, female
    employment within, 58–61
tenement houses, 45
Teresa of Ávila, 127, 149
Thomas, Elmer, 297
Time (magazine), 297–98
Tirado, Juan, 103–4
Toral, José de León, 141–42, 146–50, *148*
Trowbridge, Lady, 207
True Womanhood, 193, 198–99,
    227–28
Tymieniecka, Anna-Teresa, 128

UFCM (Mexican Catholic Women's
    Union), 170–79, 187, 222, 226
UNAM (National University), 391n24
UNESCO (United Nations Educational, Social, and Cultural Organization), xxi, 336–37
Union Internationale, 314
United Nations Educational, Social,
    and Cultural Organization (UNESCO), xxi, 336–37
United States: Cristero War and,
    359n3; economy in, 269; Gibson
    Girl and, 35; immigration in, 21,
    187; Knights of Columbus, 61, 160,
    275, 283; Latino Catholics in, xxiv;
    Mexico and, 12, 160, 169, 301–2,
    383n3; Miguel Darío Miranda's
    visit to, 111; prejudice of, 277–78;
    Sofía del Valle's travels to, 13, 155,
    265–67, 271, 305–7, 316
Universidad Iberoamericana, 338
University of Milan, 145
U.S. Marine Corps, 12

Valle, Ana María del, 16, 32, 42, 342
Valle, Clara del, 29, 32, 41, 112–13, 145

Valle, Consuelo del, 42, 205, 206, 207,
    218, 219
Valle, Enrique del, 42, 373n15
Valle, Francisco del: characteristics
    of, 22; death of, 321; family of, 21–
    22; focus of, 57; life of, 321; Miguel
    Darío Miranda and, 318–19; movement of, 41–42; photo of, 23, 29,
    29, *32*, *38*, *56*, *318*; travels of, 109,
    113; work of, 53, 69
Valle, Francisco "Paco" del, 29, 32,
    41, 87
Valle, Hortensia del, 29, 41, 43, 119,
    120, 273, 306
Valle, Matilde del: family of, 41–42,
    144, 145, 205; fashion of, 36; life
    of, 41–42; personality of, 145–46;
    photo of, *29*, *32*, *35*, *37*; responsibilities of, 234, 237, 238; Sofía del
    Valle and, 39; travels of, 258; work
    of, 39
Valle, Sofía del: activism of, 340;
    awards for, 311–12, 338, 345, 391n29;
    background of, xviii–xix; calling of,
    51; celibacy of, 38–39, 85–86, 177;
    challenges of, 74; characteristics
    of, 14, 31–32, 34, 174, 175–76, 177–
    78, 191, 193, 196, 215, 277, 347; childhood of, 28–29; Christian society
    viewpoint of, 212, 213; comportment viewpoint of, 212–13; Cultura
    Femenina and, 91, 116–17, 122–24,
    129, 153, 180–82, 185, 319; danger
    of, 291–92; death of, 346, 349–50,
    356–57; doubts of, 231–38; editorial written by, 6–7; education of,
    xix–xx, 33–34; Ericsson international and, 62, 65; family of, xix, 15–
    16, 19, 28, 29, 31, 32, 41–42, 113, 144,

234–35, 258, 321, 344–45; fashion of, 36, 70, 191–92, 213–14, 313–14; final years of, 342–43, 345–46, 348; focus of, 26, 57; fundraising by, 269, 274, 275–76, 281–82, 315–16; fundraising efforts by, 266; fundraising efforts of, 312; gender viewpoints of, 228–29; health of, 114, 124, 143–44, 224, 345–46, 348–49; home of, 28, 52; leadership of, 116–17, 120, 122–23, 129, 185, 223, 255, 258, 287, 336–38; memoir of, 178–79, 180–82; memorial of, 175; Miguel Darío Miranda and, 54, 68, 108, 109, 110, 111, 120–21, 125, 128–30, 139–40, 154–55, 160–61, 162–63, 219, 269–71, 318–19, 320–21, 345–47; miracles for, 242–45, 249–51; mission of, 98, 307–8, 310; naming of, 22; nanny of, 31; nicknames of, 291; pacifism of, 92–94, 97–98; patriotism of, 329–30, 335; personal struggles of, 124–26, 127–28, 145, 214, 216, 218, 219, 232, 236–38, 253–54, 307, 313–14, 321–22; photo of, 27, 29, 30, 35, 37, 56, 70, 73, 192, 266, 267, 318, 337, 339; possessions of, 84–85; professionalism of, 72, 310, 312; race of, xix, 278; *Regulation for the Students of Cultura Femenina*, 194–95; religious habits of, 26, 224–25; resignation of, 340; resistance to, 202–3; scandal of, 288–90; sexuality of, 37–39; spiritual direction and, 127–29; teaching of, 310–11; Thérèse Martin and, 26; travels of (Canada), 293, 296; travels of (Europe), 33–34, 204–8, 216, 220, 239–41, 245, 246–47, 249–51; travels of (Mexico), 268, 287; travels of (Rome), 256, 315; travels of (United States), 13, 155, 265–67, 271, 285, 305–7, 316; values of, 65–66; vision of, 172–73, 198–99, 226–27, 265, 293, 338–39; vocation of, 39; vulnerability of, 129–30; Warsaw conference and, 235–36, 252–55; working women and, 53–54, 64, 66; work of, 43–51, 52–53, 57–58, 309

Val Notre Dame, 206–7
Vatican, xviii, 111, 134, 158–59, 188, 256–58, 315
Vatican II, xxii
Velasco, Guadalupe Gutiérrez, 267–68, 330
victim souls, practice of, 125–26
Vidal, Carmen, 122, 123
Vidal, Trinidad, 122, 123
Vilchis, Davila, 108
Vilchis, Luis Segura, 103–4
Vilchis, Rafael Dávila, 70, 92, 234
Villa, Francisco "Pancho," 12, 40, 41
Villareal, Antonio, 292
Villela, José, 55
violence, 83, 100–101
Virgin of Guadalupe, 4–5, 267, 325, 360n4
Vogue (magazine), 207
von Hoesch, Leopold, 242, 244
von Ribbentrop, Joachim, 244
von Trapp, Maria, xxi, 338

Waldheim, Kurt, 340
Walgreen, Charles, Jr., 82
Walsh, Bishop, 286–87
Walsh, Edmund, 276
wars: Cristero War, xx, 4, 91, 359n3; Mexican-American War, 20; World War I, 133–34; World War II, 327, 328–30

Warsaw conference, 235–36, 252–55
Wells, H. G., 248
"Wild Indians," as target for conquest, 20
Williams, Michael, 301
Wilson, Henry Lane, 12
women: activism of, xxii–xxiii; Association of Catholic Ladies and, 50; benefits for, 54; Catholicism and, xxii–xxiii, 13, 26–27; celibacy of, 38–39, 336; dangers to, 198; education of, 54, 64, 69; as educators, 27; employment of, 45, 53, 58, 59, 60, 61, 61, 62, 63; Feminine Brigades of St. Joan of Arc and, 121–24; *Juventud* and, 330, 333, 335; Latin American, 26–27; rights for, 13, 63, 209–10, 336; role of, 38–39, 161–62, 227–29, 240; stereotypes of, 333, 335; traveling by, 207–8; vision for, 198–99

World Conference of the International Women's Year, 261–62
World Union of Catholic Women's Organizations (WUCWO), 254, 337, 339
World War I, Catholicism and, 133–34
World War II, Catholicism and, 327, 328–30
WUCWO (World Union of Catholic Women's Organizations), 337, 339

Yazbek, Tufic, 330–31, 390–91n11
Young Catholic Worker, 227
Young Men's Association, 55
Young Men's Catholic Association (ACJM), 100, 141, 201

Zapata, Emiliano, 40, 41, 81
Zapatistas, 81–82
Zavala, Margarita, 175, 176, 177
Ziegler, Emma, 186, 267
Ziegler, Felícitas, 267

IN THE MEXICAN EXPERIENCE SERIES

Women Made Visible: Feminist Art and Media in Post-1968 Mexico City
Gabriela Aceves Sepúlveda

From Idols to Antiquity: Forging the National Museum of Mexico
Miruna Achim

Seen and Heard in Mexico: Children and Revolutionary Cultural Nationalism
Elena Jackson Albarrán

Railroad Radicals in Cold War Mexico: Gender, Class, and Memory
Robert F. Alegre
Foreword by Elena Poniatowska

The Mysterious Sofía: One Woman's Mission to Save Catholicism in Twentieth-Century Mexico
Stephen J. C. Andes

Mexicans in Revolution, 1910–1946: An Introduction
William H. Beezley and
Colin M. MacLachlan

Routes of Compromise: Building Roads and Shaping the Nation in Mexico, 1917–1952
Michael K. Bess

Apostle of Progress: Modesto C. Rolland, Global Progressivism, and the Engineering of Revolutionary Mexico
J. Justin Castro

Radio in Revolution: Wireless Technology and State Power in Mexico, 1897–1938
J. Justin Castro

San Miguel de Allende: Mexicans, Foreigners, and the Making of a World Heritage Site
Lisa Pinley Covert

Celebrating Insurrection: The Commemoration and Representation of the Nineteenth-Century Mexican Pronunciamiento
Edited and with an introduction by Will Fowler

Forceful Negotiations: The Origins of the Pronunciamiento in Nineteenth-Century Mexico
Edited and with an introduction by Will Fowler

Independent Mexico: The Pronunciamiento in the Age of Santa Anna, 1821–1858
Will Fowler

Malcontents, Rebels, and Pronunciados: The Politics of Insurrection in Nineteenth-Century Mexico
Edited and with an introduction by Will Fowler

Working Women, Entrepreneurs, and the Mexican Revolution: The Coffee Culture of Córdoba, Veracruz
Heather Fowler-Salamini

The Heart in the Glass Jar: Love Letters, Bodies, and the Law in Mexico
William E. French

"Muy buenas noches": Mexico, Television, and the Cold War
Celeste González de Bustamante
Foreword by Richard Cole

The Plan de San Diego: Tejano Rebellion, Mexican Intrigue
Charles H. Harris III and Louis R. Sadler

The Inevitable Bandstand: The State Band of Oaxaca and the Politics of Sound
Charles V. Heath

Redeeming the Revolution: The State and Organized Labor in Post-Tlatelolco Mexico
Joseph U. Lenti

Gender and the Negotiation of Daily Life in Mexico, 1750–1856
Sonya Lipsett-Rivera

Mexico's Crucial Century, 1810–1910: An Introduction
Colin M. MacLachlan and William H. Beezley

The Civilizing Machine: A Cultural History of Mexican Railroads, 1876–1910
Michael Matthews

Street Democracy: Vendors, Violence, and Public Space in Late Twentieth-Century Mexico
Sandra C. Mendiola García

The Lawyer of the Church: Bishop Clemente de Jesús Munguía and the Clerical Response to the Liberal Revolution in Mexico
Pablo Mijangos y González

From Angel to Office Worker: Middle-Class Identity and Female Consciousness in Mexico, 1890–1950
Susie S. Porter

¡México, la patria! Propaganda and Production during World War II
Monica A. Rankin

A Revolution Unfinished: The Chegomista Rebellion and the Limits of Revolutionary Democracy in Juchitán, Oaxaca
Colby Ristow

Murder and Counterrevolution in Mexico: The Eyewitness Account of German Ambassador Paul von Hintze, 1912–1914
Edited and with an introduction by Friedrich E. Schuler

Deco Body, Deco City: Female Spectacle and Modernity in Mexico City, 1900–1939
Ageeth Sluis

Pistoleros and Popular Movements: The Politics of State Formation in Postrevolutionary Oaxaca
Benjamin T. Smith

Alcohol and Nationhood in Nineteenth-Century Mexico
Deborah Toner

*Death Is All around Us: Corpses,
Chaos, and Public Health in
Porfirian Mexico City*
Jonathan M. Weber

To order or obtain more
information on these or other
University of Nebraska Press titles,
visit nebraskapress.unl.edu.

www.ingramcontent.com/pod-product-compliance
Lightning Source LLC
Chambersburg PA
CBHW030601230426
43661CB00053B/1791